W9-BII-689

The Market Meets the Environment

The Political Economy Forum

Sponsored by the Political Economy Research Center (PERC)
Series Editor: Terry L. Anderson

The Market Meets the Environment

Economic Analysis of Environmental Policy

EDITED BY
BRUCE YANDLE

ROWMAN & LITTLEFIELD PUBLISHERS, INC.
Lanham • Boulder • New York • Oxford

ROWMAN & LITTLEFIELD PUBLISHERS, INC.

Published in the United States of America
by Rowman & Littlefield Publishers, Inc.
4720 Boston Way, Lanham, Maryland 20706
http://www.rowmanlittlefield.com

12 Hid's Copse Road
Cumnor Hill, Oxford OX2 9JJ, England

British Library Cataloguing in Publication Information Available

Library of Congress Cataloging-in-Publication Data
The market meets the environment : economic analysis of environmental
    policy / edited by Bruce Yandle.
        p.   cm. — (Political economy forum)
    Includes bibliographical references and index.
    ISBN 0-8476-9624-3 (cloth : alk. paper). — ISBN 0-8476-9625-1
(paper : alk. paper)
        1. Environmental policy—Economic aspects. 2. Economic policy—
Environmental aspects. 3. Environmental economics.   I. Yandle,
Bruce.   II. Series.
HC79.E5M3578   1999
333.7—dc21   99-27982
                                                                          CIP

Printed in the United States of America

♾™ The paper used in this publication meets the minimum requirements of American
National Standard for Information Sciences—Permanence of Paper for Printed Library
Materials, ANSI/NISO Z39.48–1992.

Contents

Figures

Tables

Preface

In the past 15 years, "free market environmentalism" (FME) has become a term of art in the field of environmental economics and policy. The phrase was first coined by Terry Anderson, executive director of PERC (the Political Economy Research Center) and then popularized in a book, *Free Market Environmentalism*, coauthored with PERC senior associate Donald H. Leal. FME gives equal weight to two important ideas: free markets–a way of organizing and managing resources that relies on private property rights and initiatives where owners bear the cost and gain the benefits of their actions–and environmentalism–a social movement in which individuals assign high value to natural and environmental resources. FME emphasizes the cooperative harmony in markets as a major force for protecting and enhancing the environment. The PERC think tank is now a burgeoning center of research, publication, and outreach activities that carry the FME theme.

Among its many activities, PERC emphasizes the important role to be played by young scholars. For example, now in its tenth year, PERC's summer student seminars annually bring to Bozeman, Montana, twenty-five or more university students to hear lectures and engage in discussions of FME ideas. The sessions emphasize economic theory and applications of FME ideas and cover topics that include hazardous waste management, endangered species protection, property rights theory, and evolving markets for rights to in-stream water flows. Institutions, how they function, and how appropriate incentives move people to protect valuable environmental assets are central to the discussions. With lectures during the week and enjoyment of Montana's fabulous nature scene on weekends, the summer programs offer a balance that reflects both parts of the free market environmentalism theme.

Each year, PERC also brings graduate students to the organization's Bozeman offices to engage in directed research that leads to a publishable paper. These visits often involve completion of a master's thesis or doctoral dissertation. Former PERC scholars are now found in national think tanks, on university faculties, and employed with foundations and in resource-based industries and other environmental activities. Another part of PERC's educational reach involves the work of senior associates who are engaged in university teaching and research.

This activity brings together faculty and students in the traditional seminar room where ideas and information are examined. In all this, FME ideas provide a productive framework for thinking about and analyzing important environmental issues.

This collection of student papers is the product of this last mentioned activity. Written by undergraduate and graduate students at Clemson University who participated in weekly environmental policy workshops, the collection reaches across the activities of several years and many discussions. Each paper represents the guided effort of a student who became excited about institutions and the FME approach. And each paper reflects a serious research project motivated by intellectual curiosity and a desire to explain the way the world works.

The collection's first two chapters represent an effort to get beyond the headline stories of two events that preceded and contributed to the passage of major federal environmental statutes. The first chapter, by Stacie Thomas and Matt Ryan, focuses on Cleveland's Cuyahoga River, which gained infamy in 1969 as America's burning river. Avoiding burning rivers became a theme for many who supported the 1972 Federal Water Pollution Control Act. References are still made to the Cuyahoga when the effectiveness of federal water quality regulation is questioned.

Stacie Thomas is currently a PERC graduate fellow. At the time this research and writing were underway, both she and Matt Ryan were graduate students in economics at Clemson. They dug into the files, gained the assistance of knowledgeable individuals in Ohio and Washington, and lined up visits to key people and places in Ohio. Thomas visited the site of the fire, met with environmental and community leaders in Cleveland, and gathered on-site information on the environmental history of the Cuyahoga. Along the way, the two researchers learned that the Cuyahoga had burned at least three times in its history and that state regulations establishing the river as an industrial stream, not the absence of regulation, contributed to the river's condition.

Thomas and Ryan's combined work explains how the institutions and property rights for managing water quality in the Cuyahoga and the nation changed across time, how previously settled property rights were redefined, and ultimately how federal legislations that virtually replaced state statutes and common law intervened to deliver polluter certainty. The detailed story they tell adds an important chapter in U.S. environmental history.

The second chapter revisits one of America's best-known environmental tragedies–Love Canal, an episode always associated with Hooker Chemical Company and unfortunate owners of residential property in Niagara Falls, New York. Credited with ushering legislation that established the Superfund program for dealing with abandoned hazardous waste sites, the Love Canal story sees Hooker Chemical Company as the villain and unwitting owners of contaminated homes as the victims.

Accepting the challenge to get to the bottom of the story, Angela Ives, a senior economics major at the time, reread the published literature on Love Canal and then made contacts and arranged a three-day visit to Occidental Chemical Company, Hooker's successor the Love Canal site and to key individuals who could explain what happened. Ives's chapter sees Love Canal as the result of failed institutions for conveying critical information. Hooker Chemical Company, the popular villain in the piece, is seen as an unfortunate victim of sorts, a firm that lost control of a hazardous waste site and then was held responsible for the cost that resulted. Again, by focusing on institutions that define and enforce property rights, Ives emphasizes the difficulty encountered when one seeks to place simple black and white hats on key characters in an important environmental episode. The third chapter, by Jeffrey C. Terry, examines the federal government's toxic release inventory (TRI) requirement, a regulation largely imposed on chemical manufacturers that resulted from another sad tragedy–the Bophal calamity in India that claimed hundreds of lives. Sometimes referred to as the federal government's most effective environmental law, the TRI simply requires firms to provide annual information on the number of pounds of specified chemicals released to the environment. Public pressure calling for emission reductions takes over at that point.

A graduate student in applied economics at the time of his work, Terry asks about the purpose of the TRI. If, as indicated in the legislation that spawned it, the TRI has to do with informing communities about potential hazards, it should be possible to build a statistical model that explains the level of TRI emissions using, among other variables, the level of educational attainment in regions where emissions occur. The argument implies that emissions will be lower where educational attainment is higher, all else being the same. The chapter presents background for this modeling effort and reports findings. The results suggest that TRI data are meaningful to highly educated people but do not inspire the lesser educated to take action.

Chapter 4, by Mariela Mercedes Nino Restrepo, a graduate student in environmental engineering, examines the TRI in yet another way. While common sense suggests that providing such information can only be beneficial, a bit more reflection on the matter raises serious questions. Just what are "toxic releases"? Are all items on the TRI list equally toxic? If ordinary citizens are led to believe that any chemical is toxic, will unduly stringent regulations follow? Restrepo addresses each of these questions by applying principles of engineering risk assessment. Her analysis shows that when TRI data are ordered on the basis of relative risk, entirely different outcomes emerge. The findings strongly suggest that this government program could be significantly improved by applying basic risk assessment principles.

Risk assessment is also the theme of George Hamrick's chapter, which focuses on an important South Carolina controversy involving the operation of a hazardous waste landfill. At issue was renewal of a state operating permit by

Laidlaw Scientific Services, the firm that managed the landfill. Political decisions involving the storage and disposal of hazardous waste understandably generate controversy no matter how much care is taken in resolving the matter. Hamrick, a senior economics major at the time of his research, spent days reviewing the filings and interviewing key participants in the administrative proceedings. Hamrick's Laidlaw case study provides background on the decision to be taken, explores the activities of various interest groups that sought to influence the outcome, and then analyzes the stringent conditions set by the state when the matter was settled. The Laidlaw story goes a long way toward explaining the economic hazards we confront in managing hazardous waste.

The next three chapters explore how market incentives and market-based mechanisms may be used for dealing with environmental problems. Chapter 6, by Stacie Thomas, explores eco-seals, consumer product labeling devices that identify just how environmentally friendly certain consumer products may be. Widely used in Europe and other parts of the world, but less common in the United Statues, eco-seals offer the promise of better consumer decision making. If consumers are concerned about the environmental impact associated with the production and use of a particular product, such as laundry detergent, eco-seals can help communicate valuable consumer information, at least in theory. By probing deeply into eco-seal background and practice, Thomas identifies the difficulties encountered when the eco-seal concept is actually applied. It turns out that determining just which products are less environmentally damaging is not a simple matter. For example, some products may "use" more environment per unit but last longer than others that appear to be environmentally friendly. In this case, the superficially more damaging product turns out to be less damaging. We learn that it is also possible for producers in one country to establish specialized environmental hurdles that favor their products over those of foreign competitors. Going for the green label can be another way of imposing trade restrictions.

Chapters 7 and 8 explore market incentives for managing water quality. In chapter 7, David Riggs, an economics doctoral student and PERC graduate fellow at the time of his research, tells the story of the Tar-Pamlico River Basin Association, a North Carolina organization that formed successfully to improve water quality in a river basin and estuary. Riggs explains how a major fish kill triggered regulatory and other actions that inspired community leaders to turn to the market in their search for a low-cost and effective process for reducing the flow of harmful nutrients into streams and rivers. By imposing discharge fees on treatment works that discharged directly to rivers and streams and by contracting with farmers to reduce their indirect discharge, the association effectively achieved a water quality goal that could not be attained through normal command-and-control regulation. Riggs 's chapter explains how the association was established and provides contact information for key people who led the Tar-Pamlico effort.

Chapter 8, by Sean Blacklocke, a doctoral student in applied economics, explores the possibilities for bringing effluent trading to South Carolina.

Blacklocke examines South Carolina data and identifies the cost savings that could
be achieved if a river basin approach were applied to the Pee Dee River, while
maintaining important water quality goals. The analysis introduces an important
consideration that was not discussed in the Riggs chapter. There are often instream locations where water quality tends to reach a low point. To be effective,
trading mechanisms must take into account these "hot spot" dynamics.
Blacklocke explains how this can be achieved.

When thinking about environmental pollution, most people may think first
about industrial plants or perhaps the local sewage treatment works. Indeed, con-
versations about environmental protection often occur on golf courses, which as
it turns out, can impose heavy environmental burdens themselves. Chapter 9, by
Alec Watson, an economics undergraduate at the time of his research, tells an
interesting golf course story. Watson explains how maintenance of greens can
impose heavy chemical loadings through runoff to streams, but then explores an
interesting market process that is now working to reward golf course managers to
take action to improve things. A new golf course certification activity developed
by the Audubon Cooperative Sanctuary Program allows conforming members to
use an Audubon logo in advertising environmental stewardship to golf course
users. Using economic analysis, Watson explains how the program works. His
later empirical research, which is not reported in the chapter, confirmed the
proposition that golfer are willing to pay a premium to play on environmentally
certified courses.

The book's last two chapters explore environmentalism itself. In chapter 10,
Brian Kropp, an undergraduate economics major at the time of his work, asks
what determines memberships in environmental organizations. Using membership
data from national environmental organizations, Kropp builds statistical models
and seeks an answer to his question. His modeling effort, which draws on data
from the fifty U.S. states, includes data on income, environmental preferences, and
religious activity. Along with other interesting findings, Kropp's work implies
that environmentalism is a substitute for more traditional religious activity, at least
for some environmental organizations. He also shows that there are significant
differences in the determination of environmental memberships as between
western and eastern states, suggesting that people in the western states are more
direct participants in environmental activities than their eastern counterparts.

Chapter 11, written by Jason Annan, a graduate student in environmental
engineering, takes environmentalism as religion more seriously. Following the
tack of other writers on the topics, Annan identifies the parallels between
traditional religions and environmentalism. He emphasizes the idea that we
cannot fully comprehend environmentalism in the twentieth century unless we
observe the movement as being essentially a new religion. Annan's final question
is the most controversial of all: If environmentalism is a religion supported by the
state, what does this say about separation of church and state?

This collection of student papers represents a major effort on the part of the students not only to complete their own work but also to assist each other as they discovered new information and research tools. Along the way, the students received financial support from many generous benefactors. These include American Farm Bureau Federation, the financial institution BB&T, Belton Industries, E. I. DuPont, Eastman Chemical Company, Charles D. Koch Charitable Foundation, Michelin of North America, PERC (Political Economy Research Center), Procter & Gamble, the Roe Foundation, the South Carolina University Research & Education Foundation, and Sonoco Products Company. Without this generous support and that provided to the Center for Policy and Legal Studies by Clemson University's College of Business and Public Affairs, the projects could never have gone forward.

Finally, two people deserve special recognition for maintaining a student-friendly environment for the workshops that produced these papers and for the careful work that brought the papers forward in publishable form. For many years, Donna Tingle has turned rough drafts into finished manuscripts while forming a link between PERC and Clemson's Center for Policy and Legal Studies. Anti Bax has assisted students, provided guidance, and performed a thousand duties that helped to hatch the papers. For all this effort and more, this book is dedicated to Donna Tingle and Anti Bax.

Chapter 1

Burning Rivers

Stacie Thomas and Matt Ryan

Introduction

In June 1969, Americans learned that rivers could burn. Cleveland's Cuyahoga River actually caught fire. The Cuyahoga was neither swimmable nor fishable, characteristics that would become key elements of future water quality legislation. The river was biologically dead. While some may have been disturbed, if not amazed, at the sight, public outrage in Cleveland was minimal. The prevailing sentiment at the time seems to have been, "So our river caught on fire. Doesn't everybody's?"

The Cleveland *Plain Dealer* ran a small six-paragraph story describing the event, using a low-key headline: "Oil Slick Fire Damages Two River Spans."[1] According to the story, the fire was reported at 11:56 a.m. and was under control at 12:20, but not before the burning slick floated under some wooden train trusses, doing $50,000 in damage. A few follow-ups were published in the succeeding days reporting on pledges made by various politicians and bureaucrats to find the source of the pollution.[2] Other than determining that the oil slick originated somewhere south of the city, the source of the problem was never determined precisely. Apparently, the condition of the Cuyahoga was not a matter of much concern.

The truth is that 1969 was not the first time the Cuyahoga had burned. It had burned at least twice before, in 1936 and 1952. Indeed, the earlier fires put the 1969 incident to shame. The 1952 fire damaged over $1.5 million in property.[3] From all indications, the Cuyahoga had long been used as an industrial sewer. In fact, it had been classified as an industrial stream by the State of Ohio.

Before becoming outraged about the insensitivities or ignorance of people in the 1930s, 1950s, and 1960s, we must remind ourselves of several important

1

differences between then and now. First, incomes were much lower sixty, forty, and thirty years ago. Employment, basic nutrition, housing, and avoidance of contagious diseases were seen as far more valuable at the margin than clean water. The environmental movement that would later fan the nation's passions was not to be seen until the early 1970s. In 1969, Rachel Carson's 1962 book, *Silent Spring*, the much-celebrated precursor to that movement, was just beginning to penetrate the national consciousness.

We must also recall that there was a legal/political environment that allowed for and even specified conditions that led to burning rivers. Recognizing this, we must remember that in terms of environmental harms, the early Cuyahoga fires were pretty insignificant when compared to other environmental threats that were being addressed. Cholera and typhoid, pervasive in waterfront communities at the beginning of the century, had been systematically eliminated. In short, there was an environmental movement at the time of the fires, but it focused on public health, science, and collective efforts to protect human health. Allowing rivers to burn gave leeway for communities to focus efforts on more pressing environmental problems.

Things have changed. Today, the burning Cuyahoga is used as a benchmark when journalists explain how far we have come in cleaning up the environment. Instead of showing pictures of oil slicks and flames, the Crooked River Association, organized and funded by private citizens along the Cuyahoga, now tells about fishing, swimming, and recreational areas. However, logs and other debris that may have contributed to the early fires are still present. In the span of some sixty to seventy years, river management has evolved in meaningful ways. Rules of law, statutes, and property rights, the institutions people build in efforts to sustain and enrich life, have changed.

At some point in the distant past, the Cuyahoga, like every other river, was a commons, an unrationed resource available to all. Then, as scarcity dictated and the prospective gains from rule change made change attractive, rules of law and custom, in this case English common law, set down fundamental relationships to be observed between polluters and downstream holders of environmental rights. Then, the river became public property, with rules of use established by state and local governments. Public law displaced private law. The rule of law was replaced by the rule of politics. The river next became subject to all encompassing federal regulation; it became national public property. And now, within the rich context of law and regulation, we see a river association, a group of private citizens seeking to claim and manage environmental rights. This private action is taking place in the context of common law, state and local statutes, and federal law.

So why did the Cuyahoga become so impaired that it caught fire not once, but three times? Many would cite the Cuyahoga River as being the classic case of market failure that posits that unregulated free market production generates external costs that are imposed on innocent parties, costs that are not recognized or accounted for by environmentally insensitive polluters. According to this view, government intervention is required to bring things into balance. Others see a property rights problem, a lack of definition or enforcement of property rights. Instead of calling for regulation and political solutions, these observers ask for enforcement and protection of environmental rights, suggesting that contracts or threats of law suits between polluters and those receiving the pollution can achieve an optimal level of pollution.[4] Common law provides such a framework.

These two competing and contrasting examples of institutional choice are helpful, but overly simplistic. As we examine the Cuyahoga, or any other American river for that matter, and peel back the institutional layers of regulation, property rights, and community action, we see a blending of institutions that has evolved over time, a blend that reflects political and economic struggles, but which also can be interpreted as embodying a search for efficient use of environmental assets.

What about the Cuyahoga River? How does it fit into this scheme? Our research on the problem suggests that the river burned because common law rights that might have precluded that event were erased by the Ohio state legislature and replaced with another set of rules. It was a matter of political choice. The state established a river classification system, defining the Cuyahoga as an industrial stream. When the former holders of common law rights went to court seeking damages for harm from pollution, they encountered the law of politics. The judge's hands were tied by legislative edict. Yes, a system of property rights was in place, a system that had transferred rights from parties downstream to polluters upstream. Political negotiations between industrialists, politicians, and other interest groups replaced transactions between polluters and the holders of downstream rights. With a state-approved permit, a Cuyahoga discharger was shielded from common-law actions.

Later, as economic pressures emerged from border states and distant but affected communities, the federal government entered the fray. Federal statutes erased the state classification system and delivered precious taxpayer dollars from Washington to improve water quality. All along, incomes were rising; the demand for environmental quality was increasing. As the federal program took hold, industrial and municipal dischargers became subject to a system of command-and-control regulation that once again allowed approved levels of discharge. Now, with growing dissatisfaction with the resulting conditions, private citizens have taken the initiative to organize an association that identifies permit violators and works to improve Cuyahoga water quality beyond the limits set and enforced by politicians.

The story of the Cuyahoga is one important episode in a much larger story, a story about the evolution of U.S. water pollution control. To facilitate the telling of the story, we rely partly on the water quality management stages developed by Bruce Yandle.[5] These support an evolutionary interpretation of events that is central to our story. Yandle's first stage is called " manna from heaven." In this stage, water quality is so plentiful that an entire community of water users can be satisfied. There is no meaningful scarcity. No allocation mechanism exists because the use of resources for rationing purposes simply cannot be justified. As scarcity enters the picture and the expected benefits of rationing exceed the expected costs, customs, traditions, and common-law rules develop that determine environmental rights. Any disputes arising among users can be settled in communities or adjudicated in common-law courts.

As populations grow, stressed water resources affect people beyond the limits of control by custom and tradition. Those seeking to follow common-law rules are frustrated in attempts to reach beyond traditional political boundaries. Longer life expectancies that emerge with higher incomes cause longer term harms to be recognized. Along the way, interest groups emerge that seek another allocation mechanism.

Burning rivers and other crises provide emotional support for efforts to change the property rights regime. Catastrophies introduce the next stage: "the age of holy water." Severe problems cause emotionally charged people to back away from the status quo and to demand a new environmental ethic. Rivers become viewed as sacred, and man is viewed as a sinner.[6] This "holy water" stage accommodates the rise of even greater control by the state over the resource. The former control system that relied on decentralized common-law and private rights plays second fiddle to the state. A discovery period emerges next where more information is gathered about the problem at hand. Is the problem being resolved? At what cost? Are all features of the environment to be viewed as infinitely valuable? The all-encompassing powers of the state become questioned. Centralized authorities become suspect. A third period emerges, "the period of economic water." The power of the command-and-control regulators erodes and important elements of water pollution control are assigned to communities, holders of private rights, and the logic of common law. All along, institutions evolve that work to balance benefits and costs.

This picture of evolving regulation is shown in table 1.1, which embodies Yandle's three stages along with the idea that movement through the stages carries elements of one stage to the next. The table shows the first stage where environmental scarcity has given rise to customs, traditions, and common law for managing environmental assets. In this stage, government plays the role of referee and enforcer of contracts and court decisions. The second stage, which emerges in the wake of little understood environmental crises, introduces regulation by local and state governments, while custom, tradition, and common law play secondary roles. Stage three introduces national regulation, with some authority being delegated to the states. Here, in the third stage, federal regulation is dominant; state and local regulations play a secondary role, and custom, tradition, and common law form a final layer in the evolving scheme.

While the elements of table 1.1 suggest easily identified discrete stages, we do not mean to give that impression at all. Instead, we suggest that at different times

Table 1.1. Evolving Water Quality Regulation

Stage One: Custom, tradition, and common law provide the basis for managing
and allocating water quality across competing users. The state plays the role of
referee and enforcer of contracts and court rulings. There are no local ordinances,
state, and federal statutes and regulation.

Stage Two: Local ordinance and state statutes provide regulations that control
water quality. Custom, tradition, and common law play a secondary and
diminished role. Previously held private rights are converted to public property
rights that are allocated and controlled by politicians and administrative agencies.
The federal government is not a part of the legal environment.

Stage Three: Federal statutes and administrative law eclipse the regulatory
powers of state and local governments, with some regulatory authority delegated
to state regulators. State and local regulation plays a secondary role. Custom,
tradition, and common law continue to operate, but at a significantly diminished
level.

in the history of water quality regulation, one can observe different institutional
arrangements with the regulatory powers of the state regularly taking the lead in
allocating and managing environmental rights. Of course, none of this takes place
in a political vacuum. Indeed, it is just the reverse. The tug and pull of politics
and markets lead and affect the evolving process.

Each and every part of this evolutionary process presents opportunities for
interest groups to gain special favors, while all along competitive forces affect the

durability of the legal institutions that evolve. At the same time, there is competition across the various institutions that seek to manage water quality. Federal regulation can be viewed as competition for state and local regulation. Common law and custom and tradition compete with all forms of formal regulation. In this sense, communities mix and mingle the different means for managing water quality, with no single approach becoming the exclusive controller of outcomes.

In the process that yields a regulatory regime, environmental catastrophes, special interest struggles, and institutional competition confront other forces that affect the relative importance of the institutional competitors. These include factors that affect transaction costs, scientific breakthroughs that enable people to understand the environmental consequences of their action, expanding national and international competition that affects comparative advantage, and technological change that provides a basis for monitoring and measuring environmental use. A careful study of the history of environmental regulation can shed light on these and other forces that give rise to the institutions that control water quality.

We are now ready to tell the rest of the Cuyahoga story, after which we will present elements of the larger story of U.S. water quality management prior to the twentieth century. The next section provides major details about the institutionally rich twentieth century, which saw the rise of federal water quality regulation. After this section, we discuss theories of regulation that seem to explain the events that transpired to form the current regulatory regime. The report closes with a discussion of the continuing evolutionary process and where it seems to be taking us.

The Rest of the Cuyahoga Story

The End of Common-Law Rights

On May 26, 1965, Bar Realty Corporation, as citizen and taxpayer of the city of Cleveland, brought suit in the Court of Common Pleas of Cuyahoga County against the mayor, the director of public safety, the commissioner of health, and the chief of police.[7] Relying on common-law logic, which protects holders of environmental rights from unwanted pollution, Bar sought to compel enforcement of the city's pollution control ordinances against some industrial plants that were discharging waste into the Cuyahoga River and its tributaries. The trial court granted the plaintiff's petition and ordered the respondents to "investigate the nature, character and extent of the activities of such persons and firms as may be in contravention of the duly enacted ordinances . . . and to order such nuisances . . . to be abated, and to do all other things necessary and proper to effectively abate such nuisances."[8] The court saw the wisdom of common law. The respondents appealed.

The Ohio Supreme Court reversed the lower court's decision, ruling first that the court could not substitute its powers for the discretion and judgment of public official charged with regulating water quality. Cutting to the heart of the issue, and announcing that property rights had indeed changed, the higher court ruled that Cleveland's ordinances were in conflict with state statutes. The Ohio Walter Pollution Control Board had granted permission to certain industries to discharge industrial wastes into the tributaries of Lake Erie. Since the commissioner had the authority to find a violation of the water pollution control ordinances, he must also have the authority to determine when permits are violated; the commissioner's discretion "cannot be controlled by mandamus."[9] The higher court saw the virtue of politics. In short, the rule of common law was erased. The Cuyahoga River was destined to burn.

Months after the 1969 fire, public officials stepped in and Interior Secretary Walter J. Hickel opened hearings in cases against four polluters charged with discharging wastes into badly contaminated Lake Erie.[10] One of the four, Republic Steel Corporation, was dumping thousands of tons of chemicals into the Cuyahoga daily. Republic bluntly challenged the Secretary's legal authority to press charges, claiming that it was conforming with a federal-state clean-up program overseen by the Ohio Water Pollution Control Board. In 1970, Cleveland Mayor Carl Stokes appeared before Senator Edmund Muskie in the Senate hearings on water pollution claiming that state statutes rendered him impotent in enforcing any sort of control over the pollution of his part of the Cuyahoga.[11] State statutes, he claimed, had given industry a license to pollute. Located downstream on the 160-kilometer river, Cleveland received the wastes from the entire 2,100 square kilometer watershed. If interstate pollution was to be controlled, the federal government would have to step in and erase the state-designed classification system and deal with upstream dischargers. In 1972, Congress passed the Federal Water Pollution Control Act that did just that.

The Cuyahoga Becomes a Symbol

The burning of the Cuyahoga became a symbol of a single state's inability to unilaterally control water pollution. Indeed, many observers credit the incident with pushing Congress to override President Nixon's veto and pass the 1972 law. Given the facts at hand at the time, the proposition that a "race to the bottom" by states allowed to set their own standards for water pollution control would occur seemed plausible. Just as now, states competed for industry to locate, operate, and expand in their jurisdictions. The race to the bottom implied a never-ending tradeoff of environmental quality for better paying jobs.

While this logic has appeal, it overlooks several important facets of the problem. First, the race to the bottom could not take place unless holders of environmental rights agreed to accept polluted waters, or unless such rights were taken by state statute. Of course, state statutes that shielded polluters from common-law suits did just that. Next, the fact that downstream cities, like Cleveland and many others, were actually at the bottom of the discharge cycle from cities upstream challenged the ability of common-law courts to go against the tide. Finally, the fact that cities were struggling to improve life at the bottom suggests that if a race had been underway, it was coming to an end.

Ignoring all this, the Federal Water Pollution Control Act took a one-size-fits-all approach to the problem, setting technology-based national standards for all dischargers into the nation's rivers and streams. The federal statute addressed the "race to the bottom" problem but pre-empted common-law nuisance suits in interstate controversies. A new and simpler property rights regime emerged, one that improved things for polluters. To develop a more complete picture of what happened, we now turn to the larger story in which the Cuyahoga was a bit player.

The Larger History of U.S. Water Pollution Control

Manna From Heaven and the Rise of Scarcity

We begin our story of U.S. water pollution at the beginning with the arrival of European settlers in the New World. Those first New England settlers established rules for protecting natural resources by means of "the ancient charters."[12] The charters incorporated the traditional English common law. These well-understood rules repeated age-old standards of behavior to be followed by one and all.[13] Recognizing the importance of water to the survival and maintenance of the colony, the charters forbade "the corrupting of any spring or source of water,"or "the destruction of fish by poisoning water."[14] Water resources were viewed as a commons to be protected from the abuse of pollution. Common-law rights, incorporated into the ancient charters and exercised by the citizens, were understood as the best protection of the common good.

The early settlers were generous in their praise of the New World and wrote of the "fresh bracing air, the vast acres of fertile land, forests full of game, and streams and lakes of pure water."[15] In 1630 John Winthrop reported to his son: "Here is sweet aire faire rivers and plenty of springes and the water better than in Eng[land]. Here can be noe want of any thinge to those who bring meane to raise out of the earth and sea."[16] The settlers no doubt felt fortunate to have arrived at a place devoid of infectious diseases and other ills they had experienced in the Old World.

As the colonial population increased, the resources needed for survival became relatively scarce.[17] Fathers could no longer rely on obtaining adequate land for their sons to cultivate. Fish populations that had once been abundant were disappearing. The resources that had once been common access, or free for all, became captured in systems of private property rights and markets. Centers of commerce, cities, emerged as places were consumers and sellers could come together and conduct transactions. Merchants bought corn, wheat, cattle, and horses from thousands of farms and fish from hundred of fishermen. Many colonists found jobs in these cities. City dwellers had problems not yet faced by other Americans: thievery, vice, city filth from human and animal wastes simply tossed into the streets, and widespread poverty.[18]

Thou Shalt Not Pollute the Holy Water

America's emergence as an industrialized society changed the landscape of the nation. What had been primarily a rural culture capable of relying on custom, tradition, and community courts, was replaced with networks of densely populated cities dedicated to entrepreneurial endeavors. The new urban centers fouled America's waters. Raw human and animal wastes, sulfuric acid used to clean iron, acids and caustic alkali from paper mills, and dyes from textile mills were routinely dumped into streams that conveniently washed the unwanted waste away.[19] Brooks, streams, and rivers that had previously been clean and full of fish were by the 1870s and 1880s blackened by industrial wastes, reeked of human wastes, and were entirely unfit to sustain aquatic life.[20]

Consider how these social forces affected the Cuyahoga. The business district of the City of Cleveland fronted on the Cuyahoga River, where steamers, schooners, and canal boats exchanged imported goods for the products of local industry. Later, discharge from oil refineries and steel factories coupled with human waste made the Cuyahoga, according to Mayor Rensslear R. Herrick in 1881, "an open sewer through the center of the city."[21]

Environmentalists to the Rescue

By the late 19th century, an early environmental movement was emerging in the nation. In 1886 James Olcott in a speech before the Agricultural Board of Connecticut called on his audience and Connecticut citizens to "agitate, agitate" in order to "cleanse" the state of the "social evil" of the pollution [and] "sewage from families and factories."[22] He urged them to halt the "raising of a polluted stream upon any body at the will of ignorant or reckless capitalists."[23] Olcott was not alone in calling for cleaning the waters of New England. Early water pollution reformers, mostly doctors and scientists from New England's leading families, held that health was related to the quality of the environment.[24] Their rallying cries included slogans such as "purity" and "anti-stream pollution," as they pushed for the creation of boards of health and associations for public health. They then would become members or commissioners of these boards and associations, calling on the citizens to clean the streams and rivers of industrial and sewage pollution, which they also believed led to air pollution.[25]

These reformers came from a background of leadership and social involvement. The Civil War experience gave them an increased appreciation for the state as an agent for change, and they believed the state would yield to their concerns because of their knowledge and social position as privileged Yankees.[26] Scientific generalists who believed in the theory of anti-contagionism, or the environmental theory of disease causation, claimed that the problem of pollution was not only an aesthetic issue but also one that involved public health, economic well-being, and political stability.[27] For example, the Connecticut legislature was told that crime decreased when sanitary conditions were provided: "We are thus led to the connection between sanitary science and political economy."[28] The Board of Health argued that not only did pollution give rise to "deadly miasmas" that "contaminate the air" and cause sickness, but it claimed that miasmas also led to the riots in Pittsburgh in 1877.[29] The reformers did admit that "communism does not originate from unsanitary conditions . . . yet it finds its recruits and most reckless supporters where sanitary reform is most needed."[30] Earlier, Connecticut citizens were reminded that "a pernicious environment in effect roots up the nobler and best instincts of our nature. It brutalizes and dwarfs the intellect, corrupts the morals, breeds intemperance and sensuality, and is ever recruiting the ranks of the vile and the dangerous."[31]

Legislatures, feeling pressure from the public health advocates, responded by creating state boards of health empowered to investigate pollution and public health. Scientific observation demonstrated the negative impact of industrial wastes and human sewage on water systems and the adverse impact of polluted water on human health. Water quality would be tested by walking downstream from a fouling source, tasting the water, and looking for swimming minnows.[32] Statisticians also used their mortality data to confirm that indeed those areas near the polluted waters had significantly higher levels of epidemic diseases.

For example, in 1878 the newly created Massachusetts State Board of Health pushed for legislative action to clean up the rivers and streams. Under the proposed law "no individual or corporation, and no authority of any city or town, or public institution, shall discharge, or cause to be discharged . . . into any stream or public pond . . . any solid refuse . . . or any polluting substance so as either singly or in combination with other similar acts . . . to interfere with its volume or flow or pollute its waters."[33] The act allowed existing polluters to continue until a "reasonable length of time to comply with the provisions of . . . [the] act."[34] Cities and towns with sewers would allow the sewage of factories "to be discharged through public sewers: provided such sewage contains no poisonous chemicals . . . or any matter injurious to the public health."[35] Despite resistance from manufacturers, the legislature followed the board's recommendations and passed "An Act Relative to the Pollution of Rivers, Streams and Ponds."[36] Three rivers of the state that had the greatest concentration of industrial use, the Merrimack, Concord, and Connecticut, were exempted from the act. Some corporations already polluting were allowed to continue either by prescription or legislative grant.[37] A river classification system with old-source/new-source rules emerged, a scheme to be repeated in 1972 when federal water pollution control legislation became law.

Sound Science and the Discovery Period

While American pollution reformers were promoting their statistical data as evidence that foul miasmas caused disease, European scientists began to suggest that invisible germs were to blame for epidemic disease. The late nineteenth-century work by the Germans Friedrich Henle and Robert Koch, the Englishman Joseph Lister and the Frenchman Louis Pasteur was gaining attention in the United States.[38] For the scientists who studied the issues of water pollution, the germ theory provided a framework that explained why disease tended to emerge only in certain areas. They discovered that it was not foul smelling water or poisonous vapors that caused disease. Invisible germs were the culprits that invaded the water system because of sewage dumping. Germs ingested by downstream drinkers caused the spread of disease.[39] The germ theory opened the door for laboratory science and graduate programs with researchers applying the latest technological instruments and chemical analysis for preventing disease.

In 1887 Massachusetts ordered the Board of Health to conduct a thorough scientific study of the state's waters. This time the effort was not led by doctors and statisticians. Ellen Swallow, an MIT laboratory-trained biologist, led the project and developed the world's first water purity tables.[40] In the early 1890s, a group of bacteriologists, chemists, and sanitary engineers at the Massachusetts Board of Health's Lawrence Experiment Station clarified the relationship between sewage in waterways and typhoid.[41] This group proved that bacteria and other germs could be eliminated by filtration through sand and exposure to air and sunlight.[42] Connecticut towns were advised to adopt quickly the Lawrence Station model for treating water. Citizens armed with scientific evidence linking specific polluters to damages reinvigorated common-law suits for protecting environmental rights. Town officials were pressured to move hastily by a number of successful nuisance actions brought by downstream residents against polluters who dumped noxious wastes into the water they used for nourishing their animals and for drinking.[43]

Balancing Benefits and Costs

Just nine years after the anti-contagionism theorists were successful in getting legislation passed barring any type of discharge into the waterways, the germ theorists dominated, shifting the concern from a focus on a combination of industrial waste and sewage waste to one entirely focused on sewage, since it was found to be totally responsible for epidemic diseases. The germ theory, modern science, and new technology had solved the problem of the spread of water-borne diseases. This new knowledge also solved a problem for industrial polluters. Some even believed that industrial wastes were helpful additions to waterways because they killed germs.[44] Early reformers pointed to streams full of fish as a sign of health, but for those opposed to clearing wastes, fish-free rivers and streams were a sign of cleaned waters. An 1888 Connecticut report put it this way: "While the impurity of water may in a measure be indicated by its poisonous action on fishes, and while water sufficiently contaminated to prevent the life of fish in it is unquestionably too much polluted for any domestic purposes, it does not necessarily follow that such contaminated streams must be dangerously polluted. Fish will live in concentrated fresh sewage, but will die when the water contains one hundred thousands part of blue vitriol."[45] More importantly, the same report that included this passage also recognized the tradeoff involved with cleaning industrial wastes, stating: "Which are of more importance, fish or the factories, there can be but one answer."[46]

Prior to these scientific breakthroughs that dealt with the direct effects of pollution, common-law nuisance actions by individuals to abate pollution were largely ignored by courts. The multiple sources of pollution and multitude of receivers made it difficult to link cause and effect. The new information, however, enabled courts once again to adjudicate nuisance torts caused by pollution. Common-law courts reemerged in competition with regulation. However, the courts replaced the pre-Revolutionary War strict liability doctrine that had been applied in nuisance suits.[47] When agriculture had dominated, land-use disputes were rare: an owner could use his land to its full capacity without inflicting a nuisance on his neighbors.[48] In contrast, entrepreneurs who operated industrial facilities were unable to use their property without emitting smoke and other effluents that infringed upon the property of others. As courts of the time saw it, granting complete primacy to a land owner to enjoin all interferences with his land conflicted with other land owners' rights to full use of their property.[49]

Instead of strict liability or strict enforcement of environment rights held by citizens downstream, the courts engaged in balancing benefits and costs. The classic formulation of the balancing doctrine was expressed in a 1900 New York case, *Riedemand v. Mt. Morris Electric Light Co.* Here, the judge said: ". . . it is the rule that, where an injunction would cause serious injury to an individual or the community . . ., and a relatively slight benefit to the party asking its interposition, injunction relief would be denied, and the parties left to their remedy at law."[50] Judges generally viewed injunctions as being more severe than damages and thus treated them as a matter of discretion rather than an automatic right. In the 1880 case of *Sanderson v. Pennsylvania Coal Co.*, the judge used the doctrine in determining what was reasonable: "We are in the opinion that mere private personal inconveniences, arising in this way and under such circumstances, must yield to the necessities of a great public industry, which although in the hands of a private corporation, subserves a great public interest. To encourage development of the great natural resources of a country, trifling inconveniences to particular persons must sometimes give way to the necessities of a great community."[51]

Common-law judges also began to consider the polluter's location and to compare it with prevailing uses in the area.[52] Following this line of thinking, judges saw some activities as being nuisances per se. Others, being lawful in the abstract, came to represent a nuisance "by reason of their location, or by the reason of the manner in which they are constructed, maintained, or operated."[53] The 1932 New York case, *Bove v. Donner-Hanna Coke Corp.*, illustrates the application of the location principle.[54] The plaintiff sought to enjoin a coke oven that deposited large amounts of soot on her house, claiming that it caused her head pain. The court denied her any relief, arguing that she had elected to move to an area endowed with a river and railroad, making it particularly conducive to industry. Under a strict liability doctrine, a polluting factory would always be considered a nuisance. "If factories inherently constituted nuisance, then the industrialization that has proceeded for the last 150 years could only have taken place through a severe laxity in the pursuit of nuisance suits."[55]

Twentieth-Century Water Pollution Control

Common-Law Strict Liability Raises Its Head

The acceptance of the germ theory at the turn of the century did not totally do away with the appearance of industrial wastes in water reform discussions. It was clear that industrial wastes were polluting streams. However, the struggle to clean up all wastes in rivers resulted in an unresolvable conflict between the concern for public health and economic development. In most states, control over water pollution rested with the state department of health because of its relation to diseases.[56] These agencies did not take action against industrial polluters because they did not feel that it was within their realm of responsibility.[57]

Some states, such as New York and Wisconsin, created conservation commissions in the 1920s, to work with the departments of health in restricting pollution and supplying technical advice to manufacturers on how to reduce their effluents.[58] Other states had fish commissions that attempted to assume a role in the abatement of industrial pollution, but were never granted enough power to take action against polluting industries.[59] Between 1917 and 1926, three industrialized states—Connecticut, Ohio, and Pennsylvania—created boards that were responsible for controlling industrial wastes.[60] These state boards believed that abatement of industrial pollution could only be achieved through cooperation with industry. They saw themselves as suppliers of technical advice to polluting factory owners and monitors of polluted streams.[61] The Pennsylvania Sanitary Water Board established three classes of streams: those that were pure, those which needed pollution control, and those that were not "economical or advisable" to clean up at that time.[62] Many sanitary engineers believed that Pennsylvania's actions demonstrated the ideal model of providing a realistic amount of environmental quality that would not hinder industrial progress.[63]

Before World War I cases where industrial pollutants damaged water supplies were reported, but it was not until 1922 that a widespread study was conducted.[64] In 1923, the Committee on Industrial Wastes in Relation to Water Supply of the American Water Works Association reported that industrial pollutants had damaged at least 248 water supplies in the United States and in Canada.[65] They specifically found that industrial wastes had profound effects on the color, turbidity, taste, and odor of water and increased the expense and level of difficulty involved with coagulation and filtration. The report provided a long list of offending industries. These included sugar refining, coal mining and washing, gas and by-product coke works, wood distillation, corn products, dye and munitions manufacture, oil producing wells and refining, metallurgical processes, and mining, textiles, tanneries, and paper and pulp mills.[66]

During the 1920s specialists believed that phenol wastes from gas and by-product coke works were the most acute problems associated with industrial wastes.[67] Pollution from gas wastes were under control by the 1920s, but difficulties with phenol, primarily odor and taste, were a post-World War I phenomenon and were largely isolated in the Ohio River Basin.[68] Concern with the effects of phenol led the U.S. Surgeon General, Hugh Cumming, to call a 1924 conference of the health commissioners of Ohio, Pennsylvania, and West Virginia to explore the interstate pollution problems related to the streams in the Ohio River Basin.[69] The conference resulted in the Ohio River Interstate Stream Conservation Agreement. By 1929, seventeen of the nineteen firms in the basin had installed phenol elimination devices, sharply reducing the most severe cases of odor and bad taste.[70] A major factor in the voluntary action by these firms was undoubtedly their concern over the possibility of legal action in the courts.

The balancing doctrine, which was a feature of particular state courts, was overturned in Pennsylvania in 1904 and in New York in 1912.[71] Once pollution abatement technologies became available, courts no longer believed that an injunction would mean the actual closing of an industrial plant. The cost of restricting pollution had fallen; injunctions were now cheaper. However, judges overturning the doctrine sometimes indicated they did so because they felt that a refusal to grant an injunction on the grounds that the cost to the polluter would be greater than the benefits to the victims was morally wrong.[72] Balancing was replaced with a return to a strict liability doctrine for nuisance, which protected property holders from their neighbors' pollution, regardless of the costs and benefits. In a 1904 Pennsylvania case, *Sullivan v. Jones & Laughlin*, a huge steel company that employed thousands of workers lost to a small group of homeowners of modest means.[73] The court required the polluter to install pollution abatement equipment or shut down. The ruling set a precedent that affected a whole set of the state's powerful manufacturing businesses; the days of the easier balancing policy were past.[74]

Strict enforcement of environmental rights is seen again in a 1913 New York case, *Whalen v. Union Bag & Paper Co*, in which a suit was brought by a farmer against a paper mill that employed more than 500 people. Pollution from the mill had damaged downstream water quality, making it unfit for a farmer's cattle. The farmer sued for $312 in damages and asked for an injunction against the mill. The trial court awarded damages and granted an injunction against the mill. An appellate court denied the injunction and reduced the damage amount, noting that the mill was an important economic asset to the area. However, the New York Court of Appeals, the state's highest court, reinstated the injunction and stated: "Although the damage to the plaintiff may be slight as compared with the defendant's expense of abating the condition, that is not a good reason for refusing an injunction. Neither courts of equity nor law can be guided by such a rule, for if followed to its logical conclusion it would deprive the poor litigant of his little property by giving it to those already rich."[75]

State Regulation and Federal Common Law

As incomes rose, people began to move into residential enclaves where industrial-related pollution problems were not prevalent. Also, the 1920s saw the rise of urban land-use planning accompanied by zoning. The classification of land accompanied the classification of rivers. Land around industry was cheap; those that thought they would move in, take the polluting industries to court, and gain a windfall were told by the courts to think again when defendants were able to demonstrate that the plaintiffs had "come to the nuisance." For example, in 1928, a Cleveland industrial firm charged in a nuisance action won the suit, arguing that it had initially been located on an isolated tract; the residents who arrived subsequently could not complain about a pre-existing condition. The court agreed and dismissed the case.[76]

Isolation was hard to maintain, however, and firms that had once enjoyed unrestricted pollution activities in isolated areas sometimes found themselves surrounded by newly developed residential communities. The "smoking car" solution to pollution no longer worked. The court system imposed costs of uncertainty on firms. Even when polluters located in areas isolated from residences, people could eventually move in and firms would often have to clean up or move. This state of affairs contrasted sharply with the balancing approach previously applied by judges with its bias toward industrial activities. The states' regulatory powers ascended.

The Tensions Generated by the New Property Rights

Early twentieth-century state regulation of water dischargers emphasized sewage rather than industrial wastes in establishing jurisdiction of boards; commissions of health were generally charged with promulgating and enforcing standards for their states' waterways. However, as the judicial treatment of industrial polluters began to enforce common-law rules that favored downstream parties, state water pollution control boards nationwide began to set standards for industrial waste dischargers.[77] The first state legislative efforts to control pollution consisted of a classification system of the sort used by Connecticut that categorized streams according to their uses. States would classify their dirtiest streams as "industrial use" and their trout streams as "recreational use."[78]

The river classification systems operated in two ways. First, total pollution was constrained to avoid harmful public health consequences. Second, the legislation served as an avenue for attracting industry by inviting them to pollute in some areas while protecting other areas for recreational and other environmental uses. The newly formed state water pollution control boards set ambient standards and administered permit programs.[79] Firms that abided by their permits were shielded from common-law nuisance suits. Only those direct dischargers that failed to obtain a permit could be charged with private and public nuisance.[80] The older system of common-law rights was displaced again. What had been a system of private rights became public property managed by public officials.

Differing standards for water quality among states sparked competition among them. A crude environmental tradeoff market emerged with communities willing to trade water quality for economic progress. However, the law of gravity caused decisions made by upstream communities to forcibly affect the quality of waterways used by people, communities, and states downstream. In some cases, interstate disputes were adjudicated by federal common law. In others, multi-state compacts were formed.

The Ohio River Compact

The success of the classification system for managing water quality depended on specialization. Some streams were assigned the role of sewage disposal while others could be maintained for providing satisfactory water supplies. The problem was more complex when rivers served competing purposes. The Ohio River is one such waterway. The management of the Ohio River was complicated because eight states border its shores with varying levels of population and industrialization. Because of heavy sewage discharge, the river became a vehicle for the transmission of intestinal-borne diseases, notably typhoid fever.[81] Sewage went downstream, but typhoid could go upstream. The disease stimulated a cooperative effort to resolve the problem. By taking a cooperative approach communities along the river developed water purifying techniques and, in the early twentieth century, installed filtration plants that ended the threat of water-borne typhoid fever.[82]

The pollution of the river was increasing, however, and the greater concentration of sewage-associated bacteria caused engineers to question their filter plants' abilities to deal adequately with the excessive burden.[83] Unwanted tastes and odors became intense and were found to be related to phenolic compounds and to the decomposition of organic materials and microscopic organisms.[84] The excessive hardness and acidity of the water during periods of low rainfall contributed to scale formation in steam boilers, corrosion of pipes, and increased fuel consumption.[85] Finally, there were sporadic outbreaks of gastrointestinal disorders, all of which displayed characteristics of being water-borne ailments.[86]

Since unilateral action by one state would yield few benefits while incurring excessive costs, the only viable approach was to secure the cooperation of all states bordering the Ohio River. In 1948 the governors of Illinois, Indiana, Kentucky, New York, Ohio, Pennsylvania, Virginia, and West Virginia met in Cincinnati to bind their states to an agreement pledging cooperation in pollution abatement through the establishment of an interstate agency.[87] They had been empowered to do this by prior action of their legislatures and the U.S. Congress.[88] As a result of the effort, several thousand municipalities and industries were motivated to invest more than a billion dollars, 90 percent locally financed, in the construction of pollution control facilities.[89]

The Ohio River Valley Water Sanitation Commission came into existence in 1948, the same year that President Truman signed the Federal Water Pollution Control Act into law.[90] The law authorized $22.5 million in annual funds designated to assist states in doing exactly what was already occurring in the Ohio River Valley. Also, two innovations specifically mentioned in President Truman's message—programming discharges in accord with variability of stream flow and continuous monitoring of river quality—were already being implemented in the regional approach adopted by those involved in the Ohio River multi-state compact.[91]

Federal Common Law: A Substitute for Compacts

Those states having interstate water quality disputes that could not be resolved in multi-state compacts could look to the body of federal common law for a resolution. In fact, the federal efforts at statutory pollution control grew out of a desire to control interstate pollution. The federal common law employed a neutral federal rule, needed because "[e]ach state stands on the same level with all the rest."[92] The Court recognized that a state "can impose its own legislation on no one of the others, and is bound to yield its own views to none."[93] This forced the

Court "to settle the dispute in such a way as will recognize the equal rights of both and at the same time establish justice between them."[94]

The 1972 case, *Illinois v. Milwaukee,* was the last major water pollution case decided by the U.S. Supreme Court under federal common law before it was preempted by the passage of the Federal Water Pollution Control Act (Clean Water Act or CWA) that same year. In this case, Illinois sued Milwaukee and other cities in Wisconsin for dumping sewage in Lake Michigan and contaminating Chicago's drinking water supply.[95] In final appeal before the Supreme Court, the Court noted that federal common law looked to state common law for guidance. Therefore, a state with high water quality standards may well ask that its strict standards be honored and that it not be "compelled to lower itself to the more degrading standards of a neighbor."[96] The Court ruled that a federal district court could grant an injunction against Milwaukee's pollution.

In 1981, the Supreme Court granted certiorari to rehear *Illinois v. Milwaukee* in order to decide "the effect of [the CWA] on the previously recognized cause of action."[97] When the case had initially been heard in 1972, Illinois alleged that the City of Milwaukee's sewer system was continuing to discharge substantial amounts of untreated sewage into Lake Michigan, which brought pollution to Illinois shores. The Supreme Court directed the state to file its case with the federal district court deciding that when it "deal[s] with air and water in their ambient or interstate aspects," federal common law controls.[98] This time, however, the Supreme Court was forced to acknowledge the historical bias against federal common law and found that it was appropriate only in limited circumstances. The Court decided that the CWA had preempted the "vague and indeterminate nuisance concepts and maxims of equity jurisprudence" and supplanted them with "a comprehensive regulatory program supervised by an expert administrative agency."[99]

The Rise of Federal Regulation and Preemption of Common Law

The nationalization of water quality that occurred in the United States during the late 1960s and early 1970s fundamentally changed the nature of control. While common law continued to operate within states, and state and local statutes remained operational, the federal blueprint that focused on inputs and technologies, instead of on outcomes, defined a new context for managing water quality.

A pivotal shift in the landscape of federal water pollution control was seen in the 1965 transfer of administrative supervision from the Public Health Service to the Interior Department.[100] The transfer shifted the focus of federal water pollution control activity from protecting public health to assuring that the nation's rivers and streams would provide recreation for people and habitat for fish and wildlife.[101] In addition, greater emphasis was placed on federal enforcement actions that some states felt superseded their own responsibilities instead of supporting them. Promises of grants-in-aid to states for construction of municipal sewage treatment facilities authorized in the statute would pay the states for their inconvenience, but states would basically remain unwilling partners of federal control.

The 1972 Clean Water Act brought sweeping changes to the basic pattern of pollution control regulation embodied in the 1948-1970 laws. Enacted over President Nixon's veto, the amendments gave federal authorities a major role in pollution control by establishing a National Pollution Discharge Elimination System (NPDES) to issue permits.[102] In addition to nationalizing water quality in the nation's rivers and streams, the law required the administrator of the newly formed Environmental Protection Agency (EPA) to establish effluent limitations at industrial point sources based on the best practicable technology (BPT). This system was to be in place and operating by 1977. It also set up a timetable for standards to be tightened to a best available technology (BAT) basis by 1983.

The 1972 law preempted state standard setting and enforcement of water quality that was less stringent than the new federal standards.[103] It also required the states to develop water quality classifications for all streams, with the expectation that all streams would become swimmable and fishable. The old classification system that provided industrial havens was no longer viable. The wishes of the national majority overwhelmed the desires of local and state majorities. This point was summarized in the conference report on the legislation: "[T]he intent of Congress is that effluent limitations applicable to industrial plant sources within a given category or class be as uniform as possible. The Administrator is expected to be precise in his guidelines, so as to assure that similar point sources with similar characteristics, regardless of their location or the nature of the water into which the discharge is made, will meet similar effluent limitations."[104]

In addition, the standards defined in the 1972 law for new sources were stricter than those for existing sources. The standard defined for new sources required best available control technology (BAT) or better-performing technology (BPT), while existing polluters faced the less strict BPT standards until 1983. Also, the EPA adopted the notion of variances, which allowed a source to operate legally in violation of BPT.[105] The granting of variances was totally under the discretion of federal authorities, which issued them not on the basis of existing water quality, but instead on the basis of "need."[106]

The 1977 amendments to the CWA addressed the key problem of the statutory deadlines that had been included in the 1972 legislation. These had either passed or were rapidly approaching with no hope of achievement in sight.[107] Further, the real cost of installing BPT and BAT had been identified as had the realities of economic hardships associated with plant shutdowns and resulting dislocations.[108] Technology-based standards were kept as the primary device for managing water quality, but the deadlines for achieving BPT and BAT were extended. A third category of control technologies was introduced and applied to the standards set for so-called conventional pollutants, or those normally treated in publicly owned treatment works (POTWs).[109] Huge sums of money were redistributed from taxpayers to municipalities for their construction of POTWs using "best conventional technology " (BCT) pollution abatement technologies.

The Clean Water Act was again amended in 1987, adding significant provision to the growing legislation of federal water quality control. Compliance dates that were outlined in 1977 were not extended even though they had not been met.[110] Provisions tightened control requirement, especially for toxic pollutants and sewage sludge, and increased the penalty amounts to be assessed against those not in compliance with the statute. Groundwork was laid for the future control of nonpoint sources of pollution, such as runoff from agriculture, forestry, construction sites, and city streets.

Assessing Outcomes

Assessing the independent effects of federal water quality programs is fraught with difficulty. After all, at the time the federal program started, every state had programs for managing water quality, as did many cities and regions. Common law, custom, and tradition interacted with the local, state, and regional rules. Standards varied from place to place, and interstate pollution problems continued to be a problem. To assess effects, we have little choice but to consider overall outcomes, recognizing the all-encompassing effects of the federal program and the crippling of other institutions that previously operated.

The CWA did not establish a system of national water quality standards as the Clean Air Act had established for air quality. Instead the CWA adopted a vague goal concerning fishable and swimmable water quality. By statute, each state had to classify streams, and other waters and develop a permitting procedure for all facilities that discharged waste in lakes, rivers, streams, and oceans. Along with these mandates came huge federal subsidies for upgrading municipal treatment works. Since 1972, some $20 billion has been spent annually to satisfy the requirements of federal programs.[111] In many cases, local treatment works, paid for with taxpayer dollars, became a substitute for, not an addition to, industry-provided pollution control paid for by consumers.

Nonpoint sources of pollutions such as runoffs from farms, construction sites, and mining operations, which still account for more than half of the waste received by the national waters, continue to be a problem.[112] The 1972 law appeared to reflect a belief that sufficient industrial and municipal waste could be controlled to offset the wastes contributed by nonpoint sources. So little attention has been paid to nonpoint source pollution that little information exists on the amount and effects of nonpoint pollution sources.

In his 1993 survey of studies reporting the effects of the federal water pollution control program, Robert Nelson reported on water quality conditions in 1972 when the Clean Water Act was passed.[113] Citing Conservation Foundation data, Nelson tells us that 64 percent of the stream miles and 84 percent of lakes and reservoirs were meeting the 1972 water quality fishable and swimmable goal when the statute was passed. In 1989 the federal government's own Council on Environmental Quality reported on the record for water pollution reduction achieved in various U.S. sectors.[114] The report indicated that industrial discharge had been reduced by 71 percent. More than 80 percent of all industrial plants were in compliance with the law. BOD levels, a common measure of water pollution, were down significantly for industry, while municipal treatment works contributed 73.2 percent of the problem nationwide, and agriculture 21.6 percent of the total. For suspended particulates, municipal waste accounted for 61.5 percent of this pollution; industrial waste, 26.6 percent; and agriculture, 13.3 percent. The pollution problem has become primarily a government facilities problem.

A recent report by the Pacific Research Institute for Public Policy provides an excellent summary of many gains in water quality.[115] For example, considerable cleanup of the Great Lakes has been achieved, which now show significantly lower levels of phosphorous, PCBs, DDT, and lead. And many people can testify that their community's river is markedly cleaner now than in 1972. Should we expect no less when $20 billion or so is spent each year and with more than $60 billion transferred to local sewage treatment plants from federal taxpayers for the purpose of cleaning up the discharge?[116]

Applying Special Interest Theory to Explain the CWA

Common-law approaches to allocating water quality focus on the actual harms placed on receivers of pollution. Injunctions and the awarding of damages, the two instruments judges have in adjudicating common-law nuisance suits, move toward a more efficient allocation of pollution by requiring those who seek to use environmental assets to bear the cost of doing so. State classification systems, which blunted common-law rights, also focused on outcomes. In some cases, rights to environmental use were allocated to polluters; in other cases, the rights went to recreationists, communities, and other clean environmental users.

In contrast, the federal statutory water quality control program and its technology-based standards emphasize inputs rather than outcomes. A one-size-fits-all approach is taken; industrial river classifications are superseded by technology-based pollution control requirements, and all water users are offered rights to clean environmental uses. At the same time, legal polluters are given the right to pollute up to limited amounts, and nonpoint source polluters have free reign. Within all this, ordinary citizens do not have to prove damages or loss of property rights to bring legal action against illegal polluters. They merely have to show that permits have been violated. At the same time, polluters who find themselves on the wrong side of the law must correct their ways, install the appropriate pollution control equipment, and pay fines, but not damages. Injunctions of the sort resorted to at common law are seldom if ever applied.

The centralized approach leaves a significant gap in the ability of people downstream to protect themselves against harms caused by pollution and to gain compensation when harms are generated. The gap suggests that the evolution of water quality management institutions is not complete. But before speculating on how the gap might be closed, we must first explain the attractiveness of the CWA's major features. Why command-and-control? Why uniformity? And why have common-law rights been taken?

Gordon Tullock and Nobel laureate James Buchanan took a major step in 1975 in answering this question.[117] Their logical explanation of the dominance of command-and-control environmental regulation purports that such regulation always represents an output restriction. That is, the total amount of goods produced by a particular industry is reduced. If such an output restriction is mandated by government fiat, the price will rise as if the industry had formed a cartel. Essentially the result is an industry cartel managed and enforced by the policing power of the pollution control authority. Finally, polluters can reap residual profits if the price increase exceeds the associated increase in cost incurred by pollution control capital expenditures.

Generally, the opportunity for reaping extraordinary profits within an industry is a temporary one because high profits will attract competition. In this case, competitors can neither enter nor expand output without first being granted permission by the pollution control authority. This story is made even more interesting with the typical command-and-control feature that requires new sources to comply with a higher standard than that set for existing sources.

Some people may discount such an argument because it sounds a little like "black helicopter"and "conspiracy theory " paranoia. However, let us compare alternative environmental protection designs that the legislators could have chosen in lieu of command-and-control. First, there is the common-law approach for protecting environmental rights. A cartel scenario would never succeed in regimes controlled by common-law courts. Judges make decisions on a case-by-case basis, and one common law judge's actions taken in one state do not necessarily bind judges elsewhere. In addition, and importantly, a judge's decision applies only to the parties to the controversy, not to an entire industry.

Even within a regulatory framework there are a variety of instruments available to the regulator: emission fees, performance standards, and tradeable pollution permits. All of these alternatives set maximum emission output standards and allow polluters the flexibility of meeting the standard in the most cost-effective way. Performance standards do not prescribe the abatement technologies to be used. Emission fees assign a price to effluent that is calculated so as to achieve the desired level of water quality. And tradeable permits allow those industries with higher abatement costs to buy permits from firms with lower abatement costs, achieving the same level of water quality but at the minimum cost per unit of pollution abated. None of these schemes bar entry to the industry; any residual profits made will be temporary.

According to this special interest theory, industry supports command-and-control regulatory approaches because it is profitable and removes the uncertainty inherent in highly competitive markets.[118] One national standard makes it easy to know what the rules will be at any location. Also, those who fear that states granted too much authority in controlling pollution will "race to the bottom," trading environmental quality for jobs, will be comforted in knowing that the same standards apply across all states and regions. Legitimizing industry's position are environmental groups that favor command-and-control over other alternatives. For these groups, anything that does not represent input controls are licenses for industries to pollute.

To make this story complete, we must consider the incentives of regulators who must implement and enforce pollution regulations. Monitoring permit compliance is less costly than monitoring environmental outcomes. Emission fees would be complicated because environmental prices would have to be determined and adjusted periodically to reflect changes in the economy. In short, command-and-control is more attractive to regulators, the regulated, and the environmental community.

Unlike common law, federal regulation of water quality distorts the incentives for polluters to think carefully of the costs they are imposing on their neighbors. As long as pollution can be imposed on people or communities because regulatory agencies control the process, rather than having polluters deal directly with affected parties, the process is wrought with politics. At taxpayer expense, subject to congressional mandates and oversight, a regulator declares what is acceptable and determines action that must be taken in the command-and-control of water pollution.

Comparing Community-Based Common Law with Federal Regulation

There are two ways to consider the purpose of federal regulation. One way views nuisance law as being inadequate in reducing emission levels so that ambient amounts of pollution decline. Statutory mechanisms that centrally plan inputs are assumed to achieve desired outcomes. The other way, and the one that fits the evidence, sees federal legislation as being created primarily to protect polluters from common-law suits. By obtaining a permit, polluters acquire an entitlement to emit some preestablished amount of various pollutants. The statute creates certainty where the unpredictability of nuisance law had previously created uncertainty. In other words, in exchange for greater limitations on emissions that perfectly enforced nuisance law would create, the polluter obtains an entitlement to emit a set amount of pollution with certainty.

While statutes do preempt common-law nuisance suits and thereby reduce uncertainty costs for polluters, this is not the argument often heard in defense of a statutory preemptive position. Most environmental groups argue for using the prior restraints of regulation as a deterrent to pollution. In this view, waiting for common law to remedy a pollution problem means encouraging environmental degradation. Command-and-control regulation offers the prospect of stopping pollution before it happens, not after it occurs. Reinforcing this argument is the notion that private enforcement fails because of high transaction costs. Pollution affects many people and often stems from multiple sources. For private action to achieve efficient levels of pollution, all of those affected would have to identify the precise sources of harm. By this argument, any scheme other than public regulation fails both to regulate pollution effectively and to provide citizens with a reasonable expectation of freedom from excessive pollution.

Comparing the two approaches requires better identification of the objective assumed in the analysis. Doing so forces the realization that common-law controls based on property rights are location specific. Federal regulation, on the other hand, is all encompassing. Common law requires facts about the situation at hand; it is a micro approach. Federal regulation generalizes site-specific facts and forms macro images of the world to be controlled. The two approaches are truly different, and therefore cannot be compared as though they were similar.

To be a perfect substitute for common-law remedies, federal regulation would have to embody all of the facts for all the nations rivers and streams, for each and every watershed, and for each and every watershed user. Then, for the federal rules to be cost-beneficial, different situations would have to be recognized. Rivers that are capable of absorbing more waste would be treated differently from others that are stressed to capacity. Pollution that imposes low costs in certain areas would be allowed. The same pollution in other locations would be denied. The federal rules would have to recognize differences. Obviously, the cost of accumulating such massive amounts of bottom-up information and then administering it would be prohibitively high. Because of these costs, those who seek to form federal rules unavoidably must skim the surface of the problem being addressed, identify goals like "swimmable and fishable," which have little empirical meaning, and then focus on administratively low-cost procedures that seem to make things better, certainly not worse.

When the resulting rules are imposed, real people who live in real watersheds must find ways to adjust the rules to fit unique situations. If these adjustment costs, or the costs of not being able to adjust, are termed transaction costs, then we have another transaction cost problem. Evidence of these costs is found in the history of variances, postponements of official water quality goals, and the fact that macro measures of water quality show little improvement since federal programs began. Evidence that communities have made micro-adjustments is seen in the marked improvements in water quality that has occurred for some rivers, lakes, and streams. All along, the economy being controlled has changed dramatically. What was a smokestack economy in the 1960s and 1970s, which produced relatively large amounts of emissions, has become dominated by services, trade, and commerce. The manufacturing sector, which is larger in terms of output, is much less involved in the production of environmentally intensive goods and much more involved in making sophisticated products that use less raw material. Hard, inflexible, smokestack regulations remain in force, while a fast-moving, dynamic economy moves forward.

The Future Path of Water Pollution Control

Life in the Cracks of the Regulatory Concrete

Industry has achieved tremendous progress in reducing the environmental impacts of their operations, and city governments have come a long way in their efforts to reduce the discharge of human waste into rivers and lakes. National environmental interest groups have much to celebrate, while local groups still have long action agendas. Yes, the Cuyahoga River is no longer burning, but Georgia's Chattahoochee is heavily contaminated by the discharge from Atlanta's faulty treatment works.

To be sure, the EPA sets national standards by prescribing the technologies to be employed by industries and publicly owned treatment facilities, and the individual states are authorized to enforce those standards and to grant the NPDES permits within their own political boundaries. States also have the power to set and enforce their own standards. Since federal regulators do not consider micro locations when promulgating standards, many states have imposed stricter standards on their trout streams in order to preserve them. The old river classification systems are still with us, but the baseline has been raised.

Working around the concrete of command-and-control regulation, often with federal regulator cooperation, some states and communities have discovered how to reduce the costly burden of regulation on industry, and ultimately the consumer, through watershed management and permit trading. Others, seeing the shift from smokestacks, mining, and timber cutting to high tech activities, tourism, and recreational demand, seek to alter the fundamental institutions that affect environmental quality.[119] In some cases, EPA is not the chief regulator confronted. The U.S. Forest Service, Bureau of Reclamation, U.S. Park Service, and other land-based regulators that represent old entrenched interests pose the most difficult challenge for accommodating changing demand for environmental quality.

The efforts to ease the evolutionary process are particulary apparent in the Pacific Northwest, where once prevalent extractive industries no longer set the pace for economic growth. With similar forces at play across the United States, rigid regulations formed with the support of industry and other interest groups are becoming all the more obsolete. Just as common-law judges shifted from strict enforcement of citizen rights to balancing employment and narrow economic benefits against absolute protection of those rights, newly evolving regulatory institutions are again favoring a new set of interest groups.

Consider Wisconsin. The state ranks in the top two states in sales of sport fishing licenses every year. Its citizens love water-related recreation. State legislators recognized the economic value of clean rivers, streams, and lakes, and so significant state funding was provided for water quality programs during the 1970s and into the 1980s. By 1983, Wisconsin's overall compliance with the CWA stood at 95 percent; compliance by industry was 100 percent. Wisconsin was the first state to address the nonpoint pollution problem using state taxpayer money. Today there are 150 county employees responsible for working with local landowners on water quality issues. The voluntary sign-up rate for these nonpoint control programs has risen to 70 percent. Those who volunteer receive funds that cover 80 percent of the cost of controlling pollution. Those who choose not to cooperate face the prospect of having to do so in the future with their own money.

On another front, communities are beginning to realize that federal and state control of water quality has left environmental protection incomplete. To fill the void left by regulation, community grassroots organizations seeking to regain control of their neighborhood rivers and streams have sprouted up all over the country. A recent search of the Internet on river associations found at least one such non-profit, community-based, organization in every state. It seems safe to say there is one for every river and stream in America.

In Atlanta, one of the South's largest cities and the site of the 1996 Summer Olympic Games, a grassroots effort to take control of the Chattahoochee River has taken hold. The Chattahoochee is rated as one of the top three most endangered rivers in the United States by the American Rivers organization. The city of Atlanta is currently paying a fine of $20,000 per day for failing to meet federal regulatory guidelines for dumping waste into the Chattahoochee.[120] Atlanta currently receives over 70 percent of its drinking water from the Chattahoochee.

The Upper Chattahoochee Riverkeeper is a nonprofit organization founded in 1994 to protect the upper Chattahoochee River. It is made up of local residents who have banded together to improve their region. Volunteers patrol the Chattahoochee, checking permits, and monitoring reports daily to make sure all dischargers are in compliance. If they detect a violation, the authorities are notified. The group has also instituted community programs designed to heighten the public's interest in the river. Hikes, canoe trips, and river cleanup days get the neighborhood involved with the river.

Interestingly enough, the water pollution problems that communities have been grappling with since the advent of federal intervention are identical to those existing today, namely, raw sewage and urban runoff. Of course water quality has improved on a grand scale compared to what it was thirty years ago, but only the most naive would attribute the outcome to federal control or water quality. The fact that the 1969 burning of the Cuyahoga River was not as bad as previous fires tells us that the river was actually improving. Just before the fire, Cleveland had successfully passed a one million dollar bond issue to facilitate a clean up of the Great Lakes tributary. Other rivers were being cleaning up as well. So what explains the elusive and unenforceable standards outlined in the Clean Water Act and the difficulty faced in moving to a more flexible and effective system of environmental protection? There is no other explanation better than that provided by special-interest theories of regulation and the rent-seeking model. Competition over property rights lie at the bottom of all this. And the competition has much to do with gaining control of assets without paying and less to do with forging strong linkages that connect the cost of human action to benefits obtained.

Over the course of the last thirty years, industrial groups have been favored in some cases, for example, by gaining certainty and shields against common law, and environmental groups have been favored in others, such as by gaining statutes that focus on all elements of environmental degradation and massive efforts to deal with past problems. Yet other economic forces now destabilize the basic institutional blueprint for managing water quality. Major advances in transportation, communication, and information delivery have opened up a global economy. Industrial firms no longer have the luxury of competing solely with those located in U.S. regions. In order to survive, they must compete with firms located in the far reaches of the globe where many nations have nothing like the U.S. Clean Water Act.

The Evolving New Order

Given this competitive environment, U.S. industry will not likely support a one-size-fits-all standard that previously restricted output and raised price. Instead, the push is for flexibility and freedom to find and apply low-cost solutions to environmental problems. Instead of throwing down the gauntlet to challenge environmental groups that might seek to support the failed smokestack regulation of the past, the new global competitors will more openly negotiate for effective controls based on outcomes, not inputs. Amassed scientific environmental knowledge will assist in this. Effects that were previously little understood and therefore always prone to encourage taking the side of precaution and "holy water" are now better known, subject to measurement and control. Environmental assets will be used and protected more effectively.

But will the zone of control shift again, as it did in the earlier days when common-law remedies gave way to ordinances and statutes, and then state controls gave way to federal regulation? Logic suggests a new division of labor that focuses again on particular watersheds, specified lakes, and well-identified shorelines. Armed with better information about benefits and costs than remote regulators and politicians could ever hope to have, citizens will again form associations and compacts for managing water quality. Well-specified property rights will of necessity play a fundamental role in the new water quality management programs. And parties to agreements about water quality will of necessity hold rights to the outcomes they bargain for. Something like common law will reemerge and become a more important component of the complex institutional tissue that will still include federal regulation of some form along with state and local rules and regulations. In short, yet another social system will have evolved, one that contains some of the traits and characteristics of the earlier ones.

C. S. Holling proposed a model to explain the dynamic of disharmony in ecological and social systems from the perspective of an ecologist. His model explains adaptive ecological and social systems as occurring in four phases: exploitation, conservation, creative destruction, and renewal. From the ecologist's perspective, these phases explain nature's way of dealing with problems of the commons. A young forest, for example, experiences a great rate of growth in its infancy. The trees flourish, giving a large endowment of fertile soil, water, and ample sunlight. Over time the trees will mature with some dying off. The forest becomes brittle and rigid until it is unable to adapt to dynamic environmental changes. Nature solves the tragedy of the commons by naturally occurring fires that make room for the new generation of trees.

Since resource management institutions define our relationship with nature, it is logical to conclude that institutional change can be mapped out according to these evolutionary stages. Institutional change constitutes cultural shifts, whereas ecological change is biological in nature. Yet the two systems are linked by human beings who are social and biological creatures. In the case of water quality management institutions, the cultural shift has been from common access to individual management and finally to collective management. These shifts characterize the reorganization phase of the adaptation model. The first initiatives involving no control or local control are representative of an approach that produced a spontaneous order for applying the appropriate scale of management. In contrast, the shift to collective management, especially at the federal level, denies individual initiative, private rights, and the spontaneous order so generated, replacing them with central planning and command-and-control. A break from the strict federal regime is akin to Holling's creative destruction, much like nature's fires that serve to prepare the forest for renewal.

The New Water Quality Management System

What does the future hold for water quality management? In the absence of major economic disruptions that destroy huge amounts of wealth and income, we will not likely see burning rivers again. The Cuyahoga's place in history will be preserved. Nor will we see a system of command-and-control seriously accepted as the appropriate way to manage all the major water systems in this vast country, though vestiges of command-and-control will remain as a dying characteristic of the new water quality management regime.

Instead, we will see a more intelligent system; after all, information is now relatively cheap. The new system will rely more on outcomes, continuous monitoring, and real effects, and it will depend less on input controls, monitoring, and speculative effects. For its operation, the new system will rely more on people closer to the waters being managed, less on those who hold remote positions of authority in government. And well understood and enforced environmental rights will play a larger role in the new water quality management system. Market forces will be more evident, and water quality will be accepted as a resource to be guarded along with other more traditional assets that form the basis of modern life.

Notes

1. "Oil Slick Fire Damages Two River Spans"(1969), p. 1-C.
2. Dirk (1989), (pg. unavailable online).
3. Van Tassel and Grabowski, eds. (1996), p. 339.
4. See Coase (1960), pp. 1-44.
5. The stages are discussed in Yandle (1989), pp. 4-7.
6. On this, see Robert H. Nelson (1993), pp. 234-255.
7. *Bar Realty Corp. v. Locher* (Ohio, 1972)
8. Ibid. The court held *MacDonald v. Cook* (Ohio, 1968) as the precedent case that directed the court to proceed in granting the preemptory writ commanding the respondents to perform their duties of enforcement under the city's pollution control ordinances.
9. See, *Foster v. Miller* (Ohio, 1940).
10. Hill (1969), p. 94.
11. Testimony of Carl B. Stokes to the Senate Public Works Subcommittee on Air and Water Pollution, April 28, 1970.
12. Cumbler (1991), p. 74.
13. Ibid., citing Steinberg (1987).
14. Cumbler (1991), p. 75, citing the *Ancient Charters* (1622) of the Plymouth Colony, ch. 63, pp. 1-2.
15. Duffy (1990), p. 9.
16. Ibid. This letter was written on July 23, 1630, in Charleston, SC. It is now part of the *Winthrop Papers* (1943), Boston, MA, 2:306.
17. See Cumbler (1991), pp. 73-91, for a discussion about how the depletion of fish in New England led to the expansion of agrarian commercialism.
18. Blum, et al. (1985), p. 69.
19. Cumbler (1995), p. 151, citing State of Connecticut (1888), which lists the industrial pollutants that were threatening Connecticut's waters. See also, State of Massachusetts Board of Health (1877, 1878), pp. 24-46.
20. Cumbler (1995), p. 151.
21. Van Tassel and Grabowski, eds. (1996), p. 339.
22. Cumbler (1995), p. 149, citing State of Connecticut (1887), pp. 239, 241, 242.
23. Cumbler (1995), p. 149.
24. Ibid.

25. Ibid.

26. Cumbler (1995), p. 150.

27. Cumbler (1995), p. 151.

28. Ibid.

29. Ibid.

30. Cumbler (1995), p. 151, citing State of Connecticut (1884), p. 48.

31. Ibid., citing State of Connecticut Board of Health and Vital Statistics (1875), p. 16.

32. Cumbler (1995), p. 152, citing State of Connecticut (1886), pp. 20-23.

33. Cumbler (1995), p. 153, citing State of Massachusetts (1874), p. 364. The board had prepared the ground for this legislation by arguing in its 1874 report that the creation of the board reflected the importance of the state as an agent for public good and that action should be extended to legislative action to protect public health. So far, these laws have had some effect in some places, but they are ineffective in others. There are manifold sanitary evils yet to be abated.

34. Cumbler (1995), p. 154.

35. Ibid.

36. Ibid.

37. Ibid.

38. Cumbler (1995), p. 156, citing Tomes (1990), pp. 509-631, for a discussion of the acceptance of the germ theory.

39. Cumbler (1995), p. 156.

40. Cumbler (1995), p. 157.

41. Tarr (1985), p. 1060.

42. Cumbler (1995), p. 157, citing State of Massachusetts (1888, 1889), pp. 32-33.

43. Cumbler (1995), p. 157, citing State of Connecticut, (1894), pp. 221-224; (1896,1897), p. 290; (1897,1898), p. 268. For an example of litigation against upstream polluters, see *Nolan v. City of New Britain* (Connecticut, 1897).

44. Cumbler (1995), p. 157, citing State of Connecticut (1887,1888), p. 196.

45. State of Connecticut (1887, 1888), p. 183.

46. State of Connecticut (1887, 1888), p. 168.

47. Heimert (1997), p. 406.

48. Heimert (1997), p. 407.

49. Ibid.

50. Rosen (1993), p. 309, citing *Reidemand v. Mt. Morris Electric Light Co.* (New York, 1900).

51. Yandle (1997), p. 93, citing *Sanderson v. Pennsylvania Coal Co.* (Pennsylvania, 1880).

52. Heimert (1997), p. 408.

53. Heimert (1997), p. 409, citing *Morgan v. High Penn Oil Co.* (North Carolina, 1953). "A nuisance *per se,* or at law, is an act, occupation, or structure which is a nuisance at all times and under any circumstance, regardless of location or surroundings."

54. Heimert (1997), p. 409, citing *Bove v. Donna-Hanna Coke Corp.* (New York, 1932).

55. Heimert (1997), p. 409.

56. Tarr (1985), p. 1060, citing "State Laws Governing Pollution by Industrial Waste" (1931), pp. 506-507.

57. Tarr (1985), p. 1060.
58. Ibid., citing "Stream Pollution and Industrial Wastes in Wisconsin" (1927), p. 664.
59. Tarr (1985), p. 1061.
60. Ibid.
61. Ibid., citing Fales (1928), pp. 715-727; Stevenson (1924), pp. 201-206.
62. Tarr (1985), pp. 1061-1062, citing Yosie (1981), pp. 266-323.
63. Tarr (1985), p. 1062.
64. Ibid.
65. Ibid., citing American Water Works Association (1923), pp. 415-430.
66. Tarr (1985), p. 1062.
67. Ibid.
68. Ibid.
69. Tarr (1985), p. 1062, citing "Results Obtained in Phenolic Wastes Disposal Under the Ohio River Basin Interstate Conservation Agreement" (1929), pp. 758-770.
70. Rosen (1993), p. 367, citing *Sullivan v. Jones and Laughlin Steel Co.* (Pennsylvania 1904) and *Whalen v. Union Bag and Paper Co.* (New York 1913).
71. Rosen (1993), p. 367.
72. Rosen (1993), p. 369, citing *Sullivan v. Jones and Laughlin Steel Co.* (PA, 1904).
73. Ibid.
74. Yandle (1997), p. 97, citing *Whalen v. Union Bag and Paper Co* (NY, 1913). Also see, Heimert (1997), p. 410, citing *Boomer v. Atlantic Cement Co.* (New York, 1970), where the judge quoted *Whalen* in his judgment.
75. Colten (1994), p. 91, citing Platt (1928), p. 30.
76. Goldfarb (1988), p. 591.
77. Ibid.
78. Goldfarb (1988), p. 592.
79. Goldfarb (1988), p. 591.
80. Cleary (1967), p. 25.
81. Ibid.
82. Ibid. Examples include Cincinnati, which began pumping water from the Ohio River in 1821, but did not provide filtration until 1907, and Steubenville, where filters were installed in 1915 after pumping from the river since 1835.
83. Cleary (1967), p. 25.
84. Ibid.
85. Ibid.
86. Cleary (1967), p. 3.
87. Ibid.
88. Cleary (1967), p. 4.
89. Cleary (1967), p. 251.
90. Ibid.
91. Heimert (1997), p. 458, citing *Kansas v. Colorado,* (U.S. 1902). The lack of alternatives for interstate disputes compelled the Court to grant jurisdiction.
92. Ibid. The Court rejected the potential alternative, noting that "[I]f the two states were absolutely independent nations it would be settled by treaty or by force. Neither of these ways being practicable, it must be settled by decision of this court."
93. Ibid.
94. Yandle (1997), p. 109, citing *Illinois v. Milwaukee,* (U.S. 1972).

95. Ibid.

96. Heimert (1997), p. 464, citing *Illinois v. Milwaukee*, (U.S., 1981).

97. Ibid.

98. Ibid.

99. Cleary (1967), p. 254, citing the Water Quality Act of 1965 (P.L. 89-234).

100. Cleary (1967), p. 255, citing "Federal Water Pollution Control Act Amendments of 1963."

101. Maloney and Yandle (1983), p. 301.

102. Maloney and Yandle (1983), p. 302.

103. Ibid.

104. Ibid.

105. Maloney and Yandle (1983), p. 305. Maloney and Yandle write that, since the variances were issued not on the basis of existing water quality but on the basis of "need, they were the handiwork of old-fashioned, pork-barrel politics."

106. Meiners and Yandle (1994), p. 3.

107. Ibid.

108. Ibid.

109. Ibid.

110. Ibid.

111. Hopkins (1992). The $100 billion estimate is that of the U.S. Environmental Protection Agency.

112 Meiners and Yandle (1994), p. 3.

113. Robert H. Nelson (1993), "How Much is Enough?" pp. 8-9.

114. Federal Facilities Policy Group (CEQ and OMB) (1995), pp. 32-35.

115. Hayward, et al., (1996).

116. Yandle (1997), p. 76.

117. Buchanan and Tullock (1975).

118. Meiners and Yandle (1994). "Let it be noted that the CWA was endorsed by the worst polluters, such as chemical and paper producers," citing *Hearings on Water Pollution Control Legislation* (1971).

119. Baden and O'Brien (1994), pp. 192-204.

120. Seabrook and Helton (1997), p. A1.

121. Holling (1992), p. 447-

References

American Water Works Association. 1923. Progress Report of Industrial Wastes in Relation to Water Supply. *Journal of American Water Works Association* 10: 415-430.

Baden, John A., and Tim O'Brien. 1994. "Economics and Ecosystems: Co-evolution in the Northwest." *Illahee* 10: 192-204.

Bar Realty Corp. v. Locher. Ohio, 1972. 30 Ohio St.2d 190, 283 N.E.2d 164.

Blum, John M., et al. 1985. *The National Experience: A History of the United States.* Sixth ed. San Diego, CA: HBJ Publishers.

Boomer v. Atlantic Cement Co. New York, 1970. 26 N.Y.2d 219, 257 N.E.2d 870, 309 N.Y.S.2d 312.

Bove v. Donna-Hanna Coke Corp. New York, 1932. 236 A.D. 37, 258 N.Y.S. 229.

Buchanan, James M., and Gardon Tullock. 1975. "Polluters' 'Profit' and Political Response."*American Economic Review* 65: 139-147.

Cleary, Edward J. 1967. *The ORSANCO Story: Water Quality Management in the Ohio Valley Under an Interstate Compact.* Baltimore, MD: The Johns Hopkins University Press.

Coase, Ronald H. 1960. "The Problem of Social Cost." *Journal of Law and Economics* 3: 1-44.

Colten, Craig H. 1994. "Creating a Toxic Landscape: Chemical Waste Disposal Policy and Practice, 1900-1960." *Environmental History Review* 18, 1: 85-116.

Council on Environmental Quality (CEQ) and Office of Management and Budget (OMB). 1995. *Improving Federal Facilities Cleanup.* Report of the Federal Facilities Policy Group, Washington, DC: October.

Cumbler, John T. 1991. "The Early Making of an Environmental Consciousness: Fish, Fisheries Commissions and the Connecticut River." *Environmental History Review* 15, 3: 73-91.

———. 1995. "Whatever Happened to Industrial Waste?: Reform, Compromise, and Science in Nineteenth Century Southern New England." *Journal of Social History* 29, 1: 149-171.

Dirk, Joe. 1989. "Fire Doesn't Still Burn on in Memories." *The Plain Dealer,* Cleveland, OH. June 21. 1989 WESTLAW (WS5850795).

Duffy, John. 1990. *The Sanitarians: A History of American Public Health.* Urbana, IL: University of Illinois Press.

Fales, A. L. 1928. "Progress in the Control of Pollution by Industrial Wastes." *American Journal of Public Health* 18: 715-727.

Federal Water Pollution Control Act Amendments of 1963. 1963. Report No. 556, Committee on Public Works, U.S. Senate, 88th Cong., 1st Sess., October 4, 1963.

Foster v. Miller. Ohio, 1940. 136 Ohio St. 295, 25 N.E.2d 686.

Goldfarb, William. 1988. *Water Law* Second Ed., Chelsea, MI: Lewis Publishers, Inc.

Hayward, Steven, Job Nelson, and Sam Thernstrom. 1996. *The Index of Leading Environmental Indicators.* San Francisco, CA: Pacific Research Institute for Public Policy.

Hearings on Water Pollution Control Legislation. 1971. Committee on Public Works, House of Representatives, 42nd Congress, December 7-10.

Heimert, Andrew J. 1997. "Keeping Pigs Out of Parlors: Using Nuisance Law to Affect the Location of Pollution." *Environmental Law* 27, 2: 403-512.

Hill, Gladwin. 1969. Hickel's Drive on Water Pollution is Challenged. *The New York Times,* New York, NY. Oct. 8: 94.

Holling, C. S. 1992. "Cross-Scale Morphology, Geometry, and Dynamics of Ecosystems." *Ecological Monographs*, 62: 447-503.

Illinois v. Milwaukee. U.S., 1972. 406 U.S. 91, 92 S.Ct. 1385.

Illinois v. Milwaukee. U.S., 1981. 451 U.S. 304, 101 S.Ct. 1784.

Kansas v. Colorado. U.S. 1902. 185 U.S. 125, 22 S.Ct. 552.

MacDonald v. Cook. Ohio, 1968. 15 Ohio St.2d 85, 238 N.E.2d 543.

Maloney, M. T., and Bruce Yandle. 1983. "Building Markets for Tradable Pollution Rights." In *Water Rights: Scarce Resource Allocation, Bureaucracy, and the Environment*, Terry L. Anderson, ed. Cambridge, MA: Ballinger Publishing Company.

Meiners, Roger, and Bruce Yandle. 1994. *Reforming the Clean Water Act.* Manufacturers' Alliance Policy Report (PR-128), March.

Nelson, Robert H. 1993. "Environmental Calvinism: The Judeo-Christian Roots of Eco-Theology." In *Taking the Environment Seriously*, edited by Roger E. Meiners and Bruce Yandle. Lanham, MD: Rowman & Littlefield Publishers.

Nelson, William E. 1995. *Americanization of the Common Law: The Impact of Legal Change on Massachusetts Society, 1760-1830*. Cambridge, MA: Harvard University Press.

Nolan v. City of New Britain. Connecticut, 1897. 38 A. 703.

"Oil Slick Fire Damages Two River Spans." 1969. *The Plain Dealer,* Cleveland, OH, June 23.

Platt, W. C. 1928. Business Protected from Encroachment of Residences. *National Petroleum News* 20, March 21, 30.

Reidemand v. Mt. Morris Electric Light Co. New York, 1900. 67 N.Y.S. 391.

"Results Obtained in Phenolic Wastes Disposal Under the Ohio River Basin Interstate Conservation Agreement." 1929. *American Journal of Public Health*, 19: 758-770.

Rosen, Christine. 1993. "Differing Perceptions of the Value of Pollution Abatement Across Time and Place: Balancing Doctrine in Pollution Nuisance Law, 1840-1906." *Law and History Review* 11, 2: 303-381.

Sanderson v. Pennsylvania Coal Co. North Carolina, 1953. 77 S.E.2d 682.

Seabrook, Charles, and Charmagne Helton. 1997. "A Fine Mess: Sewage Runoff Puts City up the Creek, Again." *Atlanta Constitution*, Atlanta, March 19, p. A1.

"State Laws Governing Pollution by Industrial Waste." 1931. *Chemical Metallurgy Engineering*, 38: 506-507.

State of Connecticut Board of Health. 1894, 1889, 1888, 1887, 1885, 1884. *Annual Report*, Hartford, CT.

State of Massachusetts Board of Health. 1889, 1888, 1877, 1874. *Annual Report*, Boston, MA.

Steinberg, Theodore. 1987. *Factory Waters: Industrialization and the Charles River.* Paper presented at the Conference in World Environmental History, Durham, NC.

Stevenson, W. L. 1924. "The State vs. Industry or the State with Industry. *Transactions* (A publication of the American Institute of Chemical Engineers), 16: 201-206.

"Stream Pollution and Industrial Wastes in Wisconsin." 1927. *Engineering News Record,* 99.

Sullivan v. Jones and Laughlin Steel Co. Pennsylvania, 1904. 208 Pa. 540, 57 A. 1065.

Tarr, Joel A. 1985. "Industrial Wastes and Public Health: Some Historical Notes, Part I, 1876-1932." *American Journal of Public Health* 75, 9: 1059-1067.

Tomes, Nancy. 1990. "The Private Side of Public Health: Sanitary Science, Domestic Hygiene and the Germ Theory, 1870-1900." *Bulletin of the History of Medicine,* Winter: 509-631.

Whalen v. Union Bag and Paper Co. New York, 1913. 208 N.Y. 1, 101 N.E. 805.

Van Tassel, David D., and John J. Grabowski. 1996. *The Encyclopedia of Cleveland History.* Bloomington: Indiana University Press.

Yandle, Bruce. 1989. *The Political Limits of Environmental Regulation.* Westport, CT: Quorum Books.

———. 1997. *Common Sense and Common Law for the Environment: Creating Wealth in Hummingbird Economies.* New York: Rowman & Littlefield Publishers, Inc.

Yose, T. F. 1981. Changing Concepts of Stream Pollution Control in Pennsylvania: Restrospective Analysis of Water Supply and Wastewater Policy in Pittsburgh, 1800-1959. Ph.D. dissertation, Carnegie Mellon University.

Chapter 2

Love Canal

Angela Ives

Introduction

Almost twenty years have passed since the Love Canal community in Niagara Falls, New York, was declared a national emergency. But the name itself still conjures up visions of pollution and distress. The darker picture is of a distressed middle-class community, parents concerned about chemical burns on the feet of small children, dying vegetation, and black sludge that somehow made its way from a large chemical plant to the basement walls of homes. Hooker Chemical Company, the firm that disposed of toxic wastes in the canal where the community was built, is viewed as the culprit. The community is seen as innocent and good. A few others have a distinctly different view of the events. To them, Love Canal was an environmental disaster that simply should not have happened. The middle-class community is still innocent in the matter. But Hooker is not the culprit. The process by which Hooker was pressured to sell land where chemical waste was stored, some twenty years before the environmental disaster occurred, is the problem.

Accounts of the losses that occurred in the 1970s at Love Canal are now widely known, but the detailed history, if ever understood, is long forgotten. Still today, Love Canal symbolizes every community's concern that homes might unwittingly be nesting on a site containing noxious chemicals. Love Canal set the tone for an adversarial relationship between industry and the individual; industry could not be trusted. The events there served as a stimulus for the passage of the 1980 Comprehensive Environmental Response, Compensation, and Liability Act, better known as Superfund. Love Canal, a disaster that should not have happened, and Superfund, a high-cost environmental cleanup program that does not work, go hand-in-hand.

Economic logic provides two ways to think about the Love Canal problem. First, there is the issue of an externality, harmful side effects that befall unsuspecting third parties when a firm produces goods to satisfy the needs of its customers. This approach to the problem was developed by A. C. Pigou in 1920.[1] When the additional cost of producing a product fails to include all costs, what is called marginal social cost, the producer tends to produce too much. That is, the producer's private costs are not equal to society's costs. The difference between these two is called an externality. Pollution of all forms is commonly, though not always accurately, called an externality.

At first glance, Hooker seems to be imposing the externality. The firm dumped chemical wastes into a canal, which twenty years later imposed costs on homeowners. The homeowners seem to bear part of the cost of Hooker's chemical production. Externality theory says that Hooker, and firms like it, should be paying the full cost of their operations, up front. In an ideal world, this can be arranged by imposing a tax equal to the expected future cost on each unit of chemical waste stored in a canal or landfill. In this way, the firm becomes conscious of all the costs of its actions and produces an optimal level of chemicals and waste products.

Another approach to the problems involves property rights considerations. This approach was developed by Ronald Coase.[2] If a chemical company holds the rights to deposit wastes on its land, and other parties prefer that the land be used in other ways, those favoring different land use can negotiate with the chemical company and purchase rights to the land. Alternately, if the rights are held by other parties, and the chemical company desires to use the land for disposal purposes, the company can negotiate with the rightsholders and purchase the land or rights to use the land for waste disposal. If private landowners hold the rights and are striving for 100 percent purity and the industry seeks 100 percent disposal, the property rights model suggests that the two parties can find an optimal point of environmental quality, which will not likely involve 100 percent control by either party. The chemical firm will purchase disposal rights up the point where the additional cost of another right just equals the benefit they obtain from it. This is also the point where the marginal cost to the community of receiving the waste is just equal to the benefit they gain from the payment. Both parties bear an opportunity cost. There is no social cost or externality. If property rights are defined, the market naturally takes care of defining an efficient degree of pollution.

On close examination, the Love Canal story is found to involve more than just a chemical company that disposed of waste and a community that was damaged by the waste. Long before the controversy arose, the waste site had been sold to the Niagara Falls School Board. Detailed information about the site and the potential hazard was provided when the land was transferred. Hooker's actions become virtually irrelevant in the application of economic theory. The board became the potential producer of externalities. Then, part of the land was sold to a real estate developer. At that point, information about the site disappeared. A new form of pollution enters the problem. The pollution that imposes an externality is a lack of information concerning the toxins buried at Love Canal.

Any analysis of the Love Canal experience, which had its origins more than fifty years ago, must recognize the importance of understanding the context of the period. The concepts of pollution and environmental protection were only vaguely recognized.

Further, as the judge observed in *U.S., State of New York, and UDC-Love Canal, Inc. v. Hooker Chemical* (850 F. Supp 997 [W.D. N.Y. 1994]), the passage of years had dulled recollections of those survivors directly involved in the original dumping and the subsequent transfers of Love Canal title from Hooker to the School Board. The sensational aspect of the case, the allegations of wholesale "poisoning of children and pets," captured the public imagination, making extraordinarily difficult any sober reconstruction of events. Although an admittedly difficult task, an effort must be made to address the question relating to the Hooker and School Board principals: "What did they know and when did they know it?"

In public policy terms, it is generally agreed that it is of paramount importance to eliminate or minimize the marginal social costs borne by the involved parties. The federal government has sought to prevent a repetition of the Love Canal situation with the Superfund program, a blunt—and expensive—instrument.[3] But it will be this chapter's contention that the government has focused on the wrong issue. The problem is not the cleanup of every polluted landfill (however profitable such activities may be to well-connected interests), but rather the failure of the principals to pass along all relevant information at the time of the transfer of landfill properties.

This chapter will first review the background of the case, presenting facts drawn from research, interviews, and visits to the site. The next section examines the main characters in the Love Canal story and provides an assessment of their actions and an evaluation of their interests and what they knew about Love Canal. The last section provides an economic analysis of Love Canal, using the failure of the information market to explain the catastrophe. Some brief final thoughts conclude the chapter.

Background

History of Love Canal

The history of Love Canal begins in the late 1890s when entrepreneur William T. Love bravely attempted to turn the sparsely populated area northeast of the city of Niagara Falls, New York, into a utopian industrial community, known as the "city of the future."[4] Love fantasized about luring major industries to his model city by offering economical hydroelectric power. The canal, in Love's elaborate scheme, was to supply power to the community. The power would be generated by water, diverted through the canal to the site of the planned community, where it would then cascade down the Niagara escarpment.[5] In the plan, the canal was to be navigable between the upper and lower branches of the Niagara River, bypassing the famous falls.

Due to the trying depression of the mid-1890s and with the advent of Tesla's alternating current, Love's dreams remained incomplete. Only a small portion of the canal was excavated, and for nearly fifty years, the canal was used as a neighborhood swimming hole and informal recreational site.[6] However, Love's ideas regarding the provision of cheap, abundant electricity did not go unnoticed. Several electric companies were attracted by the powerful flow of water in the Niagara area. Electricity production flourished. Chemical production followed. Chemical manufacturing is still the dominant industry in Niagara Falls and the surrounding area.

Elon Hooker founded the Hooker Electrochemical Company[7] in 1905 for the purpose of manufacturing bleach and caustic soda.[8] The plant began producing chlorine through a process of electrolyzing salt. Hooker then pioneered a new field, building the first monochlorobenzol plant in the United States, later to become the world's largest producer of the product.[9] Hooker expanded into other chemicals, with the primary base settling on chlorine and caustic soda.[10] The company then diversified its manufacturing production with both organic and inorganic compounds. Following World War II, Hooker enjoyed remarkable success, increasing sales from $7.1 million in 1940 to $38.7 million in 1953. And in 1970, annual sales continued to expand, reaching $450 million.[11]

Disposal Techniques

With business increasing, Hooker needed a place to dispose of its wastes. Although the firm had considered incineration as an alternative means of waste disposal, that technique could not handle the anticipated demands for heavy waste disposal. Also, the discharge from incineration would cause substantial corrosion to other machinery. In-ground waste disposal was then adopted as the most cost-effective alternative.[12] Hooker's interest was directed toward the nearby canal, a site which posed several obvious advantages. First, the canal's proximity to the Niagara Falls plant reduced transportation costs and the risk of moving large quantities of odorous, noxious chemicals. Second, the soils were composed mainly of clay, a fairly impermeable substance that would contain the wastes. Finally, there were no zoning restrictions placed on the usage of the canal.[13] These characteristics made Love Canal an ideal disposal site.

Hooker approached the Niagara Power Development Company in 1942 and obtained permission to use the site without the expense of an outright purchase. In 1947 Hooker acquired the nearby Love Canal site for the price of $1,500.[14] The canal was approximately 3,000 feet long, sixty feet wide, ten feet deep, running north and south, and filled with water supplied by rivulets and creeks stemming from the Niagara River. In 1942, Hooker obtained an operating license to begin waste disposal operations from the Niagara Power Development Corporation.[15]

Until the mid-1970s, dumping hazardous wastes was a relatively simple and cheap means of disposal. Hooker's activities not only complied with the laws set forth at the time, "but often represented a more enlightened approach to environmental safety than government or similar industry practice."[16] Regarding the time period, there was little control and virtually no public interest over landfills and disposal techniques.[17] Thus, Hooker was found to have addressed the disposal issue in a sensible and conscientious fashion.

Hooker used the northern section of the canal as a disposal site from 1942 to 1946. The U.S. Army was also found to have disposed wastes in Love Canal during World War II. No one lived near this part of the canal at the time the dumping began. More dumping occurred in the canal's southern section from the years 1946 to 1954. Six to ten homes were built in the vicinity of the section while disposal activities were under way.[18] A small amount of disposal activity then began in the canal's central section. Dams were built in the canal to separate the three areas. Also, pits, approximately twenty-five feet wide and twenty-five feet deep, were dug around the canal for added disposal.[19] The industrial waste dumped in the canal was estimated to total more than 21,000 tons.[20]

The dumping of the wastes consisted of storing over 200 toxic chemicals in metal drums or in fiber drums, originally used for filter cake residues; the drums were used or reconditioned rather than new.[21] The waste was disposed of in liquid or sludge form, being mostly water-soluble (aqueous-phase liquids). The wastes contained, among others, chlorobenzenes, chlorinated naphthalenes, thionyl chloride, benzene hexachloride (BHC), including an isomer named lindane, dodecyl mercaptan, arsenic trichloride, and trichlorophenol (which contains dioxin).[22] Hooker, according to an expert study, "definitely recognized these materials were toxic. . . ."[23] The frequency of the disposal of wastes varied. Hooker's general practice was to accumulate 500 to 2,000 drums of chemical wastes before hauling them to the site.[24]

Occasionally, according to the testimony of Hooker employees, four to five drums would break apart while dumping the wastes, and the exposed chemicals were spilled directly into the canal.[25] When a drum was broken, the material was covered right away, stated one Hooker employee.[26] Drums and waste filled the canal from one-half to four feet within the original ground's surface.[27] It was then covered with dirt or ash and sealed with a protective clay cap. This method of disposal was referred to as the "dig, bury and cover" method; a method that was not, at that time, regulated by the federal government.[28] Regardless, it has been maintained that the precautions taken by Hooker in disposing of the hazardous wastes would have satisfied the standards that followed until the early 1980s. Indeed, Hooker's disposal technique was well within the strict standards of

Resource Conservation and Recovery Act (RCRA), a regulatory law implemented in 1980.[29]

Occasionally, the employees at Hooker, working at the Love Canal site, were exposed to the chemicals. When the drums broke apart during the disposal operations, some workers were splashed by the chemicals, burning their skin and forming holes in their clothing. Sometimes, the men sought out nearby residences to wash the chemicals off.[30] Because the chemicals at Love Canal were flammable, many with a flash point of less than 100 degrees Fahrenheit, there were frequent fires in the vicinity.[31] The fire department was called out to the site several times during the 1940s; records show at least two responses to the fires in 1952 and 1953. When the fires broke out, Hooker was also notified and addressed the problems, even after the firm no longer owned the land.[32] There was no evidence that the fires harmed anyone.[33]

No fencing was erected around the central and southern sections, where 75 percent of the dumping had occurred, nor was any fencing installed around the residential property lines bordering the east and west sides of the canal.[34]   The only apparent fencing existed along the northern section.[35] Also lacking were hazard signs warning of potential dangers from the contaminants in the site.

Transfer of Land and Conditions of the Deed

The Niagara Falls Board of Education had expressed an interest in obtaining the land as early as August 1946. The School Board had plans to build a public elementary school to accommodate the needs of the area's growing population. In 1953, Hooker closed its portion of the Love Canal landfill. The canal and surrounding pits were just about full and, consequently, of no further use to the company. Shortly after Hooker officially closed its landfill in 1953, the Niagara Falls Board of Education approached the company a second time about the possibilities of obtaining the sixteen acres of property. Hooker specifically told the Superintendent of Schools, Bill Small, that the company did not desire to sell the property, and that the landfill was not a suitable area for the erection of a school. Hooker's Executive Vice President, Bjorn Klaussen immediately thought the transfer of land to the School Board was undesirable.[36] Hooker communicated to the Board that "the Hooker Company felt that [a sale] . . . was inappropriate, regardless of [their] need for it, because of the toxic nature of some materials that were being dumped there and [it] wouldn't be right for utilization for other than commercial or industrial development."[37] Hooker was, in fact, initially trying to avoid passing potential risks to another party. Hooker, according to the expert testimony of Dr. Kelley Ann Brix, "recognized a broad spectrum of serious toxic effects, including damage to the majority of major health organ systems, which could be caused by these substances."[38] Some of the chemicals, such as the HCH isomer, could poison through ingestion or skin absorption.[39] Hooker was reluctant to transfer the land.

The company disclosed to the School Board in the deed that the property was used for plant refuse containing some chemicals that were buried approximately six feet underground and covered. Again, the firm informed the board that Love Canal was not suitable grounds for the development of school buildings. There was a general consensus, at this point, that Hooker should not sell the property; the risk was too high.[40]

Hooker's warnings went unheeded; the School Board continued to press Hooker to sell the property. The board finally threatened legal action to seize the land using eminent domain proceedings. At the same time, the Love Canal property was rapidly becoming a liability to Hooker due to the increasing number of housing projects in the near vicinity.

Within a month, some minds in Hooker's corporate management had been changed.[41] Wanting "to remain a good local citizen," the company became convinced that "it would be a wise move to turn the property over to the School Board provided [Hooker] would not be held responsible for future claims or damages resulting from underground storage of chemicals . . ."[42]

Another influence on Hooker's change of heart may have been related to the results gathered from test holes dug on April 19 and 20, 1952. The purpose of digging the ten test holes was to determine whether the chemicals had moved through the soil (subsurface chemical migration). There was no hint or indication of chemical migration in any of the test holes.[43] (This evidence, however, has been determined inconclusive, and, therefore, inadmissible in court.[44]) Yet the main reason Hooker decided to transfer the property over to the School Board was probably because of the understanding that the company could not continue to use Love Canal efficiently.[45]

On April 28, 1952, the School Board did acquire the property for one dollar. The deed, which underlined the transaction, read in part:

> Prior to the delivery of this instrument of conveyance (deed), the grantee (Niagara Falls Board of Education) herein has been advised by the grantor (Hooker Electrochemical Company) that the premises above described have been filled, in whole or in part, to the present grade level thereof with waste products resulting from the manufacturing of chemicals by the grantor at its plant in the City of Niagara Falls, New York, and the grantee assumes all risk and liability incident to the use thereof. It is, therefore, understood and agreed that, as a part of the consideration for this conveyance and as a condition thereof, no claim, suit, action or demand of any nature whatsoever shall ever be made by the grantee, its successors or assigns, against the grantor, its successors or assigns, for injury to person or persons, including death resulting therefrom, or loss of or damage to the property caused by, in connection with or by reason of the presence of said industrial wastes.[46]

There was a stipulation in the deed that warned of the hazardous chemicals buried in the canal. Other conditions of the transaction included: (1) permission for

Hooker to continue dumping in unfilled portions of land, (2) Hooker's eligibility to receive a tax deduction for a charitable contribution, and (3) the continued testing of the deposited chemical waste materials at the site.[47] Hooker's willingness to transfer the land rested on the condition that the board accept the special deed provisions limiting the use of property to a school and park/recreational area.[48] Hooker later took the provisions out of the deed, settling for a verbal proviso reiterating the agreement that the School Board use the land as a school and park/recreational area only. Hooker cautioned the board about selling off the remaining acres to private interests.

On November 20, 1952, the Niagara Falls Planning Board was summoned by the School Board to evaluate and approve the central section of the canal for a new elementary school. Hooker gave a map to the chairman of the planning board depicting the locations of buried chemical wastes in the area.[49] The board, in 1953, voted that the conveyance and deed be accepted. On July 6, 1953, the transfer of land to the School Board was officially recorded.[50]

Families began gravitating to the region, and in order to satisfy the needs of the residents, the School Board built the 99th Street Elementary School on the central section of the acquired land. Hooker officials went to the School Board twice on their own initiative to remind the board of its agreement to maintain the security of the site. They strongly advised the board against selling any portion of the property to developers.[51] Mr. Arthur W. Chambers, a representative of the legal department of Hooker Electrochemical Company, restated the fact that the company had turned over the land for the sole purpose of building a school. He further stated that it was not the intent of the company to have the property divided for the purpose of building homes, and he hoped that no one would be injured. The board, Chambers asserted, had a moral obligation in this matter.[52]

Disregarding the advice, the board subsequently sold the remaining land to private interests, specifically Ralph Capone, a motel-keeper interested in building residential homes, and the city of Niagara Falls. On January 25, 1962, Mr. Capone purchased six acres of the property for the sum of $1,200 with the special provisions of the deed from Hooker included in the deed from the School Board.[53] Ralph Capone, in turn, deeded the property with references to these deed provisions to L. C. Armstrong on June 13, 1974.[54] By 1966, any surface evidence of the Love Canal landfill had been completely eliminated by residential housing.[55]

Health Problems Emerge

Over the succeeding years, the territory surrounding Love Canal showed little evidence of being a hazardous area. There were, however, a few incidents that forewarned of the perils that soon surfaced in the Love Canal region. Children occasionally came home with slight burns on the soles of their feet; dark sludge would seep into the basements of homes. But these foreshadowing events, on the whole, meant little to the unsuspecting resident of the perils that lay ahead.

It wasn't until 1976, twenty-two years after the final episode of dumping, that the residents of Love Canal began experiencing distinct, frightening symptoms of the toxic chemicals. When chemicals mix with ground water, a form known as leachate develops (a non-aqueous phase liquid).[56] Under normal circumstances, the leachates flow through the "upper slit" of the ground level, the area closest to the surface with the most permeable contents. Traveling through the upper slit, the leachates naturally gravitated southward to the Niagara River. The city of Niagara Falls disrupted this flow of chemicals with construction of the LaSalle Arterial Expressway along the canal's southern end, thus blocking the natural passage of leachates.[57] Consequently, a "bathtub effect" occurred. The leachates could no longer migrate into the Niagara; instead, as the water table rose, the chemicals neared the surface. When the Love Canal region experienced a year of unusually heavy rains and snowfall in the winter of 1975-1976, the water table was raised and the trapped leachates penetrated the ground's surface.[58]

Homes began to reek of chemicals, forms of vegetation died, and the surface where grass had once grown became exposed, oozing chemicals. Fear swept through the area, and a sense of panic gripped residents of Love Canal's stable, suburban homes. Residents quickly brought their complaints to the local officials, who merely responded that they would act accordingly. The *Niagara Gazette* reported increased incidences of sickness directly attributed to the area, thereby enhancing the growing hysteria in the community. The local government, in essence, failed to respond to the residents' pleas for help.

State health officials then came into town conducting health surveys for the residential populace. In February 1978, several studies were published noting high rates of pregnancy disorders, birth defects, and other illnesses. These studies suggested the existence of a major health hazard in the Love Canal area.[59] The health problems that emerged were grave enough to warrant serious investigation.[60] Dr. Beverly Paigen, of the Roswell Park Cancer Institute, detected a much higher incidence of illness among the individuals living above the more moist areas, where the contamination had percolated through the ground surface.[61] Among the illnesses reported were increased levels of cancer, blood and liver defects, miscarriages, low-weight births, and congenital defects in infants.[62] The Environmental Protection Agency (EPA) was summoned to perform limited cytogenetic assessments of thirty-six residents of the immediate area. The results documented an excess of chromosomal abnormalities and damage in the study group.[63] A group of scientists from the New York State Department of Health, noting the small sample size and evidence of procedural bias, concluded that it was "literally impossible to interpret" and that the reports "cannot be taken seriously as a piece of sound epidemiological evidence."[64] The studies were often mishandled and the results were insufficiently researched. There was also a lack of a control group. Consequently, few significant results, if any, have been published.[65] The New York State Department of Health and officials from the federal government, not concurring with the findings of Beverly Paigen, noted that there were no abnormalities or excessive illnesses in a community the size of Love Canal. The same number and type of illnesses would be expected in any other town of similar size.[66] Thus, there is no concrete testimony of the effects that the chemicals may have in relation to the reported ailments of the community. The causal relationship between the chemicals at Love Canal and genetic disorders or alleged medical problems of residents living in the Love Canal area could not be determined.[67]

In August 1978, the community became alarmed when Dr. Robert P. Whalen, the New York State Health Commissioner, recommended that pregnant women and children under the age of two be evacuated. He said that there was growing evidence of subacute and chronic illness, as well as spontaneous abortions and congenital malformations, enough to cause concern among experts.[68] There was no indication, however, of acute illness. Another alarming report held that the chemical pollution of the air was surveyed at two hundred and fifty to five thousand times the levels considered safe.[69]

Relocation of Love Canal Residents

On August 7, 1978, President Carter declared Love Canal a site of national emergency, the first non-natural environmental disaster. New York Governor Hugh Carey arranged for 255 families to be evacuated and their homes destroyed, as well as the 99th Street Elementary School.[70] The frenzy continued. Desperate for government aid and further evacuations, local residents took EPA officials hostage for five hours in order to pressure the government.[71] On May 21, 1980, two days later, the President announced yet another federal state of emergency. This declaration temporarily relocated 800 families who lived near the site at a cost of around $30 million.[72] President Carter offered federal funds to buy 564 more homes in the "emergency declaration area,"[73] an area reaching one mile in length and one-half mile wide; all but 72 of the 564 homeowners had chosen to move.[74]

Regulation

The Love Canal incident initiated the development of Superfund—the Comprehensive Environmental Response, Compensation, and Liability Act, also known as "the most complex set of regulations with which the Federal Government has ever come forward."[75] It was signed into law on December 12, 1980, mandating that every site achieve 99.9999 percent destruction efficiency, which is to say all sites would be cleaned to near perfection.[76] Since the evacuations of the Love Canal site in 1980, over fifteen years of cleanup efforts have plagued the area. The remediation efforts were targeted at containing the waste in the landfill, and treating the surrounding contaminated area.[77] The area is blocked off with a chain link fence and conspicuous warning signs. A 40-acre cap, intended to keep out rainwater, consists of a thick layer of clay topped with a high-density, impenetrable polyethylene membrane.[78] A leachate collection and treatment system now monitor and contain the chemicals in the canal. This system of environmental monitoring continues to ensure the long-term safety and well-being of those residing and working in the area.[79] This present system implemented by the EPA is not a permanent solution.[80] Further measures of overseeing the site consist of constantly monitoring the air, water, and soil in the area for signs of new chemical contamination.[81]

Love Canal Today

In 1988, the New York State Department of Health determined that approximately one half of the houses in the Love Canal area were fit for habitation.[82] The other half was deemed safe for industrial use. There would not be constant 24-hour exposure in these industrial areas. In 1990, the EPA finally concluded that there was no longer any danger from the toxins at Love Canal.[83] Richard Dewling, an EPA Deputy Regional Administrator, stated that based on an extensive report performed on the Love Canal environment, "[The EPA] is confident that there is no contamination in the declaration area . . . . There is no more risk living [in the Love Canal region] than in any other city."[84] The Love Canal Area Revitalization Agency (LCARA) has been renovating the homes north of the canal site containment area known as "Black Creek Village" since April 1992.[85] The quaint, brick homes in this area are being sold at 10-15% below market value; this reduced price includes renovations and repairs to be done by LCARA. Some of the new homeowners had previously lived in the Love Canal region before the evacuations occurred. The sale of "Black Creek" homes will cover about 5% of the total cleanup costs.[86] The vicinities that were not habitable for 24-hour exposure were approved for the development of commercial and light industrial needs.[87] In light of the new changes, Love Canal residents are now restoring a sense of community.

Meanwhile, Love Canal hit the courts in a series of litigious actions. Hooker was brought to court on charges of negligence and misjustices in the Love Canal disaster in *U.S. v. Occidental Chemical Corporation*, with Judge John T. Curtin presiding over the case. While the State documented many specific instances of Hooker's supposed negligence, it failed, by findings of the court, "to prove by preponderance of the evidence that Hooker's actions and omission in operating the Love Canal landfill or transferring it to the Niagara Falls School Board for use as a school and park grounds displayed a reckless disregard for the safety of others."[88] Hooker's disposal techniques, including its decision to dispose of its chemical wastes in a landfill, its choice and maintenance of the site, and its method of disposal operation, all followed the standard industry practices of the time.[89] The amount of available knowledge at the time was limited. The industry methods of disposal were primitive as compared to today's strict standards, outlined by Superfund.

Hooker disclosed to the board that many toxins were buried at the site, although they did not make known the amounts and compositions of the materials.[90] With this knowledge, the board would have had a better understanding of their newfound responsibilities. However, there is no indication that this information was sought or deliberately withheld.[91] Several times, the company warned the School Board against transferring the land to individual parties.

The court held that Hooker could have exercised better judgment in various instances. They were negligent for not warning the School Board that they had disposed of chemicals in the central section of Love Canal, where the elementary school was built. Hooker failed to mention how shallow the drum barrels were buried, which led to their later exposure.[92] The court recognized that Hooker had superior knowledge about the dangers and effects of the contaminants in the landfill; they neglected to disclose this crucial information to either the board or the community, even when residents came into contact with the chemicals.[93] The court noted that Hooker should have taken action before serious illnesses developed or more incidents of exposure occurred.[94]

The court did not approve of Hooker's conduct, but in order for Hooker to be accused of negligence and a wanton disregard for the health and safety of others, the court needed more.

This incident, the most notorious toxic dumping case of the 1970s, is almost closed. After sixteen years of battle with the federal government, a settlement was reached. The company was not fined or penalized.[95] Under the settlement, Occidental Chemical Corporation will pay the EPA Superfund $102 million to reimburse incurred cleanup costs, $27 million to the Federal Emergency Management Agency, which handled the relocation of Love Canal residents, and $375,000 for damage to birds and fish.

Occidental Chemical Corporation is continuing to flush out the remaining contaminants from the canal. The process is monitored by both Occidental and the DEC. Today, Occidental supports the U.S. chemical industries' "Responsible Care" program, which places heavy responsibility for environmental management on the shoulders of corporate managers. The Love Canal incident is seen as a learning process of "cradle to grave" control.[96] Occidental is now careful to manifest all the by-products from production, keep records, and change their method of disposing of the wastes from landfill storage to incineration, which provides better closure on materials.

Economic Considerations

The Love Canal catastrophe could have been adverted. If the School Board's pressure to sell had abated, if Hooker's original deed restrictions had survived, and if Capone had passed on information to subsequent buyers, Love Canal would not likely have occurred. The externality that grew out of Love Canal was not in the form of pollution, as would ordinarily be thought. The harm was generated by a lack of information about the hazardous chemicals contained in the canal. Many unsuspecting residents, deprived of any knowledge of the sludge underground, fell further into the ever-widening gap of ignorance. Unwitting encounters with hazardous waste were an unfortunate consequence of the true externality.

When government stepped in, the Love Canal episode moved away from environmental issues into the world of politics. The battles fought in court do not seem to be about determining the true costs borne by the parties at large and minimizing them, but rather involved attempts to reap the benefits of cleaning out Hooker's deep pockets. As a result, a high-cost solution emerged.

It has been argued that in the absence of government intervention, the environment would be insufficiently protected. Each party seeking to maximize his or her wealth would pollute rivers, streams, and lakes. Everyone would be looking out for his best interests, but none would be interested in the environment. Arguments such as this one overlook age-old common-law rules, property rights protection, and a host of informal and formal mechanisms that cause individuals to receive bills when environmental costs are imposed on unwilling recipients. When the power of these market forces are overlooked or misunderstood, there is a tendency to see command-and-control regulation as the solution to all environmental problems. The rule of politics is substituted for the rule of law. A new set of incentives enters the picture, and often, as in Love Canal, the true source of the problem—information breakdown and the exercise of eminent domain—is disregarded. Love Canal helped to deliver Superfund, a powerful package of command-and-control that did nothing to address the source of the Love Canal problem.

The School Board As the Polluter

It is important to analyze the parties that contributed to the Love Canal incident. For the sake of analysis, consider the Niagara Falls School Board as a firm in a market. The board provides educational services to the surrounding Love Canal residents. The residents, in turn, value the exchange with compensation in tax dollar terms. This transaction takes the form of Adam Smith's "laissez-faire" pure market equilibrium. There is simply a supply and corresponding demand. The complexities arise when a social cost has been imposed but is not taken into account in the model. Hazardous waste accompanied educational services and the pollution cost was not imposed on the Board.

As mentioned earlier, economist A. C. Pigou describes the difference between private costs, those recognized by the School Board, and social costs, which include the cost imposed on others by pollution. The difference between these two is an externality. Using this analytical approach, the School Board is the polluter and Hooker is no longer in the picture. Hooker has no bearing on the actions of the market after the land rights were transferred to the School Board.

Prior to the exchange, Hooker owned land that it used for disposal purposes. The chemical company was entitled to all the rights and responsibilities that came with its ownership. Accordingly, Hooker could legally dispose of chemicals, fully aware of the consequences and responsibilities that accompanied the disposal of the hazardous materials. The firm was liable for any cost it imposed on other parties. When Hooker completed its dumping and donated the site to the School Board, the chemical firm's benefits (in the long run, illusory) took the form of good will and protection against liability.

At the time the Niagara Falls School Board approached Hooker, the company was not in a political position to reject the board's bid to procure the land. Hooker was caught on the horns of a dilemma. Faced with having the property forcibly removed from its ownership through eminent domain proceedings, Hooker signed off the land for one dollar and attempted to protect itself by including protective clauses in the deed exempting Hooker from all potential future liabilities.

When the land was transferred to the school board, there were clear caveats in the deed specifying the contents of the approximated 21,000 tons of chemicals buried in Love Canal. The School Board was fully aware that hazardous materials were contained in the ground, as detailed information about the site and the potential hazard of the chemicals was provided. The responsibilities for maintaining the security of the land were transferred to the school board when the physical possession of the land was transferred.

As the operator of a public institution and responsible for the well-being of children, the board had a moral obligation not to build a school on, or near, the contaminated property. The information about the disposed hazardous wastes was then withheld by the board, which was strapped for funds and desperate to find a location to handle the baby-boomer generation.[97] Somehow, the board sold the unused portion of land to the City of Niagara Falls, without placing the strict covenants in the deed transfer. Yet the tight restrictive clauses that had accompanied the original deed from Hooker to the School Board were again placed in the deed when the land was transferred to Ralph Capone, a private housing developer. The board became the ultimate polluting party. But the chemical pollution was transformed to information pollution.

Liability Rules and Expanding Externalities

Hooker Chemical Company was very sensitive to liabilities associated with operating a chemical disposal site, and for good reasons. The rule of law imposes costs on private parties who damage others. However, public officials and organizations do not generally face the same stringent rules. It is rare indeed when a School Board member is held personally liable for harm imposed on a citizen. This lack of liability on the part of the board reduced the cost of managing sensitive information about future risks and then contributed to the birth of a new social cost.

In the case of Love Canal, the externality grew. The land was portioned off to more and more unsuspecting people interested in purchasing property in the relatively cheap, middle-class area of Love Canal. When the land was transferred from Ralph Capone to L. C. Armstrong, another housing developer, the restrictive convenants and contaminants in Love Canal were merely hinted at. Here, Ralph Capone contributed to the social costs. He had knowledge of the hazardous chemicals, but did not provide full information when he transferred the land. Consequently, the number of uninformed parties grew. The chain ran from Ralph Capone to L. C. Armstrong and continued on to each homebuyer in the community. In each deed, the restrictive covenants and caveats conveniently dissolved and the resulting community was left unaware. As the titles were transferred from owner to owner, the social cost kept increasing, pulling new variables into the formula. Depending on where the boundary is placed, the resulting marginal social cost ranges from minimal to vast.

Conclusions

Hooker, being the only innocent party but also the wealthiest, was ironically the only one served with Love Canal lawsuits. Although Hooker is not the culprit in the Love Canal story, the company is still treated as such, especially through the voice of the media. In retrospect, the one course of action that Hooker should have pursued differently was to warn the Love Canal residents as to the nature of the disposed toxins, or to have bought the land back from the School Board when it was placed on the open market. Perhaps, though, even these actions would have led to unforeseen problems.

The community of Love Canal—simple, decent, middle-class Americans—was the victim in this complex interplay of social dynamics. Uprooted homes. Emotional distress. Exposure to possible health risks. All this because the community was unknowingly living above a witch's brew of multiple carcinogens.

As it turns out, government clearly has focused on the wrong issue. The federal government's attempt to prevent another Love Canal came in the form of Superfund, a cleanup program that relies on rules of retroactive strict joint and several liability and sets unrealistic goals for cleaning abandoned sites. But the Love Canal problem is not about cleaning up every polluted landfill through strict landfill-disposal techniques. The problem that needs solving relates to the failure of parties in land transactions to pass along all relevant information each time a contaminated site is transferred.

If Superfund fails to address the real issue, how might this problem be resolved? First consider a proposal that contains an important government role.

To reduce information-borne costs, impose a requirement that liability insurance policies or guarantees be provided when industrial land is transferred by any party, public or private, and make the liabilities the same for one and all. Requiring environmental liability insurance would introduce additional market forces and provide greater safety assurance to any land purchaser. Liability insurance would serve to indemnify a person against financial loss from specified perils. Of course, the perils would include hazardous wastes, poisons, and chemicals.

Instead of national taxpayers footing part of the bill and consumers paying higher prices that include meeting unrealistic Superfund cleanup and litigation costs, the first burden would fall on property owners. With strict liability under contract, they would have an incentive to secure the least cost insurance and cleanup package; those seeking to transfer land would either absorb the cost or pass it along in competitive markets. If this policy had been in place at the time of the Hooker land transfer, the School Board would likely have not purchased the land in the first place. The costs for the insurance would have made the purchase too expensive.

Government enters the proposal as a monitor and enforcer of mandatory insurance. But competitive incentives would operate in the insurance and waste disposal markets. In essence, the market would then determine the market price for land. Private insurance companies would be more cautious than government agents who have the power to make polluters pay the cost of arbitrary cleanup programs.

Of course, insurance programs can also cause problems, if they are run by government. Consider the federal savings and loan catastrophe of the 1990s. In this case, there was an explicit government guarantee to make up depositors' losses. The government guarantee encouraged reckless and crooked individuals to make loans with no assurance of pay back. The Federal Savings and Loans Insurance Corporation (FSLIC), run by agents with no personal funds at stake, did virtually nothing to rein in the reckless operators of savings and loans. If the FSLIC had been run as a private business with an obligation to the shareholders, the results would not have been so catastrophic. Managers of competitive deposit insurers would impose rules, audits, and other conditions on their clients, raising and lowering premiums with the risks they insured.

Perhaps the simplest proposal of all is to provide support for vigorous enforcement of common-law rules against all private and public parties who impose damages on innocent victims. By expanding the use of public nuisance suits and the court system, market participants will have greater incentives to protect themselves and others from costs. With strong protection of property rights, liability insurance and other market-based activities will emerge to minimize the inevitable costs that arise when chemicals and other products are produced in a modern economy.

Final Thoughts

The misconceptions about Love Canal have generated large social costs. The expensive regulatory measures of Superfund have suppressed competitive responses to hazardous waste problems while doing relatively little to reduce the number of risky hazardous waste sites. It is always costly to install command-and-control devices in efforts to limit presumed externalities. The Love Canal syndrome could have been avoided if a strict liability insurance had been required with all transfers of industrial land or if common-law rules had been enforced rigorously against all parties.

There may be several thousand potential Love Canals in the United States and elsewhere today. In order to avoid the externality of withheld information, and to avoid future national emergencies, it is essential to find a cost-effective solution to maximize the net benefit of society. For markets to be efficient and citizens to be secure in their property, property rights must be enforced, and those who withhold crucial information when transferring land must bear the cost of their actions.

Notes

1. A.C. Pigou, *The Economics of Welfare*. London: McMillan and Company, 1920.

2. Ronald H. Coase, "The Problem of Social Cost," *The Journal of Law & Economics*, 3 (1960): 1-40.

3. On this, see Katherine N. Probst, Don Fullerton, Robert E. Litan and Paul R. Portney, *Footing the Bill for Superfund Cleanups.* (Washington, DC: Resources for the Future, 1995).

4. Andrew J. Hoffman. "An Uneasy Rebirth at Love Canal," *Environment* (March 15, 1995): 6.

5. John Deegan, Jr. "Looking Back at Love Canal," *Environmental Scientific Technology*, 21 (November 4, 1987): 329.

6. The firm was known as Hooker Electrochemical Company between 1909 and 1958; as Hooker Chemical Corporation between 1958 and 1974; as Hooker Chemicals & Plastics Corporation between 1974 and 1982. In 1968, the company was acquired by Occidental Petroleum Corp. and renamed Occidental Chemical Corp., OCC, in 1982. For our purposes, the company will be addressed interchangeably as "Hooker" and "the company."

7. *U.S., State of New York, and UDC-Love Canal, Inc. v. Hooker Chemicals & Plastics Corporation*, 850 F.Supp. 993 (W.D.N.Y. 1994) 1004. Hereafter cited as *U.S. v. Hooker*.

8. Ibid., 1004.

9. Ibid.

10. Ibid.

11. *U.S. v. Hooker Chemicals & Plastics Corporation*, 79CV9900 (W.D.N.Y.1989).

12. *U.S. v. Hooker*, 1004.

13. Ibid., 1024.

14. *U.S. v. Hooker*, 1007.

15. Ibid., 1025.

16. Ibid., 1050.

17. Ibid., 1049.

18. Ibid., 1007.

19. Hernan, p. 1 (of excerpt).

20. Clark, Mark, and Mary Hager. "Fleeing the Love Canal." *Newsweek.* (June 2, 1980): 56.

21. *U.S. v. Hooker*, 1008.

22. Hernan, p. 1 (of excerpt).

23. *U.S. v. Hooker*, 1011.

24. Ibid., 1008.

25. Ibid.

26. Ibid.

27. Ibid.

28. Hernan, p. 1 (of excerpt).

29. "Love Canal: The Facts (1892-1982)." Occidental Chemical FACTLINE. Number 13, (September 1982): 15.

30. *U.S. v. Hooker*, 1010.

31. Ibid., 1017.

32. Ibid.

33. Ibid.

34. Ibid., 1008.

35. Ibid., 1018.

36. *U.S. v. Hooker*, 1020.

37. Ibid.

38. *U.S. v. Hooker*, 1011.

39. Ibid., 1014.

40. Ibid., 1020.

41. Ibid., 1021.

42. Ibid.

43. *U.S. v. Hooker*, 1021.

44. Ibid., 1022.

45. Ibid., 1023.

46. Ibid., 1027.

47. Ibid., 1026.

48. *U.S. v. Hooker*, 1025.

49. Ibid.

50. "Love Canal: The Facts," p. 8.

51. *U.S. v. Hooker*, 1032.

52. "What Hooker Told Whom, When About Love Canal." *The Wall Street Journal* (June 19, 1980): 26.

53. "Love Canal: The Facts," p. 12.

54. Ibid.

55. Deegan, p. 329.

56. Gary McPherson, "Distributed Control at Love Canal," *Intech* (September 1994): 27.

57. *U.S. v. Hooker*, 1035.

58. Hoffman, pp. 6.

59. Eric Zuesse, "Love Canal: The Truth Seeps Out." *Reason* (February 1981): 31.

60. Bill Davidson, Kristie Hoek, Carrie Smith, and Alline Peeler. "Love Canal: An Overview of the Toxic Waste Dump that Brought the Chemical Industry to Its Knees." Internet, http://dirac.py.iu...-course/sford2.txt. Downloaded on 1/30/97. Hereby referred to as "Davidson, Internet."

61. Lewis G. Regenstein, "Love Canal Toxic Waste Contamination,"in *When Technology Fails: Significant Technological Disasters, Accidents, and Failures of the Twentieth Century,* ed. Neil Schlager (Detroit: Gale Research, 1994), p. 354.

62. Davidson, Internet.

63. Deegan, p. 329.

64. Zuesse, p. 31.

65. Davidson, Internet.

66. Davidson, Internet.

67. "Love Canal: The Facts," p. 3.

68. Davidson, Internet.

69. Regenstein, p. 355.

70. Zuesse, p. 27.

71. Hoffman, p. 7.

72. Davidson, Internet.

73. Hoffman, p. 7.

74. Davidson, Internet.

75. Ralph Blumenthal, "Bid to Curb Toxic Sites: Doubts Persist as U.S. Acts to Limit Dumping," *New York Times* (June 30, 1980): p. B1.

76. Hoffman, p. 7.

77. Hoffman, p. 8.

78. Ibid.

79. "Superfund at Work: Hazardous Waste Cleanup Efforts Nationwide," Environmental Protection Agency. Love Canal Site, Niagara Falls, NY (Spring 1996).

80. Davidson, Internet.

81. Ibid.

82. Ibid.

83. Ibid.

84. "Love Canal: The Facts," p. 3.

85. Davidson, Internet.

86. Davidson, Internet.

87. Ibid.

88. *U.S. v. Hooker*, 1067.

89. Ibid.

90. *U.S. v. Hooker*, 1068.

91. Ibid.

92. Ibid.

93. Ibid.

94. Ibid.

95. John Affleck, "Firm, feds reach $129-million pact for cleanup of Love Canal." Internet, http://detnews.com.../stories/30020.htm. Written on December 28, 1995. Downloaded on 1/31/97.

96. Notes taken from personal interview with officials of Occidental Chemical Corporation, Niagara Falls, New York.

97. "Love Canal: How Culpable Is the City?" *Science News*. Volume 119. January 17, 1981.

References

Affleck, John. 1997. "Firm, feds reach $129-million pact for cleanup of Love Canal." Internet, http://detnews.com.menu/stories/30020.htm. Written on December 28, 1995.

Blumenthal, Ralph. 1980. "Bid to Curb Toxic Sites: Doubt Persists as U.S. Acts to Limit Dumping." *New York Times*, June 30.

Clark, Mary, and Mary Hager. 1980. "Fleeing the Love Canal." *Newsweek*. June 2.

Coase, Ronald H. 1960. "The Problem of Social Cost." *The Journal of Law & Economics*, 3: 1-40.

Davidson, Bill, Kristie Hoek, Carrie Smith, and Alline Peeler. 1997. "Love Canal: An Overview of the Toxic Waste Dump that Brought the Chemical Industry to its Knees." Internet, http://dirac.py.iup.edu/ college/chemistry/chemcourse/ sford2.txt.

Deegan, John Jr. 1987. "Looking Back at Love Canal." *Environmental Scientific Technology*. 21 November, 4: 328-31.

Hernan, Robert Emmet. 1996. *Excerpt from: A State's Right to Recover Punitive Damages in a Public Nuisance Action: The Love Canal Case Study*. Internet address:http://law.touro.edu/AboutTLC/journals/environmentalj/vol1/part3.html.

Hoffman, Andrew J. 1995. "An Uneasy Rebirth at Love Canal." *Environment.* Vol. 37 (March 15): 4-9.

"Love Canal: How Culpable Is the City?" *Science News.* Volume 119. January 17, 1981.

Love Canal Site, Niagara Falls, New York. Spring 1996.

"Love Canal: The Facts (1892-1982)." 1982. Occidental Chemical FACTLINE. Number 13, September 1982.

McPherson, Gary. 1994. "Distributed Control at Love Canal." *Intech.* Vol. 4 (September): 26-28.

Pigou, A. C. 1920. *The Economics of Welfare.* London: McMillan & Company.

Probst, Katherine N., Don Fullerton, Robert E. Litan, and Paul R. Portney. 1995. *Footing the Bill for Superfund Cleanups.* Washington, DC: Resources for the Future.

Schlager, Neil, ed. 1994. *When Technology Fails: Significant Technological Disasters, Accidents, and Failures of the Twentieth Century.* Foreword by Henry Petroski. Detroit: Gale Research.

U.S. Environmental Protection Agency. 1996. "Superfund at Work: Hazardous Waste Cleanup Efforts Nationwide." Washington, DC: U.S. Environmental Protection Agency.

U.S., State of New York, and UDC-Love Canal, Inc. v. Hooker Chemicals & Plastics Corporation, 1994. 850 F.SUPP. 993 (W.D.N.Y. 1994).

"What Hooker Told Whom, When About Love Canal." 1980. *The Wall Street Journal,* June 19.

Zuesse, Eric. 1981. "Love Canal: The Truth Seeps Out." *Reason,* February.

Chapter 3

EPA's Toxic Release Inventory

Jeffrey C. Terry

Introduction

Environmental legislation, in many cases, has not accomplished its stated purpose. In most cases, environmental statutes have set ambitious cleanup goals with specific dates targeted for their accomplishment. But generally the goals have not been met, and the dates have been pushed forward. The Comprehensive Environmental Response, Compensation, and Liability Act of 1980 (CERCLA), better known as Superfund, is a prime example of lofty goals and weak performance.

CERCLA established a national priority list for cleaning up old hazardous waste sites and contaminated areas. However, since 1980 only eighty of the 1,230 targeted sites have been cleaned. Part of the problem relates to costs. On average, the cost of cleaning the eighty sites runs between $25 million to $35 million (Dalton, 1993).

CERCLA was reauthorized in 1986. When the revised Superfund Amendments and Reauthorization Act (SARA) was signed into law a new feature was added, which many assess as one of the most effective environmental rules written to date. The new addition to the law involved the public's "right to know" about emissions that come from industrial plants. This right to know was embodied in requirements for an annual report called the Toxic Release Inventory (TRI). The new rule is considered to be effective because industrial plants responded by renewed efforts to reduce the volume of emissions reported on the TRI.

The requirements for the TRI are found in the Title III of the SARA. SARA, Title III is known as the Emergency Planning and Community Right to Know Act (EPCRA), which says, "The TRI requires owners and operators of certain facilities that manufacture, process, or otherwise use a listed chemical to report annually their release of such chemicals to any environmental medium" (Federal Register, February 16, 1988, 4500).

The annual release of the TRI understandably has brought a major response from the affected industries. They must meet new challenges. The TRI arguably has shifted some risk from the public to industry. The objectives of this chapter are to give an overview of the TRI, a theoretical view to how it came about, and a discussion of the TRI's actual purpose.

The chapter begins with a background discussion of toxic release issues and policy before the TRI, taking federal and state action into consideration. The next section discusses the chemical list itself and how it works. Section four discusses how the TRI has affected the U.S. chemical industry and how the industry has responded. The next section addresses the actual purpose of the TRI. The section continues with the development and testing of a statistical model that distinguishes between hypotheses regarding the purpose of the TRI. The next section expands the statistical model to include additional forms of emissions and then focuses the model on data for the U.S. chemical industry. This section introduces a theoretical explanation of the process in which changes in toxic releases are a desired outcome. Finally, the last section offers some concluding thoughts on the chapter.

Background to the Toxic Release Inventory

Prior to the TRI

Prior to the EPCRA and implementation of the TRI, chemical releases did not claim the attention attracted after the Bhopal incident in India (discussed later). Before the early 1970s, all releases fell under the jurisdiction of common law,[1] which relied on nuisance and tort law.

In the 1970s, the Clean Air Act and the Clean Water Act were introduced to U.S. industry. In some cases, industry welcomed the acts because they established stability for the industry. Common-law injunctions became obsolete, and governmental standards on chemical releases replaced them. The standards and stiff noncompliance penalties were strict enough to induce industry pollution reductions.

The new environmental statutes did not set standards based on toxicity factors, so there was little risk-based release data accumulated.[2] Common law and statutes in the 1970s did not directly take toxicity into account, which was offered as another reason for adopting a toxic release program.

The immediate or direct reason for implementing some toxic release reporting occurred on December 4, 1984, when a cloud of methyl isocyanate (MIC) gas (extremely toxic) seeped from a Union Carbide plant in Bhopal, India. A review of the tragedy indicated that estimates of those who have died vary from 4,300 to nearly 20,000. Tens of thousands more were injured and permanently disabled.

News of the disaster rattled across the ocean, and concerns were felt throughout the United States. "Could it happen here?" was the frightful question asked. A small leak was found at Union Carbide's West Virginia MIC manufacturing plant just a week after the Bhopal incident. Although no injuries occurred, the question became a greater concern.

Before these incidents, there were groups established to deal with chemical emergencies at all levels of government, but there was no national program, nor comprehensive state and local programs to deal with chemical accidents. To fill the vacuum, the Chemical Manufacturers Association (CMA) established a voluntary program called Community Awareness and Emergency Response (CAER).[3]

State and Federal Action

Chemical Emergency Preparedness Programs (CEPP)[4] were established by state and local governments to raise state and local awareness. The efforts led to state and local emergency plans. Over thirty states passed laws giving citizens and workers access to information on hazardous materials in the workplace and community. Some state laws required reporting of chemical releases. Most notably, New Jersey and Maryland drafted chemical lists that all manufacturing facilities had to report. Not all the state laws gave accessibility to the public, however.

The federal government began to lay plans to regulate the U.S. chemical industry. Congressman Henry A. Waxman (D-California) surveyed eighty-six of America's largest chemical companies (Hanson, 1991) on January 31, 1985. The survey was the subject of a hearing held by Waxman's Subcommittee on Health and Environment in conjunction with the Subcommittee on Commerce, Transportation, and Tourism chaired by James J. Florio (D.-New Jersey). A two-week deadline was given for the survey, and sixty-eight companies replied. When the lists were in, over 200 chemicals were considered hazardous according to Waxman's survey. The survey and hearing had many opponents; problems of vagueness were pervasive.

The survey asked companies to list releases of "poison gases" (Hanson, 1991). Most companies believed that they had to reply to the congressman. DuPont supplied data on all the chemicals listed in the survey, but Bruce W. Karrh, DuPont's Vice-President for Safety, Health, and Environmental Affairs, said that all of the firm's data were supplied whether or not the chemical posed any realistic risk in terms of probability of release of toxicity.

The term "poison gases" irritated a number of companies that replied. Dow Chemical noted in its inventory of releases that the term poison gas, from a regulatory standpoint, would only include phosgene. Crowley Chemical Company simply replied that they did not use or handle any poison gases.

Republican Don Ritter (Pa.) strongly attacked Waxman's survey by saying, "We seem to make a sort of guilt by association here, and I think it's wrong. Using release data of amounts of chemicals and trying to infer that there is automatically a hazard is wrong. We must consider the concepts of concentration and exposure when looking at the volumes of releases" (Hanson, 1992).

Other proposals were made after the wake of Bhopal, but most effectively, Florio's Community Right-to-Know Bill paved the way for Congress to enact the Emergency Planning and Community Right to Know Act (EPCRA). The law does not preempt state or local laws having more stringent requirements.[5] It requires that information about hazardous substances in and around a community be made available to the public. EPCRA also imposes strict penalties on noncomplying companies.

The Chemical List and How It Works

The original Toxic Release Inventory was derived by combining the lists of chemical releases from New Jersey's right-to-know program and Maryland's background survey for air toxics regulation. The inventory was originally set for 337 chemicals. Provisions within EPCRA allow substances to be added to or deleted from the TRI as a result of petitions by private citizens, industries, state governors, or by agency initiative.

As defined in EPCRA, those required to report to the TRI are owners and operators of facilities that manufacture, process, or otherwise use these listed chemicals. A facility is one that has ten or more full-time employees, is in the Standard Industrial Classification (SIC) codes 20 through 39, and exceeds an applicable manufacture, process, or threshold.[6]

Definitions and Requirements

The Congress and EPA have defined a number of terms in order to enhance public understanding.[7] Under SARA, Title III:

> *Establishment* is an economic unit, generally at a single physical location, where business is conducted or where services or industrial operations are performed.

> *Facility* means all buildings, equipment, structures, and other stationary items which are located on a single site or on contiguous or adjacent sites and that are owned and operated by the same person. A facility may contain more than one establishment.

> *Manufacture* means to produce, prepare, import, or compound a toxic chemical.

Otherwise use or *use* means any use of a toxic chemical that is not covered by the terms "manufacture" or "process" and includes use of a toxic chemical contained in a mixture or trade name product.

Process means the preparation of a toxic chemical, after its manufacture, for distribution in commerce.

Toxic means a substance that is capable of causing either acute (short-term) or chronic (long-term) human health effects or negative effects on the environment.

The EPA interprets the SIC codes 20 through 39 to the primary facility SIC codes. If a facility has multiple establishments, coverage is based on a relative comparison of the value of products shipped and/or produced at 20 through 39 establishments versus non-20 through 39 establishments within that facility. This allows for a more defined over-all report from facilities.

Threshold levels for chemical releases are determined by the statute. For chemical processing facilities, the statute originally set reporting thresholds at 75,000 pounds in 1987. The statute went on to define reporting thresholds of 50,000 pounds in 1988 and 25,000 pounds per year in 1989 and thereafter. For toxic chemicals otherwise used (derived from the original list), the threshold level is 10,000 pounds per year for reporting purposes.

A stipulation on mixtures and trade-name products imported says that all must be evaluated for evidence of toxic chemicals. EPA applied a *de minimis* concentration limitation of one percent (or a limit of .1 percent if a chemical is a known carcinogen) on such products. If the concentration is below the *de minimis* limit, the toxic chemical does not need to be reported.

Reporting Criteria

Those facilities required to report must do so by July 1 of each year. The TRI regulation sets fines up to $25,000 per day for those facilities that fail to comply on time. EPA Form R, which is completed for each and every chemical on the list, is the annual assessment tool used by the EPA to determine amounts of emissions into the air, water, and ground. The Pollution Prevention Act of 1990 expanded the TRI and the use of Form R. In 1991 mandatory reporting of on-site and off-site source reductions, recycling, and treatment were added.

The TRI's "reporting criteria" is a responsibility mostly imposed on the chemical industry and not at all on non-manufacturers, federal facilities, and small companies. Obviously, if these unaccounted sources are substantial, estimates of risks to human and environmental health will be biased.

Problems with the Original List

As mentioned, the original toxic chemical list was formed by combining the Maryland and New Jersey chemical manufacturing and release lists. Although the state lists were established under similar community right to know programs, the lists were not based on toxicity. Hence, human and environmental health toxicity risk assessments were not conducted. Without risk analysis to test whether chemicals impose actual risks, the defining and creating of a "toxic" release list is misguided. The TRI could more accurately be called the Chemicals Release Inventory.

The U.S. Chemical Industry

The chemical industry has been under scrutiny ever since isolated incidents occurred in the early to mid-1970s. Bhopal was the final blow to the industry's credibility. The industry responded to disasters such as these in a number of ways.

The chemical industry had already established CHEMTREC in 1971, which is an emergency response center. As more incidents occurred involving dangerous chemical explosions, spills, and releases, the chemical industry began to incorporate additional responses and programs for companies and communities. The National Chemical Response and Information Center was established for both private and public use. CHEMNET, an on-site assistance program, was also adopted by the industry. Also, the industry adopted a chemical emergency response training program.

Still, through all the administrative program additions, the chemical industry's credibility wavered. Although many representatives from the industry opposed a structured reporting of chemical releases to an inventory, a statute containing requirements for such an inventory (TRI) was signed into law.

Response to the TRI

The U.S. chemical industry has been significantly affected by the TRI legislation, since it is the number one producer and releaser of listed chemicals.[8] Irrespective of the actual quantified risks associated with chemical releases, media fanfares accompanying the release of TRI data have diminished industry credibility and the brand-name capital of specific firms. The industry has reacted. In short, the TRI has given chemical manufacturers the incentive to adopt new technologies and costly plans, which might not be cost beneficial, in an effort to reduce emissions while increasing production.

According to the Chemical Manufacturers Association (CMA), its affiliates (over 90 percent of the industry) reported 6 percent TRI reductions from 1990 to

1991 and 35 percent reductions since the base year 1987. Throughout this time period (1987-1991), the industry's production rose by 11 percent, and 20 percent more facilities began reporting.[9]

Chemical Industry Costs of the TRI

The TRI has been an effective device for reducing emissions of chemical releases. Although it has spurred innovation on the part of industry, the question of costs arises in the wake of innovation and regulatory response.

It is not clear that the innovations and methods used by the chemical industry to respond to the TRI legislation are economically efficient. The chemical industry's capital expenditures for pollution abatement were relatively stable in the early to mid-1980s, but when EPCRA and the TRI were implemented, capital expenditures devoted to pollution abatement soared. In 1986, capital expenditures for pollution abatement (Chemicals and Allied Products, and Manufacturers) were $3.471 million, but when the TRI was implemented in 1987 and thereafter, capital expenditures rose each year and were $9.456 million in 1991.[10]

Of course, as individual companies comply with the TRI, expenditures may fluctuate. Arco Chemical's TRI emissions rose 20 percent from 1991 to 1992 and subsequently environmental spending rose from just over $50 million in 1991 to nearly $120 million in 1992.[11] Dow Chemical reported TRI emissions fell 7.8 percent between 1991 and 1992, and its environmental spending decreased from over $300 million in 1991 to just above $250 million in 1992.[12] But the problem is that cost-benefit analysis was not used by policy makers in forming the TRI. The TRI simply pressured industry to reduce these chemical emissions.

With a high probability of high-cost and low-benefit outcomes, two more questions can be asked:

1. Is the public really benefitting from the TRI?

2. Is the environment really benefitting from the TRI?

Subjective evaluation can be an effective method used in determining if the TRI is benefitting the public. Simply, subjective evaluation means every individual has a different conviction of what is beneficial to him or her. Individual convictions can be measured by a person's willingness to pay for reducing some toxic release. One person may be willing to give up everything he/she owns for total reduction of TRI releases, but another person is not willing to spend an additional dollar for prescription medicine (provided by the chemical industry) because of the higher costs imposed by TRI regulations. When an industry is forced to comply with environmental rules that lead to cost exceeding benefits, a misallocation of resources occurs; that is, the resources used for statutory compliance have higher valued alternative uses.

The environmental question raises similar issues. If so much money is allocated to reduce TRI emissions, monies for other environmental betterment programs will be cut, and inevitably, the environmental benefits that might spring from the other programs will be reduced.

The Purpose of the TRI

The chemical industry fought for the passage of an inventory reporting statute, but the TRI was still passed into law. Obviously, there had to have been some key groups involved in passing the law. Once the law was passed, the public became involved in its enforcement. This section addresses the political process and provides an answer to the question, "What is the purpose of the TRI?"

The TRI falls under the legislation Emergency Planning and Community Right to Know Act, which says that chemical emissions information received from industries will be made available to the public in a database. This can easily be interpreted as saying that the purpose of the TRI is to inform a broad cross section of the public, which forms a hypothesis to be considered in this section.

Alternatively, a hypothesis can be stated that the primary purpose of the TRI is not to inform the masses but to appeal to a narrow cross section of the public who will lobby to induce more pollution reductions from affected industries. It is possible to test the two hypotheses by examining empirically the determinants of changes in the level of point and nonpoint air emissions as indicated by the TRI. The operating hypothesis states that the TRI is designed to induce additional pollution control.

The Model

The level of TRI emissions reported by the EPA is the result of a political/economic process that involves producers of emissions, regulators, and interested citizens who organize to affect emission outcomes. In 1988, EPA released its first TRI emissions data set. The theory developed here argues that people in communities saw the TRI report and determined that lower future emissions were desired. Those most interested in affecting outcomes proceeded to organize interest groups to bring about change. The lower their cost of organizing, all else equal, the better the chance that they would be effective. At the same time, each state had regulatory agencies charged with controlling emissions. The regulatory agencies form a linkage between the citizen groups and the polluters.

If the TRI is driven by efforts to inform citizens, then those who are typically more informed will be more effective in inducing change. The higher the level of reading ability, for example, the more effective the group in reducing future emissions. If, however, the interest groups are organized primarily by individuals who have the highest level of educational attainment, then it is assumed that the TRI process is a special interest process, not necessarily a process designed to inform a large cross section of the population.

To develop the empirical counterpart of the story, variables were selected that proxy for key elements in the theoretical story. The logical form of the model is written:

$$EMIS = f(ENVEXP, POPDEN, LCV, VALUE92, SAT, HSGRAD, EDUC, FEDLAND).$$

There will be two specific emission release variables used as EMIS.[13] These variables are: STACK and NONPOINT.

STACK is TRI stack air emissions per capita by state for the year 1992.[14] Stack air emissions were chosen as the dependent variable because every state has numerous facilities that emit TRI emissions through air point-sources. Use of the variable allows for universal consideration in analyzing state and industrial responses to the independent variables. NONPOINT is TRI fugitive air emissions per capita by state for the year 1992. TRI nonpoint air emissions by state, on average, are slightly smaller than stack air emissions by state.

Table 3.1 gives a brief definition of each of the independent variables and the expected sign on the coefficient. ENVEXP is the amount spent on pollution abatement and environmental control per capita by state in 1990.[15] It is expected to have a negative coefficient; the more money spent on environmental control by state in 1990, the lower the stack air emissions per capital will be in 1992, everything else the same.

LCV is the average League of Conservation Voters rating for each state's two senators.[16] The greater the LCV per senator, the more environmentally aware he or she is and the "greener" the vote. It is assumed that the LCV rating reflects the preference of each state's population. The higher the average LCV of senators in each state in 1988, the lower the stack emissions per capital will be in 1992.

POPDEN is the population density (number of people per square mile) in each state in 1988. It is predicted to have a negative coefficient for the reason that higher population density in 1988 yields lower organizing costs and lower 1992 emissions.

There are three variables used to define education levels: SAT, HISGRAD, and EDUC. The education variable SAT is the average 1988 SAT score in each state, and represents data for a broad cross section of the population.[17] It is assumed that the more educated people are, the more environmentally aware they are. With this in mind, if the actual purpose of the TRI is to inform the public, the higher the average SAT scores by state in 1988, the lower the TRI stack air emissions per capita by state will be in 1992. Therefore, SAT is predicted to have

Jeffrey C. Terry

Table 3.1. Independent Variables: Descriptions

Variable	Definition	Expected Sign of Coefficient
ENVEXP	The amount spent on pollution abatement and environmental control per capita by state in 1990	negative
POPDEN	Population density per state in 1988	negative
LCV	The League of Conservation Voters rating	negative
VALUE92	Value added in manufacturing in 1992	positive
SAT	Average SAT score by state in 1988	negative
HSGRAD	% of only high school grads by state in 1988	negative
EDUC	% of people in each state with B.S. and/or advanced degrees (Ph.D.)	negative
FEDLAND	% of federally-owned land per state	negative

a negative coefficient. On the other hand, if the purpose of the TRI is to reduce emissions, SAT may have no significance at all.

HSGRAD is the percentage of a state population over the age of twenty-four who have no more than a high school education. Like SAT, HSGRAD covers a large percentage of a state's population. It can be assumed that the higher the percentage of high school educated individuals in 1988, the lower STACK will be. This predicts a negatively signed coefficient for HSGRAD. In 1988, environmental policy issues (TRI) were not discussed in detail in a high school curriculum, so this variable may have a positive or insignificant relationship with STACK.

EDUC is the percentage of individuals who have obtained bachelor degrees and/or advanced degrees (Ph.D.) in each state in 1988, a much more restrictive sample of a state's population, and a key variable in testing the hypothesis that the TRI is an instrument used by special interest groups. The higher the level of educational attainment, the more likely individuals will be politically active and environmentally aware. Therefore, a negative coefficient is expected. The larger the value of EDUC in 1988, the lower the TRI stack air emissions per capita in that state will be expected in 1992.

VALUE92 is the value added in manufacturing in 1992. The variable VALUE92 accounts for industrial production. The effect of the variable is assumed to be positive. All else equal, an increase in industrial production is assumed to generate more emissions.

FEDLAND is the percent of land owned by government for each state. FEDLAND proxies for national parks and other features of nature that are important to environmentalists. Therefore, FEDLAND is predicted to have a negative coefficient.[18]

For every independent variable a null hypothesis is stated: The coefficients of all independent variables are zero. Alternatively, the independent variables help to explain variation in the dependent variable, and therefore become significant.

The Estimation of STACK

In analyzing the relationships between the dependent and independent variables a cross-section regression was estimated for fifty observations (representing the fifty states). The model was first estimated in a linear form and then in a log-linear form. In all cases, the log-linear regression was superior.

Table 3.2 shows the results of the regression for TRI stack air emissions, where the "L" in front of every variable indicates logarithm form. LPOPDEN and LFEDLAND have negative and significant coefficients. LPOPDEN is significant at the 5 percent level, two-tailed test. The negative sign indicates that a greater population density per state in 1988 is associated with the lower TRI stack air emissions per capita in 1992. LFEDLAND is significant at the 5 percent level and

Table 3.2. OLS Regression Results for the Model Using LSTACK as the Dependent Variable

Variable	Coefficients/ (t-statistics)
LLCV	-0.2519 (-1.387)
LENVEXP	0.2669 (1.070)
LPOPDEN	-0.3775 (-2.371)[b]
LVALUE92	0.4808 (3.480)[a]
LEDUC	-0.1874 (-2.206)[b]
LSAT	0.2973 (-0.012)
LHSGRAD	0.2998 (0.202)
LFEDLAND	-0.3062 (-2.183)[b]
R^2	0.4598
Adj R^2	0.3544
F Statistic	4.3622
N	50

[a] Significant at the 1 percent level for a two-tailed test.
[b] Significant at the 5 percent level for a two-tailed test.

is negatively signed. The coefficient shows that a 1 percent increase in LFEDLAND is associated with a 0.31 percent reduction in LSTACK.

LEDUC, which proxies for informed pressure groups, has a negative coefficient and is significant at the 5 percent level, two-tailed test. The outcome supports the special interest theory. The coefficient indicates that a 1 percent increase in LEDUC is associated with a 1.87 percent decrease in LSTACK. LSAT and LHSGRAD both have negative coefficients, but are not sigificant. The combined results for LEDUC, LSAT, and LHSGRAD reject the "inform the public" hypothesis.

LVALUE92s coefficient is significant at the one percent level, two-tailed test. LVALUE92 indicates that the greater the value added in manufacturing in 1992 by state, the greater the TRI stack air emissions per capita by state in 1992. LENVEXP is insignificant.

To modify the model, LSAT and LHSGRAD were deleted and the results are given in table 3.3. The modified model assigns similar importance to LEDUC, which is significant at the 5 percent level, two-tailed test. A 1 percent increase in the number of highly educated people leads to a 1.79 percent decrease in LSTACK. Again, the result supports the theory that highly educated people drive the political process. This, in turn, supports the theory that the TRI is an emission reduction tool.

LFEDLAND is assigned more importance by the modified model. It is significant at the 1 percent level, two-tailed test. With a 1 percent increase in federally owned land per state, there would be a 0.29 percent reduction in TRI stack air emissions per capita by state in 1992. LVALUE92 remained significant at the 1 percent level, two-tailed test. With a 1 percent increase in LVALUE92, a 0.48 percent increase in TRI point air emissions would occur. LENVEXP remains insignificant in the modified model.

Additional Testing

Additional tests were run using TRI nonpoint air releases per capita by state as the dependent variable to see if the political/economic process affects other forms of pollution. Later in the section, a specialized approach to this process is introduced by using U.S. chemical industry TRI data. This will assist in determining, in a specialized way, the purpose of the TRI.

The Estimation of NONPOINT

The model was first estimated in a linear form and then in a log-linear form. Similar to the model with STACK as the dependent variable, the log-linear

Table 3.3. OLS Regression Results for the Modified Model Using LSTACK as the Dependent Variable

Variable	Coefficients/ (t-statistics)
LLCV	-0.2583 (-1.486)
LENVEXP	0.2515 (1.085)
LPOPDEN	-0.3734 (-2.692)[a]
LVALUE92	0.4837 (3.615)[a]
LEDUC	-1.7876 (-2.497)[b]
LFEDLAND	-0.2909 (-2.650)[a]
R^2	0.4593
Adj R^2	0.3838
F Statistic	6.0868
N	50

[a] Significant at the 1 percent level for a two-tailed test.
[b] Significant at the 5 percent level for a two-tailed test.

regression is superior. The letter "L" in front of each variable indicates logarithm form.

Table 3.4 shows the results of the regression on the dependent variable LNONPOINT. Once again the coefficients of LLCV, LFEDLAND, LVALUE92, and LEDUC are highly significant. LSAT, LHSGRAD, LENVEXP, and LPOPDEN are insignificant variables. The test supports the special-interest theory rejecting the hypothesis that the TRI is intended to inform a broad cross section of the public.

Table 3.5 gives the results of a modified model using LNOPOINT as the dependent variable. The modified model has LSAT and LHSGRAD deleted. The independent variables in the model explain a significant amount of the variation in LNOPOINT. LPOPDEN and LENVEXP are still insignificant.

The modified model assigns slightly less importance to LEDUC. A 1 percent increase in highly educated individuals leads to a decrease in TRI nonpoint air emissions per capita by state by 1.44 percent, all else equal. Also, 1 percent increases in LFEDLAND and LVALUE92 will lead to a 0.22 percent decrease in LNOPOINT, respectively. LLCV is highly significant and is assigned more importance in the modified model. A 1 percent increase in LLCV is associated with a 0.24 percent decrease in LNOPOINT, all else equal.

A Test Using Chemical Industry Data

The U.S. chemical industry has been a target of the TRI regulation. The approach used in modelling the chemical industry data is identical to the prior section, which used all industries (SIC codes 20-39) emissions data for each state in 1992. Estimates of the empirical model using the chemical industry data are based on the following logical model:

EMIS = f(ENVEXP, POPDEN, LCV, FEDLAND, VALUE92, EDUC),

As with the all-industry estimate, which used STACK as the dependent variable, CHSTACK is chemical industry (SIC code 28) TRI stack air emissions per capita by state in 1992.[19] Chemical facilities are found in every state.

CHFUG is chemical industry TRI fugitive air emissions per capita by state in 1992. TRI nonpoint air emissions by the chemical industry by state, on average, are less than stack air emissions, but CHFUG will assist in giving a more specific account of the theoretical model discussed earlier.

The Estimation of CHSTACK

Table 3.5 shows the results of the regression for chemical industry TRI stack air emissions, where the "L" in front of every variable indicates logarithm form.

Table 3.4. OLS Regression Results for the Model Using LNONPOINT as the Dependent Variable

Variable	Coefficients/ (t-statistics)
LLCV	-0.2218 (-1.880)^c
LENVEXP	0.8726 (0.538)
LPOPDEN	-0.1183 (-1.144)
LVALUE92	0.2445 (2.724)^a
LEDUC	-1.7542 (-3.179)^a
LSAT	-1.5477 (-0.999)
LHSGRAD	-0.9556 (-0.992)
LFEDLAND	-0.2878 (-3.158)^a
R^2	0.5318
Adj R^2	0.4405
F Statistic	5.8215
N	50

^{a} Significant at the 1 percent level for a two-tailed test.
^{c} Significant at the 10 percent level for a two-tailed test.

Table 3.5. OLS Regression Results for the Model Using LNOPOINT as the Dependent Variable

Variable	Coefficients/ (t-statistics)
LLCV	-0.2353 (-2.036)[b]
LENVEXP	0.3058 (0.199)
LPOPDEN	-0.6268 (-0.680)
LVALUE92	0.2482 (2.792)[a]
LEDUC	-1.4356 (-3.018)[a]
LFEDLAND	-0.2152 (-2.951)[a]
R^2	0.5098
Adj R^2	0.4414
F Statistic	7.4525
N	50

[a] Significant at the 1 percent level for a two-tailed test.
[b] Significant at the 5 percent level for a two-tailed test.

LEDUC and LFEDLAND have negative and significant coefficients. LEDUC is significant at the 1 percent level, two-tailed test. Its coefficient indicates that a 1 percent increase in LEDUC is associated with a 3.81 percent decrease in chemical industry TRI stack air emissions per capita by state. This interpretation, more specifically than STACK, supports the theory that the TRI is an emissions reduction tool.[20]

LFEDLAND is also significant at the 1 percent level, two-tailed test. A 1 percent increase in federally owned land by state is associated with a 0.57 percent reduction in LCHSTACK. LVALUE92 is also significant (at the 1 percent level) and has a positive coefficient. A 1 percent increase in LVALUE92 is associated with a 0.71 percent increase in LCHSTACK. LPOPDEN is significant at the 10 percent level and is negative. In this estimate, LENVEXP is significant at the 5 percent level but has a positive coefficient. One cannot infer that state regulators focus on the chemical industry. LLCV is insignificant.

The Estimation of CHFUG

A additional model was estimated using chemical industry TRI nonpoint air releases per capita by state (LCHFUG) as the dependent variable. Table 3.6 shows the results of the regression using LCHFUG as the dependent variable.

LEDUC and LFEDLAND are highly significant and have negative coefficients. LEDUC is significant at the 1 percent level, two-tailed test. It is better explained by saying that a 1 percent increase in highly educated people is associated with a 2.88 percent decrease in LCHFUG. This again supports the theory that the TRI is a means of diminishing emissions.

LFEDLAND is significant at the 5 percent level, two-tailed test. A 1 percent increase in LFEDLAND is associated with a 0.42 percent decrease in chemical industry TRI nonpoint air emissions per capita by state. LLCV also has a negative coefficient and is not significant.

LVALUE92 is significant at the 1 percent level and has a positive coefficient. LENVEXP is not significant at conventional levels of significance. LPOPDEN is insignificant.

Summary

The general models illustrated in tables 3.3 and 3.4 show significant results in estimating the relationship between the independent variables and the dependent variable.[21] The results of the regressions show that highly educated individuals drive the emission reduction process. It can be inferred that these individuals work through the political and public relations process to place pressure on industrial firms, which in turn reduce emissions. The larger the level of industrial activity, the higher the emissions.

The results also imply that individuals with only high school diplomas are not politically active in the process. This implies that the TRI is not reaching a large segment of the population.

The specific models, illustrated in tables 3.6 and 3.7, are based on TRI data from the chemical industry and allow for a more distinct analysis of the theory being tested. The results of the regressions also indicate that highly educated individuals drive the emission reduction process. The larger the state's ownership of land, the more stringent the regulation, and the larger the reduction of emissions from the chemical industry. The larger the level of chemical industry activity, the higher the fugitive emissions.

It can be inferred from the tests that the variability across states of air emissions, both stack and fugitive releases, is partially explained by a political process. Those parties that are interested in seeing pollution reduced are pushing to lower air emissions. The results say nothing about air pollution risks to human health, but the results in table 3.3, 3.4, 3.5, 3.6, and 3.7 suggest that more pressure is put on industry, specifically the chemical industry, for reducing air pollution.

Theoretical Interpretation

The empirical work suggests that the TRI's primary goal is not to reach out and inform the majority of the state populations. Put differently, the results suggest that the TRI is designed to generate pressure for emissions reductions.

The results support the notions of public choice theory:

> 'Choice' is the act of selecting from alternatives. 'Public' refers to people. But 'people' do not choose. Choices are made by individuals, and these may be 'private' or 'public.' A person makes private choices as he goes about his ordinary business of living. He makes 'public choices' when he selects among the alternatives for others as well as for himself.[22]

More simply stated, people who act in a self-interested way when making economic decisions are also the same people who vote, run for office, or are employed in the bureaucracy. Individuals bring their self-interests into politics.[23]

Rent-seeking behavior is a part of public choice theory and involves the commitment of scarce resources to capture returns created artificially.[24] Special-interest groups organize (the closer they geographically live together, the less costly it is to organize) and lobby government officials. Government officials' primary goal (their self-interest) is to stay in office, so pleasing their constituents is essential. Here government officials' self-interest comes into play by receiving

Table 3.6. OLS Regresion Results for the Model Using LCHSTACK as the Dependent Variable

Variable	Coefficients/ (t-statistics)
LLCV	-0.3682 (-1.181)
LENVEXP	0.8433 (2.030)^c
LPOPDEN	-0.4574 (-1.840)^c
LVALUE92	0.7078 (2.952)^a
LEDUC	-3.8084 (-2.969)^a
LFEDLAND	-0.5734 (-2.916)^a
R^2	0.4294
Adj R^2	0.3497
F Statistic	5.3923
N	50

[a] Significant at the 1 percent level for a two-tailed test.
[c] Significant at the 10 percent level for a two-tailed test.

Table 3.7. OLS Regression Results for the Model Using LCHFUG as the Dependent Variable

Variable	Coefficients/ (t-statistics)
LLCV	-0.4532 (-1.632)
LENVEXP	0.5695 (1.539)
LPOPDEN	-0.1897 (-0.857)
LVALUE92	0.7252 (3.395)[a]
LEDUC	-2.8838 (-2.524)[a]
LFEDLAND	-0.4211 (-2.403)[b]
R^2	0.4297
Adj R^2	0.3500
F Statistic	5.3972
N	50

[a] Significant at the 1 percent level for a two-tailed test.
[b] Significant at the 5 percent level for a two-tailed test.

contributions or promises of protest by organized groups in return for stricter regulations on industrial polluting. Both the action group and the politician are rent seeking.

A public choice picture of the TRI is painted in the empirical tests. The results clearly illustrate that the TRI is not reaching large numbers of the U.S. population. Therefore, the TRI is not living up to its community right-to-know statutory title. The TRI appears to be another regulatory tool designed to generate pressure for industrial emissions reduction.

Concluding Thoughts

Some may say that the TRI has been an effective piece of environmental legislation because it has resulted in an emission reduction response from the chemical industry. The effective response is only one dimension of the TRI, however. For the TRI to be considered a beneficial piece of environmental policy, it must incorporate elements of efficiency.

Without this efficiency criterion, the TRI is subject to many problems:

1. The original drafting of the chemical list fails to incorporate toxicity as relevant criteria.

2. The reporting criterion is very limited in accumulating accurate data and determining actual exposure risks.

3. There is no effort to assure that industry acts in cost-beneficial ways when responding to the provisions of the TRI.

These problems touch on some of the major shortcomings of the Toxic Release Inventory.

The purpose of the TRI must be reevaluated as well. The TRI was introduced and incorporated into the Superfund Amendment and Reauthorization Act for the purpose of imposing more costs on industries, primarily the chemical industry, to reduce emissions. Perhaps the list was also entitled "Toxic" so more pressure can be put on industry by the public and the media directly as well. If this is the intention of the TRI, the law can be modified to reach the same goals without imposing high costs.

Perhaps now is a more stable time, unlike when pressures were felt after the Bhopal incident, for a reevaluation of the TRI. With an actual toxicity list, industry will be able to concentrate on true risks to human health and the environment without incurring high costs by reducing emissions that limit trivial risks. Policy makers should incorporate cost effectiveness and incentives for industry into their legislative thinking. If this is done, an accurate, efficient, and cost-beneficial Toxic Release Inventory will be the outcome.

Notes

1. Common law was effective to the extent that industry would not pose extreme costs onto surrounding communities. With standing, damages imposed by the industry, the public would be granted an injunction against the industry. The threat of closure was an effective tool in reducing industrial releases (Findley and Farber, 1992).

2. Toxicity of a substance is defined as, of, or related to a poison or toxin (Webster, 1984).

3. CAER was the chemical industry's initial response to Bhopal. It is a program that establishes dialogue with citizens and involves the public as partners for chemical emergencies and managing chemical risks in the community (Chemical Manufacturers Association, 1992).

4. CRPPs are State Emergency Response Commissions (SERCs) and Local Emergency Planning Committees (LEPCs) that were established to raise public awareness and preparedness of chemical risks (U.S. EPA, 19-29).

5. *Federal Register* 40 CFR 372 (February 16, 1988) p. 4501.

6. Ibid., p. 4500.

7. Ibid., p. 4525.

8 Illustrated in EPA, *1991 Toxics Release Inventory, Public Data Release.* Washington, DC, Office of Pollution Prevention and Toxics, 1992.

9. Chemical Manufacturers Association, *Preventing Pollution in the Chemical Industry* (Washington, DC: CMA, Inc., 1992) CMA, *U.S. Chemical Industry Statistical Handbook* (Washington DC: CMA, Inc., 1993) and David Hanson "CMA Issues First Data on Pollution Prevention," in *Chemical and Engineering News,* April 1, 1985, pp. 7-8.

10. CMA, *U.S. Chemical Industry Statistical Handbook* (Washington, DC: CMA Inc., 1993), p. 136.

11. Elisabeth Kirschner "Environment Spending and TRI Up for Arco, Down for Dow," *Chemical Week,* December 15, 1993, p. 12.

12. Ibid.

13. There are problems with the TRI emissions data used to form dependent variables. Toxic release data are self-reported by the individual facility managers. The discrepancy lies in whether a manager decides to report all TRI releases. If the incentive of not reporting is greater than the cost of being caught for not reporting all data and being fined, then emission data may be manipulated and inconsistent data are reported. The costs of being caught seem to be rather low. For example, a 1991 U.S. General Accounting Office report on the TRI indicated that the EPA had only visited twenty-seven of the more than 19,000 facilities that have reported

emissions to assess the quality of data. [United States General Accounting Office, *Toxic Chemicals, EPA's Toxic Release Inventory Is Useful but Can Be Improved,* RCED-91-121, Washington, DC, U.S. GAO, June 1991].

There is no universal standard in estimating releases, so there is a discrepancy with the methods of estimating and reporting information to the TRI. EPA Form R is the universal document used by facilities to report TRI releases to the EPA, but it is very vague and confusing, which can lead to misinterpretations of data and faulty estimations.

14. The TRI emissions data for the dependent variables, STACK and NONPOINT, came from EPA, *1992 Toxic Release Inventory Public Data Release* (Washington, DC: Office of Pollution Prevention and Toxics, 1992), pp. 196-204, and the population data came from U.S. Bureau of the Census, *Statistical Abstract of the United States 1993* (Washington, DC: U.S. Governmental Printing Office, 1993), p. 28.

Also, the independent variables: POPDEN, HSGRAD, EDUC, FEDLAND, and VALUE92, came from U.S. Bureau of the Census, *Statistical Abstract of the United States 1993* (Washington, DC: U.S. Governmental Printing Office, 1993).

15. ENVEXP data came from Bob Hall and Mary Lee Kerr, *1991-1992 Green Index* (Washington, DC: Island Press, 1991), p. 148.

16. LCV data are from Michael Barone and Grant Ujifusa, *The Almanac of American Politics 1992* (Washington, DC: National Journal Inc., 1991), pp. 9-1368.

17. SAT data are from National Center for Education Statistics, *Digest of Education Statistics* (Washington, DC: U.S. Department of Education, 1993), p. 129.

18. Average per capita income for each state was originally incorporated into the model, but in estimating, income was insignificant. In evaluating the present model and the model with income as an independent variable, it is determined that income is multi-collinear with the other independent variables; more simply, income is indirectly present in the current model.

19. The TRI emissions data for the dependent variables, CHSTACK and CHFUG, are from the source, EPA *1992 Toxic Release Inventory Public Data Release* (Washington, DC: Office of Pollution Prevention and Toxics, 1992), and the population data are from U.S. Bureau of the Census, *Statistical Abstract of the United States 1993* (Washington, DC: U.S. Governmental Printing Office, 1993), p. 28.

20. An estimate was run incorporating LHSGRAD without LEDUC and LSAT, and it was found to be insignificant. The same is true when estimating LSAT as the only education variable in the model.

21. Additional tests were run using land releases and surface water releases as dependent variables. Neither estimation found a high level of significance between the independent variables and the dependent variable. LPOPDEN is the

only significant variable with land releases. The coefficient is significant at the 5 percent level of a two-tailed test and is negative.

In estimating water releases, LPOPDEN and LEDUC are the only two significant variables. The coefficient of LPOPDEN says that with a 1 percent increase in population density, an equivalent 0.37 percent reduction in water releases will result. Also, a 1 percent increase in LEDUC is associated with a 2.09 percent decrease in water releases. Although both estimates of land and water releases are weak, the variables LPOPDEN and LEDUC are still significant factors in the pollution reduction story. TRI data are from EPA, *1992 Toxic Release Inventory Public Data Release* (Washington, DC: Office of Pollution Prevention and Toxics, 1992), pp. 196-204; and the population data are from U.S. Bureau of the Census, *Statistical Abstract of the United States 1993* (Washington, DC: U.S. Governmental Printing Office 1993), p. 28.

22. Public choice is defined in Center for the Study of Public Choice, *Annual Report 1993* (Washington, DC: George Mason University, 1993).

23. Ryan C. Amacher and Holley H. Ulbrich, *Principles of Microeconomics* (Cincinnati, Ohio: South-Western Publishing Co., 1992), p. 460.

24. Ibid.

References

Amacher, Ryan C. and Holley H. Ulbrich. 1992. *Principles of Microeconomics.* Cincinnati, Ohio: South-Western Publishing Company.

Barone, Michael, and Grant Ujifusa. 1991. *The Almanac of American Politics, 1992.* Washington, DC, National Journal Inc.

Begley, Ronald. 1993. "New TRI Data Shows Chemical Industry Remains Top Toxic Polluter." *Chemical Week,* June 2: 8.

"Carbide Embroiled in Post-Bhopal Issues." *Chemical and Engineering News,* January 28.

Center for the Study of Public Choice. 1993. *1993 Annual Report.* Washington, DC: George Mason University.

Chemical Manufacturers Association (CMA). 1992. *Preventing Pollution In the Chemical Industry.* Washington, DC: CMA Inc.

———. 1993. *Protecting the Environment.* Washington, DC: CMA Inc., July.

———. 1993. *U.S. Chemical Industry Statistical Handbook.* Washington, D.C., CMA Inc.

Dalton, Brett. 1993. "Superfund: The South Carolina Experience," In Roger E. Meiners and Bruce Yandle, eds., *Taking the Environment Seriously.* Lanham, Md: Rowman & Littlefield Publishers, Inc.

Environmental Protection Agency (EPA). 1988. *Chemicals in Your Community.* Washington, DC: Environmental Protection Agency, September.

84   *Jeffrey C. Terry*

———. 1991. *1991 Toxics Release Inventory Public Data Release.* Washington, DC: Office of Pollution Prevention and Toxics.

———. 1992. *1992 Toxics Release Inventory Public Data Release.* Washington, DC: Office of Pollution Prevention and Toxics.

Federal Register, 1988. 40 CFR 372. February 16: 4501.

Findley, Roger W., and Daniel A. Farber. 1992. *Environmental Law.* St. Paul, MN: West Publishing Company.

General Accounting Office. 1991. *Toxic Chemicals: EPA's Toxics Release Inventory Is Useful but Can Be Improved.* RCED-91-121. Washington, DC: U.S. GAO, June.

Hall, Bob, and Mary Lee Kerr. 1991. *1991-1992 Green Index.* Washington, DC: Island Press.

Hanson, David J. 1991. "Toxics Release Inventory Growing More Contentious." *Chemical and Engineering News,* June 3.

———. 1992. "TRI Data Show Steady Drop in Emissions." *Chemical and Engineering News,* June 15.

———. 1993. "CMA Issues First Data on Pollution Prevention." *Chemical and Engineering News,* April 29.

Heller, Karen. 1992. "Toxics Use Reduction." *Chemical Week,* August 19.

"Industry Safety Reforms: Bhopal Inspires New Initiatives." 1985. *Chemical and Engineering News,* April 1.

Kirschner, Elisabeth. 1993. "Environmental Spending and TRI Up for Arco, Down for Dow." *Chemical Week,* December 15.

National Center for Education Statistics. 1993. *Digest of Education Statistics.* Washington, DC: U.S. Department of Education.

"Toxics Futures." 1985. *New Statesman and Society.* January 26.

U.S. Bureau of the Census. 1993. *Statistical Abstract of the United States.* Washington, DC: U.S. Governmental Printing Office.

Webster's New World Dictionary. 1984. New York: First Warner Books Printing, 1984.

Weinstock, Matthew P. 1993. "Form R: A Problem of Definition." *Occupational Hazards,* March.

Chapter 4

Evaluation of Toxic Release Inventory Data Using Risk Assessment Techniques

Mariela Mercedes Nino Restrepo

Introduction

Major environmental catastrophes often trigger federal legislation to deal with the problem. The first major piece of federal clean air legislation followed on the heels of smog in Los Angeles and inversions over Danora, Pennsylvania. Superfund followed Love Canal, and the 1986 Community Right-To-Know Act followed the 1984 tragedy at Bophal, India, where an accidental release of methyl isocyanate gas killed or incapacitated in the tens of thousands.

With similar, but not tragic, leakages having occurred in other places, national politicians sensed that there ought to be a law affecting the way toxic chemicals are used and controlled in manufacturing. The instrument designed to do that was the Toxic Release Inventory (TRI) requirement of the 1986 Act (Title III of SARA). The TRI requires an annual report of any normal or accidental release of chemicals listed by the U.S. Environmental Protection Agency (EPA). Regardless of the benefits obtained from the TRI until now, the serious policy analyst must ask if its performance could be improved, and if all the valuable information collected by EPA could be used in a superior way to address the same problem?

This report addresses these two questions and shows that a relatively simple transformation of TRI data can yield significant information for those who seek to reduce the risks associated with chemical releases. As will be explained later, the analysis raises serious questions about the efficiency (maximum benefits per dollar) and effectiveness (maximum risk reduction) associated with TRI in its current form.

The report is organized as follows: The next section provides background on the TRI and the legislation containing it. Here, detail is provided on how the TRI works and how it has evolved. The section that follows places the TRI in a risk reduction framework and offers a theoretical explanation of how an improved TRI might work. The section includes a brief discussion of some of the benefits and costs of the TRI program. The report's last major section develops a risk-based TRI model and, taking actual TRI data, shows how the data can be usefully transformed to provide superior risk-based information to those who seek to guard themselves and the environment. A set of brief thoughts concludes the report.

EPCRA and the Toxic Release Inventory

In 1986 the legislation for Superfund, known formally as the Comprehensive Environmental Response, Compensation and Liability Act (CERCLA), was reauthorized by the U.S. Congress's 1986 Superfund Amendments and Reauthorization Act (SARA). SARA modified the workings of the Superfund cleanup process and added a major new section titled the Emergency Planning and Community Right to Know Act (EPCRA). Following on the heels of the Bophal incident, EPCRA expressed the logical idea that people in communities that might be adversely affected by chemical leaks and spills have a right to know more about these risks. Leaping from risk to quantity of chemicals, EPCRA implies that if a community is informed about the quantities of toxic chemicals processed in nearby plants or emitted to the local environments, then risks can be evaluated, and the cost of taking offsetting actions will be reduced. If no other choice is available to better inform a resident, he or she can at least pull up stakes and move.

To provide this kind of information, Title III of SARA requires industries covered by the statute to provide an annual Toxic Release Inventory (TRI). The legislation states: "The toxic release inventory (TRI) requires owners and operators of certain facilities that manufacture, process, or otherwise use a listed chemical to report annually their releases of such chemicals to any environmental medium."[1] Accordingly, industrial firms and plants must annually report to EPA all environmental releases of EPA-listed chemicals, accidental or otherwise. Along with release data, each reporting facility provides data on the disposal of chemicals by removal, recycling, or energy recovery. Other information is required on the efficiency of waste treatment facilities and steps taken to prevent pollution. To give certainty to the process, fines of up to $25,000 per day are imposed on firms that fail to meet the annual July 1 deadline.

EPA developed the first TRI list of 337 chemicals by combining similar lists that had been developed by the states of Maryland and New Jersey.[2] As might be expected, the list is dynamic; SARA has provisions for adding or deleting items from the TRI, either by public provision or by EPA initiative. For example, during the period 1989-93, sixteen chemicals were added to the list and twelve were deleted, always by initiative of organizations other than EPA.

Since 1986, EPA has made three major changes in the TRI program. In an evolutionary sense, one might think of these as phases in the regulatory growth process.

Phase I: List Expansion. In 1993 EPA proposed the addition of 313 chemicals to the TRI list. The additions included 170 substances that are active ingredients in pesticides, twenty-five inorganic compounds, and 118 miscellaneous organic compounds commonly used or manufactured by industry. After considerable controversy, EPA in 1995 expanded the TRI listing to include 648 substances and twenty-two chemical categories in 1995.[3] This expansion became effective for the 1996 reports.

Phase II: Reporting Facilities Expansion. In 1995, in conjunction with the release of the 1994 TRI data, EPA announced that seven industry groups originally exempted from TRI requirements would be subject to all TRI reporting requirements. These industries were: metal mining, coal mining, electric utilities (coal and oil fired generating facilities only; natural gas and nuclear plants would be exempt), commercial hazardous-waste treatment (limited to those that fall under subtitle C of RCRA: plants that treat and dispose of hazardous waste), petroleum bulk terminals, chemical wholesalers, and solvent recovery services.[4]

Phase III: Chemical Use Information.[5] On September 30, 1996, EPA issued a notice of its intent to develop a rule to require certain facilities to report materials accounting data as to how toxic chemicals are used. The proposed rule directs facility operators to report the amounts of toxic materials entering the facility, the amounts transformed to products and wastes, and the resulting amounts leaving the facility in various forms, in effect giving a complete materials balance accounting for TRI chemicals.

Summary

Now, some twelve years after SARA, the TRI covers almost twice the number of chemicals originally listed, encompasses all but a few major stationary sources of emissions, and holds the covered industries accountable for all uses of TRI chemicals. EPA annually issues a comprehensive report ranking the states and industrial firms within states by the total number of pounds of aggregate releases of TRI chemicals. To calculate the overall toxic emissions, the EPA sums the emissions of all listed compounds from all sources for a particular plant. The overall volume of toxic emission is then used as an index of the contamination caused by the facility. Upon scanning the latest TRI data or reading a newspaper's account of the state's "dirty dozen" one is struck by the relative magnitude when chemical releases are measured in pounds.

On further reflection, one pauses to ask if the total number of pounds of aggregated data for more than six hundred chemical entities with varying degrees of toxicity is the most effective way to inform communities who wish to guard themselves from undue risk. More reflection on the problem leads one to conclude that an index based on pounds of diverse chemicals is not the desired metric. A more useful measure would provide information on the relative risk posed to human beings and the environment by releases of diverse chemicals to different environmental paths.

Risk and Risk Reduction

From the standpoint of protecting human populations and the environment from harm, the TRI should not focus on pounds of chemicals, but on the risks associated with them. If this were the TRI goal, it would consider the risk associated with *all* kinds of emissions, whether from truck tailpipes or from factory stacks. As the TRI program currently operates, more than 80 percent of emissions from TRI chemicals originate from sources excluded by the TRI program itself, with the vast majority of them coming from mobile sources.[6]

In other words, the TRI program focuses on less than 20 percent of the emissions problems. Of course, this would never happen in a perfect, but unachievable, world where anyone who imposed costs on another person, without that person's agreement, would be penalized or somehow made conscious of the costly action. In such a world, monitoring, measuring, and enforcement costs would be costless. Since these activities are costly, it is possible for a TRI-type program to improve environmental outcomes, provided the focus is on net beneficial risk reduction.

To illustrate, imagine a graph with two marginal cost curves. The upward sloping curve could be called "Social Marginal Cost." This curve measures the marginal cost imposed on a receiving community by uncontrolled risky emissions after the effects of all legal remedies have been accounted for. As more emissions are released in a given time period, exposure and cost increases. The downward sloping curve could be called "Marginal Cost of Abatement." This curve represents the marginal cost of controlling or reducing the risky emissions that would be incurred by the plant that produces the emissions. Uncontrolled release imposes no control costs. Complete elimination of emissions generates high marginal cost. In the absence of additional regulatory control, the emission source will predictably choose no additional emission control, which will impose high risks and marginal costs on the community. If, on the other hand, the community requires the plant to eliminate emissions, the original cost paid by the plant will be high, and the marginal benefit received by the community will be low. Now, consider the theory of a risk-based TRI.

Cost Consideration

If risk-based TRI data were provided to the community, additional pressure would be brought on the plant to reduce the emissions responsible for such risk. Response to this pressure could generate an outcome where the marginal cost of emission reductions equals the cost avoided by the community. In other words, marginal cost would equal marginal benefits. Straying beyond this point generates more costs than benefits. If, instead of receiving information on risk, the community receives information on pounds of emissions, it is highly likely that the plant producing the largest number of pounds of chemical emissions will be pressured first, and less likely that an efficient level of environmental protection will follow. Meanwhile, the producer of less mass but more risk may go unsullied.

An improved TRI should have reduction of risk posed by contaminant emissions as its main objective. Under the current TRI program there are no calculations of risk metrics. All chemicals on the TRI listing are treated as though they are equally risky, and all plant locations are assumed to have similar demographic, environmental, and other conditions that translate chemical emissions into human and environmental harm. As a result, valuable resources are devoted to the wrong abatement effort.

The Benefits of TRI

In terms of response generated, the TRI program may still be called the most effective environmental statute on the books. The TRI has led to voluntary programs for waste reduction from many facilities. There are at least two motivating forces supporting these efforts:

a) Image: The annual TRI report generates a large reaction among environmental and community leaders where pounds are quickly translated into risk. Major corporations concerned about public image and brand-name capital have powerful incentives to avoid membership in the "Dirty Dozen" club; they move quickly to reduce emissions. Citizen groups armed with TRI information find themselves better able to substantiate their concerns and to force reluctant companies to address these issues. For example, B. F. Goodrich reduced TRI air emissions 70 percent after TRI-equipped citizens of Akron, Ohio, brought pressure to bear on the company.[7]

b) Cost reduction: The TRI report was an "eye opener" for some industrial firms. Forced to keep track of emissions, they began to see how much material was being lost, and how much money could be saved by taking actions to reduce leakage and discharge. In many instances, managers had been unaware of the extent of pollution generated and its related financial costs until confronted with TRI information. When faced with these facts for the first time, many firms began aggressive voluntary reduction efforts.[8] As shown in table 4.1, these voluntary and other initiatives have generated significant reductions in total TRI releases.

Overall TRI emissions have fallen 60 percent from 1988 through 1994, a period when chemical production rose about 20 percent (See table 4.1.). But to paraphrase a well-known saying, "There's no such thing as a free environment."

The Cost of TRI

The overall effects of TRI are not as simple and pleasant as the previous paragraphs might lead us to believe. There are costs on the other side of the coin, in this case, large capital expenditures in pollution abatement, with no real measure of risk reduction. TRI information is stated in total pounds emitted by compound and facility; there is no measurement of the real effects of these chemicals in the surroundings.

Although the TRI has proven to be an effective tool in forcing industry to reduce emissions and innovate in community outreach, the question of costs and even more importantly, costs versus benefits arises immediately. Due to a lack of tools to evaluate the benefits of pollution abatement investments beyond the mere reduction in emissions, for example, it is not clear if the allocation of resources toward TRI emission reduction made by the chemical industry is economically or environmentally efficient. Some other allocation of control technologies or product modification could have reduced more risk per dollar spent.

Although precise data linking the effects of the TRI program on pollution abatement capital investments do not exist, we do know that the chemical industry's investment in pollution abatement was almost stable before the implementation of EPCRA and TRI. With the advent of those programs, investments devoted to control of contamination increased dramatically. In 1986, the year the EPCRA became law, the expenditure for pollution control for the industry was $3.47 billion. After the implementation of TRI, the expenditures rose every year, reaching $12.2 billion in 1994 (see table 4.2).[9]

To illustrate how the TRI might induce investments to reduce pounds of TRI emissions but not risk, consider ammonium sulfate solutions (a former member of the TRI list) as an example. Ammonium sulfate solutions are very high volume wastes, made even larger due to water content. To treat ammonium sulfate wastes, it is necessary to construct wastewater treatment plants with equalization tanks. These treatment plants require investments in land, construction, and machinery such as mixers, pumps, motors, and control devices and can yield a large reduction in reported emissions. The problem in this case is that after an exhaustive study, ammonium sulfate solutions were found to be of such low toxicity that the compound was taken off the TRI list. This implies that any induced investment failed to yield meaningful risk reduction benefits.

Table 4.1. Twenty Largest Reductions in TRI Chemicals, 1988-1994

Substance	1988 [pound X 10^6]	1994 [pound X 10^6]	% Change 1988-1994
Methanol	312	255.8	-18
Toluene	301	168	-44
1,1,1-Trichloroethane	181	38.1	-79
Phosphoric acid	177.3	78.8	-55
Xylenes (mixed)	159.5	108.9	-32
Chlorine	141.4	60.4	-57
Methyl Ethyl Ketone	141.3	79.4	-44
Dichloromethane	131.1	63.8	-51
Carbon disulfide	124.2	83.4	-33
Zinc compounds	121.8	81.8	-33
Ammonium nitrate	95.2	60.5	-36
Manganese compounds	93.5	41.5	-56
Freon 113	70.6	5.1	-93
Trichloroethylene	56.0	29.9	-47
Tetrachloroethylene	36.3	10.2	-66
Benzene	33.2	9.8	-70
Zinc	30.1	10.2	-66
Chloroform	27.2	11.4	-58
Acrylic acid	23.1	6.9	-70

Source: "Toxic Release Inventory Report Shows Chemical Emissions Continuing to Fall," *Chemical and Engineering News,* vol. 74, July 19, 1996, pp. 29-30.

Table 4.2. Expenditures in Pollution Abatement*

	1986	1987	1991	1994
Total**	3.47	4.89	9.45	12.2
Air	1.42	1.80	2.68	3.76
Water	1.28	1.89	3.66	4.24
Solid Waste	0.78	1.19	3.17	4.17
Other and Unallocated***		4.89		0.0094

*In billions of current dollars.
**Includes spending for air and water pollution abatement and for solid waste and disposal.
***Other includes business, non-manufacturing, and government spending for abatement and control of pollution. Unallocated includes business spending not assigned to media.
Source: U.S. Department of Commerce, Economics and Statistics Division.

Another TRI cost to consider is the cost of collecting the information itself. It is estimated that the average cost of reporting is about $18,500/facility/year. Some 6,400 facilities report to EPA each year; this yields $119 million/year for data gathering and reporting.[10]

A Risk-Based Model

A model that balances the additional cost of managing toxic substances and the additional benefit obtained should involve the following for each TRI chemical:

- Identification of adverse effects,

- Estimation of the relationship between exposure to hazardous substances and the response for effects of concern for human health and the environment,

- Evaluation of current exposures to the chemical,

- Combining exposure and dose-response information to predict the risk associated with the chemical,

- Identification of possible options for reducing risk,

• Evaluation of the costs and impacts of each option, in terms of the degree of risk reduction that is likely to be achieved, relative to the situation that would exist if no action is taken, and

• Selection of appropriate option.

Following each of these steps, or even some of them, would generate more useful TRI data. Indeed, if risk-weighted metrics were applied to the TRI, a very different ordering of high-risk facilities would be the result.

Consider table 4.3, which draws from the 1995 TRI report for South Carolina and shows the "Top Ten Facilities." The raw TRI data, expressed in pounds, can be usefully transformed by applying a simple toxicity weight, the threshold level value (TLV) for each TRI chemical. The TLV is defined by the American Conference of Governmental and Industrial Hygienists as "the airborne concentrations of substances that represent conditions under which it is believed that nearly all workers may be exposed day after day without adverse effects."[11] To obtain LTVs, scientists determine the dilution necessary, by water, air, or land, to cause the volume of a chemical to reach a safe LTV. The LTVs are based on information compiled from industrial experience, animal tests, epidemiological studies, and research involving human volunteers. The results obtained when the data are adjusted are shown in table 4.4. The table's last column shows diluted volume of all TRI chemicals for each of the ten South Carolina facilities.

Table 4.3. Original TRI Ranking for Top Ten Facilities in South Carolina (Reporting Year, 1995)

Rank	Facility	Air	Water	Land	Total
1	Westinghouse	5,172,000	390	0	5,172,390
2	Westvaco Corp.	3,806,150	28,833	0	3,834,983
3	International Paper	3,342,186	19,592	0	3,361,778
4	Anchor Ctal	2,793,735	0	0	2,793,735
5	Stone Cont Corp.	2,079,046	2,052	0	2,081,098
6	Devro-Teepak Inc.	1,698,000	123,364	0	1,821,364
7	Union Camp Corp.	1,633,865	85,070	12,970	1,731,905
8	Eastman Chemical Co.	1,432,151	31,423	23,738	1,487,312
9	Bowater, Inc.	1,235,777	85,977	87,110	1,408,864
10	Albemarle Corp.	778,396	100,090	405,970	1,284,456

Table 4.4. Ranking after Modification by Threshold Limit Value

Rank	Facility	Air	Water	Land	Total	Mod. by TLV
1	Int. Paper	3,342,186	19,952	0	3,361,778	190,909,091
2	Union Camp	1,633,865	85,070	12,970	1,731,905	140,909,091
3	Westinghouse	5,172,000	390	0	5,172,390	57,308,205
4	Bowater, Inc.	1,235,777	85,977	87,110	1,408,864	54,418,182
5	Westvaco	3,806,150	28,833	0	3,834,983	50,681,818
6	Stone Const.	2,079,046	2,052	0	2,081,098	42,901,515
7	Albemarle	778,396	100,090	405,970	1,284,456	32,575,758
8	Devro-Teepak	1,698,000	123,364	0	1,821,364	30,897,427
9	Anchor Ctal	2,793,735	0	0	2,793,735	25,395,345
10	Eastman Chem	1,432,151	31,423	23,738	1,487,312	21,540,909

Now, consider a specific facility in South Carolina. Suppose the concerned manager wants to minimize risk to the environment and the community surrounding the plant, using funds available for environment investment. If the manager looks at the EPA report of the TRI for his facility to decide where to invest in pollution abatement, table 4.5 depicts on what his decision will be based:

Table 4.5. Original TRI Ranking of Substances for Eastman Chemical South Carolina Facility

Chemical Name	Air	Water	Land	Total
Methanol	380,000	60		380,060
Bromomethane	378,600	3		378,603
Xylenes	209,000	1	1	209,002
Ethylene Glycol	193,000	7,700	1	200,701
Acetaldehyde	131,000	17		131,017
Hydrochloric Acid	91,000			91,000
Hydrogen Fluoride	40,000			40,000
Ammonia	54	17,000		17,054
Antimony Compounds	282	9	12,027	12,318
2-Methoxyethanol	5,500	6,000		11,500
Cobalt Compounds	95	93	9,290	9,478
Manganese Compounds	18	290	2,420	2,728
1,4 Dioxane	2,100	250		2,350
Biphenyl	1,500	1		1,501

According to this information, the obvious decision would be to try to reduce the emissions of methanol and/or bromomethane, which account for the majority of the TRI report. The management would logically allocate most of its chemical risk reduction resources to these chemicals, ignoring or making a minimum effort for the rest, because the money available is always finite. Let us now modify the original values by toxicity, applying the same parameter formerly used, the TLV. The manager now sees the list as shown in table 4.6.

Table 4.6. Ranking after Modification by TLV

Chemical Name	Air	Water	Land	Total	Mod. By TLV
Cobalt Compounds	95	93	9,290	9,478	21,540,909
Antimony Compounds	282	9	12,027	12318	11,198,182
Hydrochloric Acid	91,000			91,000	8,272,727
Hydrogen Fluoride	40,000			40,000	6,060,606
Biphenyl	1,500	1		1,501	3,411,364
Acetaldehyde	131,000	17		131,017	2,382,127
Ethylene Glycol	193,000	7,700	1	200,701	1,824,555
2-Methoxyethanol	5,500	6,000		11,500	1,045,455
Xylenes	209,000	1	1	209,002	950,007
Methanol	380,000	60		380,060	863,773
Bromomethane	378,600	3		378,603	860,461
Ammonia	54	17,000		17,054	310,073
Mangonese Compounds	18	290	2,420	2,728	248,000
1,4 Dioxane	2,100	250		2,350	42,727

After considering this information, the manager's decision would probably be different. The cobalt compounds account for the majority of the incidence in toxicity. If the manager had estimates of control costs for each of the listed toxicity-weighted chemicals, he could then compare real reductions in risk to expenditures on emission control. Then, by selecting those investments that yield the largest risk reduction per dollar spent, the manager would have achieved his goal: Maximize risk reduction subject to a budget constraint.

While this example is instructive, there is far more to the story than simply applying a measure of toxicity to the TRI chemicals, as helpful as that alone might be. For example, in this case, the cobalt compounds are solids, with low mobility. The potential for exposure to humans and the environment is low. A complete analysis would involve consideration of media through which the chemicals move, any decay in toxicity that occurs during movement and before exposure, and then the probability that human beings or environmental assets would be exposed to and damaged by the chemicals.

Other Sources of Toxic Emissions

Some critical pollutants and air toxic are not on the list of chemicals for the TRI. Substances like carbon monoxide (known depletor of hemoglobin in the human body) and nitrogen oxides (precursors of the formation of "bad ozone" in the lower atmosphere, which have no threshold), go uncounted, even though the EPA considers them toxins in the Clean Air Act. The TRI focuses on emissions from industry alone, but as we can see in table 4.7, industry is not the biggest expected polluter, at least for air emissions.

This data raises the question: If industry is not the single, not even the biggest polluter, why should it be the only target for TRI pollution control? The answer is because of the higher costs in measuring and monitoring related to controlling the other sources. But if the objective is reduction in human and environmental risk posed by chemicals, environmental policy should provide information on all major sources of toxic emissions, even though some are hard to pursue.

Final Thoughts

In 1986 Congress passed the Emergency Planning and Community Right to Know Act (EPCRA), a statute focused on the U.S. chemical industry and the potential environmental harms from chemical contamination. At the time, the idea of requiring plants to report the quantities of toxic chemicals released to the environment seemed logical and in the public interest. If, in building the TRI listing, the EPA selected a particular chemical, the EPA's decision was viewed as reason enough to consider the chemical toxic and dangerous. After that, toxicity was equated to pounds, and significant actions have been taken in the last ten years to reduce the pounds of TRI chemicals released to the environment.

With experience and improved science, we recognize that this is the time to improve the TRI, to focus on outcomes, not inputs. Pounds of chemicals are inputs to the risk creation process, but risk reduction is the desired outcome. As indicated in this report, simple transformation of the TRI data can generate meaningful discussion about what might be done to reduce risks. By taking additional and more costly steps, communities can tighten their focus on risk reduction and target their actions accordingly.

Only a group dedicated to the reduction of chemical production in the United States would continue adamantly to support a regulation that deliberately focuses on pounds of chemicals instead of risk to humans and the environment. The TRI

Table 4.7. National Emissions Estimates for 1991

Source Category	Sox	By TLV	CO	By TLV	Nox	By TLV	VOCs	By TLV	Pb	By TLV	Total	Total by TLV
Transp.	0.99	495,000	43.49	1,739,600	7.26	2,420,000	5.08		0.00162	10.8	4,654,657	4,654,610.8
Fuel Com	16.55	8275,000	4.67	186,800	10.59	3,530,000	0.67		0.00045	3.0	11,991,832	11,991,803.0
Ind. Proc.	3.16	1580,000	4.69	187,600	0.60	200,000	7.86		0.00221	14.7	1,967,616	1,967,614.7
Waste Disp.	0.02	10,000	2.06	82,400	0.10	33,333.33	0.69		0.00069	4.6	125,736.2	125,737.9
Misc.	0.01	5,000	7.18	287,200	0.21	70,000	2.59		0.00497	33.1	362,210	362,233.1
Total	20.73	10,365,000	62.09	2,483,600	18,76	6,253,333	16.89		0.00994	66.3		19,101,999.6

Note: VOCs stands for volatile organic compounds and groups all the different volatile substances based in carbon (e.g., ketones, ethers, etc.). Therefore a single value of TLV cannot be assigned to this category, and the total TLV weighting is based in the contributions of the other pollutants. (Values are in millions of metric tons per year.)

has proven to be a powerful regulatory instrument. Now is the time to adjust and improve the TRI and make it our best regulatory mechanism for risk reduction.

Notes

1. *Federal Register,* February 19, 1988, 4500 and *EPA Toxic Release Inventory.* E.P.1.2:T 66/19/pack.

2. *EPA Toxic Release Inventory.* E.P.1.2:T 66/19/pack.

3. "Tracking Toxics: Chemical Use and the Public's Right to Know," *Environment.* Vol. 38 (July/August, 1996): 4-9.

4. "EPA Proposes to Expand the TRI to Require Chemical Use Information." *Chemical Engineering Progress,* Vol. 91 (December 1996): 24.

5. "TRI Expansion Opposed by Industry Groups." *Chemical and engineering news.* Vol. 74 (August 26, 1996): 28-30; "EPA Proposes to Expand the TRI to Require Chemical Use Information." *Chemical Engineering Progress,* Vol. 91 (December 1996): 24.

6. The share of TRI emissions accounted for by manufacturing is based on data from Noel de Nevers, *Air Pollution Engineering* (New York, NY: McGraw Hill, Inc. 1995); U.S. Environmental Protection Agency, *National Air Pollution Emissions Estimates, 1990-1991,* EPA 454-R-92-013, (Washington, DC: U.S. Environmental Protection Agency, 1992); U.S. Environmental Protection Agency, *Motor Vehicle-Related Air Toxics Study,* Office of Mobile Sources, Emission Planning and Strategies Division, EPA 420-R-930-005 (Washington, DC: U.S. EPA, 1993); and U.S. Environmental Protection Agency, *Toxic Release Inventory Relative Risk-Based Environmental Indicators,* Office of Pollution Prevention and Toxics (Washington, DC: U.S. Environmental Protection Agency, 1997).

7. "Tracking Toxics: Chemical Use and the Public's Right to Know." *Environment,* Vol. 38 (July/August, 1996): 4-9.

8. Ibid.

9. *Chemical Industry Statistical Handbook,* Washington, DC: CMA Inc., 1993.

10. "TRI Expansion Opposed by Industry Groups," *Chemical and Engineering News,* Vol. 74 (August 26, 1996): 28-30.

11. Ibid.

References

Chemical Manufacturers Association. 1996. *Chemical Industry Statistical Handbook.* Washington, DC: CMA Inc.

Chemical Manufacturers Association. 1992. *Preventing Pollution in the Chemical Industry.* Washington, DC: CMA Inc.

Davis, G. A., et al. 1996. *Chemical ranking for potential health and environmental impacts.* University of Tennessee: Center for Clean Products and Clean Technology.

"EPA Proposes Expanding TRI Reporting." 1996. *Chemical Engineering Progress* (November) 91: 29.

"EPA Proposes to Expand the TRI to Require Chemical Use Information." 1996. *Chemical Engineering Progress* (December) 91: 24.

Federal Register. 33 USC&1251-1387.

Federal Register. 40CFR50.

Findley, R. W., and D. A. Farber. 1992. *Environmental Law.* St. Paul, MN: West Publishing Company: 90-96.

"Industry Safety Reforms: Bophal Inspires New Initiatives." 1985. *Chemical and Engineering News* (April 1): 6.

Jia, C. Q., and A. DiGuardo. 1996. "Toxics Release Inventories: Opportunites for Improved Presentation and Interpretation." *Environmental Science and Technology* 30, No. 2.

Nevers, Noel de. 1995. *Air Pollution Control Engineering.* New York: McGraw Hill Inc.

Terry, Jeffrey. 1994. *EPA's Toxic Release Inventory: What Is Its Purpose?* Center for Policy Studies, Clemson University, Clemson, SC.

"Toxic Release Inventory Report Shows Chemical Emissions Continuing to Fall." 1996. *Chemical and Engineering News* 74 (July 19): 29-30.

"Tracing Toxics: Chemical Use and the Public's Right to Know." 1996. *Environment* 38 (July/August): 4-9.

"TRI Expansion Opposed by Industry Groups." 1996. *Chemical and Engineering News* 74 (August 26): 28-30.

United States Environmental Protection Agency. 1996. *Chemicals in Your Community* Washington, DC: EPA. 19-29.

United States Environmental Protection Agency. 1993. *Motor Vehicle-Related Air Toxics Study.* Office of Mobile Sources, Emission Planning and Strategies Division, EPA: 420-R-930-005. Washington, DC: U.S. EPA.

United States Environmental Protection Agency. 1992. *National Air Pollution Emissions Estimates, 1990-1991.* EPA 454-R-92-013. Washington, DC: EPA.

United States Environmental Protection Agency. 1997. *Toxic Release Inventory Relative Risk-Based Environmental Indicators.* Office of Pollution Prevention and Toxics. Washington, DC: U.S. EPA.

Chapter 5

Laidlaw v. South Carolina DHEC

George Hamrick

Introduction

The handling and disposal of hazardous waste is both a risky and costly activity. Indeed, the term "hazardous waste" often conjures images of men in bright yellow space suits breathing oxygen from tanks on their backs, nuclear waste, or glowing chemical compounds with names the average person cannot pronounce, much less spell. Federal law currently defines hazardous waste as solid or liquid wastes that may "cause or contribute to an increase in mortality or an increase in serious irreversible or incapacitating reversible illness."[1] A broader definition of hazardous waste is any substance or mixture that may "pose a substantial threat to human health" and the environment.[2] However, a waste is legally determined to be hazardous if it tests "positive" for one of the following EPA-established criteria: ignitability, corrosivity, reactivity, and toxicity.[3] The definition could include anything from used motor oil to volatile organic contaminants. The risks associated with hazardous waste can vary greatly from substance to substance, but legally they are all treated as equal. However, ordinary citizens do not stop to consider the differences between the 500 substances classified as hazardous or the variations in risk that these substances pose to human health and the environment.[4] Thus, the unsettling images associated with hazardous waste have prompted many citizens to take a "not in my backyard" stance against hazardous waste. These citizens perceive the risks posed by hazardous waste to be so high that they do not want to be near them.

The concerns of citizens often are amplified by environmentalists who preach that the earth is sacred and man should not corrupt her pristine condition for the sake of greed. Accordingly, those who desecrate and waste nature's precious resources are sinners who deserve to pay dearly. Many environmentalists go so far as to call for a complete elimination of hazardous waste. However, this preposterous plea for a waste-free world of production shows very little understanding or acceptance of the modern industrial world.

Coalitions of environmentalist and citizen groups often cast a strong voice in the political arena. When such an alliance perceives that they are being forced to bear intolerably high risks to their health and/or environment, they can cause quite a political tremor. Politicians respond by talking some form of regulatory action. The regulatory action often takes the form of tighter restrictions that raise the costs of providing hazardous waste disposal. The economic costs of this regulatory backlash can be quite substantial. Thus, regulatory action can have unfortunate, unintended consequences. The problem is that it is very difficult to ascertain whether the actual risks posed by hazardous waste disposal warrant these economic costs.

Although hazardous wastes are highly undesirable, they are an unavoidable by-product of the modern industrial world. While many industries may be able to make changes in certain processes to reduce the amount of hazardous wastes generated, total elimination of hazardous waste is impossible. It is a simple fact that some products cannot be manufactured or used without rendering hazardous waste in the process. For example, at the present time it is impossible to engineer a motor oil that does not have hazardous properties because it is these properties that make it useful as a fuel. Once the oil is used, it still retains some of its hazardous properties and should be disposed of properly. It is a fact that society cannot produce and use motor oil without rendering hazardous waste in the process.

If people truly wish to reduce the risks posed by hazardous wastes, they can reduce their consumption of motor oil and other such products, thereby reducing the volume of hazardous wastes that result from the production and use of these products. However, reducing demand for such products will require a change in how people conduct their lives. People will have to reduce or eliminate many of the activities that they take for granted. Bringing about these changes is no simple matter. Also, factories facing a lower demand for their products will have to raise their prices. The prices of some products may become too high for many people to afford. When people abruptly stop buying these products, factories will close; and people will lose their jobs.

If people do not wish to reduce their demand for products whose use and/or manufacture renders hazardous waste, then some means of disposal must be found that reduces the risks posed by this waste. Safety is not free. The cost of hazardous waste disposal ranges from a high of $300-$1,000 per ton for treatment and incineration to a low of $50 per ton for landfill disposal (Dower 1993). Treatment and incineration permanently alter the hazardous characteristics of the waste, reducing the risks that it poses. Landfill disposal is meant to act as a physical barrier between the waste and the outside world. If the landfill leaks, the wastes held inside may contaminate nearby drinking water or biological systems. Society could avoid this risk by using the safer, more expensive methods of disposal. However, many industries and consumers, ultimately, cannot afford this option. For example, it is estimated that around 250 million metric tons of hazardous wastes are produced yearly. If society disposed of all of this waste using incineration ($1,000 per ton), it would cost $250 billion a year. Needless to say, the fact that hazardous wastes are an unavoidable by-product of the modern industrial world makes affordable disposal essential if society is to continue its present rate of consumption and its present standard of living.

When politicians choose to protect their constituents by arbitrarily placing greater restrictions on waste disposal facilities in order to quell the fears of citizens and environmentalists, there can be unfortunate economic consequences. By using the perceptions of citizens and environmentalists as a gauge of the actual risks posed by hazardous waste disposal sites, the costs of disposal are likely to be much higher than they should be. In fact, many would like to make them prohibitively high. Also, relying upon a commercial landfill operator's assessment of the risks posed by his landfill could result in a price of disposal that is artificially low. This can increase the risk of human and environmental exposure to hazardous waste. Thus, it is painfully obvious that a fair and accurate system of risk assessment is essential to dealing with the problem of hazardous waste.

The purpose of this chapter is to illustrate how the process of risk assessment of hazardous waste landfills is used in the current regulatory system through a discussion of a case that is currently being litigated in the South Carolina judicial system, *Laidlaw v. S.C. Department of Health and Environmental Control (DHEC)*. The first section discusses the status of landfills in the United States and the laws that relate to them. Also included in this section is some background on the Laidlaw facility and a description of its design. The second section provides an introduction to the Laidlaw controversy and gives an illustration of the role played by risk assessment by analyzing expert testimony and commissioned assessments taken from the record of the Laidlaw case. This section then translates risk avoidance to economic costs. The conclusion of the chapter offers some final thoughts on the process of risk assessment and cost determination. These final thoughts stress the need for more data on the actual risks posed by landfill operations and call for cost-benefit analysis of regulatory action and regulatory flexibility until the actual risks are better understood.

Landfills and the Laidlaw Operation

The Current Status of Landfills in the United States and the Laws That Apply to Them

Landfills currently present an affordable means of hazardous waste disposal. However, landfill disposal is viewed as "the least desirable method of disposing of hazardous waste."[5] Public and regulatory contempt for landfill disposal stems from past disposal methods that involved dumping hazardous wastes into unlined pits or lagoons. In some instances, these wastes migrated from the landfill into the local drinking water supplies. Perhaps the most publicized case of leakage from a landfill occurred in the Love Canal residential area near Niagara Falls, New York. Wastes that had been buried under the land where the residences were built seeped into the floors and walls of the houses (Dower, 1993). Since the tragedy of Love Canal in 1978, landfills have been subjected to intense public and regulatory scrutiny. Public and federal regulators have concluded that past disposal methods of dumping hazardous waste into unlined pits or lagoons have proven inadequate for protecting human health and the environment. In response, the federal government enacted the Resource Conservation and Recovery Act (RCRA 1978) to deal with the 500 commercial treatment, storage, and disposal facilities (TSDFs), the 2,500 generator-owned TSDFs, and the 75,000 industrial landfills currently in operation. RCRA established criteria for identification of hazardous wastes, as well as a cradle-to-grave system of record keeping and manifests to track and control waste from the point of generation to the point of disposal (Findley and Farber, 1992). Amendments to RCRA (1984) require new or expanding landfills to meet standards set for liners and leachate collection systems. Additionally, operators of landfill operations are required to provide assurances of financial responsibility that can be provided by one or a combination of the following: insurance, corporate guarantee, surety bond, letter of credit, and/or qualification as a self-insurer. These requirements are all enforced under the permit system established by RCRA that gives EPA broad inspection power and the power to pursue civil and criminal action against violators.

Providing all of these restrictions on landfills is by no means cheap. The yearly costs associated with restrictions on landfill disposal are estimated to be $1.6 billion (Dower, 1990). This amount may seem astronomical, but it pales in comparison to the cost estimates associated with the Comprehensive Environmental Response, Compensation, and Liability Act, enacted to clean up the estimated 2,000 abandoned hazardous waste sites that will require federal action. Obviously, regulation of landfill disposal of hazardous waste is very costly for the regulators, industries, and consumers. If society cannot find an economically feasible way to deal with the risks posed by hazardous waste, it will have no choice but to decrease its consumption and standard of living. Do the actual risks posed by landfill disposal justify such high economic costs?

The actual risks posed by landfill operations are very hard to ascertain. In fact, there is very little data that gives concrete evidence on the actual risks posed by these facilities. With such uncertainty about actual risks, we clearly cannot be certain that the benefits of stringent regulation justify the exorbitant economic costs that can result. For example, it is estimated that air emissions from landfill disposal of volatile organic compounds contribute to one of 250 cancer cases each year, and that disposal of used oil causes around eighty cases yearly. Due to the latency between exposure and the manifestation of disease or mortality, and the wide variety of potential sources for this exposure, there is no way to derive an absolute number to account for cancer cases that can be attributed to hazardous waste landfills (Benjamin, 1993). However, if we add the 250 deaths that might be attributable to volatile organics to the eighty deaths that might be attributable to disposal of used oil, and divide this figure by the $1.6 billion annual cost of landfill restrictions, we derive an estimated cost of $4,848,484 per life saved. Economists, and others who are concerned with the economic well-being of this country, might feel that the costs of these restrictions far outweigh the benefits. However, there are some people who feel that $4.8 million is not too much to spend to save a human life. Can we really say who is right?

Similarly, industrialists and those who deal with hazardous waste on a daily basis may feel that the actual risks posed by these wastes are much lower than concerned citizens perceive them to be. Is there a foolproof method to find what the actual risks are? One could consult the advice of so-called experts, but their expertise is limited by the scant supply of risk information. As such, these individuals can only make value judgments based on their own opinion. Needless to say, the opinions of experts tend to vary and even contradict one another, leaving no ultimate judgment on the risks posed by landfill operations. This leaves us with the question of how to assess risk and determine economic cost so that we can reduce the risk posed by hazardous waste without unduly destroying the standard of living that society has worked so hard to attain.

There is a case currently making its way through the South Carolina judicial system that embodies the problem of risk assessment and the determination of economic cost. The case, *Laidlaw v. South Carolina DHEC*, focuses on a landfill operation that is located 1,200 feet above Lake Marion–the largest lake in the state. After operating under Interim Status for over sixteen years, the Laidlaw landfill applied for and was issued an EPA permit.[6] Subsequently, a coalition of citizen groups, environmentalists, and governmental entities opposed the permit. One central issue of the case is the level of risk that the facility poses and the financial assurance that Laidlaw should provide based on that risk. The case has progressed through one adjudicatory hearing that produced twenty-four days of testimony, 400 exhibits, and over 5,500 pages of record. This case has also been considered in two executive sessions of the Board of Health and Environmental Control, the overseer of DHEC; it is now being appealed to the state court.

The Laidlaw Site and Its Design

The Laidlaw landfill facility is located outside of Pinewood, South Carolina, 1,200 feet above Lake Marion. Landfill operations began here in 1977 when Bennett Mineral Company obtained an industrial waste permit for its kitty litter mining operation. Bennett disposed of its waste in an unlined pit of opaline claystone until ownership was transferred to SCA Services in 1978. SCA Services transferred this waste to what is currently Section I of the Laidlaw facility in accordance with the Hazardous Waste Management Act of 1978.[7]

In 1980, GSX Environmental Services (now called Laidlaw) took over operation of the Pinewood facility. Since that time, Laidlaw has operated under Interim Status, which requires adequate recordkeeping, compliance with a manifest system, implementation of inspection programs, and groundwater monitoring. In addition, this classification required the operators to maintain adequate post-closure and financial responsibility, as well as adequate liability insurance (Dower, 1990). In 1983, Laidlaw applied for an EPA permit pursuant to section 3005 of RCRA (Findley and Farber). Laidlaw was issued a permit in 1989, "in compliance with all procedural requirements of state statutes and regulations."[8]

The Laidlaw landfill operation occupies 279 acres and currently holds over 2,300,000 tons of waste.[9] It receives approximately 135,000 tons of hazardous wastes and 100,000-200,000 tons of nonhazardous waste annually.[10] The facility consists of three holding sections that lie within the naturally occurring opaline claystone. Each section was designed, built, and opened as the preceding section reached its capacity. As such, each section was designed and built in accordance with the regulatory requirements at the time of operation. All of the sections meet or exceed these requirements.[11]

Each section contains a liner system and leachate removal system that are designed to fit the pit and to prevent leakage from the section. The leachate collection systems consist of corrugated pipes and sumps that are designed to catch the liquid that percolates downward through the landfill. This liquid consists of mainly water and some hazardous constituents.[12] The levels of leachate in each section are monitored, and leachate is pumped and removed from the landfill as required by EPA. The liner system and the low-permeable claystone beneath are meant to prevent any remaining leachate from escaping.

Section I is split into five cells, A through E. Each consists of the naturally occurring claystone, with a 30-mil hypalon system placed on top. Above the liner, the leachate collection system is situated in two feet of protective soil to prevent leachate from reaching the liner.[13] This section was closed in 1984 with a composite cover which consists of a one-foot intermediate cover, a 20-mil liner, and eighteen inches of soil material.[14]

Section II is also split into five cells, A through E. Cells A and B of Section II consist of the naturally occurring claystone, with an 80-mil HDPE liner on top.[15] Cells A and B also have the leachate detection system situated in two feet of protective soil to prevent leachate from reaching the liner.[16] Landfill Section II cells C through G, as well as Section III A, consist of a double composite liner system.[17] This system consists of the naturally occurring claystone, three feet of compacted clay of 1×10^{-7} permeability, an 80-mil HDPE liner, a geonet, filter fabric system, five feet of compacted clay, a second 80-mil liner, geonet, filter fabric, and one foot of protective soil material.[18] These sections also contain primary and secondary leachate collection systems. The primary system is used to remove any leachate in the base of the cell. The secondary system serves as a leak detection system for the landfill. Section II was also capped with a cover that consists of a one foot intermediate cover, one 30-mil synthetic liner, two feet of compacted clay, one 20-mil synthetic liner, and eighteen inches of soil.[19]

The Laidlaw facility also contains a groundwater monitoring system to detect any hazardous substances that may migrate from the landfill into the uppermost aquifer.[20] The uppermost aquifer, as defined by DHEC Reg. 61-79. 265.10, is "the geologic formation nearest the natural ground surface that is an aquifer, as well as lower aquifers that are hydraulically interconnected with this aquifer within the facility's proper boundary."[21] This monitoring system "must consist of a sufficient number of wells installed at appropriate depths to yield representative groundwater samples" as well as "comply with all other requirements of Reg. 61-79. 264.91 through 264.100 for the purposes of detecting, characterizing, and responding to releases of the uppermost aquifer."[22]

The hydrogeology beneath the Laidlaw facility is very complex. Laidlaw has performed over 300 soil borings and placed over 200 wells around the landfill in order to characterize, delineate, and monitor the site. As such, the aquifer materials are understood to be heterogeneous and of low permeability. The uppermost aquifer consists of four individual aquifer zones that lie on top of each other and are hydraulically interconnected. Each aquifer zone has "unique groundwater flow directions and hydraulic characteristics."[23] In addition, groundwater monitoring for each section of the landfill is conducted independently so that there are distinct points of compliance for each aquifer zone of each section of the landfill.[24]

The Laidlaw Controversy and Risk Assessment

The Laidlaw Controversy

The role of financial responsibility requirements as a determinant of waste disposal costs is increasing rapidly. Some refer to these requirements as a "mini-Superfund" (Dower, 1993). As financial responsibility requirements increase so does the price of landfill disposal. Although financial responsibility requirements are increasing at an alarming rate, the level of risk associated with these landfills may be the same as it always has been. Given the uncertainty of the actual risks posed by these facilities, the level of assurance that the operators of landfills are being required to provide may be well over the level that the actual risks justify. If society is to continue its present rate of consumption and standard of living it must have an affordable means of hazardous waste disposal. Providing an affordable means of waste disposal as well as providing adequate protection for human health and the environment are really the heart of the risk assessment and financial responsibility issue. This section provides a time line of the Laidlaw controversy.

On July 27, 1989, Laidlaw Environmental Services of South Carolina was issued a permit for its landfill operation. At that time, the facility had been in operation for over sixteen years and contained 2,300,000 tons of hazardous and non-hazardous waste.[25] Shortly thereafter, a coalition of citizen groups, environmentalists, and governmental entities opposed the permit. Those who initially filed were Citizens Asking for a Safe Environment (CASE), Energy Resource Foundation, Sumter County, and Sumter County Delegation. A well-known environmentalist group, Sierra Club, applied for and was granted Intervenor status. Laidlaw also filed an appeal to dispute some of the permit conditions.

On February 27, 1990, the case was referred to DHEC. Since the controlling issue of the case would be risks posed by the Laidlaw facility, DHEC was ordered to make an assessment of the risk and to issue a Final Determination of Financial Responsibility based on their assessment. This Interim Order was approved by the Board of Health and Environmental Control on April 12, 1990. The adjudicatory hearing was postponed until DHEC could fulfill the order.

The Final Determination of Financial Responsibility partly relied on a commissioned risk assessment performed by KPMG Peat Marwick, Certified Public Accountants.[26] Peat Marwick developed a list of "adverse impact scenarios" that described events that might occur, the quantitative probability that each event might occur, and the estimated cost of remediation. Peat Marwick recommended that Laidlaw maintain a $30 million environmental impairment insurance policy while in operation and that the South Carolina General Assembly raise disposal prices to generate a trust fund of $114 million (in 1988 dollars) to cover post-closure environmental liability.[27] The Final Determination of Financial Responsibility was issued on June 22, 1992. It required Laidlaw to maintain $33,588,431 environmental impairment liability insurance coverage and to establish a trust fund in the amount of $132,885,373 (in 1992 dollars) by July 1, 2000 or close the facility.[28] Both of these amounts were to be adjusted annually for inflation. Appeals were filed by Laidlaw and the Third Party Petitioners, which is how the opposing coalition is referred to in the case. The South Carolina Public Service Authority, which had expressed interest in marketing water from Lake Marion, and South Carolina Wildlife and Marine Resources were granted Intervenor Status to lend support to DHEC's financial determination. The Permit and Financial Determination issues were consolidated on April 17, 1992. Both were stayed until the issues could be resolved.[29]

Laidlaw and the staff at DHEC resolved their differences about permit conditions and financial responsibility when they entered into a Stipulated Agreement on October 5, 1992. Among other things, the agreement provides financial assurance for the following:

(1) Closure of the facility in accordance with Regulation 61-79.264.143 and 61-79.265.143; (2) financial assurance for the one hundred-year (100) post-closure care period which meets and exceeds Regulation 61-79.264.144 and 145, and 61-79.265.144 and 145; (3) third-party liability coverage of $30 million for bodily injury and property damage and costs of cleanup and restoration of environmental 79.265.147; and (4) a financial assurance package for costs of cleanup and restoration of environmental impairment ensuring $100 million, to be adjusted annually for inflation.[30]

Instead of requiring Laidlaw to build a cash trust fund to $114 million by the year 2000, the Stipulated Agreement calls for $100 million of protection immediately.[31] This amount is provided by a combination of an Environmental Impairment Fund maintained by Laidlaw and the State Permitted Sites Fund.[32] The State Permitted Sites Fund is controlled by the South Carolina General Assembly. The Environmental Impairment Fund consists of a trust fund referred to as the "GSX Contribution Fund" and a corporate guarantee from Laidlaw, Inc., a $2 billion company.[33] The GSX Contribution Fund is "funded by a quarterly contribution of $5.00 per ton of hazardous waste and $2.00 per ton of nonhazardous waste disposed at the landfill, plus earnings and profits derived from the investment of the accumulated contributions. Monies from the GSX Contribution Fund will be utilized for cleanup and restoration prior to tapping the State Permitted Fund or the Corporate Guarantee."[34] It is important to note that this agreement is binding only between the staff at DHEC and Laidlaw, Inc. The board may reject any portion of the agreement without relieving Laidlaw of its financial responsibilities. The agreement provides the highest amount of financial assurance of any facility in the nation.[35]

The adjudicatory hearing commenced on January 13, 1993. The purpose of the hearing was to determine whether the permit conditions and the financial responsibility determination were issued in accordance with regulations and were protective of human health and the environment. Testimony about the risks posed by the facility was given by experts from both sides. Experts also gave estimates of the cost of cleanup based on their evaluation of the Peat Marwick risk assessment. In the end, the administrative law judge (ALJ) ruled that the conditions and financial assurances contained in the Stipulated Agreement were perfectly legal and protective of human health and the environment.[36]

The Assessment of Risk in the Adjudicatory Hearing

Risk assessment in the adjudicatory hearing was based on expert testimony taken from both sides, as well as from the risk assessment performed by KPMG Peat Marwick. All of the experts who testified for Laidlaw had been involved with the operation of the facility for a number of years, so they had a hands-on familiarity with the facility.[37] The experts who testified for the Third Party Petitioners and Intervenors all testified that they had never visited or inspected the facility itself, that they were recently retained, and that their opinions were based solely on their review of records in DHEC's files.[38] The experts from both sides gave their opinions on the risks posed by the Laidlaw facility, as well as an estimate of cleanup costs based on their evaluation of the Peat Marwick report. These estimates of cleanup costs formed the basis for the experts' recommendation for financial assurance requirements.

Testimony from expert witnesses for the Third Party Petitioners and the Intervenors addressed the risks posed by the location, design, and operation of the Laidlaw facility. Most of the claims made by these witnesses were met with a successful rebuttal by expert witnesses for Laidlaw. In the end, the ALJ concluded that the conditions of the Stipulated Agreement were both legal and protective of human health and the environment.

One witness for the Petitioners testified that the facility was improperly sited, that there were design flaws, and that the facility was leaking.[39] Dr. Kirk Wye Brown, a professor at Texas A&M University and an expert on how liquid organic contaminants affect clay liners, suggested that the five feet of clay used in Section II C through G and Section III was too restrictive of leaks through the first composite liner into the leak detection system.[40] He testified that using three feet of clay in the cap above the wastes and five feet of clay below the leak detection system would allow rain water to drain into the landfill faster than it would leak out, hindering the performance of the leak detection system. The expert also claimed that the hypalon liner used in Sections I and II A and B was not compatible with all organic contaminants.[41] He indicated that these contaminants can absorb into the liner and migrate through.[42] It was conceded that composite liners can reduce and seal leaks, but that the liners used in these sections have turned to goo and that these sections are leaking.[43] However, Brown reached these conclusions without looking at qualitative data from the secondary collection (leak detection) layer and without reviewing data from the monitoring wells.[44] The administrative law judge concluded that "the only evidence that the landfill is leaking is speculative and uncorroborated testimony, which does not support the excavation of Sections I or II."[45]

Witnesses for the Intervenors also testified that it is not possible to effectively monitor the complicated hydrogeology beneath the Laidlaw facility. David Lang, President of Groundwater Consultants, and Dr. Joel S. Hirshhorn, former member of the Congressional Office of Technical Assessment and an expert on groundwater contamination caused by landfills, indicated that the spacing between monitoring wells could allow contamination to avoid detection if the plume was long and thin in shape.[46] This point was refuted by a witness for Laidlaw, who testified that the hydrogeology has been characterized by 300 soil borings.[47] Dr. Robert L. Powell, an expert in hydrogeology, also testified that the theoretical plume presented by the Intervenors was consistent with a homogeneous, highly permeable material like the sand used in the research of the Intervenors but not consistent with the heterogeneous, low permeable materials that make up the aquifers below the Laidlaw facility. He explained that the heterogeneous materials cause greater dispersion of the plume than do homogeneous, highly permeable materials.[48] A witness for the Intervenors later admitted that no scientific analysis had been done to show that a plume would migrate from the facility and reach Lake Marion. This was pure speculation.[49]

One witness for the Intervenors questioned whether Laidlaw was following EPA standard procedure for groundwater sampling.[50] He later conceded that he had not reviewed sufficient data to support this accusation.[51] Another witness for the Intervenors also conceded that there "has been no significant findings of contamination" at the Laidlaw site.[52] Hirshhorn also admitted that no scientific analysis had been done to show (assuming a leak occurs, there is no detection or control, and the stream actually flows toward Lake Marion) what hazardous constituents, if any, would actually reach Lake Marion and in what concentration.[53] Further testimony from witnesses for Laidlaw indicated that Laidlaw was in compliance with all U.S. EPA guidelines.[54]

Expert witnesses for Laidlaw gave testimony establishing the safety of the facility. The president of Laidlaw Environmental Services testified that the Pinewood facility is one of only two facilities in the country that has all waste on a composite liner system, that it was the first facility to use a double composite liner system, and that the facility has "consistently been ahead of the requirements and in the lead in the industry."[55] The Deputy Commissioner of DHAKA testified that he felt the facility is safe.[56] Dr. Powell testified that the groundwater monitoring data does not show "a shred of evidence of a leak from that landfill having impacted groundwater."[57] He further claimed that a leak would take 100 years from the time it reached the aquifer for it to reach the boundary of Lake Marion, and "by the time the chemicals go to that point they would be so diluted as to have no practical impact on the lake."[58]

Expert witnesses from both sides gave estimates of cleanup costs based on their evaluation of the Peat Marwick risk assessment. During the assessment process, Peat Marwick reviewed all of the information and regulatory agency documents on the site of the Laidlaw facility, visited the facility to observe and evaluate day-to-day operations and specific processes, and performed assessments of landfill design and installation methods to determine if any facets of design or installation might inherently affect groundwater.[59] Peat Marwick also evaluated each section of the Laidlaw permit that addressed closure, post-closure, monitoring, and corrective action to identify any areas of noncompliance.[60] In order to address any areas of noncompliance or other inadequacies, Peat Marwick developed a list of adverse scenarios that described events that might occur, the quantitative probability that each might occur, and the estimated cost to remediate each scenario. A short list of the scenarios developed by Peat Marwick is shown in table 5.1.

Table 5.1. Adverse Impact Scenarios
Present Worth Analysis (1988 dollars)

Scenario Description	Present Worth	Range	Prob. of Occurrence
1. Failure of Leachate Collection System	1,487,999	$1,210,000 to $1,740,000	Moderate to Low
2. Track Spill	1,228	$1,050,000 to $1,400,000	Low
3. Leachate Leak After Closure	199,890	$135,000 to $264,000	Low
4. Incompatible Materials/Fire and Fumes	197,770	$133,000 to $262,000	Slight
5. Vapor Cloud	53,765	$47,200 to $60,300	High
6. Liner Leak/Creek Contamination	1,283,839	$1,070,000 to $1,490,000	Slight
7. Earthquake/ Surface Water Contamination	1,129,400	$981,000 to $1,280,000	Low
8. Groundwater and Well Contamination	2,016,859	$1,290,000 to $3,440,000	Low
9. Partial Excavation of Site	116,443,330	$116,443,330 to $398,000,000	Low
10. Excavation of Entire Site	304,628,640	$305,000,000 to 1,400,000,000	Slight

Source: Peat Marwick Assessment of Laidlaw facility at Pinewood, p. I.6.

Looking at table 5.1, you will see a list of ten adverse impact scenarios that represent complications or events that might occur during or after the operation of the Laidlaw landfill. Beside each scenario is an estimate of the cost of remediating each event. The estimate is given in a single number as well as a range because the price of remediation varies according to the time at which it is performed and who performs the cleanup. The final column of table 5.1 assigns each scenario an index of probability. Peat Marwick based the index on a complex set of variables and assumptions, and created qualitative categories to describe the probability that each scenario might occur. The probability categories are as follows:

High - The scenario has occurred previously at the site or at similar sites; there are obvious problems in site design or the underlying hydrogeology.

Moderate - The scenario has not occurred at the site but has occurred at similar sites, and the design has potential problems.

Low - The scenario has not occurred at the site and the potential for occurrence is minimal.

Slight - It would take an unusual set of circumstances for the scenario to occur.

If one compares the first eight scenarios of table 5.1 to scenarios nine and ten, it is easy to see that there is an explicit difference between these two groups. Scenarios one through eight describe events that might occur, while scenarios nine and ten describe methods of remediation. In fact the two methods of remediation listed in scenarios nine and ten are drastic when compared to other forms of cleanup. Consequently, scenarios nine and ten should be considered worst case scenarios of remediation instead of probable events. If one adds the low-end estimates of cost for scenarios one through eight, the total estimated cost comes to $5,916,200. Coupling the low-end estimates with the high-end estimates ($9,936,300) provides an estimated range of $5,916,200-$9,936,000 to clean up all eight scenarios. However, looking at the probabilities assigned to each event one can see that the chances of all events occurring at the same time are slim to none. Despite this fact, Peat Marwick suggested that Laidlaw maintain a $30 million third-party liability insurance and establish a trust fund that will build to $130 million by the year 2000.[61]

The cost estimates for the Petitioners and Intervenors were performed by Dr. Joel S. Hirshhorn. He claimed that he was 100 percent certain that the Laidlaw facility will fail and that Peat Marwick underestimated the costs of cleanup.[62] Hirshhorn used all of the high-end cost estimates of the Peat Marwick study and arrived at an estimated total of $230 to $560 million.[63] He provided no working papers or calculations to support his work.[64] Instead, Hirshhorn claimed to use very simplistic calculations.[65] It is interesting to note that Hirshhorn criticized EPA for publishing average cost figures, claiming that they are simplistic and misleading while at the same time admitting that his own figures are "not precise brain surgery."[66] Hirshhorn also admitted that he did not perform a risk assessment, nor did he perform any site-specific analysis.[67]

The cost estimates for Laidlaw were performed by a team of experts assembled by Dr. James Dragun, president of the Dragun Corporation. Dragun claimed "that the technical basis upon which the DHEC staff had based its proposals with regard to financial assurance was flawed, and as a result of that, the overall . . . level of financial assurance is too high."[68] Dragun criticized the Peat Marwick report because it did not follow the standard approach for risk assessments as discussed in EPA manuals.[69] He further claimed that Peat Marwick failed to distinguish between the levels of risk posed by different chemicals, and he affirmed that the study did not take into consideration the chemical and biological reactions that would determine the concentration of the chemicals that the landfill contained, which would determine the potential effects on human health and the environment.[70] Dragun stated that risk to human health and the environment would have to be considered in making a decision about implementation of a remediation technology. He pointed out that Peat Marwick did not do this even though there are accepted EPA guidelines for selecting remediation technologies that incorporate this kind of risk assessment.[71] Dragun's worst case scenario focused on leaks in the liner and the resulting problems caused by chemicals from leachate and groundwater that were discussed in the Peat Marwick report.[72] Using EPA's six-step process, Dragun selected a remedial technology.[73] He opted for repair of the liner, which he estimated to cost approximately $21 million (in 1988 dollars) and groundwater remediation, which he estimated to cost $971,775. These estimates are consistent with the Peat Marwick report.[74] Dragun conceded that it would be reasonable for purposes of financial assurance to double this figure. Bringing Dragun's estimate forward to 1993 dollars at an overall 6 percent rate of inflation and doubling it gives an estimated cost of $70 million.

The process of risk assessment, as illustrated in the Laidlaw case, is quite a perilous undertaking. While testimony from experts on the risks posed by the Laidlaw facility may be evaluated with substantial success, it is very difficult to formulate precise measurements of the actual level of risk posed by the facility and to derive an exact sum that is adequate to cover the risk. As shown by the Peat Marwick assessment and the expert evaluations of this report, there are so many factors to consider that at present it is nearly impossible to ascertain an exact level of risk. As Dragun pointed out in his evaluation of the Peat Marwick assessment, regulators must understand how each chemical, metal, or organic waste reacts with every other, how they react with soils, and what processes each goes through inside the landfill or as it is migrating out of the landfill to find how the concentration of each waste material is affected. Regulators can never know what risks landfills pose to human health and the environment until they understand the materials contained inside the landfill. This dilemma brings to mind the following question: how useful is the process of risk assessment if it cannot produce precise measurements of the actual level of risk posed by landfill operations?

The Role of Risk Assessment in Risk Avoidance and Cost Determination

The fact that at the present time risk assessment is an imperfect process does not preclude its usefulness as a measure of risk. As shown by the Peat Marwick report, risk assessment does provide analytical data on the design, installation, and operation of landfills. This data is useful in assessing the exposure risk due to engineering or operational factors. However, reliable data on the different materials contained inside the landfill and how they react with one another and their surroundings is needed to show the effects that these materials have on the landfill itself and what reactions take place if and when they reach the environment. Risk assessment is only as complete as the data upon which it is based. As scientists and regulators assemble more data on the actual reactions that take place between hazardous materials and the environment, more pieces of the puzzle will be joined together to form a more complete picture. As a result, risk assessment will be more thorough and accurate and will facilitate efficient methods of risk avoidance; if regulators have a thorough understanding of the risks they face, they can devote the resources necessary to adequately address these risks while avoiding any waste of precious resources.

At the present time there are many informational gaps in the process of risk assessment. However, risk assessment does provide empirical information on complications that arise from day-to-day operations, accidents that result from faulty design or installation, and remediation costs. As shown by the Peat Marwick study, this empirical information can be used to construct worst case scenarios and derive estimated ranges of cost to remediate these complications. Of course, experts may disagree with one another on the exact cost estimates, and although the estimates provided by risk assessment are not precise, they do give regulators a good idea of what the costs would be if any of the worst case scenarios occur.

As shown in the Peat Marwick study, regulators can add a substantial margin of safety for the purposes of providing financial assurance. Until enough data is accumulated to truly understand the actual level of risk posed by landfill facilities, this financial margin of safety is needed to compensate for methods of risk avoidance based on imperfect information and to ensure that any environmental impairment that may emanate from landfill operations will be dealt with accordingly. However, supplying this financial margin of safety is not free. Any financial resources devoted to supplying a margin of safety could be used to generate profit or to improve the services that landfill operations supply. As the costs associated with supplying financial assurance and the margin of safety increase, the price of landfill disposal also increases. Bear in mind that society must provide itself with an affordable means of hazardous waste disposal if it is to sustain its present rate of consumption. As such, efforts should be made by regulators and scientists to close the information gaps that exist in risk assessment of landfills so that the financial margin of safety that landfill operators have to provide decreases. As risk assessment of landfill disposal becomes more accurate, methods of risk avoidance will become more reliable and successful. This will reduce the uncertainty associated with the amount of financial assurance needed to cover risk and thus reduce the financial margin of safety required and the opportunity cost of funds devoted to the margin of safety. Is there anything that regulators can do to reduce the opportunity cost of providing financial assurance and a financial margin of safety until enough data exists to conduct thorough and precise risk assessment?

The fact that regulators are responsible for gathering data and landfill operators are responsible for providing financial assurance and any financial margin of safety that may be required presents an interesting situation. Any uncertainty that results from information gaps inherently affects the success of any risk avoidance plan. To compensate for any areas of risk not covered by the risk avoidance plan, regulators have to pad the financial assurance requirement. However, the landfill operators and ultimately consumers are the ones who bear the financial burden caused by the information gap. However, regulators can ease this burden by allowing landfill operators to choose a combination of financial mechanisms to provide the financial assurance and any financial margin of safety that may be required. By allowing landfill operators to choose among financial mechanisms, regulators permit them to find the least costly method of supplying financial assurance. This will minimize the opportunity cost of providing any financial margin of safety that may result from lack of data.

Federal law currently allows landfill operators to choose from among a combination of financial mechanisms to provide financial assurance (Findley and Farber, 1992). The economic costs of providing a specified level of assurance vary among the financial mechanisms that are allowed by RCRA. For instance, if a company sets up a cash trust fund to cover its responsibilities, it not only loses the value of the money set aside but also all of the potential earnings that money could have gained if the company had put the money to other use. Conversely, if the company uses a surety bond, which is a written contract that legally ensures that the cash amount will be provided when the bond is called, it can use the money to earn profits while providing the specified amount of financial responsibility. Given the uncertainty of the actual risks posed by landfill operations, making use of these differences in the cost of providing financial assurance can be an essential method of providing affordable disposal until better data is assembled.

Individual states have also promulgated regulations on the use of financial mechanisms that landfill operators may use to provide financial assurance. Existing laws in South Carolina allow landfill operators to choose among approved financial mechanisms to provide the following financial assurances: closure, post-closure, and third party liability. A brief explanation of the existing laws is provided in table 5.2. Although landfill operators may choose among approved financial mechanisms to provide these financial assurances, South Carolina DHEC reserves the right to require "evidence of other financial assurance in such forms and amounts as the department determines to be necessary."[75] This gives DHEC the power to adjust financial assurance requirements of particularly troublesome sites to meet high levels of risk. Risk assessment can be used to ascertain whether the design, installation, or operation of any landfill site poses inordinate risk.

Final Thoughts on Laidlaw, Risk Assessment and Cost Determination

If risk assessment can be used to justify regulatory actions that effectively take away the right of landfill operators to choose financial mechanisms, the assessment should uncover substantial fault in the design, installation, or operation of a landfill. Looking at the expert testimony from the adjudicatory hearing and the Peat Marwick assessment, one does not observe such faults at the Laidlaw facility. It is interesting to note, however, that although federal law and existing South Carolina DHEC regulations provide landfill operators with a choice of financial mechanisms in providing financial assurance, the DHEC Board rejected the Stipulated Agreement, the conclusions of the administrative law judge, and the advice of the DHEC staff.[76] In February 1994, the board required Laidlaw to immediately provide a $30 million cash bond and to build a cash trust fund of $133 million by the year 2005.[77] Two months later, the same board reversed their decision and promulgated a law that specifically allows choice of financial mechanisms for environmental impairment responsibility.[78] Why should the board make such a drastic change in policy?

Aside from the fact that the language of federal law and DHEC regulations allows for choice of financial mechanisms, the board was able to study the potential economic effects of its February decision before the April meeting. It is estimated that the decision would have required South Carolina businesses to pay $10 million in extra disposal fees, jeopardized millions of dollars in federal funds for waste sites, and damaged South Carolina's ability to attract and keep business (Moscati, 1994). Looking at the negative ramifications of its earlier decision, the board decided to maximize environmental protection subject to economic costs. What does this say about the process of risk assessment and the determination of economic costs?

As is often the case, the assessment of risk in *Laidlaw v. DHEC* was performed by experts whose testimony tends to support a client's position. This is not to say that the testimony is false or unreliable, but merely to state that the testimony is often a little biased. In this case, the familiarity that the Laidlaw witnesses had with the Pinewood landfill and the evidence produced in the case lent considerable

Table 5.2. Existing Financial Assurance Regulations

A. Closure (R.61-79.265.142,-143)

Assures availability of funds for cost of closure. Owner or operator must submit to DHEC annually updated estimates of the costs of closure of the facility. The level of the financial assurance must meet the estimated closure cost. The owner or operator must choose from among the six optional mechanisms. Regulations have no provisions for DHEC to adjust level or mandate a particular mechanism.

B. Post-Closure (R.61-79.264-144,-145)

Assures availability of funds for post-closure care. Owner or operator must submit to DHEC annually updated estimates of the costs of post-closure care of the facility. The level of the financial assurance must meet the estimated post-closure care costs. The owner or operator must choose from among the six optional mechanisms. Regulations have no provisions for DHEC to adjust the level or mandate a particular mechanism.

C. Third Party Liability (Sudden) (R.61-79.264.147(a))

Assures availability of funds for bodily injury and property damage to third parties caused by sudden accidental occurrences arising from the operation of the facility. The level of coverage is $1 million per occurrence with $2 million annual aggregate. The owner or operator must choose from among the six optional mechanisms. The level required is not consistent with the degree and duration of risk associated with the facility. DHEC may likewise adjust the level. (R.61-79.264.147 (d)).

D. Third Party Liability (Nonsudden) (R.61-79.264.147 (b))

Assures availability of funds for bodily injury and property damage to third parties caused by nonsudden accidental occurrences arising from the operation of the facility (surface impoundment, landfill, land treatment facility, or disposal miscellaneous units only). The level of coverage is $4 million per occurrence with $6 million annual aggregate. The owner or operator may request a variance in the level of this assurance and show the level required is not consistent with the degree and duration of risk associated with the facility. DHEC may likewise adjust the level. (R.61-79.264.147 (d)).

Source: Summary of existing financial assurance regulations supplied by the McNair Law Firm.

credibility to Laidlaw's position. After twenty-four days of expert testimony and assessments of risk commissioned by DHEC, the Petitioners, and Laidlaw, the ALJ found that the evidence overwhelmingly supported the adequacy of the financial responsibilities assigned by the Stipulated Agreement. However, the DHEC Board overturned the decision and denied Laidlaw the choice of financial mechanisms allowed under federal law. How could this happen?

The DHEC Board is made up of persons appointed by the governor of South Carolina. These persons often have no more knowledge of hazardous wastes than does any other ordinary citizen. Considering the limited data on actual risks posed by landfills that is available to scientists, the knowledge of the members of the board understandably may be very lacking. When faced with a very difficult situation such as the Laidlaw landfill, they may feel pressure to take action. This pressure is elevated when a coalition of citizen and environmentalist groups opposes the landfill. The members of the board have to live among the members of this coalition, and a wrong decision could make life very unpleasant. Working with limited knowledge and under considerable political strain, the members of the board may rush into unwise decisions. The fact that the board later reversed its February decision and promulgated a law that allows choice of financial mechanisms shows that the Board can alter its position after considering all of the effects of its decision.

Risk assessment is only as accurate and useful as the body of data upon which it is based. Without a complete picture of the actual risks posed by landfill operations, there will always be uncertainty about the risks involved and the financial assurance needed to cover that risk. One thing is certain: as financial responsibility requirements increase so do the costs of waste disposal. If society wishes to continue its present rate of consumption, regulators have to find a way to permit affordable disposal of waste without sacrificing environmental safety.

Risk assessment can help reduce the costs of disposal by equating the level of financial assurance to the level of risk posed by each facility. As we have seen in the Laidlaw case, informational gaps and the political process often interfere with the ability of risk assessment to equate costs with risks. More data is needed to understand the materials contained in the landfill and how each material reacts when placed inside the landfill. Reliable data and increased knowledge will make risk assessment more accurate and more reliable and when that happens, the public will trust the methods of risk avoidance based on those assessments. Only then will the gap between perceived risk and actual risk be narrowed.

Finally, the actions of the DHEC Board clearly show that economic considerations are important to both regulators and the community. Why else would the board make such a drastic change in policy? This case clearly shows the need for cost-benefit analysis of regulations. Allowing Laidlaw a choice of financial mechanisms significantly reduces the cost of providing a specified amount of financial assurance. Until the informational gaps that are present in risk assessment are filled and until regulators are better equipped to address the risks posed by hazardous waste disposal, regulatory flexibility is the only way society can have access to affordable hazardous waste disposal.

Notes

1. RCRA 42 U.S.C. section 1004 (5) 6903; ELR STAT.42006.

2. Ibid.

3. 40 C.F.R. section 261.24, 1988.

4. 40 C.F.R. section 261.30, 1988.

5. S.C. Code Ann. 44-56-10.

6. Taken from the summary of the adjudicatory hearing at DHEC, January 13, 1993, in the matter of *Laidlaw v. DHEC,* p. 4.

7. Taken from the summary of the adjudicatory hearing at DHEC, January 13, 1993, in the matter of *Laidlaw v. DHEC,* p. 13.

8. Taken from the summary of the adjudicatory hearing at DHEC, January 13, 1993, in the matter of *Laidlaw v. DHEC,* p. 14.

9. Ibid., p. 7.

10. Taken from the summary of the adjudicatory hearing at DHEC, January 13, 1993, in the matter of *Laidlaw v. DHEC,* p. 13.

11. Ibid., p. 44.

12. Ibid., p. 15.

13. Ibid., p. 16.

14. Ibid., p. 15.

15. Ibid., p. 44.

16. Ibid.

17. Taken from the summary of the adjudicatory hearing at DHEC, January 13, 1993, in the matter of *Laidlaw v. DHEC,* p. 45.

18. Ibid., p. 16.

19. Ibid., p. 17.

20. Ibid., p. 20.

21. Ibid.

22. Ibid.

23. Ibid., p. 21.

24. Ibid.

25. Taken from the summary of the adjudicatory hearing at DHEC, January 13, 1993, in the matter of *Laidlaw v. DHEC,* p. 7.

26. Ibid., p. 31.

27. Taken from the summary of the adjudicatory hearing at DHEC, January 13, 1993, in the matter of *Laidlaw v. DHEC,* p. 31.

28. Ibid., p. 31.

29. Ibid., p. 3.

30. Taken from the summary of the adjudicatory hearing at DHEC, January 13, 1993, in the matter of *Laidlaw v. DHEC*, p. 33.

31. Ibid., p. 34.

32. Ibid.

33. Ibid., p. 33.

34. Ibid., p. 34.

35. Taken from the summary of the adjudicatory hearing at DHEC, January 13, 1993, in the matter of *Laidlaw v. DHEC*, p. 34.

36. Taken from the Conclusions of Law in the adjudicatory hearing at DHEC, January 13, 1993, in the matter of *Laidlaw vs. DHEC*.

37. Taken from the summary of the adjudicatory hearing at DHEC, January 13, 1993, in the matter of *Laidlaw v. DHEC*, p. 6.

38. Ibid.

39. Taken from the record of the adjudicatory hearing at DHEC, January 13, 1993, in the matter of *Laidlaw v. DHEC*, p. 2914.

40. Taken from the record of the adjudicatory hearing at DHEC, January 13, 1993, in the matter of *Laidlaw v. DHEC*, p. 2914.

41. Ibid., pp. 2710-2760.

42. Ibid.

43. ibid.

44. Ibid., pp. 2894, 2878.

45. Taken from the Findings of Fact #16 in summary of the adjudicatory hearing at DHEC, January 13, 1993, in the matter of *Laidlaw v. DHEC*, p. 45.

46. Taken from summary of the adjudicatory hearing at DHEC, January 13, 1993, in the matter of *Laidlaw v. DHEC*, p. 5, 2.

47. Taken from the record of the adjudicatory hearing at DHEC, January 13, 1993, in the matter of *Laidlaw v. DHEC*, pp. 1867-68, 3819, 3848-49.

48. Taken from summary of the adjudicatory hearing at DHEC, January 13, 1993, in the matter of *Laidlaw v. DHEC*, pp. 22-23.

49. Taken from the record of the adjudicatory hearing at DHEC, January 13, 1993, in the matter of *Laidlaw v. DHEC*, p. 3056.

50. Ibid., pp. 2633, 2658.

51. Ibid., p. 2724.

52. Taken from the record of the adjudicatory hearing at DHEC, January 13, 1993, in the matter of *Laidlaw v. DHEC*, p. 3045.

53. Ibid., p. 3059.

54. Ibid., p. 1644.

55. Ibid., p. 3541.

56. Ibid., pp. 371-372.

57. Ibid., p. 3855.

58. Ibid., pp. 3846-3847.

59. Taken from the Peat Marwick risk assessment of the Laidlaw landfill at Pinewood at DHEC, p. II.1.

60. Ibid.
61. Taken from the record of the adjudicatory hearing at DHEC, January 13, 1993, in the matter of *Laidlaw v. DHEC,* pp. 143-151.
62. Ibid., pp. 2934, 2937.
63. Ibid., p. 2977.
64. Ibid., p. 3089.
65. Ibid., pp. 3011-3015.
66. Taken from the record of the adjudicatory hearing at DHEC, January 13, 1993, in the matter of *Laidlaw v. DHEC,* pp. 2983, 2990.
67. Ibid., pp. 3054; 3089-3091.
68. Ibid., p. 4756.
69. Ibid., p. 4763.
70. Ibid., p. 4766.
71. Ibid., p. 4780.
72. Ibid., p. 4782.
73. Ibid., pp. 4783-4784; 4790-4797.
74. Ibid., pp. 4811-4821; 4897-4899.
75. S.C. Code 44-56-60.
76. Based on minutes of Executive Board Meeting, February 12, 1994, pp. 131-172.
77. Ibid., pp. 137-166.
78. Based on Executive Board Meeting, April 14, 1994, pp. 43-45.

References

Benjamin, Daniel K. 1993. "Risky Business: Rational Ignorance in Assessing Environmental Hazards." In *Taking the Environment Seriously,* edited by Roger E. Meiners and Bruce Yandle. Lanham. MD: Rowman and Littlefield Publishers.
Dower, Roger C. 1990. "Hazardous Wastes." In *Public Policies for Environmental Protection,* edited by Paul R. Portney. Washington, DC: Resources for the Future.
Findley, Roger W., and Daniel A. Farber. 1992. *Environmental Law in a Nutshell.* St. Paul, MN: West Publishing Company.
Minutes from DHEC Executive Board Meetings, February 12, 1994, and April 14, 1994.
Moscati, Dr. Anthony F., Jr. April 1994. "Hazardous Waste Management in South Carolina: The Cost of Being Politically Correct." South Carolina Policy Council Education Foundation.
Nelson, Robert H. 1993. "Environmental Calvinism: The Judeo-Christian Roots of Eco-Theology." In *Taking the Environment Seriously,* edited by Roger E.

Meiners and Bruce Yandle. Lanham, MD: Rowman & Littlefield Publishers.

The Record of the ALJ proceedings at DHEC, January 13, 1993, in the matter of *Laidlaw v. DHEC.*

Chapter 6

Eco-Seals

Stacie Thomas

Introduction

Some Initial Background

High profile environmental issues such as global warming, stratospheric ozone depletion, and urban smog have once again spurred public outcry for more environmental protection. Environmental issues have fueled a booming political economy in Washington since the first Earth Day in 1970. Politicians and regulators work tirelessly writing rules that will satisfy the public's overwhelming demand for environmental protection. With so much attention given to environmental issues, is it little wonder that marketers have jumped on the environmental bandwagon, attempting to translate public concern into product sales?

Some market research indicates that, given a choice, consumers prefer "green"[1] products and that they are willing to pay a premium price for those products.[2] Now more than ever, new and improved "environmentally friendly" products fill market shelves and existing products emphasize their green image.[3] The number of products with green marketing claims more than doubled between 1989 and 1990.[4] In 1990 manufacturers quadrupled their use of green marketing claims in television and print advertising.[5] It has been estimated that products bearing green claims could soon reach annual sales of $8.8 billion.[6]

Despite these numbers, actual consumer purchasing behavior fell short of the windfall response predicted by optimistic surveys. A 1996 survey conducted by Environmental Research Associates revealed that only 10 percent of the polled adults claimed, voluntarily, that they actively seek environmental information on product labels.[7] Another report conducted by Yankelovich Partners concluded that only about 10 percent of U.S. buyers could be characterized as "Evergreen" people committed to purchasing green products. All other consumers demonstrated "a basic unwillingness to translate whatever [environmental] concerns they do possess into concrete action."[8] U.S. consumers are not unique; a 1996 survey completed by the British National Consumer Council found that for "ordinary shoppers" the environment was not a big consideration.[9]

A number of possible explanations have been offered for the disparity between what consumers say and what they actually do. One explanation suggests that manufacturers have failed to provide accurate environmental information about their products,[10] or provide claims that are trivial or misleading.[11] Another possible explanation is that consumers are confused about the environmental information they are provided and either make wrong decisions or avoid buying green products altogether.[12] Yet another explanation posits that consumers are so overwhelmed by global, or even regional, environmental problems that they are convinced that their personal actions cannot possibly make a difference.[13] In some instances, consumers have opted against purchasing products that are environmentally preferable because they failed to meet price and quality expectations.[14] This confused state of affairs presents a serious problem for marketers and also reduces the potential for environmental labeling to become a reliable instrument to improve the environment.

Policy responses to the "dysfunctional green consumer market"[15] fall under two broad categories. The first is the truth-in-advertising approach in which statutes and common law set standards for non-deceptive green marketing claims.[16] Several state attorneys general have brought actions against some green marketers under generic consumer protection laws.[17] Also, various state legislatures and agencies have promulgated rules for defining specific environmental terms and have discouraged the use of broad, unverifiable claims.[18] The U.S. Federal Trade Commission (FTC) has entered the fray and issued non-binding guidelines for green marketing claims, as have agencies of other governments.[19]

The second policy response to the information problem is what the Geneva-based International Organization for Standardization (ISO) has identified as environmental labeling type I eco-seals.[20] ISO type I eco-seals are seal-of-approval type programs in which producers submit their brands to a third party for testing. If the brands meet certain criteria theoretically designed to identify a product's overall environmental excellence, producers are awarded a licensing agreement that allows them to affix a 'seal of approval' on their qualified products for a limited duration and under certain conditions. Following the intent of the *Good Housekeeping* seal, the easily recognizable seal will distinguish those products from those of the competition according to some established criteria—environmental criteria in this case.

How This Chapter Is Organized

This chapter examines the promise and prospects of eco-seals programs. The promise relates to the promotion of environmental performance improvements in highly competitive consumer markets. The prospects for accomplishing this goal relate to features of programs that have evolved and the constraints that go with them. The next section provides more extensive background to the eco-seal problem and examines the recent burst of schemes emerging worldwide, their mechanics, and purported successes. Major pitfalls are identified to explain the flaws that tend to go with product category selection and definition, and the limitations involved in extrapolating life-cycle analysis outcomes into scientifically sound ecological criteria.

The indirect and positive impacts of eco-seal schemes are subsequently examined. Eco-seals can be an impetus for encouraging the establishment of private enterprises in the business of compiling and disseminating product- and site-specific information, thus speeding up the transfer of state-of-the-art methods that could improve the environmental performance of all products. Eco-seals are not immune to unintended negative consequences, as explained further in the chapter. In fact, eco-seals could act as anti-competitive instruments that mislead consumers and stifle innovation. Finally, a brief conclusion offers some suggestions for an alternative framework that may reduce the costs associated with the inherent flaws of eco-seals.

Background

Environmental Labeling As a Market-Based Incentive for Environmental Improvement

The logic that supports the use of environmental labeling as a way to protect environment relies on an assumption that better informed consumers will seek out environmentally friendlier products in the marketplace. Improved consumer information is the fulcrum on which the market lever operates. As a result, firms producing green products will be rewarded by greater market share and profits. The lure of greater profits will invite other producers to expand pollution prevention efforts; thus, competition ensues based on development of cost-effective methods of improving environmental quality.

Environmental groups and some governments favor environmental labeling as an environmental protection device. These groups interpret survey results as a call for more eco-labels. Instead of squaring off and sparring in an anti-capitalist struggle, manufacturers and marketers could join with government and environmental groups and form productive partnerships. The more adversarial, and often costly and sometimes ineffective, command-and-control, technology-based environmental regulations typically prescribed by governments could give ground to a new approach. Environmental labeling would move environmental protection out of the regulatory realm and into the free market for goods, improving environmental performance of products and manufacturing processes beyond regulatory compliance levels. This positive vision of what might happen recognizes the value of information and emphasizes the importance of reducing the cost of transacting in the market.

In his seminal paper on social cost, Nobel Laureate economist Ronald Coase[21] suggests that the spillover costs of environmental pollution will be eliminated by market forces if transaction costs[22] are sufficiently low. Viewed in this light, the apparent divergence between survey outcomes and actual consumer behavior suggests that transaction costs are high in consumer product markets. Some economists argue that free markets cannot efficiently allocate resources in the presence of information asymmetries. Consumers faced with imperfect information about products cannot make sensible purchasing decisions. In the absence of competition many firms have little incentive to provide environmental information or may find it to be within their own interests to provide inaccurate or incomplete information. Taken on its face, this argument appears to suggest a justification for government intervention. But, as history has shown, government-prescribed solutions often provide their own negative side effects that distort otherwise free markets and make matters worse.

In theory, at least, eco-seals may solve market-distorting information asymmetries that are perceived as being inherent to self-certified manufacturers' environmental claims and credited for impeding the success of green marketing. The simplicity of the seal reduces the risk that consumers confused by environmental claims will make bad purchasing decisions. Consumer purchasing decisions are further simplified because other products will bear the same logo, creating a bundle of environmentally superior products. Promotional endeavors by certified producers and the certifying organization itself will ensure that consumers identify the seal with environmental superiority.

There are other important claims made for eco-seals. Self-declared manu-facturing claims are limited by the quantity of information they are able to provide. A manufacturer could include a pamphlet with every product, outlining all of its environmental attributes, but it is doubtful that consumers will spend time in the store aisle evaluating that information. As a result, most manufacturers' claims emphasize one medium, i.e., land, water, or air. In contrast, eco-seals are awarded to products that meet or exceed scientifically based criteria that encompass the most significant environmental impacts of the product. Products are assessed by analyzing the use of natural resources as its inputs and the environmental impacts of its production, distribution, utilization, and final disposal. This type of life-cycle analysis originated in producers' research and development laboratories as a way to cut costs caused by waste and enhance their product's position in a highly competitive and rapidly changing consumer market. Now, life-cycle analysis is gaining influence in a broader effort that seeks to quantify human impacts on the environment.

Proliferation of Eco-Seal Programs

Seals of approval for product quality and safety have existed in consumer markets since the 1940s,[23] but the Federal Republic of Germany[24] (FRG) is credited with developing the concept as an instrument for reducing the environmental impacts of consumer products.[25] In 1978, the German Blue Angel[26] eco-seal program was launched seven years after the FRG committed to the concept in a 1971 environmental program.[27] The program progressed slowly but took off in the 1980s when heightened interest spurred the establishment of more eligible product categories in response to the more than 200 category proposals received annually from interested parties.[28] By 1994, 4,200 products in eighty-one product categories were bearing the label in the German marketplace.[29]

Since the introduction of the German Blue Angel, at least twenty-four such programs have emerged. In 1988, Canada founded its Environmental Choice Program (ECP). The development of the ECP represented a fundamental shift in eco-seal programs by introducing a seal awarded not for one specific environmental aspect but against criteria based on a few significant environmental aspects derived from a complete life-cycle analysis. The explicit objective of the ECP is to spark environmental performance-based competition among producers. Therefore, criteria are set so that only a small percentage of the market can qualify.[30] As more products conform to standards, the criteria are reviewed and may become more restrictive so that only those qualified as environmentally superior are certified.

Japan's eco-labeling program began in 1989. The Project for the Promotion of Ecologically Safe Merchandise, known as the EcoMark, distinguishes itself from other programs in that its goals are directed more toward guiding consumers to products that are perceived as positively affecting the environment, e.g., solar heating systems and home composters.[31] The Japanese government promotes such industries to encourage their development and longevity and to heighten consumer environmental awareness.[32] When measured by the number of awards given and product categories established, the Japanese program is extremely successful. Since its inception, 55 product categories have been established, and there are currently 2,500 EcoMark certified products on the Japanese market.[33]

In 1989, the countries of Denmark, Finland, Iceland, Norway, and Sweden, represented by the Nordic Council of Ministers, agreed to develop a harmonized Nordic environmental label. Following the objectives and methods of Canada's ECP, the Nordic program aspires to prompt consumers into buying less damaging products and to stimulate manufacturers towards improving the environmental attributes of their products and processes.[34] The program has since developed criteria for thirty product categories and awarded 183 labels to 600 products.[35] More than half of producer participation in the program comes from Swedish manufacturers.[36]

The Nordic program coexists with at least two other eco-seal initiatives in Sweden. The Swedish Standards Institution (SSI) launched a national program in 1989 after the Swedish Parliament approved a loan for the program's establishment.[37] That same year, three of Sweden's major retailers sponsored an eco-seal program to be developed by the Swedish Society for the Conservation of Nature, Sweden's largest environmental group.[38] Products worthy of the eco-seal are identified by labels on market shelves rather than on the packaging.[39]

Also in 1989, the Austrian government introduced its eco-seal, the Austrian Hunderwasser. The eco-seal award criteria are based on entire life-cycle analysis, including raw material usage and energy consumption and a requirement that the product be at least of average quality.[40] Currently, the Austrian seal is used on forty products from twenty-eight product categories.[41]

In March 1992, the Council of Ministers of the European Union (EU) placed regulation 880/92 into force, establishing a harmonized, community-wide eco-labeling scheme.[42] The scheme does not preempt or displace existing national programs, but the European Commission (EC) regards a community-wide eco-seal as an important element of the EU's environmental policy and also a contributor to the achievement of the Single Market, which commenced in 1993.[43] The regulation requested that each member state designate competent bodies[44] to implement the scheme within six months of its entry into force.[45] The regulation became operational in October 1992.

When Regulation 880/92 was adopted by the European Council, only Germany had its own national program within the community. The accession of Sweden, Austria, and Finland into the community added at least three more programs to this list. In the wake of the establishment of the European Union program, three other national programs emerged within the Community: the French NF Environment program,[46] The Netherlands' Environmental Stamp,[47] and Spain's national program. These programs proliferated in part due to the slow development of the EU program, but also in response to national interests.[48] Of these most recent programs, the Netherlands has achieved the most success from the perspective of establishing product criteria and labeling products: twenty-five products from seventeen product categories bear the Dutch Environmental Stamp.[49] The French have given "green leaf" logo licenses to 230 products from two product categories: paints and varnishes, and garbage bags.[50] Spain has only one product category, paints and varnishes, which includes six of the ten manufacturers.[51] The European Union's community-wide eco-label now coexists with at least eight major schemes:

1. German Blue Angel
2. Nordic White Swan
3. Swedish Good Environmental Choice

4. Dutch Environmental Stamp
5. French NF-Environment
6. Spanish Environment
7. Catalan Environment
8. Austrian Hunderwasser

These programs operate in seven member states: Germany, Sweden, Finland, the Netherlands, France, Spain, and Austria.

The United States government has not yet embraced the concept of a government-sponsored eco-labeling program as an enhancement to its environmental protection initiatives with the isolated exception of the United States Environmental Protection Agency (USEPA) sponsored 'Energy Star' certification program for energy efficient computer equipment. There are, however, two independently funded and administered eco-labeling programs based in the United States: the Green Seal of Approval and Scientific Certification Systems (SCS) Environmental Report Card. While both of these programs are administratively similar, they take divergent approaches in communicating the results of life-cycle analysis studies. Green Seal sets criteria and awards seals. On the other hand, the Environmental Report Card does not signify the most environmentally preferable product, but only communicates significant life-cycle analysis results in the form of a bar graph affixed to the product's label. For comparison, a bar graph depicting the Report Card on the "typical product" is included. Theoretically any manufacturer is able to obtain a Report Card, but it is highly unlikely that a producer would submit his products for testing if they fared unfavorably in comparison with the "typical product."

Eco-seal programs now exist in China and Taiwan and in a number of developing countries, including India, the Republic of Korea, and Singapore. Unlike the criteria set in developed countries that strongly reflect national standards and values, eco-seal programs in developed countries are more outward oriented.[52] Most have emulated the eco-seal programs of developed countries.[53] Discussions are now underway for the establishment of eco-seal programs in certain countries at an intermediate level of development such as Brazil, Chile, Colombia, Indonesia, Poland, and Thailand.

The Theoretical Process of Developing Eco-Seal Programs

Generally anyone can propose a product category for labeling consideration: industry, government, consumer and environmental groups, commerce and trade. If the administrative body decides to proceed with the product category, a feasibility study of those products should first prove them to be significant from both a market and environmental perspective. If it is deemed as being significant in both dimensions, the boundaries to the product category are then defined. Ideally, boundaries are defined so that all products that are functionally equivalent, or used basically the same way, and perceived as being competitively similar by consumers are included. Most emerging programs emphasize multiple environmental impacts in their criteria; ideally the criteria are based on a full, quantitative analysis, including an inventory of all environmental factors and their corresponding relative impact on environmental themes (i.e., solid waste, water pollution).

Once criteria are set, manufacturers may voluntarily submit their products for evaluation in qualifying for the eco-label award. If the product meets or exceeds the technical environmental standards, the firm is granted the opportunity of entering into a license agreement with the certifying organization that grants the use of the seal in exchange for a small administration fee and the firm's promise to maintain those standards. A product's certification is only guaranteed for a certain amount of time. Most contracts are reviewed annually and some stipulate that criteria can be reviewed and revised as needed. Under such dynamic legal conditions it is understandable that some producers are reluctant to participate in such a scheme. Indeed, it may be more difficult for a producer to justify having the seal and losing it than to justify never having it.

Promises of Eco-Seals

The ultimate objective of all eco-seal programs, regardless of differing methods and scopes, is to protect the environment through the promotion of certain qualified products that conform to sustainable consumption principles. The consumers, if motivated by such principles, will create a niche market for seal-bearing products. Certain producers will be induced to participate in eco-seal programs by the opportunity to gain extraordinary profits that are derived from inclusion in the cartelization of its industry. If the environmentally elite products are successful in capturing a relatively price-insensitive consumer audience, a market situation may be created in which producers can sell less product at higher prices, earning greater marginal revenues on unit sales.

Successful producers are obviously attracted to the prospects of market power derived from eco-seal programs; they can set prices rather than take the price the market is willing to bear. Conforming to a set of environmental criteria may be cost-free for firms already meeting the criteria, but may be virtually impossible for nonconforming producers to accomplish. In an ideal world, eco-seals could indeed improve the environmental impacts of products and processes by isolating the external environmental costs of products and production processes that are normally imposed upon society. Command-and-control environmental regulation could accomplish a similar end but, relative to eco-seals, such regulatory approaches are generally more costly and are often ineffective.

Measures of Success

Attempting to quantify the positive effects that eco-seals have had on the environment is a problematic endeavor.[54] Eco-seals operate alongside a host of other environmental protection campaigns—government regulation, environmentally beneficial technology developments independent of eco-seals, and public environmental information campaigns. Any attempt to quantify the contribution that any eco-seal program has made in improving environmental quality would have to consider numerous outside influences. To the best of the author's knowledge, no such study exists or has been proposed. One anecdotal study conducted by Environmental Data Services, Inc., or ENDS, focuses on the longest running program—the German Blue Angel—and has reported a number of environmental successes that have been attributed to the eco-seal.[55]

The Blue Angel seems to have had an effect on consumer behavior because manufacturer nomination of product categories for eco-seal consideration is running at the pace of 150 to 200 proposals annually.[56] From the pulp and paper sector, the Blue Angel study revealed that there has been a steady increase in the recycled pulp content of paper since the establishment of an eco-label program for those products. Criteria thresholds required 51 percent recycled content in 1981. Currently, the criteria require 100 percent. In that time period, firms launched entire lines of recycled paper products, including toilet paper, hand towels, and kitchen rolls. A few manufacturers surveyed by ENDS contended that the label was helpful in establishing a market for their products. Not all manufacturers had applied for the label. The spokesman for the German Paper Manufacturing Association explained that if only one product line is labeled consumers might regard the non-labeled product lines as environmentally inferior.[57] They did not want to have to justify why one product is labeled and others are not.

One of the Blue Angel's biggest successes, in terms of environmental protection, has been its labeling of oil and gas heating appliances.[58] Within a few years of the label's introduction, the emissions of sulfur dioxide, carbon monoxide, and nitrogen oxides contributed by that product group were reduced by more than 30 percent, and the energy efficiency of products had improved significantly. However, some argue that this change was brought about by the introduction of new legislation, the eco-seal's contribution being only marginally complementary.

Another purported success of the Blue Angel is its program for low-solvent paints.[59] Since the program began, the market share for these paints has risen from 1 percent of the market to a 50 percent share. The government estimates that the label resulted in reducing the amount of solvents released into the air by some 40,000 tons annually. Even here, the question remains as to whether the reduction can be attributed directly to the eco-seal or to some other outside influence.

The Pitfalls of Eco-Seals

Arbitrary Product Category Selection

The first step in developing an eco-label award program is to select product categories to be labeled. One would assume that the expert charged with making a decision on what products to include would want only products that would yield large improvements in environmental quality. However, in practice, this would be an enormous task requiring the expert to be privy to an immense amount of data. A decision-making expert would need to know the following in order to make a benefit maximizing decision:

- The relative environmental impacts of all products and how those effects can be improved through technologically and economically feasible modifications;[60]

- The market demand of all products and related market structure (e.g., commercial versus household).[61]

Obviously, the knowledge problem is immense. It would not be practically feasible for an expert to gather all of the data required to generate this amount of information. The information problem is compounded considerably if a larger geographic span (i.e., national, rather than regional) is considered in the product category's evaluation. As it turns out, most product categories are evaluated on a case-by-case basis after they have been nominated by an interested party. Such a process inevitably results in product categories being selected arbitrarily and strongly influenced by special interests.[62]

Subjective Defining of Product Categories

Theoretically, all products that fulfill the same basic demand and are seen as competitively similar by consumers are included in the category of eligible products for the eco-label. In practice, there are at least two problems associated with this task. First, not every consumer uses the product in the same way and many products have multiple uses.[63] Household bleach is a good example. Some consumers may use bleach as an all-purpose cleaner, for use in cleaning clothes, toilets, and floors. Other consumers may limit their use of the product to serve only one function. In this case the expert must make some generalization about consumer behavior in determining the main function of the product, i.e., the primary reason for buying it.[64]

Second, no two products are seen as perfect substitutes for each other.[65] For example, before CFCs were banned in Europe, Germany established a label program for CFC-free aerosol deodorants. If the labeling objective was to guide consumers toward more environmentally benign products, it was fundamentally flawed. Consumers of roll-on deodorants, which are environmentally superior to aerosols but do not bear an eco-label, might be swayed toward purchasing the labeled aerosols.[66] However, if directing manufacturers to substitute CFCs in aerosols to an environmentally friendlier component was the objective, then it was properly established. The dual goals of guiding consumers and directing manufacturers often cannot be achieved simultaneously.[67]

Application of Life-Cycle Assessment (LCA)

Life-cycle assessment (LCA) for environmental purposes has been practiced in a number of forms since 1969.[68] The early LCAs were primarily sponsored by private interests and focused on energy and packaging issues.[69] Use of LCA in making environmental assessments did not achieve widespread use until increased consumer environmental awareness in the late 1980s encouraged a number of studies throughout North America and Europe.[70] Today, life-cycle assessment is the basis for criteria setting in most of the eco-seal programs.

LCA is a holistic evaluation of both a product's environmental impacts and the time when they occur. LCA of a product requires that an inventory be taken of all the environmental factors of the product across its life cycle, including raw materials as inputs and emissions from materials manufacture, application, product fabrication, use, maintenance, and final disposal. The effects are quantified and indexed into a table that is then used to draw a process tree in order to depict the environmental tradeoffs associated with the product.[71] The process tree is valuable for assessing the product's impact on various types of media (i.e., water, air, land, even noise) and at what stage of the product's life cycle the impacts occur.[72] Based on this assessment, areas of potential environmental improvement for that product are identified.[73]

Although LCA can be effective in comparing the environmental tradeoffs of differing technologies,[74] use of LCA to identify products with "reduced environmental impact during the entire life cycle" is not feasible.[75] There does not, and there may never, exist a method to determine the total environmental impact of a product. Additionally, a cradle-to-grave approach suggests that all raw materials used in a product's manufacture will be considered. In most cases, it will not be feasible to include all inputs in the analysis.[76] Still, even given these constraints, a detailed LCA that uses site-specific and product-specific data might come close to this ideal. However, such intensive data might not be available.

Even if such information were readily available from manufacturers and their suppliers, it is highly unlikely that they would be willing to disclose it because of confidentiality concerns and especially not if it would work against them.[77] Industry-wide data may be available but their value for the purpose of eco-seal programs is limited by how well the statistical data conform to actual technological levels that have been achieved in actual product designs and production methods.[78] All of these impediments to setting objective LCA-based criteria for products mean that eco-seal criteria cannot possibly reflect the best environmental attributes of products within a given market. Instead, programs are forced to rely on a representative sample of the market in their analysis.[79] Therefore, eco-seal programs cannot confidently identify the environmentally elite products in a given consumer market.

Information and time constraints also limit the scope of LCA studies, forcing researchers to make their own judgments as to which factors to include and which to exclude from the study.[80] If the researcher expands the scope of the study, focusing on the product's entire life cycle, enormous amounts of data will need to be compiled. Such an effort would require considerable time. An alternative is to limit the scope to specific stages of the life cycle. The tradeoff in this case is the risk of ignoring areas that could present significant environmental improvement potential.

There are other important questions to be answered. What level of detail will be used for the study? Will factors such as noise and odor be included? How will the information from the study be evaluated? Will solid waste be seen as more significant than water pollution? These questions cannot be answered scientifically. Such questions require value judgments and assumptions to be made that can be derived only from cultural and social norms. The LCA's role in the criteria setting process is limited to that of a decision support system to help the expert make subjective decisions.[81]

Setting of Specific Ecological Criteria

In setting criteria, the expert confronts a number of options. The criteria could be directly related to individual releases to, or extractions from, the environment and corresponding environmental impact.[82] These are referred to as hurdle criteria. In promulgating hurdle criteria, the analyst seeks to set an optimum environmental performance standard. Still, this approach is extremely data intensive, so standards are set according to the best available information, which often results in set standards being unrepresentative of the market and to miss optimum benchmark levels. On the other hand, criteria may be developed by relating them to the technical aspects of products and production processes, such as recycled content, paper bleached without chlorine, and detergents without phosphates.[83] This option is easier to deal with than the development of hurdle criteria; however, it tends to acquire technology-based characteristics of command-and-control regulation and its negative consequences, such as running the risk of ignoring novel technologies that may have a more profound positive effect on the environment than those identified in the criteria.[84] Both approaches are flawed in their application. Hurdle criteria present an information problem that necessitates qualitative assumptions to be made that will inevitably be influenced by special interests. Most programs mix the approaches, using hurdle criteria with data related to product or technology characteristics.

Opportunities Presented by Eco-Seals

Despite the shortcomings of eco-seals in practice, the proliferation of such programs present market opportunities for firms to develop cutting-edge methods for evaluating the environmental impacts of individual products and production processes and for pinpointing areas of potential cost savings through waste reduction, thus having a positive effect on the environment. Some organizations, namely the Organization for International Standardization (ISO) and the Society for Environmental Toxicology and Chemistry (SETC), have led initiatives for establishing a procedural framework for conducting LCA, which could facilitate an expanded role for LCA in product development and improvement efforts.[85]

The expanded role of LCA in consumer product development and improvement will generate demand for product and production specific information that will improve the quality of LCA studies. This will in turn encourage the establishment of private enterprises geared toward compiling and disseminating such information. As more complete data bases are developed, computer software could be developed for predicting environmental outcomes under various scenarios. Competitive, private sector development of improved data and analysis methods that improve LCA studies and lower their costs means that more producers can utilize such methods in their quests to cut production costs and add value to their products.

Risks of Eco-Seals

The rigid and subjective nature of recently proliferated eco-seals poses both market and environmental risks. Potential problems with eco-seals include the following:

* Eco-seals can stifle product and production innovations.
* Eco-seals may mislead consumers.
* Eco-seals are potential anti-competitive instruments.
* Eco-seals could act as de facto technical barriers to trade.

Eco-Seals Can Stifle Product and Production Innovations

Since information problems prevent award criteria from being directly related to environmental impacts, final outcomes rely mostly on technology-based product and production characteristics. This effectively codifies current technology levels, stifling the innovation of potential environmentally beneficial product designs, packaging, and production methods. By definition, inflexible technology-based standards cannot adjust to significant, environmentally beneficial technological advances that are beyond the scope of the criteria. If a particular eco-seal program is successful in terms of directing manufacturers to make modifications, those investments will be geared toward meeting the technical standards of the criteria, not in developing new, and possibly more efficient, ways to improve environmental performance.[86]

A good example of a market-driven, not eco-seal driven, innovation is seen in the development of compact detergents.[87] This innovative substitute for conventional detergents has benefitted the environment by requiring less chemicals, packaging, and transportation, and also in reducing waste during use and disposal stages.[88] In Europe alone, this technology has resulted in a net reduction of 480,000 tons of product per year that does not need to be produced.[89] Other market-driven innovations that reduce waste include high absorbency, lower fiber paper towels, recycled content and recyclable packaging, and refillable products and packages.[90] These developments could not have been foreseen in developing eco-seal criteria.

Eco-Seals May Mislead Consumers

Most eco-seal programs highlight informing consumers and heightening public environmental awareness among their key objectives. These programs also emphasize encouraging manufacturers to consider the environmental aspects of their product designs and manufacturing processes by using the eco-seal to initiate environment-based competition. As evidenced by the problems associated with defining product category boundaries and in setting award criteria, these goals cannot be achieved simultaneously.[91] A single label award cannot advertise what qualitative assumptions were made in the criteria-setting process or what particular environmental aspects were the focus.[92] Consumers will remain rationally ignorant as to what kind of actual environmental tradeoffs the product represents. Also, eco-seals discourage consumers from seeking actual environmental information about the sealed products. An environmentally motivated consumer might buy the product just because it has an eco-seal, believing that her purchase will have some positive effect on the environment. Often this is not the case.

Eco-Seals Are Potential Anti-Competitive Instruments

Eco-seals, in their idealized form, appear to be efficient tools for correcting market inadequacies. While these lofty goals are to be admired, implementation of eco-seal programs encounters a severe information problem that can distort the market process. To resolve the knowledge problem, advice and information is sought from outside sources, and those with the greatest stake in the outcome will likely become the dominant information providers.

The interaction between special interest groups and eco-seal providers can engender a scenario that is similar to that of command-and-control regulation. The scenario is that politicians, motivated by public interests, tirelessly seek methods to protect the environment by promulgating industry-wide standards for pollution control. The politician, who has limited industry-specific information, is faced with a knowledge problem and is forced to seek advice and information from outside sources. This puts the regulator in direct contact with the regulated. It is highly likely that those regulated groups will be very cooperative with the regulator, hoping that their standard will be the one set by the regulation. If the groups are successful, they have effectively captured the politician.[93]

It would be logical to assume that both groups, those that expect to win benefits from the regulation and those who expect to lose, will be highly active in trying to influence the policymaker's decision.[94] If a manufacturer can influence criteria to his advantage, he will gain a competitive edge in the market.[95] Environmental regulation, by definition, restricts output and raises the market price for those regulated goods.[96] If some producers are able to meet a standard without incurring additional costs, additional economic profits are earned. Of course, increased opportunities for profits in an industry invite competition. This is true in both performance and technology-based regulation. However, when technology is prescribed, entry to the market is effectively restricted by requiring a preliminary and often large capital investment. Performance standards, on the other hand, may yield short-term profits for some, but with firms being free to develop their own cost-effective ways to comply with the standard, those profits will be zero in the long run.

Ideally, eco-seal programs conform to a public interest theory of regulation, but the costliness of meeting this ideal, in terms of information, forces eco-seal programs to embrace a special interest theory of regulation. The criteria-setting process calls for specific and detailed information that can only come from members of the affected industry. Those best equipped to influence program managers will inevitably gain at the expense of the less influential. The special interest theory of regulation predicts that these groups will be successful in codifying their technology as criteria.[97] What begins as a public interest program can become an anticompetitive, special interest system that rewards politically adept firms. In this way, eco-seal programs can effectively cartelize an industry, restricting output and allowing those concentrated few to earn economic rents at the expense of consumers.[98] Compliance with the terms of the cartel is not a problem because it is enforced and managed by the eco-seal's governmental or quasi-governmental administrators.[99]

This is not to suggest, however, that industrial and trade interests will visibly dominate eco-seal product category selection and criteria-setting processes. Some environmental organizations and retailers have been successful in influencing outcomes that coincide with particular products and processes they have been selected as being environmentally friendly (e.g., recycled or reusable products). Involvement by environmental groups is key to the success of eco-seal programs because it lends credibility to their cause. In some cases, this influence appears to be so strong that the selection of product categories and setting of award criteria are done so successfully that industry input was either ignored or not actively pursued. Consider the following cases:

• Germany's Blue Angel program published criteria for laundry detergents that made eligible only those products sold as building blocks (separate chemicals that consumers mix in the appropriate quantities per wash). Prior to the establishment of the program, such products represented only a 1 percent market share. After, the product's market share rose to 1.5 percent, but then fell right back down to 1 percent, presumably because those consumers who bought the product became aware of its disadvantages.[100]

• Criteria set by the Swedish Society for Conservation of Nature for batteries required eligible producers not to exceed a one part per million (ppm) each of mercury, cadmium, and lead. However, the instruments specified in the criteria for measuring the quantities are only accurate at levels registering five ppm or more. The criterion is technologically impossible to verify.[101]

While the cases of industry dominated criteria and the establishment of programs that appear to be skewed toward the interests of environmental groups are well documented, at times these diverse groups work together because they often seek to achieve the same goal.[102] This coordinated effort is a key element to the seal's success. The manufacturers need support from environmental groups in order to add credibility to manufacturer's cause. Environmental groups need manufacturers because they are the ones able to promote their interests and concerns in the marketplace via labeling products that are consistent with those goals. The result could be "[a] regulatory cartel delivered and enforced by a group that takes the moral high ground."[103] As an example of this interaction, consider the lobbying process involved in the United Kingdom's hair spray criteria draft for the European Union's eco-labeling scheme. Body Works, a personal care products firm, proposed that a ban on animal testing be introduced into the criteria requirements. The United Kingdom Eco-labeling Board (UKEB) resisted at first, but finally agreed after environmental pressure groups threatened to walk away.[104]

Eco-Seals Could Act As De Facto Technical Barriers to Trade

Participation by manufacturers in eco-seal programs is totally voluntary and has not, in any circumstance, become a trade requirement by any nation's government. Still, eco-seals have recently stirred controversy in forums that discuss the adverse trade effects caused by different environmental standards, such as the World Trade Organization (WTO) and the United Nations (UN). The argument that eco-seals have the potential to become de facto trade impediments has arisen for two reasons. First, more criteria are being set covering production methods that tend to vary drastically among geographical locations.[105] Second, more product categories are being selected that are of great trade interest for exporting countries.[106] For example, programs affecting the pulp and paper sector are on the rise, and the European Union plans to include footwear and textiles (t-shirts and bed linen) as part of its scheme. The data are even more compelling; 70 percent of all products sold globally come from international manufacturers. Yet more than 80 percent of all eco-seals are awarded to domestic companies.[107]

The flaws inherent in the establishment of an eco-seal award program are central to the trade arguments of groups that feel that they have been unfairly disadvantaged by such programs in the international trading of their products. Although public participation is actively sought in the development of eco-seal schemes, this tends to be limited to that of domestic interests.[108] Also, eco-seals inevitably reflect domestic environmental concerns and priorities, causing the criteria to focus on specific environmental attributes that can be more easily met by domestic firms and may overlook the environmental advantages of imported products.[109] Testing and verification of foreign producers' products and processes can become prohibitively costly, especially if the criteria require plant inspections.[110] The proliferation of eco-seals with differing requirements increases the costs of obtaining information and investing in technology that conforms to the various standards.[111]

Summary

Recent market research indicates that some consumers are highly interested in the environmental attributes of the products they buy, and, given the opportunity, they would buy environmentally friendlier products, even at a premium price. Having discovered this, many manufacturers began including environmental information on the packaging of their products along with other information about quality, use, price, and safety. This presented an opportunity for manufacturers to differentiate their products in the marketplace by factors other than price. However, the truly environmentally friendlier products were embraced only by a small percentage of consumers relative to the number suggested by the surveys. It appears that these products have only affected those consumers truly motivated by environmental factors and have generally failed to spark interest from consumers with latent desires to buy environmentally friendlier products.

The possible explanations given for the disparity between what consumers say they want and actual purchasing behavior suggest a breakdown in the quality of environmental information given to consumers. Some manufacturers tend to provide inaccurate or deceiving claims. Other claims, it has been suggested, are too complex for consumers to easily translate into purchasing decisions reflecting their desire for green products. The environmental information problem has led to two broadly based policy approaches. The first is a truth-in-advertising approach in which manufacturers' environmental claims are regulated to ensure that they do not mislead consumers. The other approach is the environmental logo approach first introduced by the Germans but quickly emulated by other governments. In principle, the eco-seal is awarded only to those products that have demonstrated lesser impacts relative to their competition.

Eco-seals are designed to harness the desires of both the environmentally motivated consumers and those with latent environmental preferences. Manufacturers of these products are rewarded through greater market share and are able to charge a premium price for those products, recouping investments made on their green technology. Because the market promises additional profits, environment-based competition will ensue among manufacturers. Manufacturers will be directed to improve the environmental qualities of their products, packaging, and product production methods in pursuit of the eco-seal. Once the market has moved to a higher level of environmental performance, the standard is tightened again. The eco-seal can theoretically improve environmental quality by using market forces to promote sustainable consumption habits among consumers. Indeed, it appears that eco-seals have had at least some effect on consumer behavior because manufacturers are constantly nominating product groups for eco-labeling consideration. Also, some studies suggest that eco-seal programs have had a positive effect on the environment. However, it is hard to draw a concrete conclusion about the successes of eco-seals because they coexist with a number of other environmental protection tools; it is quite possible that positive environmental and market changes would have occurred in the absence of eco-seals.

While eco-seal award criteria are based theoretically on an environmental performance standard, in reality information constraints force standards to reflect current technology. The process of developing eco-seal programs requires intensive data about consumer preferences, market demand and structure, and actual environmental impacts of all products throughout their entire life cycles. At every stage of the process, the expert developing the criteria is forced to make qualitative judgments in place of quantitative judgment because the information required is not available or is not economically feasible to acquire. Even if the information were available at sufficiently low costs, the task that the process aspires to achieve is an impossible one. There currently does not exist a purely scientific method that can accurately evaluate the environmental impact of a product.

The intensive data required for doing market studies and life-cycle analysis present an opportunity for establishing a market for that information. If there is a demand for such information, there will be suppliers willing to provide that information for a price. Competition will emerge, thus increasing the quality of the information at the lowest price possible. The availability of market information and site- and product-specific information would reduce the costs involved in conducting LCA as part of the research and development of consumer products. While LCA has the potential for identifying areas for improving product quality and cutting costs by reducing waste, as a science it has absolutely no value in comparing an entire market of products to one another on the basis of environmental benignancy.

Given real world constraints, eco-seal program criteria are inevitably based on an environmental technology standard rather than a performance standard. Therefore, they are subject to the same drawbacks identified with command-and-control type regulation. The award criteria prescribe and codify current technological methods of product design, packaging, and production methods, stifling technological innovations that could enhance environmental performance beyond standards outlined in the criteria. Also, the seal of approval on products, though easily identifiable, fails to communicate all of the qualitative type assumptions made in developing the criteria. Consumers could be misled to buy only eco-sealed products that may or may not be the most environmentally preferable.

Information constraints in the development of eco-seal programs present a knowledge problem for the expert developing the program. The expert is forced to seek the advice of outside interests. Usually the entities that have the most information sought by the expert are the ones that have the most to gain or lose by the establishment of the program. The expert may be captured by special interests seeking to maximize their own self-interests. Those administering the program may be motivated to conform to those interests if they are politically motivated. Some anecdotal evidence suggests that industrial, trade, and environmental groups have been successful in influencing eco-seal development processes.

The abuses of eco-seal programs by special interests have the potential for rendering the seals ineffective. Instead of promoting the public interest, the programs promote favor-seeking behavior by industry, or as de facto, technical barriers to trade.

The central question at this point is whether eco-seal programs, with all of their inadequacies and problems, present a better solution for solving market environmental information problems than the alternative: common law and/or regulated enforcement of manufacturers' self-declared claims of products' environmental attributes. The purpose of this chapter is not to answer this question, but to present the merits of an ideal eco-seal program, explain why actual programs fall short of this ideal, present possible opportunities that could result from the proliferation of such programs, and explain how the seals can potentially harm the very things they purport to improve. Through this analysis, one can identify areas of possible improvement for reducing the potential negative effects of eco-seals. Such possible improvements could include:

• Information sharing among eco-seal programs. It is highly likely that eco-seals have already amassed large quantities of site-specific and product-specific environmental information and detailed information about their markets. If an international framework approach is taken, which is preferable, eco-seal programs can benefit by obtaining information that could provide valuable insight into how the environmental impacts of certain effects differ as a function of geographic diversity. Information sharing also provides an opportunity for the transfer and implementation of the latest in green technologies. The Global Eco-labeling Network (GEN) is an organization in which members share information about eco-seal programs.

• Graded-type eco-seals. Graded eco-seals can increase the breadth of product categories under consideration for eco-seals. Such a label would add flexibility to criteria setting and accessibility by manufacturers. Graded seals also may resolve the conflicting goals of informing consumers or directing manufacturers that inevitably arise when defining product categories and setting award criteria. The European Union just introduced such a label for its scheme. It is questionable, however, whether manufacturers will be willing to pay for a label that identifies their products as being environmentally inferior to others. The graded label may become a de facto single label.

• Third-party certification of manufacturers' self-declared environmental claims. Certification would resolve the credibility issue involved in manufacturers' self-declared claims of environmental attributes, assuming the certifying body is perceived by consumers as credible. Green Cross, a division of Scientific Certification Services, Inc. (SCS) provided such a service but this seems to be superseded by SCS's Environmental Report Card, which takes a life cycle inventory approach and communicates those results to consumers. This approach has its own methodological drawbacks that go beyond the scope of this chapter.

• Privatizing the process. Government or quasi-government institutions could be removed from decision-making positions. An independently funded and administered program is preferable, since it will not be politically motivated. Additionally, unlike governmental programs, private organizations will be, by definition, more capable of translating market conditions into action. The U.S.-based organization of Green Seal and SCS are such entities. In response to the market, they have developed other programs that promote free market approaches to environmental protection. Green Seal developed its Environmental Partners programs that put environmentally motivated commercial consumers in contact with environmentally conscious suppliers. SCS has also developed its Forestry Conservation Program (FCP), promoting sustainable forest management, and the program has been recognized internationally for its successes in that area.

• Mutual recognition agreements. Foreign producers, especially those of developing countries, are competitively disadvantaged relative to domestic producers of countries with eco-seal programs because they have higher costs of obtaining information and verifying the environmental aspects of their products and production methods. The mutual recognition of other eco-seal programs or third party certification institutions in other countries could reduce this cost.

• Acceptance of a universally accepted method for conducting and applying life cycle analysis in eco-seal programs. Developing an accepted method would reduce the inconsistencies of criteria among eco-seal programs, thus reducing the adjustment costs involved, often conflicting in separating eco-seal award criteria among different programs. The International Organization for Standardization (ISO) is in the process of developing such a framework as part of its ISO 14000 series of international standards for environmental management. ISO develops international standards in coordination with its members, who comprise over 100 different countries.

Appendix A
Eco-Seal Programs Worldwide

Location	Program	Status
Europe		
Austria	Hunderwasser Seal	Since 1991. Criteria in 28 categories with 40 awards. *Detergents:* Criteria developed, but no products awarded.
European Union	Environmental labeling program	Since 1992. Criteria developed for approximately 9 categories. Intended to "harmonize" national programs across Europe. *Detergents:* Criteria implemented in 1995.
France	NF Environment	Since 1992. Deferring to European Union.
Germany	Blue Angel	Since 1978. Historic model of all other programs. Over 81 categories labeled and over 3,600 labels awarded.
Netherlands	Stichting Milieukeur	Since 1992. Also deferring to European Union. Has 17 categories and 25 awards (2 tissue, 14 cat litter) *Toilet Tissue:* Criteria developed. *Diapers:* Delayed proposal to date. *Catamenials:* Cancelled
Scandinavia, Sweden, Norway, Finland	Nordic Swan	First criteria on the market 1991. Intended to harmonize national program in the region. 34 categories, with 800 awards. *Goals:* 85% of detergents, 45% of household cleaners, 55% of hand dish, 35% of machine dish should be ecolabeled. *Diapers:* Criteria finalized in late-1994. Three products with a seal.
	Norwegian Nature Federation (NNF)*	Since 1991. *Detergents:* Criteria developed in 1993. *Catamenials:* Criteria developed in 1993. *Dishcare Machine and Hand:* Criteria developed in 1992.
	Swedish Nature Federation*	Since 1988. *Detergents:* Criteria developed in 1993. *Diapers:* Criteria developed in 1993. *Catamenials:* Criteria developed in 1993. *Dishcare Machine and Hand:* Criteria developed in 1992.

Europe (cont.)		
United Kingdom		Deferring to European Union. Has chartered the U.K. Eco-labeling Board to run a campaign to persuade industry and consumers to favor eco-labels.
Other European Countries		All other countries plan to follow European Union lead. National programs in Eastern Europe are under consideration.
North America		
Canada	Environmental Choice	Since 1988. 2nd oldest program. Has criteria on about 30 categories with over 1,400 awards. Privatization of program underway. *Diapers:* Criteria established in 1991 favoring cloth.. *Projects Underway:* Fabric conditioners, hard surface cleaners, and personal care products.
United States	Green Seal*	Since 1989. Criteria for about 20 categories with 230 awards, mostly on "environmentally friendly" items. Involved in ISO and chairs the "Global Eco-labeling Network." *Detergents:* Project underway. *Household Cleaners:* Criteria developed.
	Scientific Certification Systems (SCS) "Claim Certification"*	Since 1989. Focuses on validating environmental claims. About 500 awards to date, especially in home goods/hardware categories.
	SCS Ecoprofile*	Since 1991. Information labled based on "life cycle inventory." Mostly in home goods/hardware categories.
South America		
Mexico	None	Government conversations underway.
Venezuela	None	Government conversations underway.
Brazil	None	Government conversations underway.
Chile	None	Government conversations underway.
Other Countries	None	No activity.
Far East		
Australia	Environmental Choice	Since 1991. Abandoned in 1993 due to industry opposition.

India	Ecomark	Since 1991. Government is reevaluating program due to lack of market impact. *Soaps and Detergents:* Criteria developed.
Japan	Ecomark	Since 1989. Criteria in 49 categories with 2,300 awards. Awards made on the basis of "inherently improving the environment," and often to whole categories.
New Zealand	Environmental Choice	Abandoned in 1994 due to industry opposition.
S. Korea	Ecomark	Since 1992. Criteria in 12 categories with 96 awards. *Tissues:* Criteria developed. *Diapers:* Criteria favor cloth.
Singapore	Green Label	Since 1992. Criteria in hygiene paper, hairsprays, mousse, gels, and diapers (criteria favor cloth).
China	Green Label	
Taiwan	Environmental Seal	

*Privately sponsored program. Others are government sponsored.
Source: Julian Morris and Lynn Scarlett (November 1996). *Buying Green: Consumers, Product Labels and the Environment,* Policy Study No. 217 (Los Angeles: Reason Foundation), p. 50.

Appendix B
The European Community Eco-Label Award Scheme

Background

On March 23, 1992, the European Council adopted Regulation 880/92, establishing the European Community's community-wide eco-labeling scheme. The scheme did not displace or preclude other existing or future national programs, but stated in the regulation's preamble the aspiration to ultimately harmonize all schemes into one community-wide eco-label.

The regulation provided the framework for the scheme and outlined its underlying principles, objectives, and scope. In order to be operational, it would have to establish product categories and set specific ecological criteria for those products. The regulation requested that member states designate competent bodies to participate in the process at the Community level and administer the program at the national level. This was to be done within six months of the regulation's entry into force. Therefore, the regulation became operational, in principle, in October 1992.

The first step in establishing the program was to identify priority product groups for the label and designate the Lead Competent Body to define product category boundaries and set award criteria. Currently, ten product groups have been established and labels have been awarded to forty-five products of six manufacturers in four product groups.

The regulation contained a provision, allowing for the review, and possible revision, of the regulation within five years of its effective date. This provision was acted upon early by the European Commission. The Commission submitted a revision to the European Council and on February 12, 1996, Revision 6 of the European Commission's draft proposal was adopted by the Council. Regulation 880/92 was repealed and replaced with Revision 6. The implementation of Revision 6 is pending the outcome of a comment period.

Revision 6 was aimed primarily at increasing the effectiveness of the scheme and streamlining the program's implementation. Some major changed include:

* The establishment of the European Eco-Label Organization (EEO) to assume the duties of establishing product categories and setting criteria that were originally the task of the Lead Competent Body.

* The introduction of a graded label that replaced the single label award. This significantly changed the appearance of the label on products and allowed increased flexibility in awarding labels and increased access of the label to manufacturers.

These changes outlined above are the most significant in achieving the goals outlined above, but they were not the only changes brought forth by the revision.

This case study outlines the European Community's eco-label award scheme and, where appropriate, makes comparisons between the original Regulation 880/92 and Revision 6.

The Label

The logo is a "European Flower" that consists of an "E" surrounded by "petals," which are stars representing the twelve member states. Information outlining the reasons for the award may be included if so specified in the award criteria.

In Revision 6, the Commission introduced the graded label as a substitute for the single label because it would "allow for greater flexibility in setting criteria and in providing information to consumers on the level of 'environmental performance' of each labeled product." The graded label would award a certain number of "flowers" as a representation of that particular product's environmental friendliness relative to its competition. A product with one flower, for example, would identify a product that meets baseline criteria standards. A product with three flowers would identify the environmental elite of that product group.

Objectives

The stated objectives of Regulation 880/92, as outlined in Article 1 of the regulation are:

* "To promote the design, production, marketing, and use of products which have a reduced environmental impact during their entire life cycle,"[112] and

* "To provide consumers with better information on the environmental impacts of products."[113]

Revision 6 clarified the concept of "products which have a reduced environmental impact during their entire life cycle."[114] Currently, no scientific methodology exists to determine total environmental impacts of a product.[115] Additionally, studying all stages of the life cycle is not feasible in practice.[116] The revision clarifies that the extent of the life cycle analysis application to product groups is limited to identifying a few environmental impacts, judged as being significant, and pinpointing possible areas of improvement as perceived by the expert doing the analysis. "Eco-label criteria are in fact based on a generic assessment of such impacts, not on a study of the actual environmental effected related to the life cycle of each specified product."[117]

Types of Products

The eco-label regulation does not set specific criteria for selecting product groups to be considered for an eco-label award. In this scheme, as in all others, anyone can nominate a product category for consideration. Specifically excluded are food, drinks, and pharmaceuticals. Excluded also are products containing harmful substances that are already subject to environmental and safety labeling requirements under other directives.

There is some indication, however, that food, drinks, and pharmaceuticals could be labeled if award criteria for packaging are set. A declaration in the Council minutes contains this suggestion, but only if "any risk of confusion between the packaging and product can be avoided."[118] Additionally, the revision recognizes that a total exclusion of products classified as "dangerous" under other directives is too stringent if applied rigidly. Such an exclusion could leave out entire categories of products for eco-label consideration such as compact detergents (classified as an irritant) and solvent-based paints (flammable). Thus, these product groups could be eligible if they correspond with the program's objectives.[119]

Product groups that are perceived as not being significant from both a market and environmental perspective will not be considered. In order for an eco-label to be successful, it must have the ability to promote environmental progress by harnessing market demand forces. This means that only products which are of major interest within the Community in terms of environmental policy and market demand will be included. An additional requirement is that environmental improvement should be technologically and economically feasible.

Participants in Establishing Product Groups and Setting Specific Ecological Criteria

The eco-label program development process under Regulation 880/92 required the participation of three main bodies: (1) European Commission, (2) Consultation Forum, and (3) Committee of Competent Bodies. In addition to these, an ad hoc working group is established and meetings are arranged with that group by the Lead Competent Body to discuss progress in various stages of the program development process.

1. European Commission: The Commission is the supranational governmental decision maker whose decisions are influenced by consultations with both the Consultation Forum and the Committee of Competent Bodies.
2. Consultation Forum: The Consultation Forum consists of five main interest groups: industry (UNICE), retailers (Eurocommerce), environmental groups (European Environmental Bureau), consumer organizations (C.C.C.), and trade unions (E.T.U.C.).
3. Committee of Competent Bodies: The Committee of Competent Bodies consists of representatives from those member states that have designated competent bodies to participate in the European Community (EC) label development process and award procedure. In the initial stages of the scheme, certain competent bodies took the lead in establishing product groups and award criteria.
4. Ad Hoc Working Group: The ad hoc working group consists of the experts designated by the Lead Competent Body, experts designated by other competent bodies, experts from the interest groups designated by the Consultation Forum, and Commission services. Outcomes of ad hoc working group meetings are non-binding but the Commission is obligated to consider the various opinions of the groups represented.

Revision 6 established the European Eco-Label Organization (EEO). As envisioned by the Commission, the EEO is a private international association of the competent bodies. Under Commission mandate, the EEO is charged with establishing and updating criteria and the corresponding assessment and verification requirements. Also, the EEO coordinates the activities of the competent bodies. The work of the EEO will be monitored by the Commission and any criteria proposals are subject to final Commission decisions.

Establishment of Product Category Definitions and the Setting of Specific Ecological Criteria

Regulation 880/92 set the groundwork for establishing an eco-label award scheme, but in order for the program to become operational, product categories had to be established and award criteria promulgated. Considerable time in the initial stages of the regulation was dedicated to this process.

After consultation with the Committee of Competent Bodies, the Consultation Forum, and other relevant Commission services, a list of priority product groups was identified for further consideration. If it was determined that the product group corresponded with the objectives and scope of the regulation, the Commission identified a candidate Lead Competent Body willing to establish award criteria and product category boundaries. Product groups and award criteria are adopted by the Commission through standard committee procedure.

Procedural Steps

The procedure for establishing product groups and corresponding ecological criteria is done in six phases:

Phase 1 - Preliminary Phase
Phase 2 - Market Study
Phase 3 - Environmental Inventory Analysis
Phase 4 - Environmental Impact Assessment
Phase 5 - Setting of Ecological Criteria
Phase 6 - Presentation of the Draft Proposal for a Commission Decision

Phase 1 - Preliminary Phase

The preliminary phase commences once initial investigations have resulted in the decision to move forward in the analysis of the product group. This phase requires that a comprehensive feasibility study be conducted as a cooperative effort among the Commission, Competent Bodies, and the Consultation Forum. Specific considerations of this study include:

* Nature of the market from an industrial and economic interest perspective
* Related environmental issues
* Potential advantages of labeling the product
* Possible negative impacts for labeling the product

Based on this study and the opinions of the groups involved, the Commission decides to proceed, postpone, or halt proceedings altogether. If the decision is to proceed, a Lead Competent Body or Bodies are identified to lead the investigative and program establishment process under a Commission-defined mandate and work program. The Commission invites the Consultation Forum to nominate representatives to participate in the ad hoc working group that will be established by the Lead Competent Body.

Revision 6 foresees the implementation of the European Eco-Label Organization (EEO) that will assume the task originally set out for the Lead Competent Bodies.

Phase 2 - Market Study

In-depth information about the market for the proposed product group is gathered, including:

* industrial and economic interests
* different types and sub-types of the product
* share amount of the Community market held by European Union and non-European Union manufacturers.

Once assembled, this information will facilitate decisions on product category boundary definitions and the appropriateness of the product for an eco-label program in terms of its visibility with consumers as a function of market share, and its conformity with the program's objectives. At this point, the Lead Competent Body or the EEO will arrange a meeting with the ad hoc working group to discuss its progress.

Phases 3 and 4 - Environmental Inventory and Impact Analysis

These two phases aim to complete an inventory and an assessment of environmental impacts by using "internationally recognized methods," in an "objective, qualified and representative manner," on a "cradle-to-grave" basis.[120] The application of life-cycle analysis (LCA) is based on the internationally recognized framework established by the Society for Environmental Toxicology and Chemistry (SETAC) Code of Practice (1993).[121] Since it is not practically feasible to consider all of the stages of a product's life cycle, a few judgment decisions must be made prior to the analysis. These include:

* the establishment of a sample group of "functionally equivalent and competitively equal" products in which to apply the LCA[122]
* formulating a definition for the functional utility of the product or, in other words, how the product is primarily used
* the scope of the life cycle analysis (LCA), or the level of detail that will be used with regard to life stages, inputs, and outputs.

The Society of Environmental Toxicology and Chemistry (SETAC) promulgates in its Code of Practice (1993) a framework for conducting LCA. In the code, there are three stages to LCA: inventory, impact, and improvement.[123]

Inventory Analysis: The goal of an inventory analysis is to identify and quantify inputs and outputs of the defined product system as they relate to the environment.

Impact Analysis: The first stage in an impact analysis is the classification and characterization of the environmental impacts of the product system, in accordance with the impact categories established by SETAC. Once this is completed, the impacts will be evaluated in order to identify the key environmental impacts associated with the product. It is important to note that there does not exist any scientific method for making this identification. Choosing a few impacts to focus on from an array of those differentiated in the study is completely subject to a qualitative assessment by an expert based on his opinion of what is important.

Improvement Analysis: The environmental inventory and impact analysis should be evaluated to consider theoretical possibilities for environmental progress. This type of analysis should consider the following:

* the feasibility modification triggering improvements from a technical, industrial, and an economic perspective
* certain consumer attitudes and preferences that may hinder or promote the label's effectiveness
* potential for environmental improvements caused by any market structure changes induced by the eco-label.

Phase 5 - Setting Ecological Criteria

The Lead Competent Body or, if functional, the European Eco-label Organization (EEO) is charged with drafting specific ecological technical standards against which candidate products will be compared. The criteria will be reflective of the environmental factors determined to be important by the LCA. The body promulgating the criteria will prioritize certain effects by assigning those effects thresholds and weighting factors. In order to be an effective market tool, the label must be made available for manufacturers' use. Therefore, criteria are set so that at least a certain amount of existing products will qualify for the label. The intention is to promote overall environmental improvements, not to create a niche market for environmentally friendly products.[124]

The introduction in Revision 6 of the graded eco-label as a replacement to the single label added flexibility to this phase of the process. Under a graded label, a greater market share would be eligible for a label without compromising any positive effects caused by environment-based competition. The criteria is prioritized in three levels: X,Y, and Z.

* Level X earns three "flowers" representing the environmental elite in that product category.
* Level Y qualifying products comply with the "baseline" criteria, earning only one flower.

* Level Z has demonstrated exceptional environmental progress, but still has not reached level X.

While the graded label makes the award accessible to more products on the market, its success is highly dependent upon an applicant's willingness to pay for a label that shows that their products are not as environmentally friendly relative to their competition.[125] The chance is that a single label may continue simply by default.

Phase 6 - Presentation of a Draft Proposal for a Commission Decision

In phase six, the Lead Competent Body, or EEO, presents a final report to the commission that contains the defined product group and corresponding award criteria. The commission forwards a copy of the proposal to the Committee of Competent Bodies and the Consultation Forum for their formal opinions. This opinion is considered by the commission in their own internal consultations for preparing a draft decision to submit to the Regulatory Committee. The final decision is made by a qualified majority vote. If the commission adopts the proposal, the draft report and draft eco-label criteria are published in the Official Journal of the European Community and are subject to a sixty-day public comment period before becoming effective.

Certification and Testing

The designated competent bodies of member states are responsible for evaluating applications for awarding the eco-label. Manufacturers, importers, and retailers[126] may voluntarily submit their applications to the competent body of the member state in which the product is manufactured or imported. Manufacturers located in their countries and importers may apply to the competent body in any of the member states in which they have, or intent to market, the product.

The commission may overrule a national authority's decision to award a label. The commission is also obligated to forward the application to other member states. If no formal objection is received, the eco-label is awarded.

Terms of Use and Fees

The eco-label is awarded upon receipt of the costs associated with the processing of applications from the applicant. The competent body concludes a civil contract with the applicant, outlining the terms of use for the label. This contract includes provisions for withdrawing the authorization to use the label. Any revision of criteria necessitates reconsideration of the contract and the contract may be revised or be terminated as appropriate.

The application processing fee is generally 500 ECU. This fee does not include testing and verification costs, which are borne entirely by the applicant. Applicants receiving the label award also must pay an annual licensing, or contract, fee of 0.15 percent of the annual sales volume[127] within the European Union, subject to a ceiling of 400,000 ECU and a 500 ECU minimum. Special consideration is given to small and medium-sized enterprises (SMEs) and manufacturers of developing countries. Application fees for these groups are approximately 250 ECU and contract fees are scaled down to 0.10 percent of sales volume. Fifty percent of the total annual fees collected will be used to finance the activities of the EEO, including information campaigns.

Other Related Issues

Confidentiality Concerns

The competent body awarding the label is required to disclose the name of the product, name of the applicant, and reasons for awarding the label and other relevant information. The commission, authorities, and other associated persons are under an obligation not to disclose other information relating to the application. However, national laws may require further disclosure.[128] The regulation does not explicitly provide for the protection of confidential commercial information. Inasmuch as the disclosure of proprietary information could threaten confidentiality concerns, no disclosure would reduce a company's ability to monitor whether its competitors are getting an unfair advantage.[129]

Involvement of Interested Parties

The "involvement and balanced participation of interested parties," at least at the community level, "are actively sought" throughout the eco-seal program development process.[130] These groups consist of industry, through their business organizations, trade unions, retailers, importers, environmental protection groups, and consumer organizations.[131] Representatives from these groups participate through the Consultation Forum and ad hoc working groups for establishing product groups and award criteria.

Transparency for Third Country Interests

The regulation does not specify exactly how foreign interests will be represented. It does state, however, that "the treatment of European Union and non-European Union interested parties shall be treated on an equal footing."[132] In a 1994 Information Meeting organized by the Consultation Forum and aimed at educating third nations about the scheme, Eurocommerce indicated that it "welcomed all comments from foreign producers and would include them in their input as appropriate."[133] The publication of draft reports by the Commission and the public comment period also provide a forum for third country interests to express their opinions. Additionally, Revision 6 requires the newly established European Eco-Label Organization to publish its work plans every six months.

Position of Interest Groups

Overall, industry has taken a rather reserved position regarding the European Community's eco-label award scheme.[134] This is not surprising considering most producers will be ineligible to receive the award's highest rating for environmental friendliness. The only element widely supported by industry is the label's potential for harmonizing existing national schemes in the long term.[135] Two groups that wholly support the scheme in their sectors are the European Association of Textile Industries and the European Confederation of Paint Manufacturers.[136] The positions of commerce, environmentalists, and consumer organizations are characterized as being "average."[137]

Other National Schemes

When Regulation 880/92 was adopted by the European Council in March 1992, only one national eco-label scheme existed within the community—the German Blue Angel. The subsequent accession of Sweden, Finland, and Austria to the Community added three more programs to the list. The French, Dutch, and Spanish have also established their own national schemes, citing slow progress in developing a community-wide scheme and heightened national interest in eco-label programs. The community label now coexists with eight major schemes:[138]

1. German Blue Angel
2. Nordic While Swan
3. Swedish Good Environmental Choice
4. Dutch Milieukeur (Environmental Stamp)
5. French NF-Environment
6. Spanish Medio Ambient
7. Catalan Medi Ambient
8. Austrian UmweltZeichen

These programs operate in seven member states: Germany, Sweden, Finland, the Netherlands, France, Spain, and Austria.[139]

While Regulation 880/92 requires that the community label be complementary to existing and future programs, Revision 6 requires that those programs coordinate their criteria with that of the European Union's scheme. In all member states with, or participating in, schemes the administering competent body also administers the community eco-label within its own country. This means that both labels would have to be promoted, often in the same product categories. Pressure groups within individual member states have more influence on national schemes that within the community program. Thus, the community label may be presented as "second choice" to competing national labels, especially if the label criteria does not correspond with domestic interests.[140] Revision 6 recognizes that although those member states that administer their own programs can contribute much to the development of the community label in the form of technical and procedural experience, the proliferation of uncoordinated national schemes "involves considerable risks of distorting the internal market."[141]

Disagreements among Member States

Many disagreements among Member States have arisen over the award criteria promulgated by Lead Competent Bodies for particular product groups.[142] This has slowed the progress of developing the label. Moreover, assigning Lead competent bodies from member countries to establish the criteria runs the risk of promoting that country's national interests through the program.[143] The European Eco-Label Organization (EEO), established by Revision 6, assumes the role originally granted to the Lead Competent Body. The commission hopes the EEO will streamline and speed up program establishment by developing criteria which will facilitate the achievement of consensus among member states.

Appendix C
ISO 14000 Series of International Environmental Management
Standards for Eco-Labeling and Life-cycle Analysis

ISO 14020	Environmental Labels and Declarations	General Principles
ISO 14021	Environmental Labels and Declarations Self-Declaration Environmental Claims	Environmental Labeling Terms and Definitions
ISO 14022	Environmental Labels and Declarations Symbols	Type II Self-Declarations
ISO 14023	Environmental Labeling	Testing and Verification
ISO 14024	Environmental Labels and Declarations Guiding Principles and Procedures	Type 1 Eco-Seals
ISO 14025	Environmental Labels and Declarations Guiding Principles and Procedures	Type III Eco-Profiles

ISO 14040	Life Cycle Assessment	Principles and Guidelines
ISO 14041	Life Cycle Assessment	Life Cycle Inventory
ISO 14042	Life Cycle Assessment	Impact Assessment
ISO 14043	Life Cycle Assessment	Interpretation

Source: European Commission (1996). Draft Proposal for a Commission Regulation, establishing a revised community-wide eco-labeling scheme, Revision 6, p.12.

Notes

1. Julian Morris and Lynn Scarlett, *Buying Green: Consumers, Product Labels and the Environment,* Policy Study No. 217, November 1996 (Los Angeles: Reason Foundation), p. 3. Noting, "There are many problems with the terms 'green' and 'environment friendly.' Here they are used simply to modify words such as 'goods' or 'products,' so as to denote the fact that such items are being presented to the consumer as having some attributes that relate to the environment."

2. Roger D. Wynne, "The Emperor's New Eco-Logos?: A Critical Review of the Scientific Certification Systems Environmental Report Card and the Green Seal Certification Mark Programs," *Virginia Environmental Law Journal,* Vol. 14 (1994): 51-149. Citing, U.S. Environmental Protection Agency (Apr. 1, 1991). *Assessing the Environmental Consumer Market,* (EPA 21P-1003); Dennis Chase and Therese Kauchak Smith, "Consumers Keen on Green But Marketers Don't Deliver," in *Advertising Age,* June 15, 1992, p. 49; The Roper Organization, Inc., *The Environment: Public Attitudes and Individual Behavior in North America: Canada, Mexico, United States,* February 1993; and *The Environment: Public Attitudes and Individual Behavior,* July 1990 (Storrs, CT:The Roper Organization).

3. Glenn Israel, "Taming the Green Marketing Monster: National Standards for Environmental Marketing Claims," *Boston College Environmental Affairs Law Review* (1993): 303-333. Citing, 137 Cong. Rec. S3034 (daily ed. Mar. 12, 1991). Statement of Senator Lautenberg.

4. Ibid. Citing "Selling Green," *Consumer Reports,* October 1991, p. 687.

5. Ibid.

6. Ibid. Citing, Hubert H. Humphree III "Making Sure Green Claims Aren't Grey," *Environmental F* (November-December 1990): 32.

7. Morris and Scarlet, sup. note 1: p. 2. Citing, Council on Packaging in the Environment, COPE Research Committee, WAVE VII Report (Washington, DC:

COPE 1996), p. 6. (Survey administered by Environmental Research Associates, March 1996).

8. Ibid. Citing *Green Market Alert,* February 1993, p. 4.

9. Ibid., p. 3. Citing, National Consumer Council *Green Claims: A Consumer Investigation into Marketing Claims About the Environment* (London: National Consumer Council, 1996) p. 45.

10. Wynne, sup. note 2, p. 122. Citing David S. Cohen, "The Regulation of Green Advertising: The State, the Market and the Environmental Good," *University of British Columbia Law Review:* 225:235-41, (describing capacity for increased cynicism among Canadian green consumers); Roger D. Wynne, "Defining 'Green': Toward Regulation of Environmental Marketing Claims," *University of Michigan Journal of Law* 24 (1991): Ref. 785: 785-88, p. 806-7 (noting the same capacity in the United States; Roger (1990), sup. note 2, p. 74-78.

11. Israel, sup. note 3, p. 304. Citing, 137 Cong Rec., sup. note 3; David J. Freeman, (June 3, 1991):18 and "Environmental Product Claims Invite New Scrutiny, Litigation." *National Law Journal.*

12. Morris and Scarlett, sup. note 1, p. 3.

13. Roper (1990), sup. note 2, p. 27, 76-78.

14. Joel S. Hirschorn, "Profiting from Sustainable Consumption," *Chemtech* (April 1995): 6. Citing such examples as a toilet tissue made from recycled paper that was filled with large holes and energy-saving light bulbs that provide less light than conventional ones.

15. Wynne, sup. note 2 (table of contents), "Introduction: The Dysfunctional Green Consumer Market."

16. Ibid., at 54.

17. Ibid. Citing Stephen Gardner, "How Green Were My Values: Regulation of Environmental Marketing Claims," *University of Toledo Law Review* 23, (1991): 31.

18. Ibid. Citing Ciannat M. Howett "The 'Green Labeling' Phenomenon: Problems and Trends in the Regulation of Environmental Product Claims," *Virginia Environmental Law Journal,* (1992): 401-2; Wynne, sup. note 11, p. 807-11.

19. Ibid. Citing 57 Fed. Reg. 36.363 (1992) (codified at 16 C.F.R. pt. 260); Australian Trade Practices Commission (Feb. 1992), *Environmental Claims for Marketing-A Guideline;* Consumer and Corporate Affairs Canada, Bureau of Consumer Affairs (1991). *Guiding Principles for Environmental Labeling and Advertising.*

20. United Nations Conference on Trade and Development (UNCTAD), Report by the UNCTAD Secretariat, *Eco-labeling and Market Opportunities for Environmentally Friendly Products* (Geneva: United Nations, 1994), pp. 5-6. ISO

categorizes manufacturers' claims as type II "Self-Declared Environmental Information." A Type III label, "Eco-Profiles," is just now under review, but it is much less developed.

21. R. H. Coase, "The Problem of Social Cost," *Journal of Law & Economics* 3 (1960): 1-44.

22. Transaction costs involve the costs of obtaining information, such as price, qualitative product aspects, and changing consumer preferences. These costs are incurred by both buyers and sellers in pursuit of each other. If transaction costs are too high, consumers will not be able to find those producers of products that cater to their desires. In the case of environmental pollution, environmentally conscious consumers will not be able to translate those concerns into sensible purchasing decisions if the costs of locating product environmental information are too high.

23. Wynne, sup. note 2, p. 59. Citing D. M. Phelps, "Certification Marks Under the Lanham Act," *Journal of Marketing* (1949).

24. The former West Germany.

25. James Salzman, *Environmental Labeling in OECD Countries* (Paris: OECD, 1991): p. 13.

26. The Blue Angel is the symbol of the United Nations Environmental Program (UNEP).

27. Salzman, sup. note 25, p. 43.

28. Salzman, sup. note 25, p. 45.

29. Update and outlook on Eco-labeling-Part I: OECD Nations (April 27, 1995). *The International Business Issues Monitor,* Monitor Bulletin No. 95-22, p. 10.

30. Salzman, sup. note 25, p. 49.

31. Ibid., p. 110.

32. Ibid., p. 53.

33. UNCTAD, sup. note 20, p. 7.

34. Salzman, sup. note 25, p. 59.

35. Update and outlook, sup. note 29, p. 15.

36. Ibid.

37. Salzman, sup. note 25, p. 61.

38. Ibid., p. 62.

39. Ibid.

40. Ibid., p. 55.

41. Update and outlook, sup. note 29, p. 7.

42. (April 11, 1992). European Council Regulation (EEC) No. 880.92 of 23 March 1992 on a community eco-label award scheme, *Official Journal of the European Communities,* Vol. 25 (1992).

43. Salzman, sup. note 25, p. 64.

44. Competent bodies are designated by separate member states to participate in decision making at the community-level and to administer the EU eco-seal at each national level. See Art. 9 of EEC 880/92, sup. note 26.

45. European Commission, Draft Proposal for a Council Regulation establishing a revised Community Eco-label Award Scheme. Brussels: European Commission: p. 4.

46. The NF Environment Label depicts a green leaf covering a sky blue globe placed over a dark blue oval.

47. The Dutch eco-seal depicts a holding stamp that prints, "environmental approval."

48. For example, of the twenty-five Dutch eco-seal awards, fourteen are for cat litter. The Netherlands has two million cats. See, Salzman, sup. note 25, p. 15.

49. Update and outlook, sup. note 29, p. 12.

50. Ibid., p. 9.

51. Ibid., p. 13.

52. UNCTAD, sup. note 20, p. 8.

53. Ibid.

54. Morris and Scarlett, sup. note 1, p. 35. Pointing out, "Since the introduction of an [eco-seal] can only be measured as a binary event (that is, either the [eco-seal] exists for a particular category at any moment in time, or it does not), any correlation, even in an apparently well-specified model, would not indicate that the [eco-seal] had caused this improvement in the environment."

55. Salzman, sup. note 25, p. 29.

56. Ray V. Hartwell III and Lucas Bergkamp, "Eco-labeling in Europe: New Market-Related Environment Risks?" *International Environment Reporter,* September 23, 1992, p. 625.

57. Salzman, sup. note 25, p. 29.

58. Ibid., p. 626.

59. Ibid.

60. Salzman, sup. note 25, p. 17.

61. Morris and Scarlett, sup. note 1, p. 14.

62. Ibid.

63. Ibid.

64. Lead Competent Body, *Guidelines for the Application of Life-Cycle Assessment in the EU Eco-labeling Programme,* second report, Leiden (1994): 8.

65. Morris and Scarlett, sup. note 1, p. 14.

66. Salzman, sup. note 25, p. 23.

67. Ibid.

68. Wynne, sup. note 2, p. 65. Citing Mary Ann Curran (1993). "Broad-Based Environmental Life Cycle Assessment," *Environmental Science & Technology* (1993), pp. 432-33; U.S. Environmental Protection Agency, Office of Research

and Development, *Life-Cycle Assessment: Inventory Guidelines and Principles* (EPA/600/R-92/245), February 1993, pp. 5-7; Robert G. Hunt et al., "Resource & Environmental Profile Analysis: A Life Cycle Environmental Assessment for Products and Procedures," *Environmental Impact Assessment Review* 12: 246-47; Society of Environmental Toxicology and Chemistry, *A Technical Framework for Life Cycle Assessment,* Environmental Data Services, Ltd., (January 1991): 3-4; *Analyzing the Environmental Impacts of Packaging: Progress and Pitfalls,* ENDS Report 192 (January 1991): 19: p. 19; World Wildlife Fund and The Conservation Foundation, *Product Life Assessments: Policy Issues and Implications,* Summary of a Forum on May 14, 1990, in World Wildlife Fund. *Getting at the Source: Strategies for Reducing Municipal Solid Waste:* p. 81-102.

69. Ibid.

70. Ibid. Citing Curran, sup. note 73, p. 434 (listing examples of actual studies performed since 1969); U.S. Environmental Protection Agency, Office of Research and Development, Background Document on Clean Products Research and Implementation (EPA/600/2-90/048), October 1990, p. 42 (listing types of LCAs performed).

71. Lead Competent Body, sup. note 63, p. 4.

72. Ibid., p. 5.

73. Ibid., p. 6.

74. Morris and Scarlett, sup. note 1, p. 16.

75. European Commission, sup. note 45, p. 11.

76. Ibid.

77. Wynne, sup. note 2, p. 67.

78. Ibid., p. 68. Citing Research Triangle Institute, *Guidelines for Assessing the Quality of Life Cycle Inventory Data, Draft Final,* June 1994 (prepared for U.S. Environmental Protection Agency, Office of Solid Waste) (presenting a brief overview of the development of the life-cycle assessment process).

79. European Commission, sup. note 45, p. 37.

80. Wynne, sup. note 2, p. 71. Citing Research Triangle Institute, sup. note 84, pp. 3-11and 3-12.

81. Lead Competent Body, sup. note 63, p. 7.

82. European Commission, sup. note 45, p. 93.

83. Ibid.

84. Ibid.

85. Update and outlook, sup. note 29, Attachment C; UNCTAD, sup. note 23, p. 18.

86. Morris and Scarlett, sup. note 1, p. 18, 43.

87. Arun Viswanath, "Perspectives on Ecolabelling Schemes for Consumer Products." *Green Business Opportunities* 1 (July-September 1995): 14-15.

88. Ibid.

89. Ibid.

90. Robert J. Shimp, Associate Director, Environmental Quality Worldwide, Proctor and Gamble. Personal Interview, February 10, 1997.

91. Salzman, sup. note 25, p. 21, 23.

92. Wynne, sup. note 2, p. 72.

93. Bruce Yandle (1996). *Creating Wealth in Hummingbird Economies: The Environment, Property Rights and Common Law,* draft copy, Clemson University, Clemson, S.C. (Center for Policy and Legal Studies), pp. 3-4. On capture theory, "publicly interested politicians and regulators will do their best to improve the well-being of all people taken together, but that they lack information on how to do this. Faced with a social problem, the politicians seek advice and information, which logically puts them into contact with the sector to be regulated . . . As the process unfolds, the regulated capture the regulators."

94. Morris and Scarlett, sup. note 1, p. 25.

95. Ibid.

96. Yandle, sup. note 92, p. 5. Citing James M. Buchanan and Gordon Tullock, "Polluters Profit and Political Response," *American Economic Review* 65 (1975): 139-47.

97. Ibid., p. 4. "Those with the most to gain, or most to protect, who have low organizing costs and specialized capital, to mention a few features, are seen as being the most successful in the struggle." Also, on the special interest or economic theory of regulation see: George J. Stigler, "The Economic Theory of Regulation," *Bell Journal* 2 (Spring 1971):3-21; Sam Peltzman, "Toward a More General Theory of Regulation," *Journal of Law & Economics* 19 (August 1976): 211-240; Richard A. Posner, "Theories of Economic Regulation," *Bell Journal* 5 (Autumn 1974): 335-58.

98. Ibid., p. 5. Stating, "If industry output is reduced by government fiat, then price will rise, just as if the industry were cartelized.

99. Ibid. "[T]he result is an industry cartel managed by the pollution control authority."

100. Morris and Scarlett, sup. note 1, p. 27.

101. Ibid.

102. This fits the definition of the theory of bootleggers and Baptists, first described by Bruce Yandle, "Bootleggers and Baptists: The Education of a Regulatory Economist," *Regulation* (May/June 1983): 12-16; and "Bootleggers and Baptists in the Market for Regulation," *The Political Economy of Regulation,* Jason F. Shogren, ed. (Norwell, MA: Kluwer Academic Publishers 1989), pp. 29-53. Also see, Bruce Yandle, *The Political Limits of Environmental Regulation,* (Westport, CN: Quorum Books, 1989). As cited in Yandle, sup. note 92, p. 33.

103. Yandle, sup. note 92, p. 12.

104. Morris and Scarlett, sup. note 1, p. 26. Citing "Ecolabels to ban testing on animals," *The Independent,* June 4, 1993; "Ecolabel programs move ahead in the EC," *U.S. Business and the Environment.*

105. UNCTAD, sup. note 20, p. 5.

106. Ibid.

107. Robert J. Shimp, Associate Director, Environmental Quality Worldwide, Procter and Gamble. Personal Interview, February 10, 1997.

108. UNCTAD, sup. note 20, p. 17.

109. Ibid., p. 5.

110. Ibid., p. 5, 14; Morris and Scarlett, sup. note 1, p. 18, 43.

111. UNCTAD, sup. note 20, p. 5.

112. Sources: European Commission, Procedural Guidelines for the Establishment of Product Groups and Ecological Criteria, Commission Information on Eco-Labeling, June 1994. Council Regulation (EEC) No. 880.92 of 23 March 1992 on a community eco-label award scheme, *Official Journal of the European Communities,* L99, Vol. 25, April 11, 1992. Ray V. Hartwell III and Lucas Bergkamp, "Eco-labeling, in Europe: New Market-Related Environmental Risks?" *International Environmental Reporter,* September 23, 1992. "Update and Outlook on Eco-labeling-Part I: OECD Nations," *The International Business Issues Monitor,* Monitor Bulletin 95-22, April 27, 1995. European Commission, Information Meeting with the EU Eco-Label Award Scheme, Commission Information on Eco-Labeling, Issue No. 8, January 1995. Lead Competent Body, Research Needs in Life-Cycle Assessment for the EU Ecolabeling Programme (Final report of second phase), Leiden: July 1995. Lead Competent Body, Guidelines for the Application of Life-Cycle Assessment in the EU Ecolabeling Programme (second report), Leiden: July 1994. United Nations Conference on Trade and Development (UNCTAD), *Eco-labeling and Market Opportunities for Environmentally Friendly Products* (Geneva: UNCTAD 6 October 1994). European Commission, Draft Proposal for a Council Regulation establishing a revised Community Eco-label Award Scheme (Revision 6), Brussels, February 12, 1996. James Salzman, *Environmental Labeling in OECD Countries* (Paris: OECD, 1991).

113. This label was decided upon before the accession of Sweden, Finland, and Austria into the European Community.

114. European Council Regulation 880/92, Article 1, sup. note 111, at 2. Also, Revision 6, sup. note 111, at 2.

115. Ibid.

116. Ibid.

117. Revision 6, sup. note 111 at 11. Also, James Salzman, sup. note 111, at 18.

118. Revision 6, Id. Also, see generally, U.S. Environmental Protection Agency, Office of Research and Development, *Life-Cycle Assessment: Inventory Guidelines and Principles* (EPA/600/R-92/245) 98-99 (February 1993).

119. Revision 6, Id., at 13.

120. Hartwell and Bergkamp, sup. note 111, at 623.

121. Revision 6, sup. note 111 at 11.

122. EEC Regulation 880/92, sup. note 60, at 2. Also, Revision 6, sup. note 111, at 29, Hartwell and Bergkamp, sup. note 111, at 623.

123. SETAC, sup. note 111, and, Revision 6, sup. note 111, at 37.

124. Revision 6, Id., at 15.

125. Salzman, sup. note 111, 23-24.

126. Retailers may submit applications for the label if those products on the application are sold under their own label.

127. Annual sales figures are based on ex-factory prices.

128. Hartwell and Bergkamp, sup. note 111, at 624.

129. Ibid.

130. Revision 6, sup. note 111, at 39.

131. Ibid.

132. Ibid.

133. European Commission, Information Meeting, sup. note 111, at 1.

134. Revision 6, sup. note 111, at 9.

135. Ibid.

136. Ibid.

137. Ibid.

138. Ibid., at 10.

139. Ibid.

140. Ibid.

141. Ibid.

142. For example, Austria opposed French-led criteria for paints and varnishes on the grounds that organic solvents should be excluded. Paints and varnishes are banned while organic solvents are regulated through national legislation in Austria. "Update and Outlook on Eco-labeling," sup. note 111, at 7. The French voted against criteria produced by Germany for laundry detergents, reasoning that the criteria focused too heavily on banning substances and not enough on real impact. "Update and Outlook," at 9.

143. Revision 6, sup. note 111, at 10.

Chapter 7

Market Incentives for Water Quality

David W. Riggs

The Tar-Pamlico Story

In 1983, local fishermen and citizens in the Tar-Pamlico region of North Carolina noticed sores on fish, algal blooms (aquatic foliage consuming water's available oxygen), and fish kills (dead fish floating to the surface due to lack of oxygen) in their local rivers and estuaries. Believing nutrients like nitrogen and phosphorus to be the cause, grassroots organizations soon expressed concern to the North Carolina state government. In 1989, the region was declared Nutrient Sensitive Waters (NSW) by the North Carolina Department of Environmental Management (DEM). The NSW legislation designated the region as being vulnerable to nitrogen and phosphorous discharge and laid the groundwork for future regulation. The prospects for control were complicated by the mix of nutrient sources. Approximately 85 percent of the nutrient loads originated with nonpoint sources, e.g., agricultural activities and natural phenomena. The remaining 15 percent came from point-source water sewage treatment facilities and local industry. Due to political and technological constraints of detecting, monitoring, and enforcing nonpoint-source nutrient reduction, impending legislation targeted point-source discharge. Old style command-and-control regulation seemed inevitable.

Publicly Owned Treatment Works (POTWs) accounted for a large percentage of the nutrient discharge from point-sources, with local industry contributing the remaining discharge. Although quantified scientific evidence regarding linkages between nutrient discharge and ultimate water quality was lacking, the DEM proposed legislation to reduce nutrient discharge from the point-source facilities. Even before the legislation was passed, some of the POTWs in conjunction with a private firm asked the state government if a better solution could be attained. Further reductions by point-source dischargers would have little effect on the basin; and many of the POTWs had previously taken measures to control nutrients, making further reductions extremely expensive. The POTWs, private firms, and interested environmental groups came up with an alternative to the DEM's plan: take the money that was to be spent on nutrient reduction from point-sources and spend it on nonpoint-source reduction. That is, rather than reduce a point-source's pollution by another 5 percent, which already has been reduced about 90 percent, the same amount of money spent on a nonpoint-source could reduce more pollution by a factor of three to four. Essentially, "more bang for the buck" could be attained if monies were spent on reducing nutrients from nonpoint sources.

As mentioned, political and technological constraints exist for reducing nonpoint discharge. What seemed logical on paper was surely not simple to implement. On the technological end, the nature of nonpoint-source pollution makes it difficult to detect, monitor, and enforce (against) nutrient discharge—by definition, nonpoint-source pollution is discharge from *diffuse* sources. The science of nutrient impact and removal is much more precise for point-source discharge. On the political end, much of the nonpoint nutrient source is from agriculture. Farmers do not look kindly when outsiders interfere in their operations and impose controls and management practices. Under the North Carolina Division of Soil and Water Conservation (DSWC), however, such practices were already being employed. The DSWC administers the Agricultural Cost Share Program (ACSP), which pays farmers to reduce nutrients and runoff. The program employs what are known as Best Management Practices (BMP). BMPs use recognized methods for controlling nutrient runoff, such as animal waste treatment lagoons. The political and technological costs associated with nonpoint nutrient reduction were diminished by the DSWC's involvement.

The group of point-source dischargers formed an organization called the Tar Pamlico Basin Association. They put their sights on funding BMPs through the ACSP at local farms. With a few refinements the state accepted the Association's alternative plan and the Association agreed to the following: fund a computer model simulating nutrients' flow and impact, take weekly samples of phosphorus and nitrogen discharge, make annual payments to ACSP, meet allowable nutrient loads, and purchase BMPs when loads exceed the allowable limit. The emergence of this "nutrient market" is exhibited at two levels:

1. *Between Point Sources.* The Association is a group of point-source dischargers with the option of members offsetting other members' discharge. In a somewhat different light, the Association also acts as an information marketplace for members. At monthly meetings, members can obtain information on scientific, political, and legal aspects of nutrient discharge.

2. *Between Point Sources and Nonpoint Sources.* "Nonpoint source trading is a new concept in which a waste-water discharger has the option of either treating its effluent to remove nutrients (phosphorus and nitrogen) or removing an equivalent level of nutrients from agricultural runoff through the ACSP."

In part, the nutrient trading strategy was accepted because environmental groups realized more nutrients were being removed than what would have been the case under the state's original plan; point sources could obtain potential cost savings; nonpoint sources, though they were more likely to be regulated due to increased funding, were being paid to reduce discharge; and the North Carolina government was maintaining federal standards and a higher level of intergovernmental cooperation.

The result of this yields a rare outcome. The primary objective of environmental quality is being pursued in a cost-effective manner. Indeed, it appears as if a fortuitous equilibrium has been reached. But why did this happen for the Tar-Pamlico Basin and not for other watersheds with similar use problems? What are the critical characteristics that set the Tar-Pamlico watershed apart from others?

Principles for the Emergence of a Water Quality Market

The Tar-Pamlico region of North Carolina offered unique circumstances for the emergence of a nutrient reduction trading strategy. The principal characteristics of this strategy are outlined below for the purpose of illustrating why a water quality market arose.

A Constraint. A binding constraint on the amount of pollution discharge must be enforced. This constraint has to be believed; dischargers must recognize that some type of pollution control is inevitable and that violation of the law is punishable.

For the North Carolina episode the constraint is evident at two levels:

1. The 1987 Clean Water Act was the federal binding constraint that affected nutrient reduction in the Tar-Pamlico watershed. A binding federal constraint will facilitate cooperation among state governmental agencies, thereby increasing the likelihood of implementing a cost-effective pollution reduction plan.

2. The North Carolina Department of Environmental Management (DEM) was the governmental agency central to the issue at the state level. Their objective was to decrease the nutrient loads in the basin, with point sources providing the low-cost means of achieving some reduction. It was DEM's flexibility and willingness to cooperate in the development of an alternative strategy that made a distinguishing difference for the Tar-Pamlico watershed. They allowed the point source dischargers (the Association) time to come up with a better plan; but, if the Association had not

come up with an acceptable nutrient reduction plan, the DEM's original strategy (constraint) was to be fully employed.

The Pollutant. When the pollutant is common to all potential transacting parties, the costs of using the market are less. Put differently, it is easier to trade oranges for oranges than apples for oranges.

In North Carolina, both point and nonpoint sources discharge nitrogen and phosphorus. The nutrients are common to all dischargers. If they were not common, costs would increase scientifically—technological difficulties of offsetting one pollutant for another—and politically / economically—negotiation and cooperation difficulties of getting two distinct parties to transact. Transaction costs are lower when the dischargers emit the same pollutant.

Science. Proper and credible assessment of the pollutant's impact and removal must be made. Scientific evidence showing adverse consequences from pollutant discharge and evidence showing positive consequences of pollutant removal will substantiate the integrity of legislative restrictions. The research that had been conducted and collected on the Tar-Pamlico prior to legislation includes the following:

> Monitoring the flow (total fluid discharge) of relatively large point sources (those with a flow greater than 0.5 MGD).

> Monitoring of total nitrogen and phosphorus discharge at these same (large) facilities.

The precise impact of nutrients and the results of their removal are unknown. In the legislation that was passed, the scientific research to be conducted and monitoring to follow includes:

> The Association funds a $400,000 computer model that simulates the flow of nutrients and forecasts impact and removal of nutrient discharge.

> Each point source must monitor and report weekly samplings of nitrogen and phosphorus discharge.

The effort to obtain scientific evidence supports the legislation's foundation and improves upon the knowledge of the feasibility of point to nonpoint tradeoffs.

Differential Costs. Differences in the cost of pollution control among potential transacting parties are required for gains from trade. Differential costs lead to an information system that supports transactions. In the Tar-Pamlico watershed cost differences are found between point sources and between the group of point-sources and nonpoint sources.

Point Sources. Key cost differential characteristics regarding members of the Association include:

80 percent of the flow from the thirteen members of the Association were from two large POTWs. Their initiative and involvement were instrumental.

The remaining eleven members were approximately the same size in terms of flow.

Pollution control cost differences among members of the Association are related to firm size. Economies of scale are present. For example, large POTWs have their own labs to perform samplings, which are required by legislation. Small POTWs must contract out for this service, thus they pay higher costs on a flow proportionate basis than large POTWs.

Point Source to Nonpoint Source. The cost differential between point and nonpoint source was instrumental for the emergence of the nutrient market. Holding constant the amount of nutrient discharge, collectively, point sources would have to spend $50 to $100 million, whereas nonpoint would require only $11.7 million. Stated differently, it would cost point sources four to five times more to reduce nutrients internally.

The Discovery Incentive. A critical feature of a flexible, market style pollution abatement program is the incentive that firms are confronted with when reducing their pollution. In the pursuit of cost minimization, firms will discover cost-effective methods of abating their pollution. Dischargers find cheaper ways to treat waste and protect and maintain the resource in the process. New methods of pollution abatement are often a consequence of such activity.

In the Tar-Pamlico watershed, the Association has found innovative ways to treat waste. The combined wealth of the Association was able to afford the hiring of a consulting firm that evaluated each member's facility. It was discovered that some facilities could be retrofitted to further reduce waste. The consulting firm discovered a cost-effective method of reducing total discharge for all members combined. Point-source discharge was minimized, while costs were also curtailed.

Inter-Group Cooperation. The market works at two levels: 1) point source to point source, and 2) point source to nonpoint source. Cooperation among the point sources at level 1 is essential if level 2 is to be attained. Some key characteristics among members of the Association that facilitate cooperation are:

The costs of nutrient reductions for POTWs are dispersed over a customer base that has few (if any) alternatives of water treatment service.

Members of the Association are homogeneous:
   1. All are point-source dischargers;
   2. Discharge comes in the form of a definable flow;
   3. Final output is the same (with the exception of the private firm);
   4. Each is a government municipality (except the private firm).

The fourth homogeneity characteristic carries many implications. The structure of the POTW industry is non-competitive—the customer base is geographically defined and enforced by law, with rates determined by a non-market process. This industrial structure may have facilitated cooperation among the Association members.

A Broker. A broker who acts as an information processor between all of the groups involved in the plan will lower transaction costs. The broker would have expertise in the legal, political, technological, and economic characteristics of a water quality market. The Association hired John Hall, an attorney with the law firm Kirkpatrick & Cody, who fulfilled the role of information broker. Hall was instrumental in developing the market strategy and still plays a critical role in the communication among Association members and between the Association and external parties (e.g., government and environmental groups).

Peripheral Groups. The actions and cooperation of environmental groups are of key concern. They commonly act as a liaison to explain and justify methods of pollution reduction to the public. The main purpose of the North Carolina Environmental Defense Fund (EDF) and the Pamlico-Tar River Foundation (PTRF) was to decrease nutrient loads. With that goal in mind, both groups supported the offset strategy and played a key role in public acceptance of the innovative plans of the Association. In addition, the environmental groups were instrumental (and still are) in many of the scientific studies.

Introduction

Controversy over the consumption and allocation of water has challenged man's ingenuity and problem-solving capacity for centuries. Externalities, or one person's use affecting another's use without compensation, are the source of controversy. Diving deeper, we find the rudimentary cause of an externality to be a lack of property rights—ownership rights to a body of water are either poorly defined or enforced, or both. Numerous methods have been used for relieving common access water use problems. The U.S. experience over the last twenty years has been one of statutory law: Property rights to many common access waters have remained undefined while the users of that water have been subjected to rules and regulations. Assuming a primary objective of water quality, one must ask, "Does this type of public policy attain the greatest benefit at least cost and, if not, does a better solution exist?"

Before this question can be addressed, and putting aside for the moment the issue of property rights, the negative consequences of an externality must be identified. What does science say about the effects different users have on a water body? What are the causes of a water quality problem? What is the natural state? What are the results of pollution reduction? Once quantifiable evidence is assembled, the issues of water consumption, allocation, and quality can be more accurately addressed.

This chapter focuses on water quality problems and proposed solutions as they relate to the Tar-Pamlico River Basin located in eastern North Carolina. A review of the water quality problems and the actions taken to alleviate them raises a number of interesting questions. First, what does science conclude about the causes and effects of the water quality problems? From where and from whom does the pollution originate? What are the effects of pollution removal? The second section of the chapter describes the scientific conclusions and ambiguities associated with the Tar-Pamlico watershed. The section identifies the sources of discharge and, to the scientific extent possible, their effect on the basin.

Next, how have industry, agriculture, environmental groups, and local, state, and federal governments addressed this issue? Section three focuses on the law that emerged from the interaction of these groups. The section describes in detail the water quality market that emerged in the Tar-Pamlico watershed. Section four enlarges on the previous section and focuses on the key features and characteristics of the Tar-Pamlico water market. The section identifies some generic qualities necessary for a watershed market to evolve. Final thoughts and conclusions are given in the last section.

Science and Politics

Water is a life-sustaining substance. It is used by an assortment of species for many different purposes—animals and plants live in water bodies; humans drink it and use it for recreational, commercial, and personal use. It is of no surprise that one species' use of water can affect another's use. This section describes the Tar-Pamlico River Basin as an estuarine system, identifies users of the system, discusses the impact that competing users have on the basin, and cites legislation that oversees and regulates dischargers in the watershed. The section is concluded with a summary of the scientific evidence and ambiguities for the Tar-Pamlico watershed.

The Tar-Pamlico Watershed

The Tar-Pamlico watershed consists of numerous rivers and estuaries, all combining into a complex basin. The Tar and Pamlico rivers are the two primary rivers from which the basin gets its name. As the figure on the following page depicts,[1] the Tar River makes up the upper portion of the watershed and is centered in the Piedmont farmlands of North Carolina. This freshwater river and its tributaries comprise about 2,300 miles of streams. The Tar drains over 4,300

Figure 7.1 Tar-Pamlico River Basin

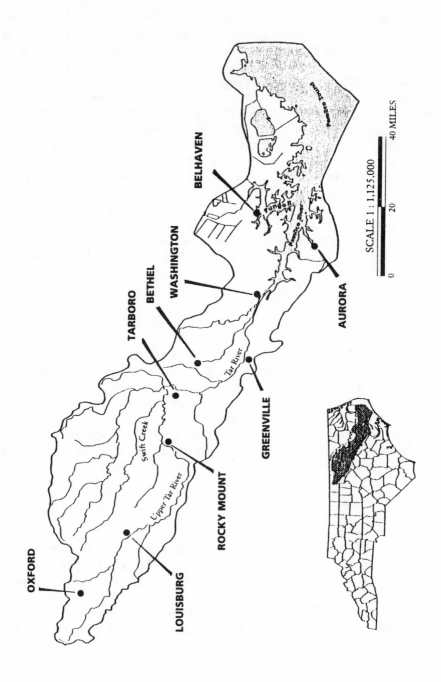

square miles as it flows southeastward 140 miles through the coastal plain cities of Rocky Mount, Tarboro, Greenville, and Washington.

The Tar River becomes an estuary, with its name changing to Pamlico, at Washington, North Carolina. The Pamlico River has wide shallow waters that do not have a constant flow and whose currents are driven by the tide and wind. It is here where the freshwater Tar mixes with the salt waters from the Atlantic Ocean. The Pamlico is known to move both easterly toward the ocean and westerly toward the Tar River. In places the estuary is up to fifteen feet deep and is five miles wide where it meets the Pamlico Sound. Approximately 1,250 square miles of the watershed is drained by the Pamlico.[2] Most of the land use in the watershed is agricultural.

The region comprises an immense ecosystem. Both the freshwater portion and estuary support important natural resources. The system contains one of the most productive estuaries in the eastern United States, with valuable commercial and recreational fishing. Indeed, it is a rich and versatile habitat for fish, wildlife, and people. Each entity's use of the ecosystem has an impact, however. Of obvious concern is the effect that man has on the system: What is man's impact on the watershed? If there are adverse consequences, what caused them? Who caused them and how? These are questions that prescribe scientific research.

Nutrients and Their Effects

Knowledge of the sources and understanding the effects nutrients have on the Tar-Pamlico's ecological system are essential if proper retroactive and proactive policy is to be implemented. Nitrogen and phosphorus are the two primary nutrients that are discharged from various sources in the Tar-Pamlico watershed. The most commonly cited problem resulting from increased nutrient loads is a process known as eutrophication—nutrients stimulate the growth of algae to a point where available oxygen is absorbed and sunlight is closed out, both necessary for other water species to exist and thrive. The nutrients are present in natural or background levels between 0.05 and 0.3 mg/l. The activities of man add to these background levels, leading to potentially adverse ecological consequences.

In addition to (or coupled with) eutrophication, other physical signs thought to be related to nutrient discharge are numerous fish kills, red sores on fish, and holes in the shells of crabs. However, it is difficult to determine the extent of man's activity causing these problems. For example, "[T]he dinoflagellate has been linked to massive fish kills and bacterial diseases that have plagued the Pamlico River and other coastal estuaries in recent years."[3] Likewise, it is uncertain that preventing nutrients from being leached in the watershed will have any positive effects on water quality, even if the source of discharge is readily identifiable. Indeed, "[T]he natural variability inherent to all estuaries complicates identifying man's effects on the estuary."[4] In short, scientific quantification of nutrient impact and removal has yet to be fully collected in the Tar-Pamlico watershed.

Nutrient Discharge

Point Source

Generally water quality problems can be defined as caused by point-source pollution, nonpoint-source pollution, or a combination of the two. Point-source pollution means "any discernible, confined, and discrete conveyance, including but not limited to any pipe, ditch, channel, tunnel, conduit, well, discrete fissure, container, rolling stock, concentrated animal feeding operation, or vessel or other floating craft, from which pollutants are or may be discharged."[5] In general, point-source pollution is discharge from a well-defined origin. Regulations to control water quality for the past twenty years have focused on point-source dischargers. The National Pollutant Discharge Elimination System (NPDES) mandates that all point-source dischargers maintain a permit to discharge into bodies of water.[6] The partial effect of NPDES and other legislation has been decreased loads from point-source dischargers. Still, these regulations have not solved most water quality problems.

The Tar-Pamlico watershed is no different. There are approximately 130 point-source dischargers in the basin. The majority of the discharge from point-sources originates with municipal wastewater treatment plants (most are publicly owned) and a few industrial dischargers. Although each pointsource in the basin has a NPDES permit, water quality problems began to arise in the mid-1980s.

Nonpoint Source

Nonpoint-source pollution is defined as any water pollution outside of point-source pollution. Basically, it is the pollution of water from diffuse sources "caused by rainfall or snowmelt moving over and through the ground and carrying natural and manmade pollutants into lakes, rivers, streams, wetlands, estuaries, other coastal waters and ground water."[7]

The types of nonpoint-source pollution in the Tar-Pamlico watershed could include agriculture, mining, hydrologic and habitat modification, urban runoff, land disposal, silviculture, construction, atmospheric deposition, and other undefined sources. According to a U.S. Environmental Protection Agency report, ecological risks posed by nonpoint-source pollution are substantially more serious than those posed by point-source pollution.[8]   Evidence from the Tar-Pamlico watershed supports this notion. As figure 7.2 displays, nonpoint discharge is responsible for 85 percent of the nutrients that are leached in the watershed. The single largest contributor of nonpoint-source discharge is agriculture, which is the sum of cropland, livestock and forestry in figure 7.2.[9] Until recently, little control over nonpoint-source pollution had been attempted relative to point-source discharge. Although science was still proceeding, federal (statutory) law already had some jurisdiction in the region and the North Carolina state government went ahead with its own rules, classifying the region as having water quality problems.[10]

Legislative Reaction

Federal

The Tar-Pamlico watershed falls under an array of legislation, ranging from the 1987 Clean Water Act (CWA) to North Carolina's Nutrient Sensitive Waters Act. Regulation of point-source discharge is politically cost-effective relative to nonpoint source because point-source dischargers are identifiable and monitoring effluent is technically feasible. The federal government has been reluctant to deal directly with nonpoint-source pollution because of the political sensitivity over land use issues. The problem centers on the lack of documented evidence about the effects specific land areas and uses have on water quality. Monitoring data is not available to address most nonpoint problems so cause and effect relationships have been difficult to establish.

A growing awareness, however, of nonpoint-source pollution's role in water quality degradation led Congress to amend the Clean Water Act of 1972. In the Water Quality Act of 1987, Congress stated:

> It is the national policy that programs for the control of nonpoint-sources of pollution be developed and implemented in an expeditious manner so as to enable the goals of this Act to be met through the control of both point and nonpoint-sources of pollution.[11]

Section 319 of the 1987 CWA addresses nonpoint-source pollution. The plan is for states to assess the water quality problems within their state and then adopt management plans to address those problems. Under the act, funds are issued by the EPA to help states in administering their management plans. By and large, however, most of the burden of developing pollution control strategies are placed at the state level, with the EPA filling a supervisory role.

Figure 7.2 1988 Tar-Pamlico Nitrogen and Phosphorus Distribution

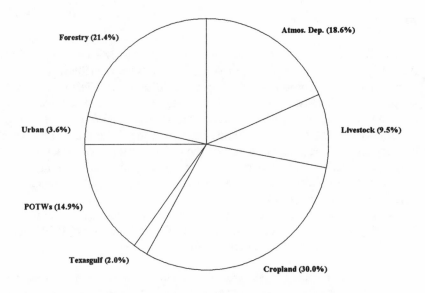

Source: North Carolina Department of Environmental Management, *Tar-Pamlico River Basin NSW Designation & Nutrient Management Strategy,* April 1989.

State

A petition was made in early 1989 to the North Carolina Environmental Management Commission (EMC) to classify the Tar-Pamlico River Basin as Nutrient Sensitive Waters (NSW). NSW is a designation used by the state of North Carolina to describe a body of water that has water quality problems caused by nutrients, e.g., phosphorus and nitrogen. The NSW designation sets separate limits on total phosphorus (TP) and total nitrogen (TN), with a year-round phosphorus effluent limit and a seasonally varying nitrogen limit: The limits were set at 2 mg/l of phosphorus and 4 mg/l of nitrogen in the summer and 8 mg/l in the winter for all expanding point-source facilities and any new facilities. These limits were set by year with the ultimate goal of reducing phosphorus and nitrogen loads by 200,000 kg/yr by 1995. The goal was based upon projections that annual loads from point sources in the watershed would reach 625,000 kg/yr by 1995.

The NSW designation allows the North Carolina Department of Environmental Management (DEM) to set stricter limits on the discharge of nutrients from *point sources*. Once the Tar–Pamlico was designated as NSW, the DEM developed a strategy to reduce nutrients entering the river.[12] It was unknown, however, what the strategy would mean in terms of reduced fish kills, sensitivity to nutrients, and historical flow of nutrients. Most of the public meetings held to discuss the NSW designation and strategy were emotional and dramatic with examples of dead fish displayed in the meetings and little discussion pertaining to the effects of the limitations on actual water quality or the costs of achieving the reductions.

Affected Sectors

Industry

Of all the point-source dischargers in the Tar-Pamlico watershed, Publicly Owned Treatment Works (POTWs) are the most visible. These facilities treat the sewage of townships in the basin and discharge the treated water.

While the NSW legislation was pending, POTWs voiced concern about how regulations would affect their costs.[13] Several point-source dischargers were facing expansion in the near future and would need to spend a large amount of money in new pollution control technology to be in compliance.[14] These POTWs and other point-source dischargers saw their long-term options limited by the state's strategy. The limitations set by the state would reduce nutrient levels by 10 to 20 percent of current discharge. The state authorities knew that the POTWs were only 15 percent of the problem but lacked the power to limit the discharge from nonpoint sources, which made up the remaining 85 percent.

Agriculture

Agriculture is the single largest contributor of nonpoint-source pollution in rivers, lakes, and wetlands for both the Tar-Pamlico watershed and across the United States.[15] The agricultural activities that cause nonpoint-source pollution are:

1. Erosion of agricultural land;
2. Concentrated animal production facilities;
3. Commercial fertilizing, animal wastes, and sludge;
4. Land receiving pesticide applications;
5. Land used for grazing;
6. Irrigated lands.[16]

The pollution resulting from these activities comes from nutrients like phosphorus and nitrogen and from sediment, animal wastes, salts, and pesticides. Nutrients are present in soil's natural state, but are often added to farmland by applying commercial fertilizers and manure to increase output per acre. Heavy rains and erosion can wash nutrients applied to a field into a stream or river.

When nutrients enter a body of water, algae consume the dissolved nutrients, often resulting in algal blooms. Sediment, animal wastes, salts, and pesticides also contribute to water quality problems due to agriculture. Sediment from topsoil erodes easier and is richer in nutrients than subsurface soil, thus sediment has a higher pollution potential. Animal waste from the fecal remains of livestock and poultry can contribute nutrients, organic materials, and pathogens to receiving waters. Not only does suspended animal waste cause nutrient concentrations to rise, but it also reduces the quantity of dissolved oxygen because of decay. Salts and other natural minerals and metals damage crop production and plant growth in aquatic environments.

Estuarine waters can be adversely affected by large concentrations of soluble salts. Pesticides applied to topsoil and plants can be washed into water bodies and become embedded into the food chain. The residue from pesticides can induce eutrophication and abortion in fish.

To varying degrees, all of these activities are present in the Tar-Pamlico watershed. The North Carolina Division of Soil and Water Conservation (DSWC) uses Best Management Practices (BMPs) in an effort to control nonpoint-source discharge. For example, with respect to the fecal wastes of livestock, animal waste treatment lagoons can be set up on site at a farm. These lagoons will greatly decrease nutrient discharge into water bodies. Use of BMPs are subject to the DSWC's discretion, however. There is very little legislation that oversees discharge from nonpoint sources.

Summary

Much has been done with regard to scientific assessment of nutrients' origins and how to remove their presence in the watershed. Scientific conclusions include the following:

- Nonpoint sources are responsible for 85 percent of nutrient loads.
- Agriculture comprises most of the nonpoint-source discharge.
- Technology exists to control nonpoint-source pollution (BMPs).
- POTWs (point source) are responsible for the remaining 15 percent of nutrient discharge.
- Technology exists (chemical and/or biological) for nutrients to be reduced at point sources.

In spite of the scientific studies that have been completed on the Tar-Pamlico watershed, a number of uncertainties remain. These include:

- What are the results of decreased nutrient loads?
- Does nutrient reduction from one area impact the entire basin?
- Are BMPs a feasible technology over many nonpoint-source sites?

As stated in the NSW Nutrient Management Strategy, "the Pamlico has demonstrated the potential for over-enrichment [of nutrients] which may become problematic. Changes in land use throughout the watershed in recent decades and problems with aquatic life measured instream have created concern for the health of the estuary."[17] To some extent the legislation has mandated that an effort be put forth to answer these scientific questions.

In the face of these uncertainties, however, the region was designated NSW, paving the way for the DEM to mandate more costly controls on point-source dischargers. With the POTWs being targeted and the scientific ambiguities remaining, an interesting development occurred. While seeking to minimize costs, POTWs realized that nutrients could be removed from the waters more cost-effectively through nonpoint sources than point sources. This discovery gave birth to the point to nonpoint trading strategy.

The Tar-Pamlico Nutrient Market

To resolve the water quality problems of the Tar-Pamlico watershed a different regulatory approach was discovered. A nutrient trading program to reduce the amount of nutrients, particularly phosphorus and nitrogen, entering the Tar-Pamlico water basin has been implemented. It originated not, per se, with the state or federal government but rather with local municipalities, industry, and environmental groups. Thus, its origins stem from the competing users, formed through their cooperation, and not from broad, sweeping statutory law. The program, now in its first phase of completion, marks the beginning of a marketable permits program that allows point-source dischargers to purchase higher nutrient emissions by paying for nonpoint-source pollution control programs. This section focuses on the development and accomplishments of the Tar-Pamlico water quality market.

The Tar-Pamlico Watershed Market

When the North Carolina Environmental Management Commission (EMC)—the board that makes decisions on environmental policy for the DEM—considered classifying the Tar-Pamlico River as NSW, the EMC asked the DEM to develop a strategy to reduce nutrients. In the summer of 1989, the DEM proposed a nutrient management strategy that emphasized strict limits on new and expanding point-source dischargers. The strategy did not address phosphate levels from current dischargers, it only imposed stricter limits on expanding facilities—those with planned design flows of greater than 0.5 million gallons per day (MGD). There were several POTWs that supported the NSW designation but opposed the DEM's strategy to deal with the designation. Doing some rough economic estimating, the POTWs found that they would have to spend between $50 - $100 million to be in compliance with the state's plan.[18] Furthermore, compliance offered no long-term assurance that the state would not impose stricter limits at a later time. Moreover, environmentalists were unhappy with the plan because it did not adequately address existing point-source discharge and nonpoint-source pollution. In summary, industry and environmental groups were unhappy with the plan because:

1. There was no baseline for judging the standards set by the strategy.
2. There was little scientific data on which to base nutrient reductions.
3. The plan was unfairly targeting POTWs, which comprised only 15 percent of the problem.
4. Implementing stricter reductions would be very costly.
5. No guarantee was given that the state would not impose stricter limits later.
6. The plan was technology based; it did not allow POTWs flexibility in how to control nutrient discharge.

A *coalition* of point-source dischargers emerged to deal with these problems. The coalition was lead by Malcolm Green, the general manager of the Greenville Utilities Commission, one of the POTWs facing plant expansion. The Greenville

Utilities Commission hired a consultant to coordinate the coalition's plans and ideas and put them into a legal framework.

In September 1989, the EMC met for its quarterly meeting and was considering acceptance of the NSW designation and DEM's strategy. The coalition accepted the NSW designation but requested that they be allowed to develop another strategy. The EMC accepted the NSW designation and referred the strategy back to the DEM to work with the coalition and environmental groups to develop a new strategy. The EMC gave the groups ninety days to develop a new strategy, or the state's original strategy would be implemented.

During the ninety-day period, the DEM, the North Carolina Environmental Defense Fund (NCEDF), the Pamlico-Tar River Foundation (PTRF), and the coalition met and worked on a plan. The first step was to develop a baseline for judging the removal of nutrients and the effects that the nutrients have on the water quality. Discharge levels were known for 1988, so it was established as a baseline year. Projections on plant discharge for 1995, which was the year the state's plan was to be implemented, were made based on the 1988 data. Plant expansions and growth were included in the projections. It was estimated that the coalition would increase discharge by 200,000 kg/yr by 1995. A simple offset/trading strategy developed among point-source dischargers to reduce the 200,000 kg/yr.

The trading strategy did not, however, address nonpoint-source pollution. The Division of Soil and Water Conservation (DSWC) was brought into the discussion to address agricultural nutrient loads. The coalition did some calculations based upon the cost of reducing agricultural nonpoint-source nutrient loads and found that they could buy three to four times the reductions of phosphorus and nitrogen from agricultural loading. That is, if it cost $X to retrofit a point-source facility, the same $X spent on reducing nonpoint-source nutrients would yield three to four times the nutrient reductions. The DSWC already was using the North Carolina Agricultural Cost Share Plan (ACSP) on farmland by implementing best management practices (BMPs) to control nutrient loading. By supplementing ACSP to implement more BMPs, the coalition realized they could meet the 200,000 kg/yr reduction for about $11.7 million, which was a significant cost savings compared to the estimated $50 - 100 million. This strategy came to be known as the Nutrient Reduction Trading Strategy (NRTS).

The baseline for nutrient load reduction was agreed upon by all parties involved. The DEM calculated the reductions based on the number of members in the coalition. To fix the nutrient goal, the coalition had to have a fixed number of members. A deadline for joining the coalition was set. The coalition became incorporated as the Tar-Pamlico Basin Association referred to as the *Association*. All point-source dischargers along the Tar-Pamlico River were invited to join.

Mostly POTWs joined the Association with one industrial firm, National Spinning, Inc., as the exception. In December of 1989, the NRTS was adopted.

Not all of the POTWs and point-source dischargers joined the Association. Some POTWs decided not to join based upon the risk involved. For instance, there was no guarantee the Association would succeed in reducing the 200,000 kg/yr by 1995. If the Association failed, the investment in BMPs, membership costs, and trading agreements would be forfeited, and the state's plan would be implemented. Some of the POTWs had already planned upgrades in plant facilities or were in the process of building them when the Association formed.[19] They could meet the state's stricter limits set for 1995 without the need to trade.

Although it is not necessary to join the Association to utilize the nonpoint-source trading concept, incentives exist for joining the Association. A discharger who is not a member, interested in trading, would not have the immediate benefit of the computer model that will be developed by the Association, which may indicate modification would be required for nutrient removal.

Texasgulf, a phosphate mining and fertilizer company, had a design flow almost as large as the entire Association but refused to join. The company was in the process of negotiating a new NPDES permit when the Association formed. By spending $30 million to redesign the operational flow of water in its facilities, Texasgulf reduced its discharge of phosphorus by 94 percent.[20] Joining the Association was not a wealth-enhancing option for Texasgulf.

The Nutrient Reduction Trading Strategy

The Nutrient Reduction Trading Strategy uses a two-phase approach: Phase I goes through 1994; Phase II begins in 1995. Phase I focuses on developing a computer model for the basin,[21] making engineering evaluations of wastewater treatment plants and implementing operational and minor capital improvements, monitoring effluent from POTWs, and using a nutrient-trading program.[22] The Association found that they could meet the allowable loads mostly by making engineering or operational changes. But in order to keep the option of trading excess load by buying BMPs, the Association agreed to make minimum payments each year. The total contribution to the nutrient trading fund is $500,000 until 1995. A transfer of $350,000 to the DSWC has already been made to demonstrate BMP effectiveness at Chicod Creek "in reducing nutrient loading as well as their cost-effectiveness as part of the Tar-Pamlico nutrient trading program."[23]

Each year a minimum payment is made and is counted toward future excess loading payments. If the Association goes above allowable loads in a given year, they must make excess loading payments. The excess loading payments are calculated based upon the following formula:

Excess Loading Payment = (Association actual annual loading - allowable nutrient loading) x $56/kg/yr - prior payments (minimum + excess loading).[24]

Prior minimum payments refers to annual contributions that were previously made by the Association to the nutrient reduction trading fund. Excess loading refers to previous annual payments to the fund.

Members of the Association may trade nutrient loads among themselves as long as the Association does not discharge more than the allowable amount. The Association allocates the allowable load by the NPDES permit design for each facility. Each facility has a NPDES permit specifying the facility's design flow. Each Association member is given a percentage of the allowable load based on its permitted flow as a portion of the Association's total permitted flow. Payments are made in the same way. Minimum payments are based upon the design flow. If the Association exceeds the allowable level of nutrient discharge, it has the option of purchasing BMP reductions through the ACSP or facing the state's stricter limits. Incentives to falsify monitoring reports are discouraged by fines and penalties enforced by the DEM.

Individual members can also expand their facility during this plan. If a member expands nutrient removal capabilities, the credit is given to the allowable amount of nutrient load. This credit is tradeable with other Association members who need to discharge higher loads.[25] New limits will not be written into an Association member's permit.

Expanding non-Association facilities can also participate in the nutrient reduction trading program through the ACSP. The nonmember must pay a one-time upfront fee:

BMP payment ($) = New Design Flow (MGD) x Excess Nutrients (mg/l) x $62/kg/yr x Conversion Factor,

where

Excess Nutrients = (TP limit - 2 mg/l) + (TN limit - 6 mg/l).

The excess nutrients are total phosphorus (TP) and total nitrogen (TN) in milligrams per liter (mg/l) added together, and the

Conversion Factor = 1382 = 3.7854 l/gal x 365 day/year.[26]

The Non-Association member must pay the one-time fee to cover modeling costs for BMPs. The higher BMP cost covers the administrative fees for implementing the BMPs. New entrants to the basin must meet a no-discharge criteria or show that it is not economically or technically feasible. If the no-discharge criteria is infeasible, the new discharger is subject to the same restrictions as an expanding facility. New dischargers will receive permit limitations based on the following schedule:

  1. If discharge is greater than or equal to 50,000 gdp: 2 mg/l TP year round.

  2. If discharge is greater than or equal to 100,000 gdp: 2 mg/l TP year round; 4 mg/l TN May-October and 8 mg/l TN November-April.[27]

New dischargers cannot participate in the nutrient reduction trading program nor can they become members of the Association.

The Association's Responsibilities

The Tar-Pamlico Basin Association is composed of the publicly owned treatment works (POTWs) of Belhaven, Bunn, Enfield, Franklin Water and Sewer Authority, Greenville, Louisburg, Oxford, Pinetops, Rocky Mount, Spring Hope, Warrenton, and Washington. National Spinning, a textile firm, is also a member. Under the trading plan, the members of the Association agree to:

  1. Develop and fund (approximately $400,000) an estuarine computer model to recommend future nutrient reductions.

  2. Do an engineering evaluation of existing water-treatment works to determine if minor improvements can be made.

  3. Begin weekly monitoring of total phosphorus (TP) and total nitrogen (TN) loads and submit them in an annual report to the DEM.

  4. Make minimum payment to the Agricultural Cost Share Program each year.

  5. Provide funding for two additional staff members of the DSWC.

  6. Meet allowable nutrient loadings each year.

  7. Purchase BMPs through ACSP, if loading is above allowable loads.

The computer model is to be used to run "what if scenarios" and to "assess the relative importance of nitrogen and phosphorus from waste water dischargers, nonpoint-sources (NPS), sediments, and atmosphere to algal growth and oxygen stress."[28] Coordinating efforts with DEM, NCEDF, and PTRF are a part of the model. The model is estimated to cost $400,000 and was scheduled for completion in July 1993. The model has been completed and will be used to track and target the best areas for implementing BMPs.

The engineering evaluation was a coordinated effort by the Association. The Association agreed to pool its resources and hire a consulting firm to conduct evaluations of each plant. The consultant suggested modifications in the operations of the facilities. When the modifications were carried out, the Association emerged 13 percent below the allowable load for the nutrients in 1991.

The Association agreed to conduct weekly samplings of water discharged from each facility. The samples are to be collected by the plant and tested either at a state approved lab or at the plant's lab, which has been a continuing point of controversy for the Association members because some members are too small to make weekly sampling cost-effective. The monitoring samples are submitted to the DEM in an annual report. DEM checks the reports for errors and misinformation. These monitoring reports are used to determine the Association's discharge of phosphorus and nitrogen. The nutrients discharged by the members are added together. If the discharge is greater than the allowable amount, the load is used to calculate the excess loading payment made into the ACSP.

The Association also agreed to make minimum payments to the ACSP for the purpose of maintaining the right to trade with nonpoint sources. The minimum payments add up to $500,000 over three years. In addition, the Association agreed to provide $150,000 for two DSWC personnel to coordinate BMPs in the Tar-Pamlico River Basin.[29] The DSWC personnel along with DEM locate problem areas in a watershed and provide assistance to BMP projects in those areas.

The North Carolina Agricultural Cost Share Program

The North Carolina Agricultural Cost Share Program (ACSP) was initiated in 1984 as a test program to address nonpoint-source pollution (NPS) problems in the "nutrient sensitive" waters of Jordan Lake, Falls Lake, and the Chowan River. Over time the plan grew to include other regions of the state, and in July 1989 the ACSP was expanded to include the entire state.[30] North Carolina is divided into several soil and water conservation districts, each of which carries out its own regional plan. State money is allocated to the districts by the Division of Soil and Water Conservation (DSWC). The allocation is based upon the district's annual strategy plan, which prioritized funding on water quality needs and limiting factors such as:

1. Availability of contractors, engineering assistance, and/or materials;
2. Landowners' agreements to complete work;
3. Length of growing season; and
4. Degree of water quality impact from BMP installation.[31]

Districts must develop alternative plans for each year to take account of weather, crop prices, governmental actions, and corporate decisions to change farming practices. The funding each district receives is determined by the DSWC by using predetermined formulas with variables corresponding to aspects of each district's need. These variables are assigned numeric values, and the formulas are run on computers to calculate the amount of funding given to each district. The funding process is subject to final approval by the Soil and Water Conservation Commission.

The process begins in one of two ways. First, landowners fill out an application based on their need to control nutrients. Non-landowners can apply provided they show a long-term written lease indicating control over the land for the life of the applied for contract. The application has a checklist of needs, which each farmer completes. Each district has a technical assistant to evaluate the water quality problem. The technical assistant walks the applicant's land and makes suggestions as to which management practices (BMPs) would best prevent the water quality problem. The farmer gets to choose how to manage the BMP. The type of BMP chosen is dependent on how the water quality problem originates on the farmer's land and the type of BMPs approved by the commission for the current program year. Each BMP selection comes from the annual Detailed Implementation Plan. This list also contains the cost figures for constructing or implementing the BMP, and the BMP's projected life. The cost is determined based upon the average cost of previous BMPs. The application is then sent to the District Board where all the cost figures for the district are totaled. These figures are used to construct the district's annual strategy plan. Based upon the district's priority for funding, a contract will be made between the district and the applicant. The district agrees to provide 75 percent of the cost, and the farmer provides 25 percent, which can be provided through in-kind contributions. The process can also begin from the district's standpoint by assigning priority to areas with high water quality problems.

When the plan has been approved, the farmer can build the BMP. It is up to the farmer to contract the work out and to ensure that the design meets the state's specifications. The farmers know how much funding they will receive from the ACSP based upon the BMP's average cost. When the farmer finishes building the BMP and the district's technical assistant reviews the BMP, the district informs the DSWC to make payment to the farmer. Knowing the amount of funding he will receive from the state, the farmer can work to minimize the cost of constructing the BMP. The ongoing management of the BMP is up to the farmer. These decisions can be instrumental in the development of the BMP because they are site specific. The district's technical assistant carries out inspections to make sure BMPs are still in place. If an applicant's BMP is found not to meet the specifications, then the applicant has thirty days to reimplement the BMP. If an applicant does not reimplement the BMP, the applicant will be required to repay the DSWC a prorated refund based on the life of the BMP. When land ownership changes, the new owner is encouraged but not forced to maintain the BMP.

The Association's contributions and payments to the ACSP are placed in a specific fund rather than in the general ACSP fund allocated by the DSWC to the districts. In the nutrient trading strategy, the Association agreed to give $150,000 to the DSWC to fund two personnel to coordinate BMP projects in the Tar-Pamlico River Basin. At this time there is only one person employed in the Tar-Pamlico River Basin to coordinate BMP implementation. The main focus is on reducing nutrient loads in watersheds where there are high concentrations of animal operations. The Department of Environmental Management helps the DSWC in locating areas with high concentrations of nutrients and possible water quality problems. The decision to implement BMPs in a particular area is left to the DSWC and the personnel funded by the Association.

Realized Gains from Trade

The nutrient reduction trading strategy has accomplished several things. First, the engineering evaluation conducted at each facility brought the Association 13 percent below the allowable loading for 1991. The Association has also been successful in getting three line-item grants from Congress to fund the strategy. The first grant was for $400,000 to document the computer model and put it into GSI format. The other two grants have gone directly into the ACSP funding. For nutrients, the state deals with the Association and not individual dischargers, lowering monitoring and enforcement costs for all involved. The cost savings from introducing the trading plan were large. Collectively, the point-source dischargers would have to spend between $50 to $100 million to meet the tighter state standards. Under the trading plan, however, the estimated cost of reducing the same quantity of nutrients was (only) $11.7 million.

The trading plan provided benefits to the state, the public, and the dischargers. The state can focus on the water quality itself, rather than the type of pollution control to be implemented. Politically, the state's efforts to control water pollution in the Tar-Pamlico River Basin can be measured by the quality of water attained and not by the technology mandated. The public was also given the opportunity to negotiate acceptable water quality standards. The environmental groups are now able to concentrate their resources on the water quality standards and the Association's compliance with those standards.

Members of the Association now have the incentive to control pollution in order to meet water quality standards. Each member has an incentive to find lower-cost ways to control pollution. Several of the members are even considering building new facilities that would allow them to trade excess control capacity with other members. There is even potential to trade outside of the Association with the farmers in the area. The payments made into the Agricultural Cost Share Program, so far, indicate that trading is economically and politically promising.

Markets and Watersheds

Issues of water quantity and quality are a major subject of controversy between users. In the recent past, attempts at controlling water quantity and quality have been through regulation. Command-and-control techniques were the typical methods employed, which focus on the technology implemented, not the results achieved, for managing the use of water rights.[32] Rarely, if ever, does this method effectively alleviate conflicts of interest between users.

In contrast, the use of a market process to harness pollution problems is a viable method of abatement and increasingly commonplace.[33] When properly implemented the benefits of pollution markets are substantial. "Properly implemented" is a critical concern because clearly what works on paper does not always hold in practice.[34] This section discusses the general characteristics of a successful pollution market, repeating some of the material given at the very beginning of the chapter. The purpose is to emphasize some key points, to explain why the market process came to be used for the Tar-Pamlico watershed, and to illustrate how this process might be implemented for other regions and pollutants.

The Assignment of Property Rights

At the root of the usage controversy is the issue of who owns the water rights and if that right is excludable. A *credit* holds such property: It is the quantity of pollution that can be discharged into a defined environmental media such as the air or water. The owner of a credit is entitled to discharge the quantity of pollution that the credit sanctions. Simply, a credit is a specified right to use the environment. When the total number of credits is controlled (i.e., limited), the credits have a value attached to them. The value of the credit is determined by the quantity of pollution a credit is worth and the total number of credits available. These credits assign property rights to the owners, who can buy more credits from other owners or sell their credits to other buyers.

When the number of credits is defined and restricted to a geographic area a pollution *bubble* is established. Inside a bubble there may be multiple discharge points. Dischargers within a bubble are allowed to buy and sell credits from one another so long as total discharge for the bubble does not exceed the legislated limit. Importantly, if ownership rights are limited and assigned, that discharger's incentive is to manage the resource to its best use. Buying and selling the right to use water results in the water rights going to the highest valued use.

Under an old-style command-and-control system, a discharger had to obtain a NPDES permit and meet specific technology standards mandated by government. The firm's focus was on lowering production costs and was of ecological importance; the technological standards caused firms to focus on the type of pollution control and not on environmental quality.

The market-style pollution abatement program in the Tar-Pamlico watershed has created a different set of incentives. The Association faces a binding constraint on total nutrient discharge. A bubble was established. Members of the Association can now buy, sell, and offset nutrient discharge of other members. A discharger is given the choice of internally controlling the pollution (retrofitting the facility) or externally offsetting (purchasing) the nutrient discharge of another facility. The enforced legislated limit coupled with dischargers given the flexibility in attaining the nutrient limit creates an incentive structure that protects and maintains the quality of the watershed while simultaneously curtailing costs. Science and legislation dictated the nutrient limits, and Association members find cost-effective pollution control methods.

The Discovery Incentive

The old-style command-and-control regulatory process involved substantial bureaucratic and abatement costs. Pollution control innovation was not encouraged. A critical feature of a flexible, market-style pollution abatement program is the incentive that firms are confronted with when reducing their pollution: Firms will discover cost-effective methods of abating pollution when attempting to minimize costs and maximize profits. Dischargers will seek the least cost method to treat waste because excess pollution credits can be sold for profit. New methods of pollution abatement are often a consequence of such activity.

The Association has discovered innovative ways to treat waste. The combined wealth of the members enabled the Association to afford the hiring of a consulting firm that evaluated each member's facility. It was found that some POTWs could be retrofitted to further reduce discharge. The consulting firm discovered a cost-effective method of reducing total discharge among all members. Point-source discharge was minimized, while costs also declined.

Cost Differences

A market-based credit system is driven by the costs of controlling pollution, with an emphasis on environmental quality. A firm is given a choice to pollute or to control the pollution. If the cost of controlling pollution within the firm is less than the cost of a credit, the producer will choose to control the pollution and sell its credits. The opposite holds as well—purchase credits and expand operations. Science, via legislation, determines environmental quality by limiting the amount of credits, and a credit holder is penalized for violating the law if it discharges more pollution than it has in credits.

The market system vanishes, however, if cost differences between dischargers are not present. When two potential transacting parties have equal marginal abatement cost functions, the net gains from trade are zero. Trading discharge permits presents no advantage. If, on the other hand, two firms face different marginal abatement cost schedules, tradeable discharge permits enable gains from trade. Having the lower-cost firm increase its pollution abatement by one increment and simultaneously having the higher-cost firm reduce its pollution abatement by one increment, environmental quality is maintained (the additional abatement exactly offset the reduced abatement) and the cost savings to the higher-cost firm exceed the rise in costs to the lower-cost firm. The higher-cost firm compensates the lower-cost firm for reducing discharge. The cost differences lead to an information system that supports transactions.

In the Tar-Pamlico watershed, the cost differences are found between point sources and between the group of point sources and nonpoint sources, with the latter providing the initial spark for the emergence of a market. The group of point-source dischargers estimated their costs of reduction to be $50 to $100 million collectively for compliance with pending legislation. In contrast, for the same amount of nutrient abatement, nonpoint-source reduction was estimated at $11.7 million. Stated differently, it would cost point sources four to five times more than nonpoint source to reduce nutrients. The gains from trade and cost savings were substantial.

The cost differential between point sources was also instrumental for the emergence of a nutrient market. The differential is evident in terms of plant size between members of the Association. Eighty percent of the discharge flows from the thirteen members were from two large POTWs; the remaining eleven members were approximately the same size in terms of flow. Economies of scale are present. The large POTWs have their own labs to perform water samplings, which are required by legislation. Small POTWs must contract out for this service, thus they pay higher costs on a flow proportionate basis than do large POTWs.

Transaction Costs

When using a credit market, several hurdles or costs must be incorporated by the potential transacting parties. In general, these costs are referred to as transaction costs. A transaction cost is the "friction" in the transfer of a good or service across a separable user.[35] This friction is similar to the friction found in machine parts. The more the machine parts grind, the less efficient is the machine. In a market, transaction costs are part of a firm's decision to produce internally or purchase in the market. Some types of transaction costs are finding suppliers, writing contracts, and monitoring the quality of parts needed for production. The lower the transaction costs, the smoother the market mechanism works.

Under command-and-control regulation, a producer who creates pollution has to control it internally. The only choice for the firm is to reduce the internal cost of control given specific technology standards. The market approach gives a producer the option to control or discharge the pollution based on relative costs. If the transaction costs of doing business in the market are low enough, the firm will choose to use the market, thereby lowering the firm's cost of pollution control.

A credit market has transaction costs. Depending on idiosyncratic circumstances, different transaction costs would be incurred for different markets. Some of the key transaction costs for a water quality market are:

1. The waterbody (market) has to be geographically defined.
2. A water quality goal for the market has to be established.
3. Dischargers with similar pollutants must be identified.
4. Government restrictions on trading cannot make transactions too costly.
5. Trading terms and values of credits have to be established.
6. An institutional structure needs to allocate credits, monitor discharge, and penalize violators.[36]

Each of the six transaction cost factors is found in the Tar-Pamlico market. The terms of trade have to be defined and contracts have to be written based on the location and area of the market used. The geographic definition of the Tar-Pamlico watershed market is shown in figure 7.1. The physical boundaries of the market accord with the flow and contours of the watershed.

Once the physical market is delineated, a water quality goal can be mandated. The goal is based on what science dictates to be the total quantity of nutrients to be released into the water body. A binding constraint on the amount of pollution discharge must be enforced. This constraint has to be believed. Dischargers must recognize that some type of pollution control is inevitable and that violation of the law is punishable. The constraint is evident at federal and state levels for the Tar-Pamlico watershed:

1. The 1987 Clean Water Act was the federal binding constraint that fostered cooperation among the North Carolina state governmental agencies. The federal constraint ensured a state government water quality objective.

2. The North Carolina Department of Environmental Management (DEM) was the governmental agency central to the issue at the state level. Their objective was to decrease the nutrient loads in the basin, with point sources providing the low-cost means of achieving some reduction. It was DEM's flexibility and willingness to cooperate in the development of an alternative strategy that made a distinguishing difference for the Tar-Pamlico watershed. They allowed the point-source dischargers (the Association) time to come up with a better plan; but, if the Association had not come up with an acceptable nutrient reduction plan, the DEM's original strategy (constraint) was to be fully employed.

Trading will work best between dischargers who have similar production types and pollution discharge. When the pollutant is common to all potential transacting parties, the costs of using the market are less. If firms and governing bodies must convert one type of pollution into another for the purpose of transacting, costs will rise relative to the situation where identical pollutants are offset. Put differently, it is easier to trade oranges for oranges, than apples for oranges.

In North Carolina, both point and nonpoint sources discharge nitrogen and phosphorus. The nutrients are common to all dischargers. If they were not common, costs would increase scientifically due to the technological difficulties of offsetting one pollutant from another, and politically/economically due to negotiation and cooperation difficulties of getting two distinct parties to transact. Transaction costs are lower when the dischargers emit the same pollutant.

Government restrictions on trading could raise the cost of transacting above the cost of internally controlling pollution. The Association and other groups central to the Tar-Pamlico market helped to reduce these bureaucratic costs, which are shown below:

• *Inter-Group Cooperation.* The market works at two levels: 1) Point source to point source, and 2) Point source to nonpoint source. Cooperation among the point-sources at level 1 is essential if level 2 is to be attained. Some key characteristics among members of the Association that facilitate transactions are:

• The costs of nutrient reductions for POTWs are dispersed over a customer base that has few (if any) alternatives of water treatment service.

• Members of the Association are homogeneous:

1. All are point-source dischargers;
2. Discharge comes in the form of a definable flow;
3. Final output is the same (with the exception of the private firm);

4. Each is a government municipality (except the private firm).

The fourth homogeneity characteristic carries many implications. The structure of the POTW industry is non-competitive—the customer base is geographically defined and enforced by law, with rates determined by a non-market process. The members are not competing with one another for consumer dollars. Hence, intra-industry transfers through regulation are not as likely. This industrial structure may have facilitated cooperation within the Association.

• *A Broker.* A broker that acts as an information processor between all of the groups involved in the plan will lower transaction costs. The broker would have expertise in the legal, political, technological, and economic characteristics of a water quality market. The Association hired John Hall, an attorney with the law firm Kirkpatrick & Cody, who fulfilled the role of information broker. Hall was instrumental in developing the market strategy and still plays a critical role in the communication among Association members and between the Association and external parties (e.g., government and environmental groups).

• *Peripheral Groups.* Participants such as environmental groups commonly act as a liaison to explain and justify methods of pollution reduction to the public. The main purpose of the North Carolina Environmental Defense Fund (EDF) and the Pamlico-Tar River Foundation (PTRF) was to decrease nutrient loads. With that goal in mind, both groups supported the offset strategy and played a key role in public acceptance of the innovative plans of the Association. In addition, the environmental groups were instrumental (and still are) in many of the scientific studies. Support from these groups will help to lower transaction costs.

Once the first four transaction cost factors are sufficiently low, the number of credits that will be traded can then be determined. The ongoing monitoring and enforcement of water quality will have to be handled by some institutional structure. This, again, was one of the primary functions of the Association, which acted to ensure that each member monitor and perform water quality samplings.

Trading pollution permits or rights offers the prospect for reducing pollution control costs and for achieving the goals of water quality statutes. In the absence of property rights, pollution control will continue to be costly and controversial. Water quality goals will not be achieved. But while we understand these things, we also know that organizations are costly to form and markets are costly to use. Transaction costs stand as a barrier to the promise of lower costs. As the cost of transacting rises, the less efficient a market alternative will be for controlling pollution costs. Stated differently, the gains from markets are only theoretical if transaction costs are insurmountable.

Concluding Thoughts

When allowed to operate as designed, water quality markets can demonstrate the effectiveness of economic incentives in achieving environmental improvements. In particular, a market strategy creates incentives for industry to further reduce pollution, since dischargers can directly benefit from developing cost-effective methods of nutrient abatement. Also, these policies have afforded savings to the consumers of products made with nutrient discharging production processes. The market strategy allows for nutrient reduction to be achieved at a lower cost, which translates into lower prices. These are the accomplishments and results often heralded by proponents of a market strategy. But the Tar-Pamlico watershed market offers this and more.

Confronted with higher water quality standards and imminent command-and-control regulation, nutrient dischargers were motivated to find lower cost alternatives. In their search for an alternative, a system of property rights was established. The nutrient dischargers formed the Association and were allocated a limited right of discharge. The nutrient bubble of the Association formed through the threat of regulation, not through mandated legislation. Simply, the industry caused the structure of the current regulation.

The next logical step was to find the low-cost alternative. Agriculture was targeted. But why would nutrient offsets ever take place between point sources (the Association) and nonpoint sources (agriculture)? Answering this question was perhaps the most novel consequence of the Tar-Pamlico watershed market. Because the point sources were faced with imminent nutrient reductions, they formed the Association to act as an intermediary between them and agriculture. Agriculture, foreseeing possible nutrient regulations in their near future, realize the potential gains from trade. By modifying their operations, the farmers are paid to reduce nutrient loads.

The future holds the possibility for more pollution trading markets to arise. The Neuse River Basin of North Carolina, located immediately south of the Tar-Pamlico, is just one example of a developing market. The sources of discharge and potential market participants are quite similar to those in the Tar-Pamlico watershed. One can only hope that many of the principles and characteristics of the Tar-Pamlico watershed market will be recognized and incorporated in the Neuse and other potential markets—our quality of life and environment depend on it.

Appendix
Acronyms

ACSP	Agricultural Cost Share Program
BMP	Best Management Practices
CWA	Clean Water Act
DEM	Department of Environmental Management
DSWC	Division of Soil and Water Conservation
EMC	Environmental Management Commission, North Carolina
EPA	Environmental Protection Agency
GDP	Gallons per Day
kg/l	Kilograms per Liter
MGD	Millions of Gallons per Day
mg/l	Milligrams per Liter
NCEDF	North Carolina Environmental Defense Fund
NPDES	National Pollutant Discharge Elimination System
NRTS	Nutrient Reduction Trading Strategy
NSW	Nutrient Sensitive Waters
PTRF	Pamlico-Tar River Foundation
TN	Total Nitrogen
TP	Total Phosphorus

Market Participants in the Tar-Pamlico Watershed

Beth McGee
NC State Dept. of Environment, Health and Natural Resources
Dept. of Environmental Management
512 N. Salisbury St.
Raleigh, NC 27604
919 733-5083 or 919 733-7015
FAX 919 733-9919

Buster Tawell
NC State Dept. of Environment, Health and Natural Resources
Division of Soil and Water Conservation
512 N. Salisbury St.
Raleigh, NC 27604
919 733-2302
FAX 919 733-2622

Malcolm Green
Chairman, Tar-Pamlico Basin Association
Greenville Utilities Commission
P.O. Box 1847
Greenville, NC 27835
919 551-1500
FAX 919 551-1597

Dave McNaught
Pamlico Tar River Foundation
P.O. Box 1854
Washington, NC 27889
919 946-7211
or 919 946-9492

Russel Waters
Public Works Director
City of Washington
P.O. Box 1988
Washington, NC 27889
919 975-9302
FAX 919 946-1965

Bill Reynolds
Director of Engineering
National Spinning Co., Inc.
West 3rd Street
P.O. Box 191
Washington, NC 27889
919 975-7111
FAX 919 975-7194

Notes

1. The figure was computer regenerated from Pamlico-Tar River Foundation, Inc. *A River of Opportunity: A Pollution Abatement and Natural Resource Management Plan for the Pamlico Basin.* Washington, NC, April 1991.
2. Ibid., pp. 3-4.
3. The dinoflagellate is a single-celled aquatic plant algae. It only reproduces sexually when it is in mid-kill of fish. Although research is ongoing at North

Carolina State University about "dino's" origin and capabilities, at least some of the fish kills are linked to this creature. See M. E. Pellin, "Killer Algae too Strange for Fiction: Weird Creature Plays Part in Fish Kills in Pamlico River, Expert Says," *Washington News,* July 1, 1993.

4. North Carolina Department of Natural Resources and Community Development, Division of Environmental Management, Water Quality Section. *Tar-Pamlico River Basin Nutrient Sensitive Waters Designation & Nutrient Management Strategy,* April 1989, p.3.

5. The United States Clean Water Act as amended by the Water Quality Act of 1987, PL 100-4, Doc. No. 73-355, Section 502(14), United States Government Printing Office.

6. See Section 402 of the Clean Water Act.

7. U.S. Environmental Protection Agency, Office of Water, *Proposed Guidance Specifying Management Measures for Sources of Nonpoint Pollution in Coastal Waters* (WH-553), May 1991, p. 1-1.

8. U.S. Environmental Protection Agency. *Comparing Risks and Setting Environmental Priorities,* Washington, DC, August 1989.

9. The data on phosphorus displayed in figure 7.2 is from 1988. Since that time Texasgulf has reduced its phosphorus discharge by over 90 percent.

10. For a similar scenario of federal legislation that moves ahead without respect to scientific analysis, see David W. Riggs, "Acid Rain and the Clean Air Act: Lessons in Damage Control," in *Taking the Environment Seriously,* Roger E. Meiners and Bruce Yandle, eds. (Lanham, MD: Rowman and Littlefield, 1993).

11. U.S. EPA, *Proposed Guidance Specifying Management Measures for Sources of Nonpoint Pollution in Coastal Waters,* op. cit., p. 1-2.

12. The proposed legislation was: NCDEM, Water Quality Section, *Tar-Pamlico River Basin Nutrient Sensitive Waters Designation & Nutrient Management Strategy,* April 1989.

13. One previous designation of a river basin as NSW in North Carolina, the Chowan basin, resulted in POTWs using land application instead of discharging into the river. The smaller towns could not afford the higher costs of building new facilities to control the nutrients at the lower levels.

14. The towns of Greenville, Rocky Mount, Belhaven, and Pinetops, for example.

15. U.S. EPA, *Managing Nonpoint Source Pollution: Final Report to Congress on Section 319 of the Clean Water Act (1989);* January 1992, pp. 15 - 29.

16. U.S. EPA, *Proposed Guidance Specifying Management Measures for Sources of Nonpoint Pollution in Coastal Waters,* pp. 2-8 and 2-9.

17. NCDEM, Water Quality Section, *Tar-Pamlico River Basin Nutrient Sensitive Waters Designation & Nutrient Management Strategy,* April 1989, p.3.

18. Personal conversation with Malcolm Green, Chairman of the Association, February 11, 1993.

19. The towns of Tarboro and Robersonville, for example.

20. Telephone conversation with Rann Carpenter and Jeff Furness of Texasgulf, Inc., January 29, 1993.

21. The computer model is designed to monitor the flow of phosphorus throughout the basin. It identifies the quantity of phosphorus entering the basin and pinpoints high concentrations.

22. U.S. Environmental Protection Agency, *Incentive Analysis for Clean Water Act Reauthorization: Point Source/Nonpoint Source Trading for Nutrient Discharge Reductions,* April 1992, p. B-8.

23. Memo from Steve Tedder to David Sides, February 10, 1993. Available upon request.

24. *Tar-Pamlico Nutrient Sensitive Waters Implementation Strategy,* adopted December 14, 1989, revised February 13, 1992, p. 5.

25. Greenville and Washington POTWs are anticipating banking excess credits.

26. *Tar-Pamlico NSW Implementation Strategy,* p. 7.

27. Ibid., p. 5.

28. Ibid., p. 2.

29. Details of Association responsibilities are included in North Carolina Department of Environmental Health, and Natural Resources, Division of Environmental Management, Water Quality Section, *Attachment B: Tar-Pamlico NSW Implementation Strategy An Estimation of Major Requirements.* September 13, 1990.

30. Established under North Carolina General Statutes Chapter 143 Article 21 Section 149. (a), effective May 1, 1987. The details of the plan are found in North Carolina Administrative Code Title 15, Chapter 6, Section 6E, June 4, 1992.

31. James R. Cummings, Nonpoint Source Section Chief for Division of Soil and Water Conservation *"North Carolina Agricultural Cost Share Program For NPS Pollution Control: Soil & Water Conservation District Prioritization,* Memo, March 27, 1989.

32. The reasons for mandating this type of environmental legislation go beyond the scope of this report. The interested reader is referred to Bruce Yandle, *The Political Limits of Environmental Regulation: Tracking the Unicorn* (New York: Quorum, 1989) and for a more general assessment of the theory of economic regulation see Sam Peltzman, "The Economic Theory of Regulation after a Decade of Deregulation," in *Brookings Papers on Economic Activity: Microeconomics* (Washington, DC: Brookings Institution, 1989).

33. See, for example, Title IV of the 1990 Clean Air Act, where a market of sulfur dioxide permits has been created to control acid rain. Use of the market for pollution control has its origins in J. H. Dales, *Pollution, Property and Prices.* (Toronto: University of Toronto Press, 1968).

34. Some past attempts at using a market-style pollution abatement program have been unsuccessful. In theory the programs worked well but upon implementation failed. The Fox River of Wisconsin is an example, see Erhard F. Joeres and Martin H. David, eds., *Buying a Better Environment,* Land Economic Monograph No.6 (Madison: University of Wisconsin Press, 1983) and Bruce Yandle, "A Primer on Marketable Permits," *Journal of Regulation and Social Costs* 1(1991): 25-41.

35. Oliver E. Williamson, *The Economic Institutions of Capitalism: Firms, Markets, Relational Contracting* (New York: The Free Press, 1985), p. 1

36. U.S. EPA, *Incentive Analysis for Clean Water Act Reauthorization: Point Source/Nonpoint Source Trading For Nutrient Discharge Reductions,* April 1992, pp. 8 - 11.

References

Alm, Alvin L. "Nonpoint Sources of Water Pollution." *Environmental Science Technology,* 24 (1990): 967.

Coase, Ronald H. "The Problem of Social Cost." *Journal of Law and Economics* 3 (October 1960): 1-44.

Cummings, James R. *North Carolina Agricultural Cost Share Program For NPS Pollution Control: Soil & Water Conservation District Prioritization,* Memo, March 27, 1989.

Dales, J. H. *Pollution, Property and Prices.* Toronto: University of Toronto Press, 1968.

Environmental Reporter (ER). Selected References, Vol. 22. p.117, p. 663, p. 2190, p. 2439, and p. 2534.

Hahn, Robert W. "Critical Issues for Implementing Restoration Credits." *Economists Incorporated,* December 15, 1992.

Industrial Economics, Inc. *Case Studies on the Trading of Effluent Loads in Dillon Reservoir.* Prepared for the U.S. Environmental Protection Agency, 1984.

Joeres, Erhard F., and Martin H. David, eds. *Buying a Better Environment.* Land Economic Monograph No.6. Madison: University of Wisconsin Press, 1983.

Levitas, Stephen J., and Douglas N. Rader. "Point/Nonpoint Source Trading: A New Approach to Reducing Nutrient Pollution." *Environmental Permitting* (Winter 1992/1993): 5-19.

Macaulay, Hugh H., and Bruce Yandle. *Environmental Use and the Market.* Lexington, MA: D. C. Heath and Company, 1977.

North Carolina Administrative Code, Title 15, Chapter 6, Section 6E, June 4, 1992.

North Carolina Division of Environmental Management, Water Quality Section. *Tar-Pamlico River Basin Nutrient Sensitive Waters Designation & Nutrient Management Strategy.* April 1989.

North Carolina Department of Environmental Health, and Natural Resources, Division of Environmental Management, Water Quality Section. *Attachment A: Tar-Pamlico NSW Nutrient Management Strategy.* September 13, 1990, p.1.

————.*Attachment B: Tar-Pamlico NSW Implementation Strategy An Estimation of Major Requirements.* September 13, 1990.

North Carolina General Statutes Chapter 143. Article 21. Section 149. (a), effective May 1, 1987.

Pamlico-Tar River Foundation, Inc. *A River of Opportunity: A Pollution Abatement and Natural Resource Management Plan for the Pamlico Basin.* Washington, NC, April 1991.

Pellin, M. E. "Killer Algae too Strange for Fiction: Weird Creature Plays Part in Fish Kills in Pamlico River, Expert Says." *Washington News,* July 1, 1993.

Peltzman, Sam, "The Economic Theory of Regulation after a Decade of Deregulation." In *Brookings Papers on Economic Activity: Microeconomics.* Washington, DC: Brookings Institution, 1989.

Riggs, David W. "Acid Rain and the Clean Air Act: Lessons in Damage Control." In *Taking the Environment Seriously.* Roger E. Meiners and Bruce Yandle, eds. Lanham, MD: Rowman and Littlefield, 1993.

Tietenberg, Tom. *Environmental and Natural Resources Economics.* Third Edition. New York: Harper Collins Publishers Inc., 1992.

Water Quality Act of 1987. PL 100-4, Doc. No. 73-355. Section 502(14). United States Government Printing Office. U. S. Environmental Protection Agency.

U.S. Environmental Protection Agency. *Comparing Risks and Setting Environmental Priorities.* Washington, DC, (August 1989).

————. *Incentive Analysis for Clean Water Act Reauthorization: Point Source/ Nonpoint Source Trading For Nutrient Discharge Reductions.* Office of Water and Office of Policy, Planning, and Evaluation. Washington, D.C., (April 1992).

————. *Managing Nonpoint-Source Pollution: Final Report to Congress on Section 319 of the Clean Water Act (1989).* January, 1992.

————. Office of Water. *Proposed Guidance Specifying Management Measures for Sources of Nonpoint Pollution in Coastal Waters.* WH 553, May 1991.

U.S. Government Accounting Office. *Water Pollution: EPA Budget Needs to Place Greater Emphasis on Controlling Nonpoint Source Pollution.* GAO/T-RCED-92-46, April 7, 1992.

————. *Water Pollution: Pollutant Trading Could Reduce Compliance Costs If Uncertainties Are Resolved.* GAO/RCED-92-153, June 1992.

Williamson, Oliver E. *The Economic Institutions of Capitalism: Firms, Markets, Relational Contracting.* New York: The Free Press, 1985.

Yandle, Bruce. *The Political Limits of Environmental Regulation: Tracking the Unicorn.* New York: Quorum, 1989.

————. "A Primer on Marketable Permits." *Journal of Regulation and Social Costs* 1(1991): 25-41.

Chapter 8

Effluent Trading in South Carolina

Sean Blacklocke

Introduction

Effluent trading is a simple and beneficial incremental adjustment to current United States and South Carolina water pollution control policy. Subsequent to an equitable initial wasteload allocation of a permitted level of a pollutant, one that has been determined to be safe for human and ecological exposure, wastewater dischargers can be allowed to trade pollution reduction requirements to reduce pollution abatement costs while maintaining or improving water quality.

Effluent trading has bipartisan support at the national level. In 1995, the U.S. House of Representatives passed the Clean Water Act Rewrite, H.R. 961. The proposed Republican legislation supports this market incentive for water pollution control. In May of 1996, the U.S. Environmental Protection Agency (EPA) published a *Draft Framework for Watershed-Based Trading* in response to President Clinton's Clean Water Initiative of February 1994 and the administration's proposed 1994 Clean Water Act (CWA) Reauthorization Amendments.

The Clinton Initiative's emphasis on controlling polluted runoff alone is estimated to improve the water quality of 52 percent of the nation's rivers and 63 percent of the nation's lakes. The EPA estimates that $700 million to $7.5 billion in control cost could be avoided in the United States if states adopted effluent trading among point-source, nonpoint-source, and pretreating dischargers.[1] South Carolina accounts for 2 percent of the annual total U.S. expenditures on water pollution control.[2] Effluent trading might save South Carolinians an estimated $14 million to $150 million while improving the water quality of their rivers and lakes.

This chapter first presents a theoretical discussion that explains the underlying logic of effluent trading. This first discussion is based on the simple notion that the participating dischargers seek to meet a collective water quality constraint. The analysis does not take into account the likely fact that certain segments of a receiving stream ultimately determine the constraint to be met. This part of the analysis comes later. After developing the theoretical points, the discussion then introduces a number of real world conditions and explores policy implications. The second section of the report focuses more sharply on the water quality constraint and the transfer function that translates the impact that dischargers may have on a particular stressed component of a receiving stream. This section shows how the first theoretical model is modified to meet the water quality challenge. Section three discusses applications of effluent trading and what we have learned from these limited experiences. Finally, the fourth section describes the Pee Dee River trading study and the results derived from it. A short conclusion addresses the fundamental policy challenge: How do we get from the current system of control to one that incorporates effluent trading and the gains that come from it?

Effluent Trading: The Analytics

Some Background

Allowing facilities that discharge wastewater effluents to receiving streams the flexibility to trade pollution reduction requirements is a minor and simple incremental change in state water pollution control policy consistent with policy adjustments at the federal level. But while the policy adjustments are minor, the ultimate benefits to be realized from effluent trading may not be minor at all. Criticisms by those who are experienced with effluent trading in theory and practice are extremely rare. Much of the reason this policy adjustment has not already been employed in all states is that state policy makers, municipality and industry representatives, and other citizens are not familiar with the economics and applications of effluent trading.

Under current regulations, point-source dischargers and certain nonpoint-source dischargers ultimately have to prevent the violation of ambient water quality standards. Industries pretreating wastes that discharge to a publicly owned treatment works (POTW) must not contribute pollutants at levels to which the POTW will be out of compliance with its own permit. These point-source dischargers, nonpoint-source dischargers, and pretreating facilities generally adhere to a floor of technology-based standards for pollution abatement. Pollution reduction requirements beyond these effluent standards intended to prevent ambient standards violations are often distributed in a way that attempts to achieve equity among dischargers. But, equating reduction requirements often does not result in the most cost-effective allocation of pollution control, and water quality improvements beyond minimum ambient standards are rarely achieved. Further investigation of related costs and benefits associated with facilitating effluent trading generally leads to estimates of net benefits.

The Economic Gains from Trade

Two factors contribute to the lack of cost effectiveness in traditional command-and-control wasteload allocation policies: dischargers of different varieties have different marginal control costs for removing pollutants from their waste streams, and dischargers have different effects on the water quality limited portion(s) of the streams into which they discharge. Dischargers thus have different marginal control costs for instream pollutant load reductions.

In an effluent trading program, a pollution source that is able to treat additional pollutant load at a low cost is allowed to accept payment from another source for excess treatment. The other pollution source will typically be one that is only able to treat additional pollutant load at a high cost. In such a scenario, a more cost-effective allocation of pollution control can be achieved. This is to say that among dischargers, the respective dollar figures for treating one additional unit of pollution in excess of the current level of treatment (marginal costs) are closer to being the same amount for all dischargers at the aggregate reduction requirement level. In economic terms, when the marginal costs of reducing the required pollutants for each discharger are equated, the overall cost of achieving the reduction requirement is minimized.

Each point-source, nonpoint-source, and pretreating discharger will likely have a different marginal control cost curve. A graphical representation of varying marginal control costs is provided in figure 8.1.

If the goal is to reduce five pollution units (PU) overall, there are four different combinations of reduction requirements that yield this outcome. However, there is only one combination of reduction requirements that produces the least-cost, or cost-effective, outcome. This is where the two marginal control cost curves intersect. Both facilities have an incentive to trade requirements at every other combination of reductions totaling five PU, as indicated in table 8.1.

If the initial allocation of PU reduction requirements is for Facility 1 to reduce its first PU and Facility 2 to reduce its first, second, third, and fourth PU, for a total reduction of five PU, there will be an incentive to trade. If Facility 2 pays Facility 1 $50, Facility 1 can reduce its second PU for $10, thereby earning $40. Facility 2 will save $50, because it would have cost $100 to reduce its fourth PU. Facility 2 would likely also opt not to treat its third PU and pay Facility 1 to treat its third PU. If exchanged at a price of $40, Facility 1 will earn $20, because it will only cost Facility 1 $20 to treat this PU. Facility 2 will save $10 because treating its own third PU costs $50. What results is the least cost combination of PU reductions. Facility 1 reduces its first PU in compliance with its initial requirement, and further reduces its second and third PU earning $60. Facility 2 treats its first and second PU, but pays Facility 1 $90 to reduce the additional two

Figure 8.1. Pollution Reductions and Marginal Control Costs for Two Facilities

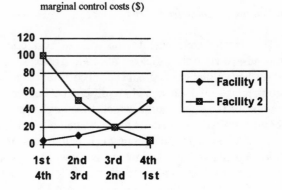

marginal control costs ($)

reduction of pollution units (PU)

Table 8.1. Pollution Reductions and Marginal Control Costs for Two Facilities

Reductions (PU)		Marginal Control Costs ($)	
Facility 1	Facility 2	Facility 1	Facility 2
1st	4th	5	100
2nd	3rd	10	50
3rd	2nd	20	20
4th	1st	50	5

PU that it was initially required to reduce. Facility 2 must pay out $90, but treating its own third and fourth PU would have cost it $150. Facility 2 thus saved $60. Trading allowed for cost savings of $120, and five PU were still reduced.

Another allocation may be to require Facility 1 to reduce its first and second PU and Facility 2 to reduce its first, second, and third PU. This again results in a total reduction of five PU, and again there is an incentive to trade. Facility 2 can pay Facility 1 $30 to treat its third PU and save $20. Facility 1 will earn $10. The third reduction requirement scenario would entail Facility 1 reducing its first, second, third, and fourth PU, and Facility 2 reducing its first PU. Facility 2 can make $25 if it treats Facility 1's fourth PU at an exchange price of $30. Facility 1 will save $20.

If Facility 1 is required to reduce its first, second, and third PU, and Facility 2 is required to reduce its first and second PU, there will be no incentive to trade. Both only spend $20 on their last unit reductions. This is the cost-effective allocation of a five PU reduction requirement. Under market conditions of perfect information and perfect competition, any initial allocation of pollution reduction requirement will eventually arrive at this cost-effective allocation. These market conditions are rare, but if trading is allowed, some of these cost savings can be realized. Furthermore, water quality improvements can result if a trading partner that has a large impact on the water quality portion of a stream treats a portion of wasteload for a facility that has a small relative impact on this stream segment.

It is important to note that in this hypothetical example, the marginal control costs increase at an increasing rate. In other words, marginal control costs can increase with each additional level of pollution reduction. The reason for this is obvious. Removing the bulk (90%) of most pollutant loads from waste streams might be accomplished with common procedures such as aerobic biodegradation or sedimentation. As additional amounts (91%, 92%, 93%...100%) of pollutants are removed, more expensive techniques will need to be employed. For instance, addition of expensive chemicals might yield 91% removal, whereas further addition of even more expensive chemicals may need to be added to get 92 percent removal. High-cost distillation might be necessary to go from 98 percent to 99 percent removal.

Often in reality, graphed marginal control costs for sources look more like steps than curves because large capital expenditures for significantly more effective pollution controls are often required for additional pollutant load removals. In such cases where segments of marginal cost curves can be undefined, incremental costs (IC) should be compared. An incremental unit cost of reduction is simply the total cost (TC) of that bulk reduction divided by the pollution units reduced (PUR). In other words, incremental cost is the average cost of only the additional reductions.[3]

$$IC = TC / PUR$$

Effluent trading is simply the allowance of dischargers with different marginal or incremental costs to trade reduction requirements for savings and profits. Pollution loadings can also be reduced if lesser savings and profits are realized.

Cost Differentials

EPA has promulgated technology-based effluent standards for fifty-one categories of point-source dischargers and thirty-nine categories of pretreating industrial dischargers.[4] The costs of removing equal levels of pollutants in waste streams vary significantly among these sources due to several reasons. First, different processes or activities generate different quantities and types of pollutants requiring different appropriate control technologies. Second, treatment technologies of differing age are not equally efficient. Third, facilities with higher flows can have larger economies of scale. Fourth, some facilities have superior ability to recycle waste residuals. And, finally, prices for required land, power, and water for treatment can vary among sources.

Every pollution source generates pollutants unique to that process or activity in varying amounts. The process or activity of the source has a bearing on the type of pollution abatement the source will employ. For instance, a paper mill, a POTW, and a logging operation might all contribute an equal amount of five-day biochemical oxygen demand (BOD5) loading to a stream. However, the cost of removing the pollutants that exert this equal oxygen demand will likely not be the same if the pollution abatement technique is not the same. More specifically, if the paper mill employs an aerobic lagoon to remove solids, it may cost the mill less per pound to remove these solids than the POTW removing solids via activated sludge. The logging operation may simply make use of retention ponds to remove an equivalent amount of BOD5 at a cost lower than the paper mill and POTW. Different technologies are employed because the amounts of the waste and complexity of the waste molecules are different.

A facility with a twenty-year-old plant is probably not employing an abatement technology that is as efficient as a modern one. The plant will therefore have higher per unit reduction costs. If the technology is not outdated, the age of the equipment might affect its performance, yielding the same inefficiency.

Two facilities of the same type may treat identical types of waste, but if the volume of wastewater is significantly different, the cost per pound of waste treatment will likely also be different. POTWs exemplify this. To meet 85 percent removal requirements, two municipalities might construct POTWs. A POTW with a large service area will generate revenues large enough to support efficient treatment technologies that require large capital expenditures but allow for expansion of the service area, thereby creating lower long-run average total costs. The smaller municipality will not be able to generate funds to employ the efficient technology and will have higher per unit costs associated with treating the same types of pollutants.

In many situations, the residuals that are discharged via the waste stream are particles of the very product the manufacturer is producing. Some processes in manufacturing are more amenable to reassimilating these residuals as usable product. Recycling waste before it is sent to the endpipe can have a significant effect on pollution abatement costs. Wastewater treatment requires land and can also require power and water. Charges for land, power, and water can vary significantly depending on the location of the discharger. These costs are incorporated into the cost per pound treatment of wasteload.

EPA has long recognized that each type of water polluting source faces different unit costs for waste removal. In fact, exhaustive cost-effective analyses and economic impact assessments are performed prior to promulgating the effluent standards that each pollution source is required to meet. EPA compiles data on compliance expenditures for each category of discharger and arrives at estimates on the per-unit costs of meeting the standards. Throughout the past twenty years, when ambient state standards were largely not being met with these control requirements, EPA performed cost tests to determine which industry category is required to pay the least to comply with effluent standards. More stringent controls are then assigned to that industry.

But these attempts to equate control costs between industry categories at the federal level have failed to achieve a cost-effective distribution of pollution control costs. Control costs vary so significantly between categories of sources that cost estimates for removal of wasteloads from waste streams are largely meaningless when applied to individual facilities. Furthermore, the relative effects of discharges on pollution stressed portions of streams are not considered. Variability in these effects can be significant.

Relative Impacts on Water Quality Limited Streams

The pollution control cost of real interest is not that of removal of pollutant load at the source, but rather the control cost of reducing pollutants in the water quality limited portion(s) of receiving waters. Wasteload composition, amount, and point of origin all affect the degree to which respective discharges impact water quality limited stream segments.

Oxygen-demanding constituents, in particular, can have a significant impact on large and distant portions of a stream. Toxic pollutants and metals often have impacts closer to the discharge point itself. Trading to redistribute portions of an allocated aggregate load (with the exception of pretreated wasteloads) is most appropriate for oxygen-demanding constituents. Carbon and nutrients, mostly nitrogen and sometimes phosphorous, are the two pollutants of concern in cases where a stream segment is water quality limited due to low dissolved oxygen (DO). Sources contributing larger amounts of these constituents will obviously have larger impacts.

In many cases, the point of origin of the BOD5 or Ammonia-Nitrogen (NH3-N) may offset the effects of higher loadings. A wastewater discharge containing a particular amount of carbon and nitrogen has a unique dissolved oxygen critical point, or sag point, associated with it. This sag point will typically be downstream of the discharge in the absence of tidal influence and is graphically the point in which the deoxygenation and reoxygenation curves intersect (see figure 8.2).[5]

Each discharger's individual sag point can result in a similar aggregate sag point downstream. The cost that is really of interest is the cost of reducing BOD5 and NH3-N at this aggregate sag point. Although it is true that if loading is redistributed, the stream's sag point will likely shift, if origins stay the same, the sag point DO should rise on redistribution. Effluent trading creates an economic incentive for those who have a high impact on this sag point to accept payment to treat other dischargers' wasteloads, because their true marginal control costs, the marginal costs of decreasing wasteload at the sag point, are low. If a coefficient

Figure 8.2 Stream Oxygen Sag Point

DO (mg/l)

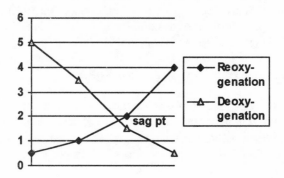

(a) is derived to represent percent contribution to DO depletion at the sag point, the marginal control cost at the endpipe (mcc) of a one pollution unit reduction at the sag point is:

mcc/a

Building a water quality model can obtain a transfer or impact coefficient for every discharger by simply performing a model run with the discharger "turned off."

The resultant decrease in ultimate biochemical oxygen demand (BODU), a derivation of BOD5 used in modeling, allows a ratio of end-of-pipe loading to sag point loading to be calculated. Exchanges in a water pollution market under perfect market conditions on a DO limited stream with this type of sag point would result in the mcc/a's for each facility being the same. This would achieve the cost-effective, or least-cost, allocation of pollution control. This same concept can be applied to different endpipes at a single facility.[6]

The Cost-Effective Allocation of Pollution Control

A mathematical formula to determine BOD trading opportunities is presented in figure 8.3. The formula minimizes the total cost of meeting the state ambient standard for DO. It accounts for end-of-pipe marginal control costs, relative DO

Figure 8.3. The Cost-Effective Allocation of BOD

$$\min Z = \sum_{i=1}^{n} \sum_{j=1}^{x} mcc/a_i \ (BODr_j)$$

$$\text{s.t.} \ \sum_{i=1}^{n} \sum_{j=1}^{x} BODr_{ij} \geq BODs$$

Z = total cost of complying with the DO ambient standard
i = point-source or nonpoint-source discharger
j = increment of BOD reduction at sag point
mcc = marginal control cost at endpipe
a = impact or transfer coefficient
BODr = BOD reduction
BODs = BOD reduction necessary at sag point for DO $\geq$ ambient standard

sag point impacts, and the U.S. Code of Federal Regulations-Title 40 (40 CFR) effluent limitations.

Unfortunately, little information on the marginal control costs, or even incremental control costs, of removing pollutants from waste streams is readily available at this time. This is a direct result of the current command-and-control effluent standards. Facility engineers have little incentive or reason to calculate these costs because they have never had the option of reducing or increasing abatement efforts in pursuit of cost savings. General information on cost per pound removals for varying industry categories are often meaningless in practical applications to facilities of interest due to the very reasons they are sought. If general numbers represented the true specific marginal costs of each facility in an industry, EPA economists would be able to better predict the cost-effective allocation of pollution control in their development documents for effluent guidelines and standards, and effluent trading might not yield significant cost savings.

Impact coefficients, on the other hand, are easily obtainable, and as markets for water pollution control develop, marginal and incremental control cost data will become more readily available. A maximum allowable industrial loading (MAIL) is the total loading of a pollutant that is allocated to facilities discharging to a POTW. A cost-effective allocation of a MAIL can be determined for indirect dischargers, just as a total maximum daily load (TMDL) is determined and allocated to direct dischargers.

Costs, Benefits, and Externalities

An analysis of the costs and benefits of effluent trading details the cost savings and water quality benefits associated with trades. It must also consider the increased administrative costs and trading transaction costs, as well as any spillover costs and benefits. Cost savings to municipalities and industries for pollution abatement translate into cost savings to citizens as taxpayers and consumers on water and sewer rates and consumer goods.

There are several studies that support and quantify this. One study found families with annual incomes between $20,700 and $29,000 could expect to contribute $175.79 every year toward POTWs meeting CWA requirements.[7] Studies have also been done to place dollar values on the environmental benefit of increments of improved water quality. Improvements in water quality due to effluent trades can translate into increased revenues for the tourism industry, the commercial fishing industry, the outdoor recreation industry, and can increase the market values of homes bordering streams. The Delaware Estuary Study found that instream DO increases of 4.0 mg/l to 5.0 mg/l, 5.5 mg/l, and 6.5 mg/l entailed increases in monetized water resource recreational benefits of 5%, 15%, and 28%, respectively. Refer to table 8.2.[8]

Table 8.2

INSTREAM OXYGEN INCREASES AND ASSOCIATED BENEFITS

DO (mg/l)	Index of Recreational Benefits
6.5	128
5.5	115
5.0	105
4.0	100

Administrative costs to oversee effluent trading can be large or small depending on how proactive an approach the administering agency takes toward regulating trading terms or facilitating the flow of information between potential trading partners.

Discussions of government costs to regulate such things as monopolies or collusion in pollution trading are premature and irrelevant at this point in water pollution markets. Effluent trading is in the early stages of development and does not require the same regulatory controls as more advanced and established commodities markets. Initial allocations must still be decided on by the administering agency, which accounts for the individual circumstances of each facility. Initial wasteload allocations remain as they are, the result of competing political forces seeking equity. If anything, the ultimate option of effluent trading may help to expedite the process of achieving equitable distribution in wasteload allocations. Any trades subsequent to initial allocations will only benefit trading partners.

If the administering agency responsible for initial allocations were to collect fees for effluent trades, this might cause some mistrust among dischargers as to the motives of initial wasteload allocations. This may not be an appropriate way to fund an effluent-trading program.

Administrative expenditures on providing a clearinghouse for the exchange of cost and relative impact data might be significant, although cost savings to the beneficiaries as a whole would likely be far in excess of these costs. Many cost savings trades could occur with the current information already available. A model can produce impact coefficients and outputs resulting from adjusted model inputs in minutes. Facility engineers can often approximate costs in seconds. If most trades are only allowed over five-year periods coinciding with basin-wide repermitting, very little extra effort on the part of permit engineers will be required. Some effluent trading could certainly be done directly between facilities without third-party brokering.

As effluent trading becomes more developed and widespread, if administering agencies cannot locate the resources to broker trades, it may become profitable for private brokers to assimilate trading criteria and administer trades. This might reduce profits and saving among dischargers, but could increase private sector revenues in a newly created industry.

Any policy analysis of effluent trading is likely to fail to account for some of the spillover costs, or externalities, associated with the policy adjustment. The major spillover cost would be in the form of resource requirements by administering agencies to educate industries and citizens on the true ethics, economics, legality, and management of pollution markets.

There are also other benefits that might be gained external to an analysis of effluent trading. A trade between a point-source discharger and a nonpoint-source discharger for an equivalent load is likely to have spillover benefits. For instance, construction of a retention pond at a small concentrated animal feed lot could provide habitat for wildlife and decrease sediment loading to a stream. Also, if nonpoint-source pollution data is shared with other interested parties, resources can be freed for these parties to engage in other pollution abatement activities.

Additional future water quality improvements are also likely if effluent trading is permitted between point sources. Point sources will now have an economic incentive to innovate advanced pollution control measures, which will eventually lower the price of exchanges, but will probably not result in a retreat from the water quality improvements that have been made.[9] In situations where communities in watersheds are seeking to locate new industries that must be accommodated by a stream's assimilative capacity, the benefits of ensuring that water quality problems do not inhibit the location of new enterprises can be substantial. The same is true in situations in which an indirect discharger is seeking to locate in a municipality, and the POTW has allocated its entire maximum allowable industrial loading (MAIL). Perhaps the greatest external benefit to effluent trading is the fact that agency administrators, municipality and industry representatives, and affected citizens will more likely participate in cooperative efforts to achieve water quality goals in a way that is not in conflict with other social and economic goals.

Applying the Trading Concept

Effluent trading can be easily done within a facility with multiple outfalls and between point-source dischargers. Effluent trading can also occur between point-source dischargers and nonpoint-source dischargers and between indirect dischargers that pretreat wastewater that is sent to a common POTW.

Point-Source Trading

A point-source effluent trade is simply a point-source discharger of any standard industrial classification or size faced with costly new reduction requirements beyond those specified in EPA regulations, paying another point source to treat all or a portion of this reduction requirement. The facility that accepts the requirement will likely do so at a lesser cost and will accept payment from the high-cost facility in some amount greater than its cost but less than the high-cost facility's cost.

As long as a point-source trade is not predicted to result in a violation of state water quality standards or a breach of minimum effluent standards limitations, the CWA will have been complied with fully. The anti-backsliding requirement in Section 402(o) of the CWA requires that point sources not reduce control measures. However, Section 303(d) of the CWA allows backsliding when a facility is facing high costs to treat waste at advanced levels on water quality limited streams, where it can be demonstrated that a reduction in treatment requirement will not result in a decrease in water quality.[10] Typically, point-source trades will occur within the framework of a TMDL, where a post-trading model can be run to better ensure water quality goals will be met.

Trading pollutants on a 1:1 scale will usually result in water quality improvements in situations where the effluent seller has a larger impact coefficient. If water quality improvements beyond ambient standards are thought to be less beneficial than cost savings, ratios can be used to reflect the relative values of load removals from sources with different impact coefficients. This results in mcc/a's being small for high-impact facilities and large for low-impact facilities. Any altered requirements can be remodeled and represented on the wastewater permits that are issued every five years. The time frame for contracted agreements between facilities can vary.

An effluent trade between point sources has occurred between dischargers on the Fox River in Wisconsin. The Fox River case study estimated that annual cost savings of $6.8 million could be realized from effluent trading, but the program's barriers to trading have been prohibitive of any other market activity. Point-source to point-source trading is currently being considered as an alternative to meet total maximum daily loads for copper in South San Francisco Bay.[11]

In intra-plant effluent trading, a single plant with multiple outfalls can redistribute wasteloads among their respective discharges in order to meet a facility-specific wasteload allocation cost effectively. This could also occur subsequent to an initial wasteload allocation for a facility or could be requested prior to an allocation.

At least ten iron and steel facilities have utilized the flexibility of the EPA intra-plant trading rule. They have been able to increase loadings of conventional pollutants and metals at some endpipes while decreasing a greater amount at others for pollution reductions from 10 percent to 15 percent and estimated cost savings of at least $123 million over ten years.[12]

Nonpoint-Source Trading

Nonpoint sources of water pollution, those sources that contribute to runoff pollution and are usually assigned a collective load allocation in a wasteload allocation, are excellent partners for point-source traders due to the low relative cost of treating nonpoint-source pollutants. Nonpoint sources are generally not regulated and are thus not required to reduce percentages of the total maximum daily loads set by regulation, meaning that they are currently treating waste at a very low point on their marginal control cost curves.

For example, cost discrepancies can be large between a new facility locating on a stream and an existing streamside hog farm. The new facility may be faced with reductions in excess of New Source Performance Standards (NSPS) requirements, while the hog farm employs no measures to control nutrient and carbon runoff at all. Significant cost savings might be realized if the new facility were to install structural nonpoint-source control devices such as retention ponds or grassy swales on the hog farmer's property. This could be done in lieu of meeting the advanced requirements. Engineers can calculate the anticipated removal performances of such control measures, and a margin of safety can be used to represent the relative uncertainty in the calculation. This margin of safety can be accounted for in a trading ratio, where one unit of reduction at a point source is worth some number greater than one at the nonpoint source. Relative impacts can also be represented with trading ratios.

The model can then account for that portion of the load allocation as it would for a point source. The altered requirements for the point-source facility can be reflected in its five-year permit issuance, although the contract agreement would likely be for a longer period of time. Nonpoint sources could theoretically trade with one another, but in the absence of strong regulatory requirements for these sources, trading incentives would be rare. Three nonpoint-source to point-source trading programs have been established in Colorado and one in North Carolina to achieve net reductions in nutrient loading at a lower overall cost. Eleven other programs are being considered currently nationwide.[13]

Indirect Discharger Trading

Industrial facilities that discharge to a POTW can be thought of in an effluent-trading scenario as point sources discharging into a stream. POTWs have maximum allowable headworks loadings (MAHL), much like a stream has a total maximum daily load. Industries discharging to a POTW are allocated a maximum allowable industrial loading (MAIL). Indirect dischargers have categorical limits for their effluents just like other dischargers. Beyond these limits, there are general and specific limitations that prohibit the discharge of pollutants that can pass through the POTW untreated or that can impair the POTW's ability to treat wastewater. POTWs that have limited MAILs must set local limits on indirect discharges. Usually, the MAIL is divided by the total industrial flow for each pollutant. This concentration is the local limit. Each indirect discharger is required to meet this limit.

Just as is the case with point-source direct dischargers, indirect dischargers have different marginal control costs for meeting advanced limits. If one facility can reach a concentration limit at a lesser cost than another, effluent trading allows the high-cost facility to pay the low-cost facility to treat its portion of the MAIL. The trades are reflected in POTW-issued permits. These permits are also generally reviewed every five years prior to the POTW's basin-wide reallocation.[14] The town of Oxford POTW in North Carolina currently negotiates loadings with its indirect dischargers following the establishment of a MAIL. Although not a true trading program, this municipality has recognized the potential benefits of a more cost-effective allocation of its MAIL.[15]

The ability of market forces to allocate resources in a cost-effective way is well established. The allowance of effluent trading between sources of water pollution would hardly result in a market of pure competition and perfect information, but significant cost savings and water quality improvements can be realized if effluent trades are allowed to be made. Control costs and relative impacts have been demonstrated to vary significantly between sources of water pollution in a watershed. Effluent trading allows these differences to be minimized, thereby freeing resources for water quality improvements or other endeavors by industries, municipalities, and consumers. The benefits of effluent trading that are external to a typical analysis are also thought to be significant. Allowing point sources, nonpoint sources, and indirect dischargers the flexibility to improve water quality more cost effectively is a policy adjustment with large overall benefits and low costs.

Pee Dee River Case Study

A case study is presented that investigates some of the potential benefits of effluent trading in the Pee Dee River Basin in South Carolina. The five-year wasteload reallocation for the Pee Dee River Basin was to be conducted in 1996, and a TMDL was to be established pursuant to Section 303(d) of the CWA. The Pee Dee River is water quality limited for dissolved oxygen (DO) at a particular stream segment down-stream from the city of Florence, river segment 34. This is the river's DO sag point. The location of dischargers and the sag point are shown in Figure 8.4. The study identified which dischargers had the greatest impacts on the river's DO sag point and which facilities were faced with relatively high costs to meet assigned effluent limits. These estimates were then considered to determine what mix of effluent limitations, within the confines of CWA provisions, could achieve an instream DO equal to or greater than 5.0 mg/l, the state's ambient standard, at the least cost. Stone Container, the town of Marion, Smithfield Foods, and the city of Florence were all identified as potential trading parties.

How the Study Was Conducted

The standard water quality modeling procedure, Qual2E, run at 7Q10 (seven-day, ten-year low flow conditions) was employed to predict instream pollutant concentrations resulting from the anticipated upcoming wasteload allocation loading scenario. Relative contributions to DO depletion at the river's DO sag point were obtained for each point-source discharger by "turning off" the dischargers' modeled flow and observing the rise in DO. Total DO depletion at the most critical river segment (34,16) was 2.06 mg/l, calculated by adding the individual mg/l DO rises with each discharger turned off. (Refer to figure 8.4 for modeled discharger locations and sag point.)

Each discharger's modeled impact on sag point estimate was calculated by dividing the rise in DO with its discharge turned off by 2.06 mg/l. The percent below 40 CFR guidelines for required BOD5 and NH3-N removal was determined for each discharger by consulting current draft permit rationales and 40 CFR.

Figure 8.4 Pee Dee River Point-Source Dischargers

Pee Dee River Dischargers
Proposed 1996

Cost information was then sought for those dischargers determined to be candidates for trading. Effluent buyers are those facilities that are being required to reduce loading beyond 40 CFR guidelines that generally have low relative impacts on the sag point and relatively high costs for meeting advanced limits. Sellers are those facilities that have a significant impact on the sag point that can meet further loading reductions at a lower relative cost. No cost information was available for reducing only NH3-N.

Stone was identified as an effluent seller. Marion, Smithfield, and Florence were identified as effluent buyers. Cost estimates for meeting advanced BOD5 removal requirements were furnished by engineers at these facilities, with the exception of Florence.

Florence's cost for meeting advanced limits was reported to be minimal initially but was anticipated to possibly rise an unknown amount in the latter part of the five-year period. EPA furnished a cost test spreadsheet with an estimate for $/lb BOD5 removal expenditures associated with going from secondary to advanced secondary requirements (30 mg/l BOD5 to 20 mg/l BOD5). The figure was $.48/lb (annualized 1995 dollars). This is thought to be a reasonable estimate due to the fact that the town of Marion estimate was $.50/lb. Florence was required to reduce from 30 mg/l to 24 mg/l. The number used as the cost estimate for Florence's reduction requirement was $.12/lb.. This figure was arrived at by calculating half of $.48/lb to represent the approximate 50 percent of advanced secondary requirement, and half of the resulting $.24/lb to account for the $0.00/lb estimate for the first 2.5 year period of the requirement. Increasing marginal costs should result in this figure being a low estimate.

Stone Container has a very unusual treatment process. Stone employs a 1,600-acre lagoon to treat the waste they generate. Stone believes that they could simply utilize the lagoon's three feet of freeboard to treat the extra wasteload requirement that they would sell. The cost of doing this was reported to be negligible.

Initially, marginal control cost matrices were requested from facility engineers for each endpipe, detailing the $/lb for removing increments of BOD5 and NH3-N from their waste streams. These data did not seem to be readily available, as no marginal control cost estimates were submitted. General estimates on $/lb BOD removal from EPA effluent guidelines development documents and industry technical documents were considered, but, with the exception of Florence, were not used due to the uncertainty of the applicability of these numbers to these facilities.

The Results

The benefits of effluent trading on the Pee Dee River include pollution control cost savings to dischargers and improved water quality. The costs of effluent trading in the basin consist of the South Carolina Department of Health and

Environmental Control's (DHEC) additional administrative costs, facilities' engineering and opportunity costs, and any brokerage or contract fees. The study found that the net benefit of allowing effluent trading on the Pee Dee River under this modeled scenario was roughly $1.6 million in cost savings over the five year permit reissuing period and a 3 percent increase in DO above the ambient standard at the river's sag point. The model was run to confirm that the market-driven wasteload allocation would not result in a violation of the ambient standard on any river segment (refer to table 8.3).

Table 8.3. 1996 Proposed Pee Dee River BOD Wasteload Allocations

Buyer/ Seller (B/S)	Pre-Trading BODU(mg/l)	Post-Trading BODU (mg/l)	Savings from Increment Change($/yr)
Smithfield(B)	23.0	101.7	+ 210,787
Marion(B)	30.0	45.0	+ 76,285
Florence(B)	36.0	45.0	+ 32,850
Stone(S)	180.8	131.1	- 0

Total Cost Savings: $210,787 + $76,285 + $32,850 - $0 = $319,922/yr (5 yr) = $1,599,610
Administrative Costs: $28,000/yr / 1950 hrs/yr = $14.36/hr (67.5 hr) = $969
Brokerage Costs: $21,000/yr / 1950 hrs/yr = $10.77/hr (37.5 hr) = $404
Net Cost Savings: $1,599,610 - $969 - $404 = $1,598,237
Net Water Quality Benefit: 3% Dissolved oxygen increase above ambient standard at sag point.

Three cost savings trades were identified. Trading resulted in Florence paying Stone some amount greater than $0.00 to treat 750 lbs/day of BOD5, Marion paying Stone some amount greater than $0.00 to treat 418 lbs/day of BOD5, and Smithfield paying Stone some amount greater than $0.00 to treat 600 lbs/day of BOD5. The scenario entails Stone receiving some amount less than $32,850/year from Florence, $76,285/year from Marion, and $210,787/year from Smithfield. The remodeled inputs for BODU for Florence, Marion, and Smithfield were 45 mg/l, 45 mg/l, and 101.72 mg/l, respectively. Florence's and Marion's post-trading limits are those required by the secondary treatment rule, and Smithfield's limits reflect NSPS. Stone's load was further reduced to 131.08 mg/l, which is 47 percent below BPT (Best Practicable Control Technology). The model run reflecting the traded loads resulted in a DO rise at river segment (34,16) from 5.00 mg/l to 5.15 mg/l (5.14 mg/l slightly upstream).

DHEC managers' time to produce model runs was estimated to be 7.5 man hours, and permitting time for revisions was estimated to be 15 man hours x 4 (for

4 permits). Salary calculated was $28,000/year at 37.5-hour weeks. DHEC cost for effluent trading on the Pee Dee River was estimated to be $969.

Facility costs for trading are considered to be $0 in this scenario, because cost estimates were not arrived at as the result of any original calculations. Typically, there will be engineering costs associated with dischargers calculating their own marginal or incremental control costs, and possibly opportunity costs associated with these calculations and time spent making inquiries about other facilities' costs. These more refined cost estimates can increase or decrease net benefits.

Brokerage time for this very simple analysis was estimated to be 37.5 man-hours. Salary calculated was $21,000/year. The brokerage fee for effluent trading on the Pee Dee River was estimated to be $404. Contract fees are not estimated in this analysis.

Summary

Two of these facilities, IBP and Smithfield, will likely not locate in South Carolina. It is doubtful that this is due exclusively to their wasteload allocations. However, if the facilities were to locate on the Pee Dee River, according to Pete Rogers of Marion County Development, they would generate $1.6 million in tax revenues and invest $160 million in land and capital. This illustrates that accommodating such enterprises in the future with the option of effluent trading could have substantial external benefits.

Other facilities have requested limits revisions based on facility modifications since the time of this model. Cost savings estimates from facility engineers were not the result of rigorous engineering estimates, and the engineering and brokerage costs are arguably low (although relatively insignificant). The case study was not intended to provide a true dollar figure for benefits associated with effluent trading in the Pee Dee River Basin so that trading would be immediately undertaken. The study aimed to illustrate the ease in which such future trading can be facilitated and the potential benefits of effluent trading. It is noteworthy that a model run confirmed that IBP could have also traded with Stone to reduce 72 percent of the 77 percent below guideline NH3-N loading IBP was initially allocated, and a modeled standards violation would still not have occurred.

It may seem that the simple solution to minimizing costs in a situation such as this is to require low-cost facilities like Stone to reduce all of the necessary loading. Some, probably not Stone, would agree that this is also an equitable wasteload allocation given the circumstances. But, DHEC does not generally have this cost information. And, even if it did, this approach sends a message to all dischargers that if they have or install low-cost, highly effective control technologies, they will be forced to carry a disproportionate burden in meeting state water quality goals. This type of economic disincentive for pollution reduction is what most modern policy analysts are attempting to remedy in the CWA.

Other such case studies of point-source to point-source trading of BOD have found similar or higher annual cost savings: Fox River, $6.8 million; Delaware River, $46,000-$9.2 million; Holston River, $3.7-$27.2 million; Houston Ship Channel, $4.56 million; Lake Lena Run, $1.34-$1.66 million; Mohawk River, $560-$970 thousand; Willamette River, $340 thousand-$1.4 million; Upper Hudson River, $40-$450 thousand.[16]

Final Thoughts on Effluent Trading Policy in South Carolina

Allowing those who contribute to the water pollution problem the flexibility to exchange pollution reduction requirements among themselves might seem to many to be a step in the wrong direction toward a cleaner environment and a higher quality of life. In South Carolina, many people may feel that polluters simply do not have the right, moral or legal, to buy and sell portions of the state's water quality. A closer look into the economics of effluent trading may convince some that they already inadvertently support this approach to water pollution control on normative grounds. On legal grounds, the right to trade pollution reduction requirements in the United States is already established in common law and statutory law.

Ethics

As evidenced in many South Carolina policies, the state's citizens largely have an anthropocentric view of moral rights. In other words, South Carolinians do not ascribe moral rights to beings other than humans. Many statesmen hunt and fish and farm animals and plants, and feel that in doing so they are right by God or their own sense of reason. The biocentric view that humans are only an equally functioning part of a world with no species-specific center is not prevalent in South Carolina.

With respect to water pollution, human health risk is the major factor in determining acceptable levels of toxic pollutants. Conventional water pollutants that deplete oxygen in streams are allowed at levels that will not result in significant ecological damage, but the rights of individual organisms that suffer the ill effects of this allowable level of pollution are not recognized. The only rights that are recognized with respect to conventional pollutants are the rights of citizens to an abundant supply of surface water in which to drink, fish, or recreate. These rights are considered maintained when waters are not impacted to the point that these uses will not be sustained. Beyond this, the only moral right a South Carolina citizen might claim with respect to a stream's assimilative capacity is the right to utilize it for the accommodation of domestic and industrial wastewater.

If the majority of South Carolinians feel they have a moral right to zero discharge from wastewater treatment plants, they have not made themselves heard. Those who do take this stance and also seek to maximize their own economic well beings may have a conflicting ethic.

Economics

Beyond the protection of certain implicit moral and legal rights, many South Carolinians would agree that a good policy adjustment is one that maximizes the well-being of the state as a whole. This utilitarian ethic is the basis for much of the economic policy analysis that is done to determine the most appropriate ways to spend tax dollars.

Most policies are considered desirable if rights are not infringed on, and the marginal costs and marginal benefits of the policy are equal or further equated. In water pollution control, state ambient water quality standards are based less on monetized benefit estimates and are grounded more on less quantitative criteria of acceptable stream conditions, such as "fishable and swimmable." This is to say that achieving economic efficiency is not the direct goal of water pollution control policy. In fact, if economic efficiency was the policy goal of the CWA, some studies predict that water pollution expenditures might decrease in an attempt to equate marginal costs and marginal benefits.[17]

Most would agree, however, that given acceptance of a characteristic goal for each water body, it would be sensible to minimize the cost of achieving this goal. This would free resources for other endeavors, like employing wastewater engineers to remediate Superfund sites or make infrastructure improvements. The cost-effective allocation of resources is the least-cost way to achieve a specified goal. Effluent trading allows for this more cost-effective allocation of resources.

In economic terms, policies with Pareto optimal outcomes are those that, after an initial allocation of resources, provide benefits to some without reducing the utility of others. The normative Pareto Principle is a Pareto efficient policy that does not allow for the infringement of any moral rights. A policy adjustment that does not infringe on widely accepted moral rights but can provide benefits to some without detracting from others, and can do so in such a way as to have some of the benefits redistributed to those who do not gain, is arguably a good policy adjustment. Much of the ethics and economics that national and state laws are founded on embody the normative Pareto Principle with a subsequent redistribution of benefits.

Effluent trading exemplifies this normative Pareto Principle in that, following an initial wasteload allocation, no one suffers losses but some make gains. Those cost savings gains of municipalities and industries can be redistributed to affected citizens in the form of marginal water quality improvements.

Law

Many characterize effluent trading as the buying and selling of pollution rights. The terms in which the policy adjustment is characterized are important for reasons of public perception, but to the judges, legislators, and administrators the legality of such an adjustment are of more concern.

There have been numerous common-law settlements of disputes over citizens' rights to clean water versus industries' rights to maximize profits on their own properties. The courts have set a general precedent. Above a floor of protection of certain basic entitlements, the extent that streams can be polluted is directly related to the relative costs and benefits of the varying levels of pollution. In essence, with the exception of streams already designated as outstanding resource or shellfish harvesting waters, this means that wastewater dischargers are entitled to utilize the assimilative capacity of a stream. In other words, at this time the courts view the zero discharge goal as prohibitively expensive.

In addition to this, there is a popular strain of legal scholarship associated with the University of Chicago School of Economics that views the proper assignment of rights as that which promotes the most efficient use of resources. In other words, these scholars feel that if an entity has a legal right that is not being used in its most productive sense, others should have the legal right to purchase it.[18]

Common-law precedent has a resounding effect on administrative law judges' interpretation of statutes. In interpreting the legality of incorporating an effluent-trading policy into the current framework of South Carolina water pollution control policy provided by the CWA and S.C. Pollution Control Act, three considerations would likely influence a judge's decision. Canons of statutory construction, statutory interpretations with common -law characteristics, and pre-emption-ouster of state common law by federal public law would be determinants.

Canons of statutory construction are determinations by administrative law judges regarding the meanings of statutory language. Determinations are based on findings of meanings of other similar statutes. If a precedent has been set in the rulings on a sister statute, such as is the relationship between the Clean Air Act (CAA) and CWA, statutory interpretation with common-law characteristics would likely yield rulings similar to that of the sister statute.[19] A judge ruling on a state-sponsored contest of the national interpretation of a federal public law would likely rule to oust the state common-law interpretation in favor of the established federal law.[20]

Given the opportunity, it is unlikely that an administrative law judge would somehow find the allowance of effluent trading in South Carolina illegal. There are no state or federal statutory prohibitions to effluent trading, and no special act of state congress is necessary to implement such a policy. At the federal level, market incentives for water pollution control have bipartisan support and are likely to be incorporated into the CWA's reauthorization. Several other states in the

United States have employed effluent-trading programs successfully and without contention. State administrators, municipality and industrial representatives, and other private citizens are the final elements in the policy process of implementing an effluent-trading program in South Carolina.

Water Quality Management

Many state administrators might agree that there are no ethical or legal obstacles to accommodating effluent trading in South Carolina, but, most would also agree that management resources are scarce, and management by objective strategies are labor intensive and prohibit additional activities.

As an incremental adjustment to current monitoring, modeling, permitting, and wasteload allocations, an effluent-trading program in its simplest form could be implemented with minimal personnel resources. If point sources are allowed to trade wasteload allocations after an initial load is allocated, models can be rerun to ensure water quality goals are met, and draft permits can be revised. The marginal effort should not be in excess of one modeler and two permitter days per trade. If most trades are only made every five years, and significant cost savings and water quality improvements can come out of every basin-wide reallocation involving effluent trading, such a program should easily be self-perpetuating and could possibly gain substantial financial backing.

Most South Carolinians seem to have a baseline anthropocentric environmental ethic above which they seek to maximize their own economic well-being without detracting from their neighbors' respective utilities. The allowance of the use of the assimilative capacities of streams and, furthermore, the ability to utilize it at least cost is consistent with South Carolina ethics and economics. Many judges view the cost-effective allocation of resources as a function of public law. Judges also look to sister statutes or federal law for statutory interpretations. Given the well-established trading program of the CAA amendments of 1990 and the growing number of effluent-trading programs currently being implemented in states, it is unlikely that an effluent-trading program in South Carolina could be contested successfully.

Conclusion

In reviewing South Carolina water pollution control policy, it can be argued that a policy adjustment by DHEC administrators to allow for effluent trading in South Carolina watersheds would be consistent with the wishes of the citizens the agency aims to protect. South Carolina ethics, economics, and law support more cost-effective ways to achieve state goals, including state water quality goals.

The only real contention to such a policy change is that state resources are not available to facilitate trading. The case study demonstrates what little resources are necessary to implement a very basic effluent-trading program. A more elaborate or proactive effluent trading program, one that encompasses nonpoint sources and pretreating industries, would likely yield even greater relative benefits. Such a program will never occur if an initial effort is not put forward.

Given the current attitude surrounding water pollution control at the national level, it seems inevitable that South Carolina will eventually have to develop an effluent-trading program. At the present time, South Carolina has the opportunity to lead the nation in innovative water pollution control policy and demonstrate to other states that environmental agencies, municipalities, industries, and citizens can cooperate to improve water quality while promoting economic development.

Notes

1. M. Luttner, *President Clinton's Clean Water Act Initiative: Costs and Benefits*, http://www.epa.gov/docs/epajrnal/summer94/12.txt.html/, 1996. The EPA study estimate of $700 million to $7.5 billion is based on 50 percent participation in trading.

2. U.S. Department of Commerce: Bureau of the Census, *Current Industrial Reports: Pollution Abatement Costs and Expenditures, 1991*, 1993. U.S. water pollution abatement capital and operating costs (including payments to governmental units for sewerage services) in 1991 totaled $9.16 billion. South Carolina water pollution abatement capital and operating costs (including payments to governmental units for sewerage services) in 1991 totaled $186.2 million.

3. U.S. Environmental Protection Agency, *Draft Framework for Watershed-Based Trading*, 1996.

4. Ibid, 3.

5. D. Stephenson, *Water and Wastewater Systems* (Amsterdam: Elsevier, 1988).

6. T. Tietenberg, *Environmental and Natural Resource Economics* (New York: Harper Collins, 1992).

7. G. E. Lake, W. M. Hanneman, and S. M. Oster, *Who Pays for Clean Water?* (Boulder: Westview Press, 1979). Figure is projected in 1985 dollars.

8. U.S. Environmental Protection Agency, *The Economics of Clean Water*, 1972.

9. CWA anti-backsliding requirements will prevent water quality degradation.

10. U.S. Environmental Protection Agency, *The Economics of Clean Water*, 1972, 3.

11. Ibid., 3.

12. Ibid., 3.

13. Ibid., 3.

14. Ibid., 3.

15. Ibid., 3.

16. Industrial Economics Inc., *Benefits and Feasibility of Effluent Trading*

between Point Sources; An Analysis in Support of Clean Water Act Reauthorization, prepared for EPA, (1992).

17. T. L. Anderson and D. R. Leal, *Free Market Environmentalism* (San Francisco: Pacific Research Institute for Public Policy, 1991). Anderson and Leal cite a 1985 study with benefit estimates ranging from $3.8 to $18.4 billion and costs of $15 to $20 billion.

18. Z. L. Plater, R. H. Abrams, and W. Goldfarb, *Environmental Law and Policy: Nature, Law, and Society* (St. Paul: West Publishing Co., 1992).

19. Pollution trading became a part of statutory law with the 1990 amendments to the Clean Air Act. Bubbles, netting, and offsets allowed facilities located or locating in areas in which ambient standards were not being attained to buy and sell reduction requirements.

20. Z. L. Plater, R. H. Abrams, and W. Goldfarb, *Environmental Law and Policy: Nature, Law, and Society* (St. Paul: West Publishing Co., 1992).

References

Anderson, T.L., and D.R. Leal. 1991. *Free Market Environmentalism.* San Francisco: Pacific Research Institute for Public Policy.

Industrial Economics Inc. 1992. *Benefits and Feasibility of Effluent Trading between Point Sources; An Analysis in Support of Clean Water Act Reauthorization*, prepared for Environmental Protection Agency.

Lake, G. E., W. M. Hanneman, and S. M. Oster. 1979. *Who Pays for Clean Water?* Boulder: Westview Press.

Luttner, M. 1996. *President Clinton's Clean Water Act Initiative: Costs and Benefits*, http://www.epa.gov/docs/epajrnal/summer94/12.txt.html/.

Plater, Z. J., R. H. Abrams, and W. Goldfarb. 1992. *Environmental Law and Policy: Nature, Law, and Society*, St. Paul: West Publishing Co.

Stephenson, D. 1988. *Water and Wastewater Systems.* Amsterdam: Elsevier.

Tietenberg, T. 1992. *Environmental and Natural Resource Economics.* New York: HarperCollins.

U.S. Department of Commerce, Bureau of the Census. 1991. *Current Industrial Reports: Pollution Abatement Costs and Expenditures.*

U.S. Environmental Protection Agency. 1996. *Draft Framework for Watershed-Based Trading.*

U.S. Environmental Protection Agency. 1996. *The Economics of Clean Water*, Vol. I.

Chapter 9

An Economic Analysis of the Interaction between Golf Courses and the Environment

Alec Watson

Introduction

There is nothing abnormal about an environmental issue creating controversy. In fact, it seems unusual when two groups' differences over environmental practices fail to generate public debate. Most issues involve questionable methods of water pollution, air pollution, waste disposal, or depletion of natural resources. A typical scenario includes an environmentalist's calls for the offending party to adopt a particular solution that will reduce or eliminate the specific environmental problem. What is not as common is an issue that encompasses all forms of pollution, yet has no definite solution. Such a diverse problem would appear to apply only to some mysterious organism or hazardous practice that endangers human lives.

Obviously, a golf course is not the first topic that comes to mind when searching for an issue that fits this description. A closer look reveals that golf courses have the potential to do such harm. How can a seemingly simple game have such negative consequences? Do golf courses actually have such an adverse impact on the environment? If so, why is there no explicit solution, and what can be done to minimize this impact?

This chapter addresses these questions and more. The next section examines the nature of the conflict between golf courses and environmentalists, including a look at why this friction has emerged. The following section focuses on the new methods developed by golf course operators designed to reduce the negative environmental consequences that result from building and maintaining a golf course. Included in that section is a close examination of a golf course that is dedicated to maintaining and improving environmental quality at its facilities. An economic analysis of the entire situation forms the next section. It applies economic thinking to each side of the story in determining motives and actions. The benefits and costs of environmental cleanup are considered in an effort to ascertain an "optimal" level of pollution for golf courses. Next is an overview of an important program that is changing the way both golf course operators and environmentalists behave. That section is followed by some general thoughts on the situation, containing some proposals designed to resolve this conflict. Finally, some brief thoughts on the interaction of golf courses and the environment conclude the chapter.

Establishing The Problem

When considering golf and pollution, one must first decide what, if any, problem exists. In the United States alone, there are over 15,000 golf courses, covering nearly 1.5 million acres of land.[1] Because they are found in so many locales, it is certain that golf courses have an impact on the environment. What is not as certain is whether this impact is positive or negative. Although golf courses have existed in the United States since 1888 when the St. Andrews Golf Club was founded in Yonkers, New York,[2] concerns expressed by people who felt courses were harming the environment were not heard until the 1970s.[3] These initial concerns stemmed from a major drought in the western states, particularly California. Critics complained that golf courses were utilizing scarce water resources that would better serve elsewhere. Once the subject was first broached, course management practices across America became more scrutinized.[4] In the following years, these four crucial aspects of golf course management practices have been examined in search of their environmental repercussions:

- the potential for water pollution from runoff containing pesticides, herbicides, and fertilizers;

- the use of irrigation where water resources are scarce;

- the tendency of golf courses to displace and eradicate wildlife, erase valuable agricultural lands, and devastate ecosystems; and

- the impact of golf course practices on golfers.[5]

Chemical and Pesticide Misuse

When people think of potential hazards associated with golf courses, damage to water sources from chemical runoff is the first issue to come to mind. A survey of environmental groups (including the EPA, Sierra Club, Audubon Society, etc.) in the February 1996 issue of *Golf Course Management* revealed that pesticide/herbicide/fertilizer use on golf courses was indeed a critical matter to these groups. Typical among complaints from environmental activists was the comment from Diana Post, executive director of the Rachel Carson Council:

> The maintenance of most courses is tied, by choice, to the use of synthetic chemicals for fertilization and pest control. In practice, many of them prioritize the technological support system over the ecosystem support services in order to maintain turf areas unnaturally smooth and green.[6]

Mark Massara of the Sierra Club is even more critical of golf course management practices. He asserts that today's beautiful courses do not come without cost. "Use of pesticides and fertilizers has been taken for granted," says Massara. "Until very recently, use of dangerous chemicals was unrestrained until all weeds were gone, all disfavored animals disappeared."[7] Though there is very little evidence linking golf course mismanagement to water pollution, several fish and bird kills have occurred, and many environmental groups continue to criticize courses.[8] All sides agree that potential problems exist if pesticides, herbicides, and fertilizers are not used properly.

Too Much Irrigation?

Irrigation systems are another controversial aspect of golf course management. Some irrigation is essential in the ordinary maintenance of almost any golf course. Nearly all greens are irrigated, as are most tees. In addition, there is a growing number of fairways being irrigated, and the trend is to apply the same techniques to roughs.[9] Water is obviously a scarce resource, especially in some western states experiencing swift population growth combined with extended drought. Therefore, a premium is placed on water usage. Some are concerned about the possibility of too much irrigation. Consider the comments of James Beard, author of *Turf Management for Golf Courses*:

> Unfortunately, irrigation practices are widely abused, misused, and mis-understood. Many golfers tend to rate the golf course superintendent's abilities by how green the turf is maintained. Too frequently a lush, green golf course is expected at all times; however, such a turf is not necessarily healthy and wear tolerant. Proper irrigation practices are essential for good playing conditions and are of greater concern than whether irrigation produces a lush, green cover.[10]

Beard raises an important issue; golfers seem to demand a splendid, green surface throughout the entire course. Attempting to satisfy this demand can lead to over-irrigation, which can be detrimental to all parties. Too much irrigation is not healthy for the turf; the practices can result in the misuse of valuable water resources.

Golf Course Siting

The siting and construction of new golf courses is currently the most hotly debated topic.   Just as the inappropriate utilization of pesticides and other chemicals originally raised the ire of environmental groups, the manner in which new courses are being built has done the same.   Again, Mike Massara expressed the Sierra Club's opinion on this situation:

> While the desire of golfers to recreate in clean, open-space environments is laudable, their cookie-cutter approach to construction of courses throughout the 19th century (sic) has cost future generations untold losses of sensitive habitats and endangered species. In particular, we hope to eliminate future loss of habitat in sensitive coastal areas, wetlands habitats, fragile deserts, rain forests, mountains and prime agricultural soils.[11]

Massara also contended that all land is not suitable for golf courses, and he expressed his discontent at the "unreal, Disneyland-like beauty" for which many courses seem to aspire.[12] Because of the recent boom in golf course development in the United States (over 2,000 built in the past decade), it is certain that careful attention needs to be paid to the siting and construction of these new courses, particularly to the effect on the wildlife habitat and plant species in the area.[13]

Excess Golfer Exposure to Pesticide

The fourth and final point raised by environmentalists is about the effect of certain course management practices on golfers. Foremost among these concerns is the potential for harm to golfers from exposure to pesticides. In any given round of golf, an individual will come into close contact with the turf in a number of ways: through the ball, clubs, shoes, tees, or by picking up loose grass or leaves. Very few golfers know with any certainty how the course they are playing applies pesticides, herbicides, or fertilizers, and some courses are surely more liberal applicators than others. With so much contact between an individual and a chemically treated surface, there is good reason for apprehension on behalf of any golfer.

Currently Implemented Solutions

Currently, vast strides are being made to ensure that golf courses are operating in harmony with the environment. Across the country, hundreds of golf course superintendents are experimenting with both old and new methods that should allay the concerns of environmental groups everywhere. The first issue involves the misuse of fertilizers, pesticides and other chemicals, and the potential for damage to the water supply.

Fertilizers

The fertilizer issue has to do with nutrient runoff contaminating both groundwater and surface water. Most turf fertilizers contain nitrogen (nitrates), which fosters leaf growth and green color, and phosphorus (phosphates), which enhances root development. To begin with, the amount of fertilizer that most golf courses use is much less than the amount that most people perceive. In addition, studies have shown that golf course turf has a remarkable ability to absorb water and these nutrients. In a series of tests at Pennsylvania State University, turf saturated with both fertilizers and pesticides was subjected to heavy rainfall in an attempt to determine the level at which runoff and/or leaching will occur.[14] Runoff from the tested turf was unmeasurable until the slopes had been irrigated at over twice the intensity of a 100- to 125-year storm. Runoff was also collected from an induced rainfall of six inches per hour, an extremely improbable circumstance. In each case, the nutrient concentration in both runoff and leachate were well below the public drinking water standards. Golf course turf is by no means the open soil of a farm, which is somewhat prone to surface water runoff and groundwater leaching.[15]

Best Management Practices

Regardless of these findings, many golf courses are taking additional steps to ensure that their fertilizer use has no negative impact on the local water supply. Attempts by golf-course managers to further minimize the amount of nutrients in runoff and leachate are known as Best Management Practices (BMPs). Courses have BMPs for the design and construction phase, as well as the operational phase.[16]

BMPs vary from site to site, depending on the topography and other geographic features of the course. Design and construction of BMPs include:

- a closed drainage system that catches much of the runoff from rainfall and returns it to the course's irrigation reservoir, eliminating any chance of that runoff leaving the site;

- planning construction around seasonal rains in an effort to control erosion;

- further limiting erosion with silt fences and silt basins;

- choosing a turf grass that is well adapted to the climate and resistant to drought;

- strategically placing putting greens, which call for the most care, in areas not prone to turf disease; and

- designing an irrigation system that is flexible enough to handle variations in turf need.[17]

In addition to those BMPs implemented during the design and construction phases, many courses have adopted operational BMPs that are in effect throughout the daily activities of the golf course. These include:

- carefully label all fertilizers, pesticides, and other chemicals;

- store these chemicals in an area that can easily contain any potential spills; and

- irrigate only up to the amount required by the plants, adjusting this amount for any rainfall.[18]

Although fertilizer use on golf courses has been criticized as a potential cause of surface water and groundwater pollution, recent studies have shown that these fears are likely unfounded. Nevertheless, numerous golf courses have implemented a series of best management practices in hopes of eliminating the risk of nutrient runoff and leachate in the water supply.

Pesticides

Contrary to popular opinion, pesticides are not intended for aesthetic use. According to the Golf Course Superintendents Association of America (GCSAA), pesticides are designed to "ensure a healthy playing surface for the game" and to "protect a valuable and ecologically important piece of land."[19] The image of a greenskeeper flooding his entire course with pesticides is utterly inaccurate. According to a 1990 GCSAA survey, 97 percent of golf courses managed by GCSAA members employed at least one licensed or certified pesticide applicator.[20]

Integrated Pest Management

The most popular practice regarding turf management today is known as Integrated Pest Management (IPM). Among the applicants for the GCSAA's 1996 Environmental Steward Awards, 92 percent used some sort of an IPM program, the highest of any idea or program.[21] Ted Horton, Vice President of Resource

Management at Pebble Beach Company, describes Integrated Pest Management as "a management plan that utilizes a variety of control measures to keep turfgrass pest populations below levels that are economically and aesthetically damaging, without creating a hazard to people and the environment."[22] This procedure involves targeting and eliminating pests through a careful inspection of the course, without random, haphazard pesticide application.   Horton's Pebble Beach Company takes seven steps to implement a successful IPM program.

1. Choose grasses for your tees, fairways, greens, and roughs that are least susceptible to insects, drought, and disease.

2. Ensure continuous research of pest activity on your course, including checks of the responsiveness of the turf to previous control procedures.

3. Implement sound cultural control methods, such as mowing and irrigation methods, traffic control, pH management, etc.

4. If possible, use natural biological control methods rather than chemical procedures.

5. "Spray only when necessary": when pesticides are used, attempt to employ those that are least harmful to the environment, i.e., less toxic and less mobile.

6. The location of pesticide application should be closely monitored.

7. Any areas prone to ground or surface water contamination should be identified and closely supervised.[23]

While these guidelines are fairly general and should be kept in mind with any IPM program, the design of an IPM for any one course is an individualistic process that relies on an examination of the characteristics and features inherent to that particular golf course. Aside from eliminating the use of pesticides, which is an inefficient and unrealistic option for most courses, the best way to minimize their potential harm is likely to be through the careful development and implementation of an Integrated Pest Management System.

Water Conservation Efforts

The second concern of environmentalists discussed earlier was the abuses of irrigation, in light of the fact that water is a scarce resource. Water is valuable, and many courses are looking into ways to better utilize their water supply. One such method is through the development of grasses that can thrive with less water. With this goal in mind, the USGA has sponsored turf grass breeding programs at eleven universities across the country. The results have been encouraging, and many of these new turfs should begin to appear in the market shortly.[24]

Another solution involves a more careful study of the irrigation system. Computerized irrigation systems are emerging as a viable alternative. By combining such a system with an on-site weather station, a superintendent can avoid watering the course immediately before rainfall.[25] In addition, irrigating only to the plant roots can limit ground and surface water runoff while conserving water.[26]

One of the biggest steps toward greater water conservation is being taken by courses that use treated wastewater effluent for irrigation. Wastewater effluent has several nutrients that can benefit turfgrass, and it costs significantly less than potable water. This is water that may ordinarily be wasted because it cannot be used for agricultural purposes, but is perfectly fit for turf.[27] Golf course superintendents face budget constraints and therefore recognize the value of the water they use. Responsible irrigation practices, including all of the above, are being utilized today to help golf courses get the most out of their water supply.

The Environmental Principles

As the number of golf courses being built continues to grow, more attention is being placed on the construction and siting of these courses. Environmentalists realize that their influence can be larger when concentrating on the development of newer courses rather than attempting to change existing ones. Partly in response to this pressure, the Center for Resource Management, *Golf Digest* Magazine, the National Wildlife Federation, and the Pebble Beach Resort Company decided to hold a summit on topics concerning the interaction between the environment and golf. With representatives from many powerful golfing and environmental organizations in attendance, the first meeting was held at Pebble Beach in January 1995. The group decided to pen a set of principles that would act as guidance in the planning, building, and management of a golf course. This document, known as the *Environmental Principles for Golf Courses in the United States*, was adopted at the Second Conference on Golf and the Environment in March 1996.[28]

These principles described many ways that can and are being used to plan a golf course that works in harmony with the environment. Developers are encouraged to work with local groups in the community and government to discuss the environmental impact of the new course while it is still in the planning stage. All sites should be looked at carefully by experts from the golf and environmental industries, and this feedback should be weighed heavily in the development of the golf course. Special attention should be paid to sensitive environmental areas, such as wetlands or habitats of endangered species, plants or animals. Developers are encouraged to enhance the environmental aspects of their course, and not just accept the status quo. Another idea that has long been supported by environmental groups is the building of golf courses on reclaimed land, land that has been previously scarred by sites such as landfills, mines, or quarries.[29] The possibility of constructing golf courses on old landfill sites is covered in-depth later. These and other procedures are being employed across the country every day, and newer courses are considering their surroundings like never before.

Human Risk from Pesticides

Though it is commonly thought by some to be a problem, a golfer's safety from pesticides on the course is a non-issue. The testing of a new pesticide is extremely rigorous. Before new pesticides hit the market, the product is put through a series of up to 120 different tests and studies by the EPA. These tests can last up to ten years and cost upwards of $50 million.[30] A University of Florida study attempted to show how minimal a golfer's risk of harmful exposure to pesticides actually is. This risk assessment was done on putting greens treated with pesticides. Their assumptions were:

- The golfer kneels on every green to align putts.
- He handles golf grips that have been laid on the green.
- He contacts the soles of his leather shoes when cleaning them.
- He cleans his ball after every hole by licking it.
- The greens are sprayed every day with three insecticides.
- The golfer plays 365 days a year for seventy years.

Even with these assumptions, the golfer would have received only one-third of the safe dosage for a lifetime set by the EPA after seventy years.[31] Once the pesticides dry and are watered in, there is almost no chance that they could be rubbed off.[32] It is clear that the chance of a golfer being harmed due to contact with pesticides on a golf course is minuscule, at best.

The Links at Spanish Bay: A Model of Excellence

On California's Monterey Peninsula in the Del Monte Forest lies a prime example of a golf course working in harmony with the environment. The Links at Spanish Bay, owned and operated by the Pebble Beach Company, is a golf course run with a commitment to improving the environment. This 18-hole course situated on the Pacific Ocean was recognized in 1994 with the National Environmental Steward Award from the GCSAA. The environmental efforts were evident from the start, as the course was built on an old sand mine in 1987. The turf for the entire course was planted with the idea of minimizing the amount of water needed while still being able to tolerate the salty ocean breezes. Existing sand from the mining plant was used throughout the course, wherever possible.[33]

Everyday management of Spanish Bay is done with this same environmental commitment in mind; its pest and irrigation practices are sensitive to its surroundings. As mentioned above, Spanish Bay's IPM program is a model for all such programs across the country. In the drought-prone western states, water availability is at a premium, and this course treats it as such. The Pebble Beach Company engineered a wastewater reclamation project designed to free up 800 acre-feet of potable water for community and residential use by using 800 acre-feet of reclaimed water for its golf courses. This $34 million project was implemented in 1994 at no taxpayer cost.[34] Spanish Bay's irrigation program is remarkably efficient. Reconstructed sand dunes and reduced acreage for roughs are among the features designed to keep water use at a minimum. Watering schedules were created and are constantly being monitored by the company for their effectiveness. Moisture content readings are taken daily, and the results are examined to determine the current need for irrigation. In an effort to prove itself as a careful consumer of water, statistics on water use are kept and shared.[35]

What makes the Links at Spanish Bay unique are the many environmental programs that supplement the on-course efforts. Spanish Bay was the first California course to gain full certification as a sanctuary golf course by the Audubon Society of New York, a program to be discussed more fully later.[36] Since 1993, the Pebble Beach Company has operated a green-waste composting program designed to reduce landfill material. Through this plan, 90 percent of the company's 2,500 tons of green waste (grass, pine needles, leaves, shrubs, and tree trimmings) is redistributed throughout the Del Monte Forest. The green waste composting program works in conjunction with Monterey County to reach a state-mandated goal of 50 percent reduction in solid waste disposal by the year 2000. In further cooperation with the state mandate, the Pebble Beach Company runs an extensive recycling program. The company recycles glass, paper, plastic, cardboard, motor oil, cooking oil, and batteries. In 1994 alone, Pebble Beach collected over 610,000 pounds of recyclable goods.[37] Other approaches intended to benefit nature include an endangered plant species propagation program, a lily garden containing over 120 species of California lilies, a harbor seal pup protection program, and a series of educational signs on the environment along 17 Mile Drive, a scenic trail through the Del Monte Forest.[38]

The Pebble Beach Company is also concerned about automobile pollution. An alternative fuel conversion program began in 1995, replacing ordinary gasoline-powered cars with the much cleaner natural gas powered automobiles . At least twenty of the 100 vehicles used by the Pebble Beach Company have already been converted to bi-fuel cars that run on natural gas normally, but can operate on gasoline in an emergency. The remainder of the vehicles will be replaced with bi-fueled models over the next decade. Since 1987, the company has run an employee rideshare program designed to minimize the number of single-occupant cars on the roads. Their Trip Reduction Program has grown yearly, offering incentives for employees to car pool to work.[39]

This commitment to improving their surroundings has placed the Pebble Beach Company at the forefront among environmental innovators in the golf course industry. The management has not been content with simply eliminating harm to their environment; they are determined to enhance it. Tom Oliver, President of the Pebble Beach Company, expressed this philosophy:

> If we are to create the means whereby these resources can be appropriately managed and maintained, we must also achieve economic goals. The most heartening aspect of making this commitment is that technology and research have improved to the degree that now, more than ever, it is possible to find and implement creative solutions to environmental and economic challenges.[40]

As they have shown at Pebble Beach, technology has made it possible to meet these environmental challenges, and still operate a premier golf course.

Economic Analysis

Benefits of Providing an Environmentally Sensitive Golf Course

For any golf course superintendent to choose to manage in an environmentally sensitive manner, the course and its operators must benefit in some way. And while the Golf Course Superintendents Association of America lists many benefits, most of them are public benefits that accrue to the community, not to course operators. Some are private benefits that are personally valuable to superintendents. Then, some of the benefits reach to the bottom line; they affect profitability.

Many superintendents get into the business because they are lovers of nature. Others try to improve their surroundings because, as one superintendent said, they feel they "owe it to God and to the Earth."[41] Building a golf course is an excellent way to restore an environmentally ravaged site, such as a landfill or a mine. Golf courses can also act as "air conditioners," producing oxygen, cleansing the air, and cooling the atmosphere.[42] Watering a golf course can be beneficial to the entire community. An irrigated course can attract tourist and property dollars. Turf grass can be irrigated with wastewater effluent. This allows courses to irrigate using recycled water, freeing up potable water for other purposes. This irrigated turf is very valuable; it prevents erosion, acts as a filter for pollutants, and is conducive to groundwater.[43] Often, a golf course acts as a desperately needed habitat for both wildlife and plant species in an otherwise urban setting. Other benefits of golf courses include:

- recreational opportunities for activities such as jogging and walking;

- prime areas for real estate developments;

- both part- and full-time jobs;

- a host for many charitable benefits; and

- wetlands preservation areas.[44]

Costs of Managing an Environmentally Sensitive Golf Course

There are clearly benefits associated with managing a golf course with the environment in mind. However, there are also some significant costs of doing so. Many superintendents believe that the federal and state pesticide registration programs have formed one of the largest hurdles. Any new pesticide goes through years of costly testing. With the severe backlog of new pesticide applications at the EPA, many innovative proposals get bogged down with major delays. Another obstacle is the amount of training needed to properly operate an IPM program. An IPM approach is extremely complicated, and many superintendents just cannot invest the time necessary to learn the intricacies of the system. In addition to the increased educational costs that go along with an IPM program, there is also an increase in the amount of time it takes to operate an IPM, or any other environmentally sensitive program.[45] It would be much easier for a superintendent to carelessly spray his pesticides wherever he deems it necessary. Watering practices could be simplified by installing more sprinklers throughout the course and paying no attention to limiting water use. Developers would find it easier to construct a new course by destroying environmentally sensitive wetlands and wildlife habitats rather than working around them. Recycling green waste takes substantially more effort than hauling it off to the landfill. All of these practices are time consuming; it is up to the superintendent to decide whether he wishes to take these measures.

Marginal Benefit/Marginal Cost Analysis

When determining which environmental choices to adopt, the superintendent must weigh the benefits of cleaning up against the costs of doing so. Rather than looking at the total benefits and total costs, they will examine the marginal benefits and marginal costs. Figure 9.1 shows a typical marginal benefit/marginal cost curve for a golf course superintendent.

Basically, there are three options a superintendent can choose from in terms of environmental cleanup. The superintendent can choose to clean up nothing (point A), cleanup everything (point B), or clean up somewhere in between. It is obvious that no rational superintendent would choose to cleanup nothing. At point A, the marginal benefits of cleaning up just a little clearly outweigh the marginal costs of cleaning up that fraction. It is also apparent that no superintendent would choose to clean up everything. At point B, the marginal benefits of cleaning up

Figure 9.1. Marginal Analysis

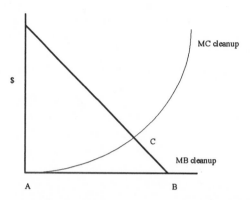

that last bit are much less than the cost of cleaning that last unit. The logical superintendent would decide to cleanup somewhere between point A and B. That somewhere should be at point C. Point C is the place where the marginal benefit curve intersects with the marginal cost curve. At point C, if any more cleanup occurs, the marginal costs will outweigh the marginal benefits. Similarly, if cleanup is cut back, the marginal benefits of cleaning up will exceed the costs of the lost cleanup.

It is easy to see that the optimal level of cleanup at any given golf course would be at point C, where the marginal benefits equal the marginal costs. The actual amount of cleanup that renders point C is not as easy to determine. There is no magic solution that equates marginal benefits and marginal costs. No one can say that, for example, by implementing an IPM program and using wastewater effluent, you are at point C. This solution will be unique to each course.

There are several factors that will affect the decision of how much to cleanup, and there are legitimate explanations for a golf course to choose to cleanup both large or small amounts. A sound case could be made that any rational golf course owner would instruct his superintendent to take maximum care of the facilities. To the owner, a golf course is a very valuable asset that has an extended life. With any property that valuable, there is an incentive to take care of it, because the price at which the owner could sell it in the future will be higher if the property has been carefully maintained.

To illustrate this concept, imagine that you currently own a ten-year-old Honda Accord: a good car, but nothing spectacular. One day, your rich uncle comes to visit you and promises that one year from that day, he will give you a brand new Lexus automobile. You have every reason to believe your uncle, who has done similarly outrageous things in the past. Now that you know you will have this magnificent car in one year, does it mean you will scratch the paint off your Honda, never change the oil, and kick a dent in the side every time you get in the car? Of course not. You know that when you are given the Lexus in one year, you will be able to sell the Honda. The price you will receive for the Honda will be much higher if the car is properly maintained for the entire year. The same goes for a golf course. If the facilities are sufficiently conserved, the land kept fertile and clean, and the wildlife habitats sustained, the future selling price will be much higher. The ability to sell property encourages people to preserve and maintain their property.

With that rationale, one should expect that all golf courses are managed with proper care given to the environment and the course's surroundings. This is obviously not the case, or there would be no issues for discussion here. There must be reasons that some courses choose to disregard environmental welfare in their everyday maintenance. It is possible that the golf course owner is not aware of the course superintendent's routines. Another explanation is that the owner may be short-sighted, and chooses to sacrifice future riches for current fortune. One thing to remember is that nearly every golf course exists to make a profit. Thus, they will choose their level of environmental cleanup based on their ability to earn rents. A 1996 National Golf Foundation study showed that most golfers would not tolerate moderately poorer landscape conditions in return for lowering amounts of pesticides and water used.[46] Many golfers seem to demand immaculate, green courses. By implementing some of these environmental programs, courses may risk losing customers, which could lead to diminished profits. In this scenario, the golfer's demand for a perfect course encourages environmental hazards. The superintendent could choose to restrict cleanup efforts for fear that their actions will hurt their bottom line.

A Contrast in Golf Course Styles

This situation is evident when the typical American golf course is compared to the typical European golf course. Most Americans share a vision of an ideal golf course that embodies the picturesque, floral surroundings of Augusta National Golf Club in Georgia, home of the Masters. Golf developed in Scotland, and the majority of the courses found on that side of the Atlantic, are nothing like their American counterparts. The term "links" refers to Scottish courses located on sand dunes covered with rich, alluvial soil deposits left behind by a river.[47] Nature exclusively designed the earliest Scottish links, and this trait remains evident in many European courses. These courses often contain many more bunkers, and the grasses are not the vast, closely manicured green landscapes seen throughout America. The only water found on most Scottish links is natural rivers and lakes, and trees are practically nonexistent, a stark contrast to the majority of American courses.

A series of new American courses were built following the 1930s, and the key features to this development were the increasingly innovative methods of landscaping. According to renowned golf course architect F. W. Hawtree, "the art was now assisted by earth-moving capabilities which turned the old approach to natural feature upside down. Instead of using what natural feature the site possessed, the site could now be endowed with whatever natural feature the architect fancied."[48] The majority of American golfers have grown to expect their courses to resemble the exquisite landscapes they see the professional golfers play on weekly.

A group of members of both Audubon International and the European Golf Association's Ecology Committee presented a series of environmental seminars during a tour of European golf courses. Many of those at the seminars expressed the feeling that golfers in the United States are spoiled. They perceive American courses as over-manicured and over-watered, and felt that the "game was to be played on grass, not color."[49]

Two major explanations exist for the differences in style among European and American golf courses. Part of the reason for this variation relates to the distinct climates of the two regions. American courses, especially those in the south, are much more suited to growing decorative vegetation and greener grasses. On the other hand, traditional European courses are located throughout Scotland, England, Sweden, and Belgium, where the climate is less acclimated to such course management practices.

Consider a marginal cost/marginal benefit curve similar to the one used earlier, this one measuring the visual appeal of a European golf course (figure 9.2).

Assume that 100 percent visual appeal (point B) represents a golf course similar to Augusta National Golf Club, with dazzling flower beds, tall shade trees, and striped, dark green fairways. Remember, a golf course superintendent will choose to maintain a level of visual appeal where the marginal cost equals the marginal benefit. Again, the superintendent will choose the level of visual appeal at point C. If European golf course superintendents try to create and maintain a course with 100 percent visual appeal, they will seek point B. There, the marginal costs of operating a golf course at that level far exceed the marginal benefits. No rational superintendents would choose to "Americanize" their course due to the unnecessary costs of doing so.

The second explanation behind the contrasting styles of European and American golf courses is that the issue is a simple matter of tastes and preferences. The demand for these Americanized, visually appealing courses is found by using the following function, $Qd = f[EP, Pg, M, Ps, Pc, tastes]$, where EP is environmental protection, Pg is the price of golf, M is the individual's income, Ps is the price of substitutes, Pc is the price of complements, and tastes represents the golfer's preferences. Tastes are positively correlated with the quantity demanded;

Figure 9.2. Marginal Analysis

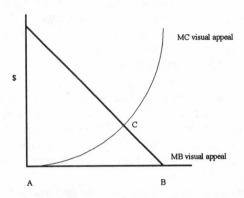

that is, if golfer's preferences for these closely manicured courses increase, the quantity demanded will also increase. According to a National Golf Foundation survey, the majority of American golfers prefer this type of immaculate course condition. The study revealed that the majority of golfers would not accept somewhat poorer playing conditions in exchange for a reduction in water and chemical usage, although most believe in protecting the environment.[50] Therefore, American golfers' tastes promote the continued existence of these resplendent golf courses.

In contrast, it can be assumed that most European golfers do not have the same preferences as their American counterparts. Both the demand function and positive effect of the tastes variable remain the same overseas. However, most European golf courses do not share a similar appearance with most American courses, thus implying that European golfers do not share this same taste for these closely manicured, impeccable golf courses with American golfers.

Public Knowledge of Course Management Practices

Another consideration that must be made when determining the level of environmental cleanup at any course is the uncertainty of many golfers surrounding the course's management practices. With all of the social pressures for a golf course to be managed in an environmentally friendly manner, it is conceivable, even plausible, that an individual course would take extraordinary environmental measures to avoid the negative publicity associated with being a polluter. The problem with this behavior is the apparent lack of knowledge on the golfer's behalf concerning a golf course's environmental programs.

A 1995 survey by NYT Sports/Leisure Magazines questioned 1,000 subscribers to *Golf Digest* and 1,000 subscribers to *E* Magazine, a national environmental publication, about issues involving the way golf courses interact with the environment. One of the most telling responses came from the question, "Are golf courses in your area taking actions to mitigate environmental problems?" A full 65 percent of the *Golf Digest* subscribers and 71 percent of the *E* Magazine subscribers replied "unsure" to that particular question.[51] If this large a percentage of individuals do not know if their local course is attempting to minimize environmental hazards, then the incentive to take care of their surroundings is assuredly diminished. These earlier worries about negative publicity, and even hopes of positive publicity, are irrelevant, because neither side is getting the message out sufficiently. Furthermore, if the percentages listed above are accurate, then it can be assumed that the general public (those who do not golf regularly or identify with environmental groups) knows even less about the management practices of their local golf course. Golfers and environmentalists are the major parties affected by this issue, and you would expect them to be more cognizant of the situation than the rationally ignorant public. It is costly to take care of the environment, and the realization that the public may not know if their course is environmentally conscious may prompt some courses to sacrifice environmental quality in return for larger profits.

The Audubon Cooperative Sanctuary Program

Lack of public information on environmental action seems to be a major problem in golf course management. How will the managers and owners reap rewards for good environmental management, if those who value such actions know nothing about them? A potential answer to this dilemma is found in the Audubon Cooperative Sanctuary Program for golf courses. Formed in 1990, the program represents an effort by the Audubon Society of New York State and the United States Golf Association to work together with golf course developers and superintendents to improve environmental quality and educate others about what is being done.

At the outset, a course will register with the Audubon Society of New York. The course will then complete a resource description form, with a complete inventory of the property and distinctive features. The Audubon Society of New York will reply, sharing thoughts and suggestions on ways the course can improve its overall environmental quality, from watering methods to wildlife preservation. It is then up to the course to plan and implement these new methods. Once the new ideas are set in motion, the course will detail its accomplishments to the New York Audubon staff, and they will decide if the acts deserve certification. The Audubon Society of New York awards certification in the following six categories:

- Environmental planning;
- Integrated Pest Management;
- Public involvement;

- Wildlife and habitat management;
- Water conservation; and
- Water enhancement.[52]

Currently, over 2,100 golf courses are registered with the New York Audubon Society. Participation in the program requires only a $100 annual fee.[53] About 220 courses across the country have been certified in one or more of these areas, and sixty-seven courses, including the Links at Spanish Bay, have been recognized as "certified cooperative sanctuaries" by earning credit in all six categories.

With the idea of promoting environmental work from the start, there is also an Audubon Signature Cooperative Sanctuary Program. It operates just like the Audubon Cooperative Sanctuary Program, except the course registers during the planning stage. Ideas are shared on the best possible way to develop the course, and greater environmental quality can be achieved. Once designed, the New York Audubon staff and the course continue to work together to realize Signature status. Attaining status as an Audubon Signature Cooperative Sanctuary course means that the course has achieved the highest environmental standards, and should be viewed as "an environmental model of national significance."[54]

Part of the purpose behind the Audubon Cooperative Sanctuary Program is to educate the public on issues involving golf course management practices and the environment, which provides a critical insight into the reasons this program is succeeding. Both the Audubon Society of New York and golf courses faced risks from participation, but both had something to gain. The Audubon Society of New York placed their image in jeopardy. Many environmental groups consider golf courses the enemy. Even the National Audubon Society has viewed golf courses with disdain, once commenting, "Few suburban landscapes are as pretty, or as toxic, as your typical golf course. If you scraped a golf course green and tested it, you'd have to cart it off to a hazardous waste facility."[55] The New York Audubon Society took the risk of losing some of their credibility among their environmental counterparts for this cooperation with these "polluters." Similarly, the participating golf courses placed themselves at risk. By joining this program, the golf course lets the New York Audubon staff examine their practices, and allows them to gain an in-depth look behind the scenes at a golf course. There was nothing to stop the Audubon Society of New York from informing the public about these courses and broadcasting any unsafe management procedures throughout their respective communities. However, each side felt they had more to gain from the partnership than they stood to lose. For the Audubon group, this was a chance to gain some influence in the everyday management of these golf courses, and to help them increase environmental quality. For the golf courses, it was a chance to increase environmental quality while increasing profits at the same time. It was earlier argued that the increasing costs of cleaning up at a profit-maximizing golf course, combined with the public's lack of knowledge about course management practices, could lead to that course's choosing to sacrifice environmental quality for continued profits. This Audubon program makes it possible for courses to increase both simultaneously.

In this regard, the public's demand for golf can again be summarized in the following function: Qd = f [EP, Pg, M, Ps, Pc, tastes], where EP is environmental protection, Pg is the price of golf, M is the individual's income, Ps is the price of substitutes, and Pc is the price of complements. These are the factors the public will consider when determining their demand for golf. For this case, everything except environmental protection (EP) and the price of golf (Pg) will be held constant. Figure 9.3 shows the supply and demand curves for golf.

The supply curve is represented by Sgolf, and the original demand curve (before the Audubon certifications) is marked as D1. The quantity demanded before the certifications is Q1, and the price of golf before these certifications is P1. If both the Audubon Society of New York and the participating golf courses are correct, their assigning certifications to golf courses should increase the demand for golf, since environmental protection is part of a golfer's demand function. With this increase, the demand curve for golf will shift out, to D2. This increases quantity demanded to Q2, and the price of golf (greens fees) rises to P2.

Figure 9.3. Supply and Demand Analysis

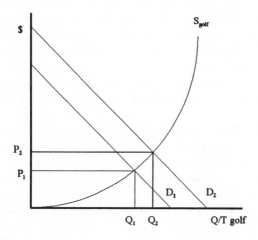

With this increase in greens fees, the course earns more money than before (Q1*P1 < Q2*P2). Some of this extra money can be used to make environmental improvements to the courses. This way, both sides benefit. The course earns the extra money they desire, and the Audubon Society of New York secures an increase in environmental quality at participating courses. The entire program is based on the ability of each side to let the public know about their efforts. By educating the public on golf course management practices, each side gains something they value.

Landfill Golf Courses

Earlier it was mentioned that the *Environmental Principles for Golf Courses* recommends examining old landfills as potential sites for new golf courses. With a finite supply of land available in this country, the idea should become an increasingly viable option. With these conversions, a community gets rid of an unsightly landfill, while the addition of a golf course increases property values, provides a stream of revenue for the community, and makes the area more attractive. However, since the first landfill course was built in Brooklyn, New York, in 1961, only sixty such projects have been undertaken.[56] To understand the reasons for this apparent lack of interest in landfill golf courses, an insight into the process of closing a landfill, along with some of the potential hazards associated with these ventures, is essential.

When a landfill reaches its capacity, it is the responsibility of its owner to close the landfill. Landfill closure is a complicated process that requires a great deal of planning in the months prior to closing. At closure, a thick clay cap is placed over the refuse, in an attempt to seal in all remaining water.[57] Next is a two-foot layer of soil, followed by the top soil. Signs must be posted, and fences must be erected. In the months to come, a gas collection system, drainage control structure, leachate control facility, and groundwater monitoring device must be installed. Finally, the topsoil must be covered with some sort of vegetation to prevent erosion.[58]

Covering the landfill is by no means the end of the story; several potential hazards remain. Landfills produce leachate, which is water that tends to percolate through the remaining trash. Careful monitoring must ensue to guarantee that no leachate contaminates the groundwater supply. The clay cap is one of the best defenses against leaching. The second by-product of landfills is landfill gas, which is a mixture of methane, carbon dioxide, and percaptins. Landfill gas is extremely light, and will often rise through the trash to the surface, occasionally resulting in underground fires or explosions. Another complication results from the instability of landfills. Settling often occurs, from pockets of landfill gas or unsteady mounds of trash. This can become a major problem, as one Los Angeles landfill golf course found out, when they had a putting green sink twenty-seven feet.[59] These issues are undoubtedly of some concern to any developer planning on building a golf course on a landfill site. However, with careful control systems designed to limit escaping leachate and landfill gas, these difficulties can be minimized.

Since these obstacles are by no means catastrophic, one must wonder why there have not been more landfill golf courses built. The major reason for this lack of new course development, which relates to the various complications listed above, can be illustrated in terms of supply and demand. The supply of golf courses is determined by the function $Qs = f$ [Pg, Cs, Co, M, Pl, OC, tastes], where Pg is the price of a round of golf, Cs is the startup costs of a new golf course, Co is the operating costs of a golf course, M is the level of incomes, Pl is the price of land, OC is the opportunity cost of investing in a golf course, and tastes represent individuals' preferences. Figure 9.4 shows the supply and demand for golf courses.

Consider two identical plots of land, one the site of a closed landfill and the other having never been disturbed. It can be safely assumed that the price (Pl) of the closed landfill will be cheaper than the price of the other lot because of the additional risk that comes with the closed landfill site. Using this reasoning, a decrease in the price of land (Pl) should lead to an increase in the supply of golf courses. Since this drop in land price results from a lower price for closed landfill sites (and not a lower price for unblemished land), this increase in the supply of golf courses should be a direct result of an increase in the supply of landfill golf courses. With just over sixty such courses having been built in the past thirty-six years, this is obviously not the case. The reason for this is the same reason that the price of landfill sites is lower: the additional risk. Although the price of land is

Figure 9.4. Demand and Supply Analysis

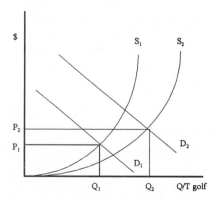

reduced, this benefit is more than offset by the increase in startup costs (Cs) and operating costs (Co). Both costs are above what they could be for a normal tract of land due to the potential hazards of closed landfills. Landfill gas and leachate must be continually monitored, and there is a constant threat of sinkholes. In addition, irrigating a closed landfill is often more difficult due to areas of settlement. Over time, these additional costs will likely surpass the one-time gain from the price of land. Rising costs would force golf courses to raise their prices. If you recall the golfer's demand function, a rise in the price of golf (Pg) leads to a decrease in quantity demanded at that course. Therefore, the landfill golf course has higher costs and is losing golfers, because of their need to increase prices.

There may be a way to solve this problem. What is needed is something similar to the Audubon Cooperative Sanctuary Program, but one that recognizes landfill golf courses. This program would be sponsored by some environmental group, who would act as a clearinghouse for landfill courses. In return for a membership fee, the sponsoring organization would keep a register of landfill golf courses, while publicizing efforts to improve the environment. The benefits for these member courses are twofold. First, remember that environmental protection is part of a golfer's demand function. If these courses are recognized for their commitment to the environment, there should be an increase in demand to play at such registered courses. Second, the sponsor would gain information on management practices from both its research and from these courses, and provide golf-course operators with more efficient methods of leachate and landfill gas monitoring and control. Finally, the environmental organization would benefit by seeing new golf courses located on sites where their impact on the environment is unquestionably an improvement over the previous tenant. Figure 9.4 illustrates the overall impact of this program on the supply and demand for golf.

This program produces an increase in quantity demanded (Q2>Q1) from the increase in environmental protection (which caused a shift right in the demand curve, just as with the Audubon program). Once new methods for landfill gas and leachate control are shared, startup and operating costs are lowered, causing a rightward shift in the supply curve. This means higher revenues for golf courses, as (Q2*P2) > (Q1*P1). Like the Audubon Cooperative Sanctuary Program, both environmentalists and golf courses will benefit from this proposal.

Additional Thoughts

There is no optimal level of environmental cleanup that every golf course in America should attain. There are certain minimal pollution control practices that all courses must adhere to, and these are regulated by the United States Environmental Protection Agency. Any measures that go beyond the regulated procedures should be determined by each individual course. No one knows each particular course better than its owners and superintendent, and they will choose to pollute at a level where the marginal benefits of environmental cleanup are equal to the marginal costs of environmental cleanup. Environmental groups that campaign for increased environmental quality on golf courses play a part in this in that they draw attention to the situation and force golf course operators to consider their course's reputation in determining their level of environmental cleanup.

Both environmentalists and members of the golf industry seem to be moving in an efficient direction with the Audubon Cooperative Sanctuary Program. This approach could be the closest thing available to a solution to their problem. During the Kapalua Invitational golf tournament on ESPN on November 7, 1996, one announcer mentioned that all three courses used during the Kapalua Invitational were certified by the Audubon Society of New York as Cooperative Sanctuaries. This publicity is exactly what is needed to advance the environmental aspects of golf course management.

For the Audubon Cooperative Sanctuary Program to function properly, golfers need to be informed as to what the program is about and how the system works. Both sides reason that holding all other things constant, a golfer would choose to play at a course that is Audubon certified rather than one that is not accredited. For this scenario to hold true, the golfer must know about this plan. Both environmentalists and golf courses need to educate the public on this matter. One way to get the word out is being used by Bruce Wolfrom, superintendent at Treetops Sylvan Resort in Gaylord, Michigan. His course is Audubon certified, and was selected as the winner of the 1996 Environmental Steward Award in the resort class from *Golf Course Management*. At his course, every golfer is handed a card explaining that Treetops has been certified as a sanctuary course by the Audubon Society of New York.[60] If the information is valuable, all certified courses should do something similar. Once the golfing public learns more about the Audubon certifications, pressure will be placed on non-certified golf courses to register with the Audubon Society of New York in order to remain competitive with these Audubon sanctuaries.

The same circumstances apply to the suggested landfill golf course program. Currently, potential developers seem hesitant to build their next golf course on the site of a closed landfill. This reluctance is understandable, in light of the potential hazards and ensuing high costs. If these costs can be reduced, more closed landfill sites may be utilized. By launching this proposed plan, all sides gain something important to them.

Conclusions

The conflict between golf course operators and environmentalists is unique. A seemingly harmless recreational activity has been targeted by environmental groups and said to pose a danger similar to that of a toxic waste dump. This deleterious reputation has followed golf courses for the majority of the past two decades, but course operators seem to be working to erase this harmful image. Ideas for cleaning up their golf courses are being spread by superintendents across the country, and more and more courses are adopting these new practices. The expanding use of Best Management Practices and Integrated Pest Management programs are just two ways that superintendents everywhere are showing that they care about their environment. Courses are following the innovative example of individuals such as Ted Horton from the Pebble Beach Company and reaching out to improve not only the environmental quality of their golf course but also that of their community. Approaches such as the Audubon Cooperative Sanctuary Program appear to be improving both environmental quality and environmental awareness among golf courses and the general public. With the evidence of increasing cooperation between each group, it seems that definite progress is being made, and there is no reason to believe that this progress will not continue in the coming years. Through increased research and collaboration, technological advancements, and expansion of educational programs, the environmental hazards associated with golf courses should gradually diminish, until the day when such a unique issue is no longer relevant.

Notes

1. James. T. Snow, *An Overview of USGA Environmental Research* United States Golf Association, Internet, 1996, p. 1.

2. James B. Beard, *Turf Management for Golf Courses* (New York: United States Golf Association, 1982), p. 5.

3. Snow, *An Overview,* p. 1.

4. Ibid.

5. Ibid.

6. "Environmental Activists Tee Off," *Golf Course Management,* (Lawrence, KS: Golf Course Superintendents Association of America, February 1996), p. 36.

7. Ibid., p. 26.

8. Snow, *An Overview,* p. 3.

9. Beard, *Turf Management,* p. 317.

10. Ibid.

11. "Environmental Activists," p. 24.

12. Ibid., p. 26.

13. Snow, *An Overview,* p. 4.

14. John Millhouse, "Golf Courses and Our Water Resources," *Ronald Fream's Golfplan* (Santa Rosa, CA: Ronald Fream Design Group, Ltd., 1997), p. 1.

15. Ibid.

16. Ibid., p. 2.

17. Ibid.

18. Ibid.

19. "The Facts About Golf Course Pesticides," *Greentips* (Lawrence, KS: Golf Course Superintendents Association of America, March 1996).

20. *GCSAA Environmental Stewardship Strategy for Golf Courses,* (Lawrence, KS: Golf Course Superintendents Association of America, April 1996), p. 6.

21. W. Lee Berndt, "For the Record . . .," *Golf Course Management* (Lawrence, KS: Golf Course Superintendents Association of America, February 1996), p. 68.

22. Ted Horton, "Pebble Beach Golf Course Integrated Pest Management (IPM)" (Pebble Beach, CA: Pebble Beach Company, March 1996), p. 2.

23. Ibid., pp. 2-3.

24. Snow, *An Overview,* p. 2.

25. "Water Conservation," *Greentips.* (Lawrence, KS: Golf Course Superintendents Association of America, March 1996).

26. Horton, "Pebble Beach," p. 3.

27. "Water Conservation."

28. *Environmental Principles for Golf Courses in the United States,* (Salt Lake City, UT: The Center for Resource Management, 1996), p. 1.

29. Ibid., p. 7.

30. "The Facts About Golf Course Pesticides," *Greentips.*(Lawrence, KS: Golf Course Superintendents Association of America, March 1996).

31. Snow, *An Overview,* p. 6.

32. "The Facts About Golf Course Pesticides."

33. "A Taste of the Past," *Golf Course Management* (Lawrence, KS: Golf Course Superintendents Association of America, January 1995), p. 26.

34. "CAWD-PBCSD Wastewater Reclamation Project in Pebble Beach."

35. "A Taste of the Past," p. 32.

36. *Pebble Beach Company Environmental Annual Report, 1994-1995,* (Pebble Beach, CA: Pebble Beach Company, 1995), p. 4.

37. Ibid., p. 9.

38. Ibid., pp. 11-12.

39. Ibid., p. 7.

40. *Pebble Beach Company Environmental Report, 1993,* (Pebble Beach, CA: Pebble Beach Company, 1994), p. 2.

41. Kay Hawes, "Environmental Heroes," *Golf Course Management* (Lawrence, KS: Golf Course Superintendents Association of American, February 1996), p. 11.

42. *Golf and the Environment.* Golf Course Superintendents Association of America, Internet, 1996.

43. Ibid.

44. Ibid.

45. GCSAA, p. 5.

46. Ibid.

47. Geoffrey S. Cornish, and Ronald E. Whitten, *The Architect of Golf* (New York: HarperCollins Publishers, Inc., 1993), p. 16.

48. F. W. Hawtree, *The Golf Course: Planning, Design, Construction and Maintenance* (London: University Press, 1983), p. 48.

49. Ron Dodson, "The Old Course and the Environment," *Golfcourse* (www.golfcourse.com.org/interzine:InterZine Productions, Inc., 1997), p. 1.

50. GCSAA, p. 5.

51. Roger Schiffman, "Changing Attitudes on the Environment," *Golf Digest* (Turnbull, CT: NYT Sports/Leisure Magazine, April 1995), p. 9.

52. *The Audubon Cooperative Sanctuary Program for Golf Courses,* Golf Course Superintendents Association of America, Internet, 1996.

53. Snow, *An Overview,* p. 4.

54. *The Audubon Cooperative Sanctuary.*

55. Bob Costa, "Golf and the Environment: Initiating Change," *Golf Course Management* (Lawrence, KS: Golf Course Superintendents Association of America, February 1996), p. 176.

56. Doug Saunders, "Landfill Golf Courses: A Fresh Solution to Discarded Problems," *Golfweb and Sportsline USA,* (www.golfweb.com, 1997), p. 1.

57. Ibid.

58. Philip O'Leary, and Patrick Walsh, "Landfill Closures and Long-Term Care, Lesson 10," *Waste Age Magazine*, March 1992, updated January 1995, p. 3.

59. Saunders, "Landfill Golf Courses," p. 1.

60. "The View at the 'Top,'" *Golf Course Management* (Lawrence, KS: Golf Course Superintendents Association of America, February 1996), p. 96.

References

The Audubon Cooperative Sanctuary Program for Golf Course. 1996. Golf Course Superintendents Association of America, Internet.

Beard, James B. *Turf Management for Golf Courses.* 1982. United States Golf Association, New York.

Berndt, W. Lee. 1996. "For the Record . . .," *Golf Course Management,* Lawrence, KS: Golf Course Superintendents Association of America, February.

"CAWD-PBCSD Wastewater Reclamation Project in Pebble Beach." 1994.

Cornish, Geoffrey S., and Ronald E. Whitten. 1981. *The Golf Course.* New York: The Rutledge Press, New York.

———. 1993. *The Architects of Golf.* New York: HarperCollins Publishers, Inc.

Costa, Bob. 1996. "Golf and the Environment: Initiating Change." *Golf Course Management.* Lawrence, KS: Golf Course Superintendents Association of America, February.

Dodson, Ron, 1997. "The Old Course and The Environment." *Golfcourse* www.golfcourse.com.org/InterZine: InterZine Productions, Inc.

"Environmental Activists Tee Off." 1996. *Golf Course Management*. Lawrence, KS: Golf Course Superintendents Association of America, February.

Environmental Principles for Golf Courses in the United States. 1996. Salt Lake City, UT: The Center for Resource Management.

"The Facts About Golf Course Pesticides." 1996. *Greentips*. Lawrence, KS: Golf Course Superintendents Association of America, March.

GCSAA Environmental Stewardship Strategy for Golf Courses. 1996. Lawrence, KS: Golf Course Superintendents Association of America, April.

Golf and the Environment. 1996. Golf Course Superintendents Association of America, Internet.

"Golf and the Environment." 1996. *Greentips*. Lawrence, KS: Golf Course Superintendents Association of America, March.

"Golf Courses and the Environment." 1996. *Greentips*. Lawrence, KS: Golf Course Superintendents Association of America. Lawrence, Kansas, March.

Hawes, Kay. 1996. "Environmental Heroes." *Golf Course Management*. Lawrence, KS: Golf Course Superintendents Association of America, February.

Hawtree, F. W. 1983. *The Golf Course: Planning, Design, Construction, and Maintenance*. London: University Press.

Horton, Ted. "Pebble Beach Golf Course Integrated Pest Management (IPM)." Pebble Beach Company.

Ingram, Candy. 1995. "Pebble Beach Company's Alternative Fuel Conversion Program." *Scoreboard*, January/February.

"Landfill Golf Course." 1996. *EnvironMinute Home Page*. Finger Lakes Productions, Inc., May 16.

Millhouse, John. 1997. "Golf Courses and Our Water Resources." *Ronald Fream's Golfplan*. Santa Rosa, CA: Ronald Fream Design Group, Ltd.

O'Leary, Phillip, and Patrick Walsh. 1995. "Landfill Closure and Long-Term Care, Lesson 10." *Waste Age Magazine*, March 1992, updated January.

Pebble Beach Company Annual Environmental Report 1993. 1994. Pebble Beach, CA: Pebble Beach Company.

Pebble Beach Company Environmental Annual Report 1994-1995. 1995. Pebble Beach, CA: Pebble Beach Company.

Saunders, Doug. 1997. "Landfill Golf Courses: A Fresh Solution to Discarded Problems." *GolfWeb*.

Schiffman, Roger. 1995. "Changing Attitudes on the Environment." *Golf Digest*, Trumbell, CT: NYT Sports/Leisure Magazines, April.

Snow, James T. 1996. *An Overview of USGA Environmental Research*. United States Golf Association, Internet.

"A Taste of the Past." 1995. *Golf Course Management*. Lawrence, KS: Golf Course Superintendents Association of America, January.

"The View at the 'Top.'" 1996. *Golf Course Management*. Lawrence, KS: Golf Course Superintendents Association of America, February.

"Water Conservation." 1996. *Greentips.* Lawrence, KS: Golf Course Superintendents Association of America, March.

What Are the Environmental Principles? 1996. Golf Course Superintendents Association of America, Internet.

Chapter 10

Environmental Organizations: What Makes Them Tick?

Brian Kropp

Introduction

Today's national environmental organizations, like the Sierra Club, the Nature Conservancy, and the Environmental Defense Fund, are recognized far and wide as key elements in the U.S. environmental movement. Indeed, we cannot understand the movement itself unless we understand the rapid growth of national environmental organizations.

We know that the 1970s and the 1980s saw unprecedented growth for environmental groups. For example, the Nature Conservancy saw more than a fourfold increase in membership during the 1970s, with membership rising from 21,442 in 1970 to 98,910 in 1980.[1] After that, growth accelerated to yield a fivefold increase in the 1980s, with membership reaching 577,604 in 1990. Other major environmental groups experienced similar growth patterns. But recent evidence suggests that these boom times have passed. The Sierra Club and the National Audubon Society both saw membership dip by over 11 percent in 1993.

Consider the data in figure 10.1, which describe annual memberships for three major environmental organizations. Notice the rapid increase in the earlier years and the recent peaking of memberships for the Sierra Club and the Audubon Society. What explains this growth?

Figure 10.1. Environmental Membership: 1970-1994.

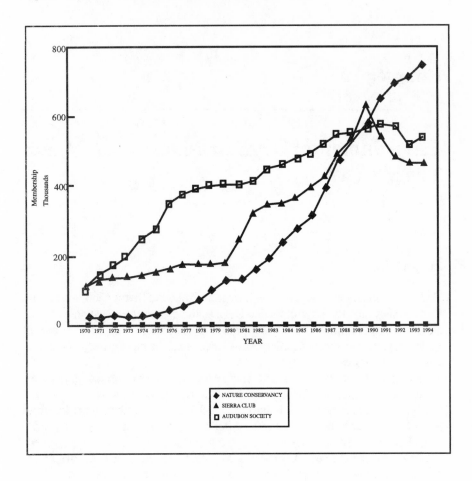

At least five general arguments can be offered to explain why people join environmental groups. All else equal, memberships will increase:

- If people become richer;
- If they become more educated;
- If momentous environmental events occur;
- If environmentalism takes on the trappings of a religious movement, and
- If political forces favor a growth in environmental organizations.

Are these arguments valid? What about other factors? Are memberships of environmental groups larger in urban or rural areas? Does close proximity to national parks play a role? Are people in the western United States more concerned about the great outdoors than people in the East? Surely some important insights can be gained by modeling the economic determinants of environmental group memberships. But is it possible to examine environmental groups as substitutes for religious organizations, as has been suggested by several writers? (Easterbrook 1995, Nelson, 1993) Indeed, Frederick Turner has suggested that if one crosses out God from the traditional religious creeds and substitutes Earth, one would have a religious creed for environmentalists (Nash, 1990). Religion to one side, can we, as other writers suggest, determine the extent to which the organizations gain and lose when Democrats or Republicans control the White House or Congress?

Drawing on economic logic and statistical models, this chapter addresses each of these questions. The next part of the chapter gives a brief overview of the history of the environmental movement. That is followed by a theory section, which develops a framework for thinking about the demand and supply of environmental group memberships. Statistical modeling of environmental group memberships is the focus of the next section, while the last section offers some final thoughts.

A Brief Sketch of the Environmental Movement

By most popular accounts, Earth Day–April 1, 1970–marks the beginning of the U.S. environmental movement and the start of environmental regulation. Earth Day is surely an important event in the history of the movement, but regulation began several centuries earlier. In 1626 the Plymouth Colony passed ordinances that regulated the cutting and sale of timber on specific tracts of land (Nash, 1990). In 1652 Boston established a community water system, a move followed by Pennsylvania shortly thereafter (U.S. EPA, 1992). Throughout the late 1600s regulation developed concerning timber operations in Pennsylvania and around the Massachusetts Bay (Nash, 1990).

During the 1700s New York, Connecticut, and Massachusetts all passed legislation that protected deer and other animals from hunters (Nash, 1990). By 1800 seventeen municipalities had governmentally controlled water systems. (U.S. EPA, 1992) The 1800s saw the rise of congested cities along with rising incomes, the birth of outdoor sports magazines, and the coining of the term "ecology." One of today's major environmental organizations emerged in the late nineteenth century; the Sierra Club was founded in California by John Muir in 1892 (Switzer, 1994). Finally, the first piece of federal environmental law emerged in that period when the Rivers and Harbors Act was passed in 1899 (Downing, 1984).

The National Audubon Society was formed in 1905. At the same time, the Progressive Movement, a social force that had a dramatic effect on natural resource management, was taking shape. It was during this period that two competing environmental concepts emerged that split the budding environmental movement into two factions–preservation and conservation. The preservationists, led by John Muir, believed that nature should be left untrampled by man. The conservationists, led by Gifford Pinchot, the first director of the U.S. Forest Service, sought to harness nature and create a sustainable use of natural resources (Cohen, 1988). In 1935 Franklin Roosevelt created the Soil Conservation Service, and in 1937 the Pittman-Robertson Act established funds for state wildlife protection (U.S. EPA, 1992).

The post-World War II period saw the Nature Conservancy emerge in 1951 as an acquirer of land either by donation, purchase, or trade and the emergence of two powerful books: *Silent Spring* and *The Population Bomb*. Rachel Carson's 1962 book, *Silent Spring*, raised the nation's sensitivities to chemical poisoning generally, and more specifically to the adverse effects of DDT. *The Population Bomb*, written by Paul Ehrlich in 1968, described a Malthusian scenario about overpopulation, famine, and disease. By this time, environmentalism was becoming a national phenomenon. The 1960s saw the start of a flurry of federal environmental legislation. The first Clean Air Act became law in 1963; the Federal Water Pollution Control Act was enacted in 1965; and a more rigorous Air Quality Act was adopted in 1967. The highlight of the era came with the creation of the EPA, which opened its doors on December 2, 1970. The 1970s also saw the birth of many new environmental interest groups.

With the passing of extensive federal legislation, the attention of environmental groups shifted away from educating local groups and state legislatures and focused on the national government. With new legislation, which was strongly supported by environmental groups, the federal courts and national politics became more important in affecting environmental policy rather than in generating discussion of natural resources and proper farming and production techniques. For example, the National Audubon Society redirected its mission from supporting the activities of dedicated bird watchers and backpackers to seeking to affect national legislation and policy. Redirection of mission was also observed in 1971 when the Sierra Club formed the Sierra Club Legal Defense Fund to litigate on behalf of environmental causes. In 1968, the relatively more confrontational Environmental Defense Fund was created; it was joined in 1970 by the Natural Resources Defense Council (NRDC), which also specialized in litigation (Schnaiberg and Gould, 1994). As the environmental movement set its sights on Washington, demand for information on congressional voting increased. The League of Conservation Voters (LCV) responded. Founded in 1971 by Marion Eddy, the LCV developed an annual index based on votes cast by each member of Congress and funneled contributions to political action committees in an effort to affect election outcomes (Gottlieb, 1993).

Environmental crises seem to have added fuel to the interest group engines. For example, Congress passed the 1980 Superfund legislation on the heels of the Love Canal episode, a New York event that focused the furor of environmentalists. Other episodes no less emotional than Love Canal captured the nation's attention. There was the Alar pesticide scare, the Exxon Valdez, the deadly Union Carbide plant leak in India, and other environmental catastrophes. Most major environmental legislation was in place by the decade of the 1980s, but 1990 saw the Clean Air Act amendments gain legislative approval, and 1992 saw the adoption of the Energy Policy Act.

On the occasion of the twenty-fifth anniversary of Earth Day, *U.S. News and World Report* published a list of significant events believed to have defined key milestones in the environmental movement. The abbreviated list in table 10.2 includes some of the items mentioned there along with others believed to have added to the momentum of the environmental movement.

There can be little doubt that some of these events energized the political forces needed to push through federal statutes. It is also likely that events like these contributed to the growing interest in environmental protection and recognition of the value of environmental organizations. But these statements are simply refutable hypotheses. Saying these things gains little ground in explaining the fundamental forces that underlie the decisions made by many ordinary people to join the environmental movement. Clearly, a review of history is crucial to understanding the movement. But a more general model is needed and statistical testing is required if we are to understand the demand and supply of memberships in environmental organizations.

Table 10.1. Significant Events in the Environmental Movement

1970	EPA Created. Clean Air Act and National Environmental Policy Act passed by Congress.
1972	DDT banned.
1973	Endangered Species Act passed.
1974	Safe Drinking Water Act passed.
1978	Love Canal crisis.
1979	Three Mile Island crisis.
1980	"Superfund" legislation passed.
1984	Union Carbide plant leak resulting in death of over 2,800.
1985	Discovery of ozone hole.
1986	Meltdown of Chernobyl nuclear plant.
1989	Exxon Valdez runs ashore off the coast of Alaska.
1990	Spotted Owl listed as threatened species.
1992	California condors reintroduced into the wild.
1994	California Desert Protection Act passed.
1995	Gray Wolves reintroduced to Yellowstone National Park.

Explaining Environmental Interest Group Growth

Some Theoretical Considerations

Major environmental organizations are first and foremost firms that succeed in the marketplace when their services are purchased voluntarily by dues-paying members. Like all firms, environmental organizations must generate revenues large enough to cover all costs. Seen as membership maximizers, environmental groups must develop services and products that appeal to a large population cross-section. As indicated earlier, some organizations specialize in litigation. Others focus on the acquisition of sensitive land. These and still others provide educational products and recreational experiences that focus on natural resources. One and all engage in political lobbying, attempting to influence emerging environmental policy.

Environmental organizations are multiproduct firms that provide members with outdoor experiences, books, magazines, and fellowship. These are private experiences that individuals can choose exclusively for themselves. But one major category of activities suffers from a public goods characteristic that makes rationing, and therefore excluding non-payers, impossible. Once passed, a desired environmental statute can be celebrated by all environmentalists, whether they are dues-paying members or not. Successful litigation generates the same problem. When a major case is won, all who favor the outcome receive a benefit. In short, it is easy for environmentalists to free ride, to let someone else provide benefits that cannot be rationed once they are produced.

Perhaps this public goods characteristic of environmental organization services explains the effort put forth to reach deep into the psyche of potential members, to appeal to the individual's sense of what is right. If environmentalism successfully takes on the trappings of religion, then environmental organizations can better deal with the tendency of some to avoid paying for things they might get anyway.

Demand and Supply of Memberships

When thinking about the environmental marketplace where memberships are bought and sold on the basis of lobbying, individuals are pictured as hearing messages with varying degrees of appeal. When the messages relate to important national legislation that addresses something as ubiquitous as water or air pollution, individuals nationwide will likely attach more importance to the issue than when the proposed rule applies to a state, county, or region. However, when national issues cease to be as pressing, but local issues seem unaddressed, the same individuals will refocus their attention to problems in their own backyards. National memberships may suffer. The relevant group varies for particular issues.

Incomes and levels of understanding have a major bearing on decisions to join volunteer organizations. Having a higher than average income offers the means to focus on issues, whether national or local. Having a higher than average level of education equips the individual to understand or be intrigued by the complex issues that emerge.

The potential member of an environmental group has a demand for membership that is driven by income, education, and interest in environmental matters. The person is likely to be even more interested, all else equal, if he or she is aware of problems that might be addressed by an active national government. Of course, there are costs associated with membership, but these are generally small. They and commitments of time are voluntary. Still, the potential member is seen as weighing the benefits and costs of joining. The lower the costs for a fixed benefit, the larger will be the commitment.

It is costly to organize and operate an environmental organization. In this analysis, the supply of memberships offered by environmental organizations is seen as representing constant costs, which is to say the cost of having one more member does not vary with the size of the group. In the earlier organizing period, it is likely that average and marginal costs fall as more people join, since there is a fixed overhead that can be spread across the group. But after some point, the environmental firm encounters constant costs.

There is yet more to the story about environmental organizations when theories of regulation are considered. Extensive work has been done on other fronts in the study of interest groups and the factors that affect their formation. George Stigler (1971) presents work that argues that interest groups seek regulation that allows them to capture well-defined economic benefits. Stigler (1973) has also examined the free rider problem mentioned earlier. Buchanan, Tollison, and Tulluck (1980) have argued that interest group lobbying, while benefitting highly concentrated groups, generally imposes even greater costs on the mass of unorganized consumers and voters. These and other economists see interest group actions as a vital part of the larger political process. But while some powerful general theories of regulation have been developed, very little work has been done to explain the varying fortunes of particular groups.

Murrell (1984) was one of the first scholars to examine factors that are important in the actual formation of interest groups. He examined such factors as the size of government, the length of time that a country has been a democracy, as well as demographic characteristics such as age and population density. His work helps to bring focus to the task reflected in this chapter, which is to explain membership in major environmental groups across the United States and across time. Following the path of Murrell, the model to be presented here seeks to explain memberships in four major environmental organizations by examining economic and political variables, religiosity, and regions of the country. The estimates to be discussed identify just which variables are most important and how activities seem to differ across specific environmental groups and regions of the country.

The Statistical Models and Findings

Using ordinary least squares regressions, several estimating models were developed for explaining membership in major environmental organizations. The first estimates examined data across the fifty states for the years 1990 through 1993 for a total of 200 observations. These cross-sectional models draw on the theories discussed in the previous section and take the general form of:

$$INT = f(PCY, YG, EDUC, POPDEN, AGE, LCV, HAZWAS, TRI, FEDLAND),$$

where the dependent variable, INT, is a per capita measurement of membership by state for four national environmental organizations. Data for the variable were provided by the Sierra Club, the National Audubon Society, the Nature Conservancy, and the NRDC.[2]

These four organizations were chosen for several reasons. First, they all are national organizations. They all lobby for political change, yet each has some degree of specialization. The Nature Conservancy participates in real estate conservation; the NRDC participates in extensive litigation; the National Audubon Society, until recently, has been an organization that focuses on issues concerning camping and wildlife; while the Sierra Club is a multi-issue group (Bosso, 1994). Each group defines a member differently. For this study, a member is someone who has paid a membership fee to receive some benefit from the environmental interest group.[3] INT is formed by summing membership per state across groups and dividing by total state population. The variable is scaled in thousands.[4]

The first independent variable, PCY, is state per capita income. Economic theory and related empirical work tell us that people with higher incomes consume more luxury goods. Other researchers have found demand for environmental quality to be very sensitive to income, with demand rising 2.5 percent for each one percent increase in income (Coursey, 1992). This high income elasticity places environmental quality in the same category as luxury goods such as BMW and Mercedes automobiles. The coefficient on PCY is expected to be positive. YG measures the rate of growth in state per capita income. The sign on its coefficient is expected to be positive, which implies that memberships rise when incomes grow at an increasing rate.[5]

EDUC measures the percent of the state population with at least a college degree; its coefficient is predicted to be positive. That is, we expect to see memberships rise as advanced education makes the population more aware of the environment and more politically involved. POPDEN is population per square mile. Economic theory tells us that organizing costs are lower for individuals in close proximity to one another, which suggests a positive coefficient. However, environmental organizations are national in scope and their gains from state population density may be nonexistent. It could also be the case that environmental interest groups are a rural phenomenon and not an urban one, in this case the sign on population density would be negative. The competing theories for the sign on this variable must be settled empirically.

AGE is the percent of the states' population in the 18 to 34 age group. The variable tests to see if the environmental movement is somehow more responsive to younger populations, who may have become sensitive to environmental issues in their earlier years. If environmental interest group formation is responsive to the size of this group, we would expect the sign on this variable to be positive.[6]

The next set of variables are all environmentally specific. LCV is the League of Conservation Voters average score for a states' entire congressional delegation. The LCV rating is an unbiased score based on how each state's delegation voted on pertinent environmental issues. It is generally argued that politicians act in ways that reflect the preferences of their constituents. If voting "green" is valuable to their constituents, the resulting LCV rating will rise. In this way, LCV indirectly reflects voter ideology, and its coefficient will be positive.

HAZWAS introduces environmental events that may trigger an interest group response. In a recent survey reported in *Science*, respondents were asked about certain environmental problems, and were then asked to indicate what they thought should be described as "very serious" (Roberts, 1990). From this, one can argue that the problems that people report as "very serious" are the problems with the highest expected cost to those people. As expected costs of pollution rise, the affected population is more likely to join an environmental group.

The two largest concerns reported in the *Science* survey were active and abandoned hazardous waste sites, with a response of "very serious" for 67 and 65 percent of the respondents, respectively. Hazardous waste sites per square mile is included in the model to account for this concern. The variable is the sum of the number of federal and state hazardous waste sites per square mile in each state. The sign on the coefficient is predicted to be positive.

The third and fourth problems ranked "very serious" were industrial water pollution and occupational exposure to toxic chemicals. Sixty-three percent of the respondents reported each of these problems as "very serious." Data for total releases as reported in the Toxic Release Inventory (TRI) are used. The variable is reported in thousands of total release pounds, and the coefficient is expected to be positive.

FEDLAND is a measure of the percent of land in a state that is owned by the federal government. This variable proxies for parks, rivers, mountains, forests, and other environmental amenities that are valuable to environmentalists. All else equal, people in close proximity to these amenities are expected to be more sensitive to federal preservation efforts; the sign on the variable is expected to be positive.

The Estimates

The model was run for the years 1990 through 1993 for all fifty states with the years 1991 through 1993 being dummied.[8] Two transformations were made in preparing for the estimates. First, the dependent variable, INT, was put in the logistic response form, since its values are bounded by one and zero. Then, all models were run in log-linear, double-log, linear-log, and non-log forms. In every case, the results were more robust in the double-log form. All tests of significance are two-tailed tests, assuming a normal distribution. These results are reported and discussed.

Table 10.1, equation 1, presents the regression results of the full model where the L before variables indicates that natural logs have been taken. ONE represents a constant term. Several variables of interest emerge from the full model. Examining societal variables first, we find no surprises in LPCY. LPCY is positive and significant at the 5 percent level and suggests that a 1 percent increase in per capita income creates an 0.31 percent increase in environmental group membership. For South Carolina, this implies that a \$310 increase in per capita income will yield a 1 percent increase in environmental interest group membership. LYG however is not significant at any level, which implies a zero valued second derivative for interest group memberships with respect to per capita income.

LPOPDEN is significant at the 1 percent level. The negative size indicates that a one percent decrease in population density is associated with a 0.19 percent increase in environmental interest group membership. The result implies that interest group formation is not affected by the reduction in transactions costs that are associated with an increase in population density, which is to say that group memberships are produced by some national production process. The negative sign suggests that the environmental movement is more rural or suburban than urban.

LEDUC is the strongest of the societal variables and is significant at the 1 percent level. The coefficient indicates that a 1 percent increase in LEDUC is associated with a 1.48 percent increase in the membership of environmental interest groups. For South Carolina, this indicates that if 21,000 additional people were to obtain a bachelor's degree, we would expect to see an increase in the combined membership of the four groups of over 1,600 new members. LAGE is not significant, implying that the environmental movement is not a youth movement.

Interesting results are also seen in the coefficients of the environmental variables. LLCV is significant at the 5 percent level with, as expected, a positive sign on the coefficient. As the states' political delegations score increases by 1 percent, the environmental interest groups experience a corresponding increase of 0.12 percent in their membership.

Table 10.2. The Full Model

Equation 1 Dependant Variable: LINT Full Model		Equation 2 Dependent Variable: LINT Revised Full Model	
Variable	Coefficient	Variable	Coefficient
ONE	-11.3983 $(5.551)^c$	ONE	-10.1974 $(8.465)^c$
LPCY	0.310670 $(2.419)^b$	LPCY	0.312724 $(2.518)^b$
LYG	0.002303 (0.177)		
LEDUC	1.48094 $(9.670)^c$	LEDUC	1.491 $(10.942)^c$
LPOPDEN	-0.198254 $(4.489)^c$	LPOPDEN	-0.185043 $(4.683)^c$
LAGE	0.432632 (0.766)		
LFEDLAND	0.139950 $(6.770)^c$	LFEDLAND	0.141872 $(7.072)^c$
LHAZWAS	0.208814 $(5.912)^c$	LHAZWAS	0.201331 $(6.052)^c$
LTRI	-0.001109 (0.062)		
LLCV	0.126010 $(2.651)^b$	LLCV	0.118819 $(2.602)^b$
Y91	0.082359 (1.039)	Y91	0.061547 (0.904)
Y92	0.058227 (0.707)	Y92	0.020924 (0.307)
Y93	-0.028508 (0.322)	Y93	-0.072777 (1.077)
R-Squared	0.63442	R-Squared	0.63183
Adj R-Squared	0.61096	Adj. R-Squared	0.61439
F-Stat	27.0428	F-Stat	36.2298
N:	200	N:	200

(T-Statistic in Parentheses).
[b]Significant at the 5% two-tailed level.
[c]Significant at the 1% two-tailed level.

LHAZWAS is significant at the one percent level, and has a positive coefficient. The coefficient indicates that a 1 percent increase in the hazardous waste sites per square mile causes a 0.20 percent increase in environmental group membership. For the state of South Carolina, this would mean that one more state or national hazardous waste site in the state would increase environmental group memberships by 1.1 percent.[9] LTRI is insignificant. This questions the importance of the TRI in the minds of environmental interest groups. If there is no response from an increase or a decrease in TRI emissions, then the incentives for firms that fall under EPCRA to decrease toxic emissions are reduced.

LFEDLAND is also significant at the 1 percent level, and has a positive coefficient. The coefficient indicates that a 1 percent increase in the share of land owned by the government causes a 0.13 percent increase in the membership of environmental groups. In South Carolina, if the government were to purchase 301 square miles and convert that area into state or national parks, we would expect to see a membership increase in the four interest groups of 0.13 percent. Equation number two in table 10.1 shows the results of the model with YG, AGE, and TRI removed. As indicated, there is little change in the coefficients.

Estimates for Individual Groups

As mentioned earlier, each of the four organizations included in the sample came from a specific market niche. The Nature Conservancy participates in land transactions and conservation; the NRDC specializes in litigation; the Sierra Club is a multi-issue group; and the National Audubon Society originated as an organization that focused its attention on bird watching and camping, but has recently become a multi-issue group. Recently, with the exception of the Nature Conservancy, most environmental groups have increased litigation activities.

There are two competing hypotheses about the behavior of these organizations. The first is that they all produce the same product and are competing on the basis of some sort of brand-name capital. The second is that each group specializes in some particular aspect of environmental policy. If the first hypothesis holds, then estimates for each organization will have similar coefficients and t-statistics. On the other hand, if each organization has actually specialized, then the coefficients and the significant variables will vary across organizations.

Estimates of the full model for each individual environmental organization are reported in table 10.2. While there is some fluctuation, the magnitudes and significance of LEDUC, LFEDLAND, LPOPDEN, LHAZWAS, and LLCV all remain relatively the same. LTRI is the most interesting variable that arises when the model is separated into the individual groups. For the Sierra Club, the variable becomes significant at the 1 percent level. LTRI becomes significant for the National Audubon Society at the 10 percent level. The variable attains borderline significance for the NRDC, and is insignificant for the Nature

Table 10.3. Membership by Individual Groups

Variable	Nature Conservancy Dep. Var: LNATCON Coeff.	NRDC Dep. Var: LNRDC Coeff.	Sierra Club Dep. Var: LSIERRA Coeff.	Audubon Society Dep.Var: LAUD Coeff.
ONE	- 10.2193	- 19.4074	-20.3896	-9.70864
	$(3.755)^c$	$(7.402)^c$	$(11.213)^c$	$(5.114)^c$
LPCY	0.219220	0.766175	0.611327	0.393613
	(1.288)	$(4\ 671)^c$	$(5.375)^c$	$(3.314)^c$
LYG	-0.013576	-0.012334	0.0101324	0.0128329
	(0.787)	(0.742)	(0.879)	(1.066)
LEDUC	1.61845	1.76505	1.30946	1.03933
	$(7930)^c$	$(\ 8.977)^c$	$(9.603)^c$	$(7.300)^c$
LPOPDEN	-.218443	-0.258743	-0.03066	-0.294553
	$(3.732)^c$	$(4.582)^c$	(0.784)	$(7.123)^c$
LAGE	-0.1137480	0.706011	1.42177	.0207018
	(0.152)	(.979)	$(2.842)^c$	(0.040)
LFEDLAND	0.158832	0.108325	.189966	0.035519
	$(5.797)^c$	$(4.104)^c$	$(10.378)^c$	$(1.859)^a$
LHAZWAS	0.228853	.258743	0.077987	0.233190
	$(4.889)^c$	$(5.737)^c$	$(2.494)^b$	$(7.141)^c$
LTRI	0.027282	-0.036868	-0.044109	-0.03140
	(1.142)	(1.602)	$(2.764)^c$	$(1.884)^a$
LLCV	0.135296	0.271631	0.177819	0.149934
	$(2.147)^b$	$(4.475)^c$	$(4.224)^c$	$(3.411)^c$
Y91	0.131484	0.002570	0.264351	.058301
	(1.252)	(0.025)	$(3.766)^c$	(0.796)
Y92	0.136179	-0.388241	0.190246	-0.032705
	(1.247)	$(3.691)^c$	$(2.608)^c$	(0.429)
Y93	0.120076	-0.503661	0.0924721	-0.248955
	(1.024)	$(4.457)^c$	(1.180)	$(3.042)^c$
R-Squared:	0.57368	0.71355	0.75117	0.62078
Adj. R-Sq:.	0.54632	0.69516	0.73520	0.59645
F-Stat:	20.9697	38.8175	47.0433	25.5102
N:	200	200	200	200

(T-Statistic in Parentheses).
[a]Significant at the 10% two-tailed level.
[b]Significant at the 5 % two-tailed level.
[c]Significant at the 1% two-tailed level.

Conservancy. Recall that LTRI was not significant for the combined four group estimate.

When significant, the coefficient on LTRI carries a negative sign. The result implies that a 1,000 thousand pound decrease in TRI emissions yields a 0.03 percent increase in the National Audubon Society membership and a 0.04 percent increase for the Sierra Club. This result is intriguing.

In the theory section, the sign on TRI was predicted to be positive, arguing that the more toxics that are released, the greater the cost to members of the community, and therefore, the more people who would join interest groups in an effort to reduce emissions. The negative sign indicates that the more toxic releases there are, the fewer the number of environmental interest group members. A possible explanation for this sign revolves around the argument that firms that emit toxics behave rationally, and that they equate at the margin. In deciding how much and how many pollutants to release, the firm looks around and attempts to estimate the amount of political pressure that might be generated for each specific level of emissions. Where there is already a large concentration of environmental interest groups, the political pressure is greater. Here, the costs of reducing emissions may be less than the cost of having to work with the environmental interest groups. When there is not a large concentration of environmental interest groups, the political pressure would be less. Here, the costs of the political pressure could be less then the cost of decreasing chemical emissions that fall under the TRI.

LAGE, which was not significant in the combined estimate, proves more interesting for the Sierra Club; the coefficient on LAGE is significant at the 1 percent level. The result implies that the Sierra Club markets memberships to a distinct demographic group. LPCY is significant for all the organizations except the Nature Conservancy, which implies no income sensitivity for that organization. Again, we see distinct differences across the four organizations.

The dummy variables for year also gain significance for some of the organizations. For the Nature Conservancy the dummy coefficients are borderline significant and positive, which suggest a shift in that organization's growth path. The dummy variables for the NRDC become increasingly negative and more significant through time, which suggests that support for litigation activities has become weaker. A similar pattern is observed in the National Audubon Society estimate. In summary, the individual estimates provide evidence that each group has distinctive features that set it apart from the others. At the same time, some social forces, as revealed by other variables in the model, seem to have similar effects on memberships.

Religion and Environmentalism

The second set of estimates delves further into the membership process and examines the effects of religion on the environmental movement. Many modern environmental writers argue that the environmental and religious movements have many similarities. For example, Nelson states that "over large areas of environmental policy there is a large theological content." Nelson also points out that environmentalists "ground commitment to protect the environment in traditional Judaic and Christian tenets of faith" (Nelson, 1993). Other writers comment that the parallels between the two movements are "instructive" (Rubin, 1994).

If these and other writers are correct in their beliefs that environmentalism is grounded in religion, two possible arguments emerge. Environmentalism and religion are either substitutes or complements. If environmentalism is the new religion born from the Puritanical beliefs of the last century, then it is possible that these two goods are complements. States that have large religious communities could have already laid the groundwork for other possible religious organizations to move in and prosper. If environmentalism is a religion, then it could be the case that the more conducive certain states are to other religious beliefs, the more conducive they are to environmentalism. In this case, in states that are highly religious we would expect to see a larger degree of environmentalism.

On the other hand, if environmentalism is a religion, then we would expect it to compete with other religions for membership, and be a substitute. Environmentalism could be a substitute for Methodists, just as being Methodist is a substitute for being Episcopalian. When one religion is experiencing an upswing in support, the other religion should be experiencing a downswing, all else equal. If this argument defines the relationship between environmentalism and religion, then we would expect to see environmentalism stronger in states where other religions are weak, and weak in states where other religions are strong. Environmentalism and religion could be substitutable goods, just like Coke and Pepsi. The competing theoretical debate must be settled empirically.

The Estimate

The religion cross-sectional model is run in ordinary least squares, where the dependent variable is adjusted to fit the logistic response function. The model states:

$$INT = f(REL, PCY, YG, EDUC, POPDEN, AGE, LCV, HAZWAS, TRI, FEDLAND)$$

This model contains the same variables as the full model from table 10.1, but contains fifty observations that correspond to all fifty states in 1990. REL is measured as the percent of a state's population reported as either of the Christian or Jewish faith. According to theory, we are unsure of the sign of the coefficient. We expect the signs on the remaining coefficients to be similar to those that were discovered in the original full model from table 10.1. Again the model was run in linear, double-log, log-linear, and linear-log forms, with the double-log results

Table 10.4. The Religion Model

Equation 1 Dependant Variable: LINT Full Model with Religion		Equation 2 Dependent Variable: LINT Full Model Without Religion	
Variable	Coefficient	Variable	Coefficient
ONE	-5.2556	ONE	-7.68464
	(1.084)		(1.839)[a]
LREL	-0.2649		
	(0.990)		
LPCY	0.2572	LPCY	0.3195
	(1.619)		(2.191)[b]
LYG	0.0016	LYG	0.0042
	(0.080)		(0.199)
LEDUC	1.4462	LEDUC	1.410
	(4.989)[c]		(4.905)[c]
CLPOPDEN	-0.2106	LPOPDEN	-0.2367
	(2.375)[b]		(2.795)[c]
LAGE	0.9460	LAGE	1.192
	(0.772)		(0.993)
LFEDLAND	0.1003	LFEDLAND	0.1224
	(2.052)[a]		(2.812)[c]
LHAZWAS	0.1992	LHAZWAS	0.2102
	(2.897)[c]		(3.099)[c]
LTRI	0.0252	LTRI	0.0241
	(0.703)		(0.669)
LLCV	0.2495	LLCV	0.3086
	(1.791)[a]		(2.450)[b]
R-Square	0.73189	R-Square	0.72515
Adj R-Square	0.66314	Adj. R-Square	0.66331
F-Stat	10.646	F-Stat	11.726
N:	50	N:	50

(T-Statistic in Parentheses).
[a]Significant at the 10% two-tailed level.
[b]Significant at the 5% two-tailed level.
[c]Significant at the 1% two-tailed level.

being more robust. The estimation results are found in table 10.3, equations 1 and 2, with and without religion in the model.

In the original religion model from table 10.3, equation 1, the sign on LREL is negative, but the t-statistic is not significant. This implies that religion could be a substitute, but at this point there is not enough significance attached to the t-statistic to make this statement with any strength. In contrast to the full model from table 10.1, LPCY is not significant in the religion model. The significance and the coefficient on LPOPDEN, significant at the 1 percent level, and LEDUC, significant at the 1 percent level, imply the same educational and population effects on group formation as the full model from table 10.1. Again LAGE and LYG are insignificant. The environmental variables in the religion model create similar implications as the full model from table 10.1. LLCV is positive and significant at the 10 percent level. As the state's political delegations' LCV increases by one percent, environmental group membership will increase by 0.24 percent. Again LTRI is insignificant. LHAZWAS is significant at the 1 percent level, and the coefficient is consistent with the value in full model. LFEDLAND is significant at the 10 percent level in the religion model, and has the same coefficient as it does in the full model.

With the current variable of interest being LREL, we omit the variables that were not significant in table 10.3, equation 1, with the exclusion of LREL, and compute the regression. The results can be found in table 10.4, equations 1 and 2. The variable of interest then becomes significant at the 10 percent, two-tailed, level. The coefficient on LREL implies that a 1 percent increase in religion causes an 0.46 percent decrease in environmental interest group membership. For the state of South Carolina, this implies that if 100 more people considered themselves as being of either Christian or Jewish faith, than we would expect to see forty-six fewer members in conservation organizations. The results of the remaining variables are generally consistent with the religion model from table 10.3; LEDUC is significant at the 1 percent level with a strong coefficient; LPOPDEN is still negative and significant at the 10 percent level; LHAZWAS is positive and significant at the 1 percent level. LLCV is the only variable that experiences significant changes in the modified religion model from table 10.4, as it losses its significance as an explanatory variable.

Estimation of the Religion Model for Each Environmental Group

Individual estimates were made for each environmental group to examine the question: are all environmental groups similar or do they specialize and find their market niche in the market for religion? The results of the first individual estimates are found in table 10.5. Then, the same variables are eliminated that were eliminated in the earlier market niche test, and those regression results can be found in table 10.6.

Table 10.5. Modified Religion Model

Equation 1
Dependent Variable: LINT
Revised Model with Religion

Equation 2
Dependent Variable: LINT
Revised Model without Religion

Variable	Coefficient	Variable	Coefficient
ONE	-5.94699 (3.815)[c]	ONE	-7.90194 (6.385)[c]
LREL	-0.464543 (1.963)[a]		
LEDUC	0.63471 (6.200)[c]	LEDEC	0. 64839 (6.061)[c]
LPOPDEN	-0.151288 (1.880)[a]	LPOPDEN	-0.185004 (2.281)[b]
LFEDLAND	0.102635 (2.203)[b]	LFEDLAND	0.147451 (3.519)[c]
LHAZWAS	0.182762 (2.772)[c]	LHAZWAS	0.205514 (3.068)[c]
LLCV	0.148018 (1.182)	LLCV	0.231771 (1.907)[a]
R-Square	0.70836	R-Square	0.68223
Adj R-Square	0.66766	Adj. R-Square	0.64612
F-Stat	17.4069	F-Stat	18.8930
N:	50	N:	50

(T-Statistic in Parentheses).
[a]Significant at the 10% two-tailed test.
[b]Significant at the 5% two-tailed test.
[c]Significant at the 1% two-tailed test.

Table 10.6. Membership by Individual Groups in the Religion Model

	Nature Conservancy Dep. Var: LNATCON	NRDC Dep. Var: LNRDC	Sierra Club Dep. Var: LSIERRA	Audubon Society Dep. Var: LAUD
Variable	Coeff.	Coeff.	Coeff.	Coeff.
ONE	-12.9932	-14.6131	-13.4614	-7.65545
	(1.916)[b]	(2.608)[b]	(7.414)[c]	(1.677)[a]
LREL	-0.118945	-0.739619	-0.42869	0.680302
	(0.318)	(2.391)[b]	(1.985)[a]	(2.700)[c]
LPCY	0.364449	0.307563	0.307940	0.047250
	(1.639)	(1.674)	(2.892)[c]	(0.316)
LYG	-0.021070	-0.020063	-0.002403	0.03409
	(0.708)	(0.817)	(0.140)	(1.704)[a]
LEDUC	1.51046	1.81040	1.37278	1.0935
	(3.723)[c]	(5.401)[c]	(5.866)[c]	(4.005)[c]
LPOPDEN	-0.269729	-0.139378	-0.00316	-0.232726
	(2.173)[a]	(1.359)	(0.044)	(2.786)[c]
LAGE	0.359735	0.910277	1.77808	0.941805
	(0.210)	(0.642)	(1.797)[a]	(0.815)
LFEDLAND	0.127215	0.029239	0.140468	-0.023214
	(1.859)[a]	(0.517)	(3.558)[c]	(0.504)
LHAZWAS	0.232467	0.165240	0.040739	0.188347
	(2.416)[b]	(2.078)[b]	(0.734)	(2.908)[c]
LTRI	0.0645711	-0.006343	-0.009564	-0.0264493
	(1.273)	(0.152)	(0.319)	(0.780)
LLCV	0.248254	0.352217	0.309240	0.208511
	(1.273)	(2.186)[b]	(2.748)[c]	(1.588)
R-Square	0.60994	0.76676	0.82682	0.71016
Adj. R-Sq.	0.50993	0.70695	0.78242	0.63584
F-Stat:	6.0985	12.8209	18.6201	9.5555
N:	50	50	50	50

(T-Statistic in Parentheses).
[a]Significant at the 10% two-tailed level.
[b]Significant at the 5% two-tailed level.
[c]Significant at the 1% two-tailed level.

Brian Kropp

Table 10.7. Membership by Individual Groups in the Modified Religion Model

	Nature Conservancy	NRDC ety	Sierra Club	Audubon Soci-
	Dep. Var: NATCON	Dep. Var: LNRDC		Dep. Var:
		LSIERRA	Dep.Var: LAUD	
Variable	Coeff.	Coeff.	Coeff.	Coeff.
ONE	-9.52642	-11.4145	-12.9497	-4.54682
	$(3.171)^c$	$(4.248)^c$	$(6.722)^c$	$(2.002)^b$
LREL	-0.245757	-0.818750	-0.509868	-0.786887
	(0.752)	$(2.791)^c$	$(2.425)^b$	$(3.175)^c$
LPCY	0.235679	0.3037283	0.352131	0.0705314
	(1.136)	$(1.761)^a$	$(2.815)^c$	(0.478)
LEDUC	1.65134	1.91163	1.52173	1.19544
	$(4.530)^c$	$(6.323)^c$	$(7.022)^c$	$(4.679)^c$
LPOPDEN	-0.168716	-0.142545	0.016257	-0.254299
	(1.578)	(1.495)	(0.238)	$(3.157)^c$
LFEDLAND	0.134467	0.016071	0.142505	-0.048228
	$(2.139)^b$	(0.305)	$(3.774)^c$	(1.084)
LHAZWAS	0.186577	0.169634	0.027574	0.206570
	$(2.051)^b$	$(2.276)^b$	(0.523)	$(3.279)^c$
LLCV	0.186577	0.316493	.248798	0.183763
	$(2.139)^b$	$(2.167)^b$	$(2.376)^b$	(1.489)
R-Square:	0.57747	0.75956	0.81233	0.67838
Adj. R-Sq:	0.51851	0.71948	0.78106	0.62478
F-Stat:	9.7947	18.9539	25.9716	12.6556
N:	50	50	50	50

(T-Statistic in Parentheses).
[a]Significant at the 10% two-tailed level.
[b]Significant at the 5% two-tailed level.
[c]Significant at the 1% two-tailed level.

When the organizations are separated and religion is incorporated into the model, the significance of religion becomes very interesting for the NRDC, the Sierra Club, and the National Audubon Society. LREL is negative and significant at the 10 percent level for the Sierra Club, negative and significant at the 1 percent level for the National Audubon Society, and negative and significant at the 5 percent level for the NRDC. At the same time, LREL is insignificant for the Nature Conservancy. This result strengthens the argument that there are differences in the market perceptions of these organizations.

The NRDC, the Sierra Club, and the National Audubon Society are substitutes for religion. The coefficient on the Sierra Club indicates that a 1 percent increase in religion causes a 0.42 percent decrease in membership for the Sierra Club. In the Audubon model, LREL suggests that a 1 percent increase in religion causes a 0.68 percent decrease in Audubon membership. The strongest religion effect occurs for the NRDC, where a 1 percent increase in religion causes a 0.73 percent decrease in membership for the NRDC. In fact, the NRDC and religion are fairly close to being perfect substitutes.

Note that the coefficient on LAGE again becomes significant for the Sierra Club, this time at the 10 percent level. This reinforces the argument that the Sierra Club is a movement of young people, while the other organizations are not. The remaining variables are generally consistent with the full model from table 10.1. LEDUC is significant for all the organizations at the 1 percent level, except for the NRDC. LPOPDEN and LHAZWAS are significant for the Audubon Society and the Nature Conservancy. This result further supports the argument presented earlier.

A Comparison of Eastern and Western Environmentalism

Many environmental studies have argued that there are differences between the eastern and western parts of the United States in their approach to environmental policy. In an attempt to see if this is true of environmentalism, additional tests were done to compare the East with the West. This model takes the same form as the full cross-sectional model and covers the same years, but is run on states west of the Mississippi River, excluding Hawaii and Alaska, for a total of ninety-two observations. The eastern model is run for all four years on states east of the Mississippi River for a total of 100 observations. The results of the western model are reported in table 10.7, equation 1, where the modified regression can be found in equation 2. The results of the eastern model are given in table 10.8, equations 1 and 2.

Table 10.8. Western Model

Equation 1		Equation 2	
Dependant Variable: LINT		Dependent Variable: LINT	
Western States Model		Revised Western States Model	
Variable	Coefficient	Variable	Coefficient
ONE	-8.62852 (2.926)[b]	ONE	-8.58445 (6.341)
LPCY	0.0811982 (0.669)	LPCY	0.135316 (1.141)
LYG	-0.0062153 (0.379)		
LEDUC	1.58867 (6.298)[c]	LEDUC	1.52810 (7.514)[c]
LPOPDEN	-0.127018 (1.300)	LPOPDEN	-0.139218 (2.450)[b]
LAGE	0.215203 (0.204)		
LFEDLAND	0.247844 (10.357)[c]	LFEDLAND	0.243075 (11.375)[c]
LHAZWAS	0.159209 (2.168)[b]	LHAZWAS	0.177989 (3.619)[c]
LTRI	-0.043747 (2.409)[b]		
LLCV	-0.055521 (1.054)	LLCV	-0.040100 (0.813)
Y91	0.0319476 (0.260)	Y91	0.0248716 (0.285)
Y92	0.0169456 (0.127)	Y92	-0.0209234 (0.238)
Y93	-0.0933416 (0.626)	Y93	-0.089628 (1.042)
R-Square	0.80510	R-Square	0.79380
Adj R-Square	0.77550	Adj. R-Square	0.77116
F-Stat	27.1950	F-Stat	35.0737
N:	92	N:	92

(T-Statistic in Parentheses).
[a]Significant at the 10% two-tailed level.
[b]Significant at the 5 % two-tailed level.
[c]Significant at the 1% two-tailed level.

Table 10.9. Eastern Model

Equation 1 Dependant Variable: LINT Eastern States Model		Equation 2 Dependent Variable: LINT Revised Eastern States Model	
Variable	Coefficient	Variable	Coefficient
ONE	-13.1471 (3.123)^c	ONE	-15.178 (5.028)^c
LPCY	.1.07595 (2.851)^c	LPCY	0.936248 (2.596)^b
LYG	0.014698 (1.171)		
LEDUC	1.39759 (6.453)^c	LEDUC	1.33576 (7.148)^c
LPOPDEN	-0.468711 (8.4l6)^c	LPOPDEN	-0.454243 (7.978)^c
LAGE	-1.19543 (1.844^a)		
LFEDLAND	-0.061174 (2.329)^b	LFEDLAND	-0.061904 (2.273)^b
LHAZWAS	0.176086 (5 555)^c	LHAZWAS	0.174431 (5.277)^c
LTRI	0.065080 (3.440)^c		
LLCV	0.320161 (4.652)^c	LLCV	0.341354 (4.768)^c
Y91	0.0745984 (1.064)	Y91	0.126118 (1.890)^b
Y92	0.0441105 (0.589)	Y92	0.0830370 (1.245)
Y93	-0.0292589 (0.259)	Y93	-0.0144207 (0.217)
R-Square	0.85762	R-Square	0.83562
Adj R-Square	0.83798	Adj R-Square	0.81918
F-Stat	43.6709	F-Stat	50.8353
N:	100	N:	100

(T-Statistic in Parentheses)

^{a}Significant at the 10% two tailed level.

^{b}Significant at the 5% two tailed level.

^{c}Significant at the 1% two tailed level

From the results, it appears that there are vast differences between environmentalists in the East and the West. For the western model LPCY, LPOPDEN, and LLCV become insignificant. LHAZWAS, LEDUC, and LFEDLAND all remain significant and maintain their coefficient signs. However, the coefficient on LFEDLAND becomes more significant for the western model than the full model, and actually becomes negative for the eastern model. This result implies that people in the western states maintain an even higher value for the ability to camp and engage in other activities that involve parks. In the eastern model LPCY and LLCV remain significant, and LAGE becomes significant at the 10 percent level and negative. This result points to another difference in the environmental movement across states. Environmentalism in the East does not coincide with a youth movement. In fact the sign and significance of LAGE in the eastern model point out that environmentalism in the East is a movement of people older than the 18 to 34 age group. The other variable of interest is LTRI. For the western states LTRI is negative and significant at the 5 percent level. This result is consistent with the earlier discussion about the effects of TRI. However, for the eastern states LTRI is positive and significant at the 1 percent level. The eastern result is consistent with the original hypothesis that as the amount of TRI chemicals released increases, so do the number of environmentalists. This result points out even greater differences between environmentalists in the East, and in the West.

The explanation for the income, federal land, and League of Conservation Voter effects can be attributable to the way that easterners and westerners observe value. A consumer can gain three types of value: use value, existence value, and option value. Yellowstone National Park is used as an example to explain the different types of values. Some consumers will actually hike and camp in the national park. They will climb the mountains and touch the trees. The utility that they gain can be measured in the use-value category. They are gaining utility from being in the woods. Other consumers never have a chance to visit the forest or see a spotted owl, they do not gain any use value from these things. However, they gain utility just from knowing that somewhere out there, there are old growth forests that are not being cut down. This utility can be measured in existence value. Option value is a slightly more abstract concept. Certain people, if they could, would buy an option to visit Yellowstone at some point in the future. If they can buy this option, then they would be able to preserve the natural resource.[10]

These different types of values help explain the difference among the coefficients and the significance of the variables between the eastern and western models. In the western half of the United States, there are greater amounts of national parks and amenities than there are in the East. Westerners are able to gain use value out of these amenities. They swim in the rivers and camp in the mountains. This explains the increased significance of LFEDLAND in the western model.

Easterners, in general, are not able to appreciate the same natural resources that westerners do. The value that they receive from nature is of the existence and option value types. They are willing to absorb the costs of joining an environmental group to know that there are spotted owls alive in the Pacific Northwest. Easterners express their existence and option values through the two variables LPCY and LLCV. As they become richer they are more willing to spend money to assure that the Grand Canyon stays clean, even though they may never visit. The expression of their existence and option values also takes shape through the effect on the LLCV variable. Environmental interest group members in the East support legislation that is "green" in nature. They support this legislation even though they may never see the benefits from it. According to this theory, supporting this legislation just makes them feel good. Second, eastern environmentalists, by supporting "green" legislation are, in effect, buying an option to visit the natural amenities that they are voting to protect today.

LFEDLAND being negative in the eastern model is consistent with this argument. Potential environmental interest group members in the East, who are already in states that have access to national parks, have no incentive to spend resources in order to gain existence or option values. They can gain use value from the national parks that are close to them, and they will not join environmental groups.

Estimates for Individual Groups in the Eastern and Western Models

Tables 10.9 and 10.10 present results for western and eastern estimates for each individual group. Results from these models not only support the argument that each group has found their own market niche, but that each group has found its own market niche in each half of the country, and that those niches are different.

The Nature Conservancy model result has some variables that are similar in both the eastern and western models, but has other variables whose estimates change. LPCY and LAGE become borderline significant in the eastern model, but they stay insignificant in the western model. LLCV is insignificant in the western model, but significant at the 1 percent level in the eastern model. The dummy variables for year become significant and positive for the eastern model, but remain insignificant for the western model. LTRI has the same signed coefficients as it did in the combined eastern and western models.

The NRDC also experiences similar changes in the eastern and western models. LYG becomes significant in the western model at the 5 percent level, and the coefficient of 0.04 gives the slope of the second derivative of the per capita income line. The coefficient on LYG in the eastern model is insignificant. LHAZWAS also becomes insignificant for the western model, but is significant at the 1 percent level for the eastern model. Much like the results for the Nature Conservancy estimate, the sign on LTRI is significant and positive for the

Table 10.10. Membership by Individual Groups in the Western Model

Variable	Nature Conservancy Dep. Var: LNATCON Coeff.	NRDC Dep. Var: LNRDC Coeff.	Sierra Club Dep.Var: LSIERRA Coeff.	Audubon Society Dep.Var: LAUD Coeff
ONE	-9.09838 (2.167)[b]	-7.50671 (2.259)[b]	-14.6414 (4.640)[c]	-2.92994 (1.124)
LPCY	0.093312 (0.540)	0.206458 (1.509)	0.287330 (2.211)[b]	0.142979 (1.332)
LYG	-0.0130385 (0.558)	0.041238 (2.231)[b]	0.027038 (1.540)	0.0061260 (0.422)
LEDUC	1.61879 (4.506)[c]	1.97564 (6.950)[c]	1.76585 (6.541)[c]	1.15270 (5.167)[c]
LPOPDEN	-0.269247 (1.935)[a]	0.0422748 (0.384)	0.247009 (2.362)[b]	0.128970 (1.492)
LAGE	0.330708 (0.220)	-2.01483 (1.692)[a]	-0.277057 (0.245)	-1.66630 (1.783)[a]
LFEDLAND	0.272074 (7.983)[c]	0.278181 (10.316)[c]	0.283579[c] (11.072)[c]	0.129715 (6.129)[c]
LHAZWAS	0.246232 (2.354)[b]	0.0209294 (0.253)	-0.110893 (1.411)	0.125751 (1.936)[a]
LTRI	-0.017152 (0.564)	-0.115881 (4.817)[c]	-0.103325 (4.522)[c]	-0.0781684 (4.140)[c]
LLCV	-0.122516 (1.633)	0.065618 (1.106)	0.082633 (1.466)	0.0397610 (0.854)
Y91	0.0823093 (0.470)	-0.258329 (1.864)[a]	0.121037 (0.920)	-0.175591 (1.615)
Y92	0.101604 (0.536)	-0.598354 (3.992)[c]	0.086853 (0.610)	-0.211637 (1.799)[a]
Y93	0.084569 (0.398)	-0.851861 (5.066)[c]	-0.157898 (0.989)	-0.486726 (3.689)[c]
R-Squared:	0.73709	0.81300	0.80010	0.71007
Adj. R-Sq:	0.69716	0.78460	0.76974	0.66604
F-Stat:	18.4572	28.6222	6.3503	16.1236
N:	92	92	92	92

(T-Statistic in Parentheses).
[a]Significant at the 10% two-tailed level.
[b]Significant at the 5 % two-tailed level.
[c']Significant at the 1% two-tailed level.

Table 10.11. Membership by Individual Groups in the Eastern Model

	Nature Conservancy Dep.Var: LNATCON	NRDC Dep. Var: LNRDC	Sierra Club Dep. Var: LSIERRA	Audubon Society Dep.Var: LAUD
Variable	Coeff.	Coeff.	Coeff.	Coeff
ONE	-10.4867 (1.925)[a]	-36.1156 (6.396)[c]	-25.2548 (6.737)[c]	-9.47502 (2.188)[b]
LPCY	0.617229 (1.264)	3.09925 (6.122)[c]	1.65455 (4.922)[c]	0.952182 (2.453)[b]
LYG	0.012640 (0.778)	0.000458 (0.027)	-0.000978 (0.088)	0.0247928 (1.921)
LEDUC	1.54649 (5.519)[c]	1.22799 (4.227)[c]	0.910227 (4.719)[c]	1.38087 (6.199)[c]
LPOPDEN	-0.509046 (7.064)[c]	-0.616061 (8.247)[c]	-0.207081 (4.175)[c]	-0.511379 (8.927)[c]
LAGE	-1.20831 (1.472)	-0.758167 (0.891)	0.169134 (0.299)	-1.96056 (3.004)[c]
LFEDLAND	-0.088319 (2.645)[c]	-0.074198 (2.143)[b]	0.034316 (1.493)	-0.0641792 (2.417)[b]
LHAZWAS	0.178519 (4.353)[c]	0.215605 (5.070)[c]	0.0839788 (2.975)[c]	0.104472 (6.305)[c]
LTRI	0.079219 (3.237)[c]	0.095638 (3.769)[c]	0.034461 (2.045)[b]	0.0630645 (3.241)[c]
LLCV	0.436302 (4.900)[c]	0.474667 (3.769)[c]	0.237340 (3.872)[c]	0.220836 (3.120)[c]
Y91	0.155878 (1.718)[a]	0.076229 (0.810)	0.279608 (4.476)[c]	-0.100874 (1.398)
Y92	0.208022 (2.145)[b]	-0.432327 (4.301)[c]	0.118575 (1.777)[a]	-0.071883 (0.933)
Y93	0.222383 (2.108)[b]	-0.482341 (4.409)[c]	0.085251 (1.174)	-0.271135 (3.232)[c]
R-Square	0.79673	0.89300	0.86671	0.83283
Adj. R-Sq	0.76870	0.87824	0.84833	0.80977
F-Stat:	28.4172	60.573	47.1430	36.1190
N:	100	100	100	100

(T-Statistic in parentheses).
[a]Significant at the 10% two-tailed level.
[b]Significant at the 5 % two-tailed level.
[c]Significant at the 1% two-tailed level.

eastern model, and significant and negative for the western model. If we recall from the full model that LYG was insignificant and LHAZWAS was significant at the 1 percent level for the total organization, we realize that the NRDC has found two different market niches based on regional location. Some of the results for the Sierra Club are consistent with those of the Nature Conservancy, and the NRDC. LTRI has the same effect as it did on the other organizations. LFEDLAND is significant at the 1 percent level for the western model, and insignificant in the eastern model. The most interesting variable for the Sierra Club becomes LHAZWAS, which is positive and significant at the 1 percent level for the eastern model, and border line significant and negative in the western model.

The estimates for the National Audubon Society shows effects that are similar to those for the NRDC. In the eastern model, LYG becomes significant at the 5 percent level with a coefficient of 0.02, which provides a slope to the second derivative of the per capita income line, but LYG is insignificant in the western model. The estimates for LLCV and LTRI are consistent with the estimates for the full eastern and western models, and the estimates for each organization.

A Political Theory of Environmental Interest Group Formation

Some environmental scholars argue that the recent downturn in support for environmental interest groups is nothing more then a cyclical phenomenon based on the national political makeup. After all, President Clinton and Vice President Gore are card-carrying environmentalists; interest groups can relax a bit. But as the previous estimates indicate, there is more to the story. Data tell us that the first upswing in environmental group membership occurred during the late 1960s and early 1970s. By some accounts, the first Earth Day, held in 1970, was the galvanizing event. Richard Nixon was in the White House.

Memberships continued to expand through the 1970s, while Gerald Ford and Jimmy Carter, two very different politicians, were presidents. Membership growth weakened in the early 1980s and then expanded later during the Reagan and Bush years (Smith, 1995). The cycle seems to be random with respect to the party of the president. Perhaps, other components of the political apparatus need to be considered.

In an effort to estimate political effects, a time series model was constructed using data on per capita national memberships in the four environmental organizations and national data on the other variables. The model tested, which provided the best fit in double-log form, is written:

INT=f(EDUC, PCY, PRES, SRATIO, HRATIO, Y70)

In this model INT is the percent of the national population that are members of the Nature Conservancy, The Sierra Club, or the National Audubon Society.[11]

INT was adjusted logistically. Once again PCY is the national per capita income; its coefficient is expected to be positive. EDUC is the national percentage of people that have a bachelor's degree. The coefficient is expected to be positive according to previous theory.

PRES is a dummy variable that becomes one if a Republican is in the White House, and is zero otherwise. The expected sign is positive, indicating that environmental interest group formation will increase with a Republican president. HRATIO is the ratio of Republicans to Democrats in the House of Representatives. As the number of Republicans increases relative to Democrats, we expect an increase in environmental interest group formation; the coefficient should be positive. SRATIO is the same ratio for the Senate. We have the same expectations about the sign on this coefficient. Y70 represents a dummy variable to account for the period when major national environmental statutes were written. The variable has a value of one for 1970 and for the following years. The full time series model was adjusted for first order serial correlation. The model is run on the years 1950 to 1994 for a total of forty-five observations.

The results of the estimate shown here do not provide support for a political theory.

LINT=ONE	LEDUC+	LPCY+	PRES-	LSRATIO-	LHRATIO+	Y70
-30.7172	1.55770	2.16598	0.05419	-0.190047	-0.081733	0.140313
(6.843)	(4.184)	(3.699)	(1.284)	(1.098)	(0.695)	(1.117)

R-Squared: 0.83621
Adj. R-Square: 0.80436

The coefficients on LPCY and LEDUC are positive and significant at the 1 percent level, but none of the remaining variables are significant. Other adjustments were made in an effort to find significant political variables, all without success.[12]

This unsuccessful modeling effort should not be interpreted to mean there is no relationship between the political makeup of the White House or Congress and environmental interest group membership. In any time series analysis numerous problems can arise, which may account for the apparent lack of a relationship. Popular literature does seem to argue that people make environmental decisions based on which political party holds the White House. Clearly, there is a difference in political beliefs among Nixon, Reagan, and Bush; however, in this type of modeling all of those presidents are treated as being equal. Second, as the presidents vary in their level of conservatism, people might respond not only by deciding to join an environmental interest group but also by switching membership among environmental interest groups. The more anti-environment the perception of the president, the more pro-environment group they will join.

Another family of problems arises when we start examining the supply side of the question. During the period of the estimate, splinter groups pulled away from some of the three organizations to form other groups. An example of this is when the Izak Walton League and Friends of the Earth left the Sierra Club. This effect is difficult to measure, and presents another problem in the time series estimation of interest groups.

The rise of environmental interest groups in the 1970s and 1980s not only made them larger national policy players but also made them less responsive to local problems (Smith, 1995). Some writers contend that this caused them to become less responsive to local needs and issues, providing openings for local environmental groups. Potential interest group members make rational choices about which group to join. With this in mind, they might believe that they will receive a higher benefit if they join local groups over national groups.

Conclusions

National environmental organizations form an important part of the U.S. environmental saga. They and their local counterparts transmit information to their members and to politicians, regulators, and industrialists. Although they are not-for-profit organizations, successful environmental interest groups must still gain revenues to fund their wide-ranging activities. This chapter has made the simple assumption that to maximize revenues, environmental interest groups must maximize membership.

The research reported here identifies economic forces that affect memberships. There is little doubt that events like Three Mile Island and the Bhopal chemical release give people incentives to join environmental interest groups. But waiting for catastrophic events to occur is not a viable strategy for interest group managers who seek to increase memberships.

Five major arguments for explaining environmental interest group formation were offered in section one of the report: educational attainment, rising incomes, environmental events, religiosity, and political cycles. The research reported here support all but the political cycle.

From this study, and every model that it has examined, it is clear that as populations become more educated or richer, they are more likely to join environmental interest groups. There is also strong evidence that memberships respond to incidents that do occur. As the number of hazardous waste sites increase, so do the incentives to join environmental interest groups. The evidence from this chapter suggests that some environmental interest groups are substitutes for religion. This result supports the argument that some types of environmental groups are in fact religions, and that some organizations are more religious than other organizations. Therefore, environmental interest group managers and those that have to work with environmental groups need to behave accordingly.

The analysis from this chapter shows that not all environmental groups are alike. Some are more responsive to income and education; others are more responsive to age or hazardous waste sites. For politicians and managers of firms, this implies that they need to tailor their behavior in accordance with the type of environmental group they are working with. More work needs to be done to find what the actual differences are across organizations that cause some to be more religious than others.

Additional evidence from this study suggests that not only are there religious differences across organizations but also there are differences across organizations based on geographic location. Western environmentalists are more concerned with the use value of federal lands than are easterners. Eastern environmentalists are more income responsive, and are more responsive to existence and option values than are western environmentalists. More work needs to be done to explain why there are differences between the East and West.

This chapter fails to reach a conclusion about the cyclical nature of the environmental movement. While the popular literature argues that there is a relationship between who controls the White House and the strength of environmental groups, a statistical analysis of the data does not support or contradict the argument with any strength. More work needs to be done attempting to find the relationship, if there is one, between the cyclical nature of the presidency and the environmental movement.

This chapter also provides strategic information to environmental interest groups managers who seek to build memberships. A marketing strategy would focus on those states or locations where the population is richer, more educated, have more national parks, more hazardous waste sites, a less dense population, and are less religious. The coefficients found in the various models provide response information for each of the characteristics. By knowing something about the cost of marketing, the efficient manager could equate at the margin and allocate effort where marginal gains are equal to marginal cost.

This chapter also provides information to any group that works with or receives pressure from environmental interest groups. For interest groups that work in conjunction with environmental groups, information is provided on where to concentrate efforts. For groups that receive negative pressure from environmental interest groups, this chapter supplies information about states and regions that exert the least pressure. Information is also provided to potential political candidates. Those involved in industrial development may also find the chapter useful. Finally, if potential politicians wish to pursue either a "green" or "anti-green" platform, they now have information as to where those efforts would be the most effective.

E.G. Nisbet (1991) wrote that "it is entirely possible that when the history of the twentieth century is finally written, the single most important social movement of the period will be judged to be environmentalism." This report identifies major forces that, in some cases, support and, in others, weaken the movement.

Notes

1. Membership data provided to author by the environmental organization noted.

2. A potentially better measure of environmentalism would be to use the dollar amount of donations from each state. Each organization has several different types of members dependent on the amount of their donation. This data would have been a more accurate measure of environmentalism because it could be the case that two states that have equal number of members have different levels of donations. If this were the case, then the state with a larger amount of donations, by some measures, would be a more pro-environment state. However, these data were not available.

3. There are two important points that need to be made. First, there are questions concerning the hardness of the data. Due to the membership collection techniques of the environmental groups, state membership numbers, though very close to accurate, may be slightly incorrect. Then, there are incentives for every volunteer organization to exaggerate their membership. To deal with this problem we assume consistency. If this is the case, then the implications of the model do not change, but the magnitudes of the coefficients do change.

4. This technique is consistent with environmental interest group membership as reported in periodicals such as the Green Index.

5. This analysis is consistent with previous work on environmental issues. See Randall (1987).

6. PCY, YG, EDUC, POPDEN, and AGE were all gathered from *The Statistical Abstract of the United States*, various issues, 1991-1994.

7. In 1986 the Emergency Planning and Community Right to Know Act (EPCRA) was enacted. The EPCRA legislation created a national data base that requires that the owners and operators of chemical facilities file reports on the release of certain chemicals to a national data base that is known as the TRI. For a full discussion of the TRI see Terry (1994).

8. Additional tests were performed dummying other years. While this did slightly change the magnitudes of the coefficients and the t-statistics, no new insight was gained.

9. There are two important points that need to be made. This variable could actually be more important than implied by this model. In this model, national environmental groups see an increase in membership with the addition of hazardous waste sites. However, concerns about local sites are higher for local than national groups (See Schnaiber and Gould, 1994). Second, there could be some correlation across states. For example, the Barnwell low level radiation plant is on the border between Georgia and South Carolina, and its location gives incentives for people to join environmental interest groups in both states. The type of modeling in this paper does not account for this fact.

10. For a further discussion of existence and option values see Randall (1987), Lindsay (1969), or Bishop (1982).

11. Again problems with the data need to be identified. In discussions with the employees of the environmental organizations, they state that due to their record-keeping techniques the membership data is generally accurate, but slightly soft. The actual membership data might be slightly lower or higher than reported. The NRDC is eliminated because it did not come into existence until 1970.

12. Following these results additional tests were run using the political variables. Additional regressions examined tests of other types of income, the effect when the presidency and the Congress are controlled by the same party, different measures of education, and a test using dummy variables instead of the ratio for which party controlled which house of Congress. No new insight was provided from these tests.

References

Baden, John. 1994. *Environmental Gore*. San Francisco, CA: Pacific Research Institute for Public Policy.

Bishop, Richard. 1982. "Option Value: An Exposition and Extension. *Land Economics*. (February): Vol. 58, pp. 1-15.

Bison, Michael, and D. Schap. 1995. "Regional Conflict and Environmental Legislation." Working Paper, Department of Economics, College of the Holy Cross.

Boerner, Christopher, and C. Kallery. 1995. *Restructuring Environmental Big Business*. St. Louis: Washington University, Center for the Study of American Business, January.

Bosso, Christopher. 1994. "After the Movement: Environmental Activism in the 1990s." In *Environmental Policy in the 1990s: Toward a New Agenda*, edited by Norman Vig and Michael Kraft. Washington, DC: Congressional Quarterly Press.

Buchanan, James, R. Tollison, and G. Tullock. 1980. *Towards a Theory of the Rent Seeking Society*. College Station: Texas A&M University Press.

Carson, Rachel. 1962. *Silent Spring*. Boston, MA.: Houghton Mifflin.

Cohen, Michael. 1988. *The History of the Sierra Club 1892-1970*. San Francisco, CA: Sierra Club Books.

Coursey, Don. 1992. "The Demand for Environmental Quality." Working paper, Department of Economics, Washington University.

Dalton, Russell. 1994. *The Green Rainbow*. New Haven, CT: Yale University Press.

Downing, Paul. 1984. *Environmental Economics and Policy*. Boston, MA: Little Brown and Company.

Easterbrook, Greg. 1993. *A Moment on the Earth*. New York: Viking Press.

The Economist. 1990. "Seeing the Green Light." October 20, pp. 88,93.

The Economist. 1994. "As Green Turns to Brown." March 5, pp. 27-28.

Ehrlich, Paul. 1968. *The Population Bomb.* New York: Bamantine Books.

Gottlieb, Robert. 1993. *Forcing the Spring.* Washington, DC: Island Press.

Hall, Bob, and Mary Lee Kerr. 1991. *1991-1992 Green Index.* Washington DC: Island Press.

Hansman, Henry. 1980. "The Role of Nonprofit Enterprise." *Yale Law Journal.* Vol. 89, (April): pp. 835-901.

Hoose, Philip. 1981. *Building an Ark.* Covelo, CA: Island Press.

Ladd, Everett, and K. Bowman. 1995. "Attitudes Toward the Environment: Twenty Five Years after Earth Day." Washington DC: American Enterprise Institute for Public Policy Research.

Landsburg, Steven. "The Religion of Environmentalism." *Across the Board.* (March 1994): 41-43.

Lindsay, Matt. 1969. "Option Demand and Consumer Surplus." *Quarterly Journal of Economics.* Vol. 83, (May): 344-346.

Lipford, Jody. 1990. Religious Organizations As Nonprofit Firms: A Study in Organizational Theory. Ph.D. Dissertation, Clemson University, Clemson, South Carolina.

Long, Bill. 1994. "Global Competition: The Environmental Dimension." *Business Economics*, April, 45-50.

Maloney, Michael, and Robert McCormick. 1982. "A Positive Theory of Environmental Quality." *Journal of Law and Economics.* Vol. 25 (April): 99-124.

Murrell, Peter. 1984. "An Examination of the Factors Affecting the Formation of Interest Groups in the OECD Countries." *Public Choice.* Vol. 43 (Spring): 151-172.

Nash, Roderick. 1990. *American Environmentalism: Readings in Conservation History.* New York.: McGraw-Hill.

Nelson, Robert. 1995. "Environmental Calvinism: The Judeo-Christian Roots of Eco-Theology." In *Taking the Environment Seriously*, edited by Roger Meiners and Bruce Yandle. Lanham, MD: Rowman and Littlefield Publications.

Nisbet, E. G. 1991. *Leaving Eden: To Protect and Manage the Earth.* Cambridge, MA: Cambridge University Press.

Olson, Mancer. 1965. *The Logic of Collective Action.* Cambridge, MA: Harvard University Press.

Peltzman, Sam. 1976. "Toward a more General Theory of Economic Regulation." *Journal of Law and Economics.* Vol. 2 (August): 3-21.

Randall, Alan. 1987. *Resource Economics.* New York: John Wiley and Son.

Roberts, Leslie. 1990. "Counting on Science at EPA." *Science* (August 10): 616-618.

Rose-Ackerman, Susan. 1986. "Introduction." In *The Economics of Nonprofit Institutions: Studies in Structure and Policy,* edited by Susan Rose-Ackerman, Oxford: Oxford University Press.

Rubin, Charles. 1994. *The Green Crusade.* New York: Free Press.

Schnaiber, Alan, and K. Gould. 1994. *Environment and Society, the Enduring Conflict.* New York: St. Martin's Press.

Smith, Zachary. 1995. *The Environmental Policy Paradox.* Englewood Cliffs, NJ: Prentice Hall.

Stigler, George. 1971. "The Theory of Economic Regulation." *Bell Journal of Economics and Management Science.* Vol. 2 (Spring): 3-21.

———. 1974. "Free Riders and Collective Action: An Appendix to the Theories of Economic Regulation." *Bell Journal of Economics and Management Science.* Vol. 5 (Autumn): 359-365.

Switzer, Jacqueline. 1994. *Environmental Politics.* New York: St. Martin's Press.

Terry, Jeff. 1994. "EPA's Toxic Release Inventory: What Is Its Purpose?" Center For Policy Studies, Clemson University, September.

United States Environmental Protection Agency. 1992. *The Guardian: Origins of the EPA.* Washington DC.

Chapter 11

Is Environmentalism the New State Religion?

Jason Annan

Introduction

Today's modern environmental movement possesses many of the traits of an organized religion. There exists a dogma of an impending environmental apocalypse, a vocal and extremely faithful cadre of environmentalist prelates, and, in unspoiled nature, the cathedrals of worship. But is environmentalism a "religion" in its own right? How does environmentalism relate to Christianity? To what extent has "eco-theology" impacted environmental policies? The questions are myriad. The first part of this chapter examines the "environmentalist" theology of Christianity. This provides a springboard for assessing the words and actions of the leaders of the modern environmentalist movement to determine if their cause can be deemed an alternative religion in its own right. The second part of this chapter brings religious "speak" into the realm of substantive policy issues. How has environmental dogma impacted policy, and what threats or benefits does it pose to a rational, secular system of policy making?

The Religious Nature of Environmentalism

Environmentalism: The Eleventh Commandment

The Bible has been interpreted as requiring good environmental stewardship of man. Perhaps the most referenced scriptures are found in the creation story of Genesis. In the book of Genesis, God gives dominion over the earth to man (Gen.

1:28). Likewise, some theologians reference the book of Job as compelling evidence for environmentalism. God asks Job, "Where were you when I laid the Earth's foundation?" (Job 38:4). God goes on to describe the mysteries of the Earth, asking Job why rain falls on uninhabited ground (Job 38:26). Environmentalist and ordained minister Bill McKibben interprets these passages as meaning "that God is quite happy with places where there are no people" (McKibben, 1989). In Job 12:7-10, Job tells the lessons to be learned by asking animals, "birds of the air...fish of the sea." Man may "speak to the earth and it will teach you." These scriptures have been interpreted to mean that God values all of creation–the land, sea, animals, and plants. Similar environmental theologies can be interpreted from the Old Testament story of Noah and the Ark.

Tom Hayden, a prominent environmentalist and self-described eco-theologian, blames traditional Christian theology for what he describes as the environmental chaos that plagues the earth (Stamer, 1996). He is representative of a growing number of people who believe the church has misinterpreted God's gift of "dominion" over nature, using this privilege as "a license to pillage the planet" (Stamer, 1996). "For the most part Western religion excluded the environment from what was considered sacred and the drama became centered on the human and how to live a good life according to good values...The universe and rocks, trees, and the Earth were background," says Hayden (Stamer, 1996). Hayden, like McKibben, insists that God meant for man to be ecologically sensitive. He cites the book of Genesis, where God says "it is good" after creating the sea, the earth, and "all the living things that move on this Earth" (Gen. 1:1-28) (Stamer, 1996). To Hayden, and others, this is proof positive that God intends for man to revere the Earth as "holy" (Stamer, 1992).

The rise of modern environmental consciousness has spawned a brand of Christian theology known as creation spirituality or theology. This theology is represented by the scriptural interpretations of McKibben. The view holds that "God is all things rather than in one Supreme Being...while there is one Supreme Being, created things also have divinity" (Witham, 1992). Thus, "love of nature is honoring God and the 'gracious gift' the Creator gives," says Rev. Donald Conroy, president of the North American Council on Religion and Ecology (Witham, 1992).

Viewing nature as an extension of God is not new. There is a strong undertone of environmental consciousness in the prayers of St. Francis of Assisi. In the *Canticle of Brother Sun*, St. Francis gives praises to "Brother Sun," "Sister Water," and "Mother Earth" asking for the gift of sustenance for "all your creatures" (St. Francis, 1997). Likewise, the modern ritual of the Blessing of the Animals, practiced in many Christian churches, traces its origin to St. Francis. Noted nature theologians include John Muir, the founder of the Sierra Club. Muir, though raised in a strict Presbyterian home, wrote that he took "more intense delight from reading the power and goodness of God from the things which are made than from the Bible" (Nelson, 1992). Muir often referred to forests as "temples," and "sought to preserve the wilderness" as it constituted "terrestrial manifestations of God" (Nelson, 1992).

It is interesting that nature theologians claim to remain within the Christian tradition. They have not sought to remove God from nature, nor have they sought to devalue man's special place in creation. Rather, nature theologians stress the fact that since God loves nature so too must man. Man's moral purpose remains to glorify God, and this may be done by treating His creations with respect. There is a fine line, however, between a Christian environmentalism and outright worship of nature.

God on the Rocks

Not surprisingly, nature theology has generated considerable controversy within the Christian church. Opponents claim that such spirituality leads not to faith and worship of God but rather to worship of nature. "This leads to saying that you can pray to God by walking in the woods, not by actually talking to the Creator," says minister Lawrence Adams (Witham, 1992). Detractors claim that nature theology is a brand on animism, a form of religion that gives "conscious life to nature or the natural world" (Thomas, 1996). Likewise eco-theology has been branded as a so-called New Age religion or as a modern form of pantheism, a belief that there is no one God, but that all of the universe is spiritual.

The statements of environmental leaders lend strength to these claims. Hayden is quoted in the *Los Angeles Times* as saying, "religion is about defining what we should consider sacred and treat accordingly... You can't think of it in terms like what conception of God would be useful... There's either a God or there's not" (Stamer, 1996). Hayden goes on to state that, "even if you believe in one God or one sacred being it's evident that the being manifests itself in multiple forms... There's one creation with an infinite variety of forms" (Stamer, 1996). By Hayden's words environmentalist theology is at odds with conventional Christian thought. Is God a spirit found in rocks, birds, or trees?

In 1967, environmentalist Lynn White published an article in *Science* in which she stated that a religious grounding for environmentalism would start with the theologies of Asia or of Native Americans, religions that teach either spirit worship of animism (Nelson, 1992). White's words were not the mere pontifications of a scholar. They have been put into practice. At an Earth Day religious celebration in 1994, prayers from the Iroquois Indians were distributed by the National Religious Partnership for the Environment. "We return thanks to our mother, the Earth, which sustains us," reads the prayer (Sirico, 1994). "We cannot let our Mother die. We must love and replenish her," reads another (Sirico, 1994).

The Iroquois prayer illustrates another interesting facet of eco-theology; that is, the tendency to refer to the Earth as an entity itself. James Lovelock, a prominent British environmentalist, developed the Gaia Hypothesis in the 1970s

(McKibben, 1989), which states that all life on Earth is interconnected. The sea, land, air, animals, and plants are all twined together so that an impact on one is felt by the whole. "The basic premise of Gaian theory is that the Earth itself is a superorganism that is both living and divine" (Sirico, 1994). Lovelock admits that "Gaia is a religious as well as a scientific concept" (Chase, 1992). The religious implications of the theory are profound and smack of earth worship. There has even been a choral mass written in praise of Gaia, the *Missa Gaia* (Sirico, 1994).

Ironically, the God of Christianity is a powerful being, as omnipotent as He is caring. But the "god" of eco-theology, if it is to be construed as nature, the earth, or endangered wildlife, is a fragile entity. Environmentalists hold that nature is constantly threatened by man, and can even be destroyed. In fact, eco-religious dogma maintains that man is even killing himself through environmental destruction such as ozone depletion or deforestation. As Bill McKibben explains, environmental dogma has profound implications for Christianity (McKibben, 1989). For if God created nature, and holds it as divine, then surely man cannot destroy it. Furthermore, what does it say of God if man, created in His own image, would be allowed to destroy himself? Environmentalism dodges these questions by supplanting nature with God.

Environmentalism dogma is not based on rational thought or scientific grounding. Alton Chase writes that the science on which environmentalists' beliefs rest is "weak or non-existent" (Chase, 1992). It is a religious faith, assigning man a moral purpose–not of glorifying God, but of "saving" the earth. Robert Nelson has even compared environmental religion to the strict Christian Calvinists. Both view man as inherently evil and full of sinful desires. To wit, environmental leaders have branded man a "cancer" and a "virus" (Nelson, 1992). Paralleling the dogmatic times of Europe's church-dominated Middle Ages, any challenge to the dogma can be met by claiming that the challenger cares not for the environment, and is indeed anti-environment, regardless of what these terms actually mean. As will be explained later, the commandments of environmentalist dogma have profound policy implications.

It seems apparent that environmentalism strains the confines of Christian theology. Indeed, environmentalism has been branded a secular-religion: possessing the religious aspects of Christianity from which it was derived, but devoid of any mention of God the Creator. Secular religions, like Marxism or environmentalism, profess to offer truths about life and society, just as organized religions do. Nelson references the words of environmental writer Theodore Roszak, who states that "Environmentalism . . . will have to provide answers to 'ethical conduct, moral purpose, and the meaning of life,' and thereby help to guide 'the soul' to the goal of 'salvation'" (Nelson, 1992). Statements of similar religious character are heard from environmental policy makers, as will be discussed later.

Environmentalists have not always been successful at convincing other Americans of the veracity of their faith. As Nelson describes, rational environmentalists began by explaining how good environmental behavior could help man lead cleaner, healthier lives and fuel the economy. Apart from the rational environmentalists are the religious environmentalists, who believe in the dogma described above. Religious environmentalists hold that helping the environment is reason enough for action, regardless of whether or not it helps man. They have sought allies in the Judeo-Christian churches of America. And why not? With 90 percent of Americans indicating a belief in God, what better way to spread the environmental faith than aligning it to the mainstream faith of the nation? If environmental imperatives are given the weight of biblical commandments, then the environmentalist dogma becomes more convincing to otherwise disbelieving Christians. This casts a shadow on the legitimacy of Christian nature-ecology. Is it really a Christian theology, or rather a formulation designed to promote the motives of radical (religious) environmentalists?

Policy Implications of Eco-Religion

How have religious beliefs about the environment influenced policy? One might believe that environmental policy is dominated by rational environmentalism: pollution laws to protect public health, for example. If environmental rules and regulations are influenced by a religion, then what does this mean for cost-effective, rational policy? Likewise, if religious environmentalism has influenced policy, is this an infringement of the disestablishment clause of the Constitution?

Cost-Conscious Policy Making

The core of faith for the religious environmentalist is to protect the earth from man. Quite ironically, environmentalism holds that man, Earth's "virus" and "cancer," holds the keys to the salvation of nature. Aside from advocacy groups, it can be argued that environmentalists most often appeal to government for actions and policies commensurate with their dogma. If nature is sacred, it must be protected. By extension, there can be no compromise on sin. By equating nature, the wilderness, and the earth with the divine, environmentalist dogma has constructed a moral imperative, and in turn a system of values that must be obeyed. In short, there is a very high price (or no price at all) to be placed on any part of nature; for what value can be placed on the divine?

Roger Starr states that the overriding desire of religious environmentalism is not cost-effective policy, but "deliberate sacrifice by individuals" (Starr, 1979). To illustrate the point, he cites examples of federal regulations on wastewater discharge that are set stringently without regard to cost (Starr, 1979). Discharge requirements have more than tripled wastewater treatment costs, according to Starr, without a corresponding gain in the water quality of the receiving waters (Starr, 1979).

While inefficient command-and-control regulation may well represent the notion of punishing sinners, the policy effects of eco-religion are perhaps best demonstrated by case studies. The Endangered Species Act, for example, seeks to protect those animal or plant species that are threatened by extinction. From a strictly cost-benefit point of view, endangered species should be protected only if saving those species provides some net marginal economic value. Such cost-benefit appeals are often made in attacking rain forest destruction: the ever disappearing species of the rain forest may provide the cure for cancer, or some other valuable miracle drug to save countless lives. Also, as Robert Nelson has summarized, man often places an "existence value" on a species or unspoiled wilderness even though few might ever see them (Nelson, 1992). However, to obey completely the dogma of religious environmentalism means that *every* species is divine, that every part of nature must be saved. Immediately, the protection of any part of nature must trump new factories, homes, roads, or even facilities that may affect far-away areas with pollution. The economic conse-quences could be enormous. Robert Nelson cites studies performed at the University of Maryland that show that "the marginal economic value to society of protecting one more endangered species may be nothing" (Nelson, 1992). Nelson goes on to claim that for the most part, the economic benefits of modern environmental regulations have been minimal (Nelson, 1992). If such analyses are true, then one must consider that environmental regulations are devoid of economic foundation, and constitute rather an institutionalization of eco-religious beliefs.

Religious environmentalists never argue their cause in terms of cost-effective policies. For example, when Bruce Babbitt, U.S. Secretary of the Interior and perhaps the nation's chief promulgator of environmental policy, attempted to add 239 new species to the endangered list in 1995 (Nelson, 1992), he cited the biblical story of Noah. Babbitt said that God "did not specify that Noah should limit the ark to two charismatic species, two good for hunting, two species that might provide some cure down the road" (Nelson, 1992). In short, Nelson summarizes, "Babbitt concludes the Endangered Species Act must not be altered to take costs into consideration" (Nelson, 1992).

Polluters: The Environmental Anti-Christ

Another aspect of policy that reflects eco-religious tendency is the treatment of polluters. Central to the environmentalist dogma is the role of pollution: eco-religion's anti-Christ. All pollution is evil and must be stopped. The cost implications of this belief have been discussed above. As pollution has been equated to sin, then polluters, the sinners, should be handled in a way befitting a sinner. In its treatment of polluters, or even would-be polluters, eco-religion takes on a strict, eco-Calvinistic attitude (Nelson, 1992). Polluters should be dealt with harshly, in the forms of fines or even imprisonment. Consider again the

Endangered Species Act. Killing just one specimen of the endangered Delhi Sands fly, native to suburban San Bernardino, California, calls for fines of up to $200,000 and one year in jail (Sugg, 1997). Similarly, municipal wastewater treatment plants that exceed pollution discharge standards for just one day may be fined, even though the temporary lapse may cause little environmental harm. The punishment system surrounding American environmental regulations parallels the Calvinistic attitude that man is full of evil intent and "in need of strict management" (Nelson, 1992).

The Spanish Inquisition won converts on the torture bed. The depth of the newfound faith is arguably correlated to the severity of the impending conversion "technique" employed. But does the constant threat of punishment to the polluter really protect and preserve the environment? Consider the case of the Delhi Sands fly mentioned above (Sugg, 1997). The fly spends just one week of its life in the adult, non-larval, stage. When eight specimens were found on a one-hundred acre tract of land in San Bernardino, California, protection of the insects reached a religious fervor. A hospital scheduled for construction was forced to relocate and land owners were required to set aside sizable chunks of their property and donate hundreds of thousands of dollars to "mitigate" habitat destruction. U.S. Fish and Wildlife Service policy makers even called for the speed limit on a nearby interstate to be lowered to a fly-splattering-proof fifteen miles per hour during peak fly mating periods (September and October). Protection of the fly is estimated to have cost San Bernardino County $4.5 million. What was the net effect of the efforts? The fly was given a maze of protected "corridors," often measuring only a few dozen feet wide, for mating purposes. Corridors met and intersected at right angles, forcing flies to make sharp turns to remain within their preserve (Sugg, 1997).

To the casual observer, the story of the Delhi Sands fly is environmental protection gone awry. Focus on the environmental sinner hinders true protection of the environment. Holistic solutions to environmental problems, such as with the Tar-Pamlico River in North Carolina in which pollution regulations have been waived in order to institute a river-wide quality control system, have been successful, but are more an exception than the norm. Furthermore, examples of policy silliness, such as the Delhi fly, are fodder for a knee-jerk reaction that holds all environmentalists as crazed "tree-huggers." As the standards of environmental lunacy are raised, it becomes more difficult for rational conservationists, whose policies may be well grounded, to champion their causes.

Eco-Socialism?

Within the environmentalist dogma is a strong undercurrent of anti-development, if not anti-capitalism content. Environmental writer Loren Wilkinson states "the tragedy is that the standard of 'development' to which those billions of people in the Third World aspire is set by us in the 'developed' world" (Sirico, 1994).

Are Westerners to feel uncomfortable in an air-conditioned car? That's the hope of religious environmentalism. "A child born into an average American family will use up to fifty times as many of the Earth's goods—and leave at least that much more in waste—as a child born into a poor family in the developing world," states Wilkinson (Sirico, 1994).

Mikhail Gorbachev, the Soviet Union's last communist leader, is now an environmentalist, and president of the International Green Cross. This is indeed ironic, for the environments of the former Soviet Union, and much of eastern Europe, were ravaged by communism. Writer Andrew Furguson states that environmentalism encourages Gorbachev and his colleagues to "sustain the moral equivalence that was their chief rhetorical safeguard during the cold war" (Ferguson, 1995). The "global ecological crisis proves that capitalism . . . has failed" (Ferguson, 1995). "The most profound need is to move away from a technology-centered to a culture-centered way of living. We must change the nature of consumption so that it is geared towards our cultural needs," says Gorbachev, though the words could be coming from any environmental leader (Ferguson, 1995).

Is there any industry that a religious environmentalist would sanction? Development can cause pollution and the potential for environmental damage. By enforcing strict pollution discharge standards, regardless of cost or marginal benefit, industry can be made to respect the environment. Implicit in the demonization of consumptive culture is a suspicion of private industry. This is reflected in policy. Past and current environmental regulations, shaped during the rise of environmental consciousness in the 1970s and 1980s, explicitly spelled out the types of pollution control technology to be used by industry. Within the philosophy of command-and-control policy is the belief that, if left to their own devices, industry may not achieve pollution standards. Alternative, and perhaps more cost-effective, technologies proposed by industry are compared not in their own right but against the standard technologies set by government that environmentalists are more apt to trust.

Environmentalism, like socialism/communism, also harbors distrust of property rights in general. Recent actions by the federal government have sought to severely limit, and even prohibit, private property owners from developing their lands in order to protect the habitats of endangered or threatened species, to preserve wetlands, or otherwise to preserve what the government classifies as environmentally sensitive areas. Such actions dovetail nicely with eco-religious thought as explained above. Indeed the concept of property rights fits uncomfortably with and is even alien to a radical religious view of the environment. Though individuals may own the land, they have a moral obligation to preserve the nature on their property. More importantly, should the individual be unwilling to obey this moral dictate, the government, under the control of a state eco-religion, is morally obligated to save it from him.

Separation of Eco-Religion and State

Interior Secretary Bruce Babbitt is an embodiment of religious environmentalism, and he has used his bully-pulpit to advance the faith. Babbitt had a religious awakening while visiting a Hopi Indian reservation in his native Arizona. From that time on he molded tribal faith with his own Catholicism to produce an eco-theology. Babbitt states that "the land ... all the plants and animals in the natural world are together a direct reflection of divinity" (Nelson, 1992). When Babbitt proposes environmental policies, he hopes that "he is carrying out God's instructions" (Nelson, 1992). Alston Chase writes, "the real significance of Babbitt's talk is that it admits the obvious: that environmentalism is a religious movement. And this observation carries profound constitutional implications" (Chase, 1992).

Other environmental policy makers have mixed policy with eco-theology. Vice President Al Gore is a noted environmentalist and author of the green best seller *Earth in the Balance*. Gore has called for "a new reverence for the environment as a whole" and urged Americans to stop "heaping contempt on God's creation" (Nelson, 1992). The director of the National Park Service in the Clinton administration, Roger Kennedy, received attention in 1995 for his statement that wilderness was "a religious concept" and that creating national parks would be "a profound religious act of gratitude to the Almighty" (Epstein, 1995). Kennedy calls legislation to preserve nature "an acknowledgment of our sins" (Epstein, 1995).

The religious ethic that is entering environmental policy making has drawn the attention of some lawmakers. Representative Helen Chenoweth of Idaho has claimed that the administration of President Bill Clinton is pushing religious beliefs about the environment too far. She charges that current policies violate the First Amendment's requirement for a separation of church and state (Barker, 1996). Chenoweth states that federal environmental policies are instituting a state religion that is "a cloudy mixture of new age mysticism, Native American folklore and primitive earth worship" (Barker, 1996). Though Chenoweth's words may constitute grandstanding, in part because of her conservative constituents, scholarly writers have recognized the principle of her claims.

Robert Nelson raises some interesting points about the establishment of environmentalism as a state religion:

> If environmentalism does literally teach a religious message how can the active teaching of this message in the public schools be justified, when traditional Christian beliefs—from which the environmental message is in major part originally derived—are not allowed similar proselytizing? If a wilderness is literally a church of environmental awakening, why is it permissible for the government to maintain this type of place of worship but not an ordinary Christian church? (Nelson, 1992)

Alston Chase also warns that a "growing, unholy alliance of theologians, environmentalists, politicians, and scientists is gradually demolishing the walls that separate church from state and science from theology" (Chase, 1992). Already, school children learn of "a dying earth," and are taught environmental orthodoxy, according to Chase. "It may be only a matter of time before America becomes a complete theocracy—a place where, in the name of environmentalism, science and religion fuse with civil authority to rule the populace" (Chase, 1992).

Perhaps a certain amount of Orwellian forecasting is warranted here. For a state eco-religion would surely mean imposing limitations on the freedoms Americans have traditionally enjoyed. Full, unrestricted use of property will certainly be curtailed, and the establishment of an extensive "church" bureaucracy will be needed. Church bureaucrats will not only lead educational programs to instruct people in "correct" environmental behavior but would provide guidance in the form of myriad permits, inspections, and testing agencies required to ensure that no part of the environment is harmed. Inspectors could, as they do now, arrive unannounced to test for environmental damage and be empowered to levy stiff fines and jail time. It would be up to the property owner to prove the allegations of "environmental mismanagement" incorrect. As with any state religion, the entrenchment and preservation of the bureaucracy will be a priority. Environmental protection will become an adequate, but not predetermined, result of regulations.

Conclusions

Modern environmentalism has taken on a religious aspect. Some environmentalists hold that God values the earth and that man must treat it as sacred. Others have adopted a more animistic religion. The earth is treated as the center of creation, a fragile, even divine, entity that must be saved from the sins of man. Man, on the other hand, is a "cancer," a "virus" who is killing the earth. Though there is little to no scientific evidence to substantiate the view, environmentalists have adopted it as a dogma. Animistic environmentalists may be allying themselves with liberal Christians in order to advance their own beliefs. By using the weight of biblical interpretations, environmentalists have been more successful at convincing Americans of the value of protecting nature than they have in the past.

The environmental dogma has profound implications for policy. As pollution is equated to a sin, there can be no compromises. Waste emission limits must be continuously lowered, no matter what the cost. Polluters must be made to pay for their sacrilege against sacred Mother Nature. Of course, all types of industry are highly suspect in the environmental dogma. The cause of man must necessarily take a back seat to the protection of endangered species or of unspoiled nature. Some lawmakers and scholars feel that the environmental dogma has already become a state religion: leading policy makers like Interior Secretary Bruce Babbitt and Vice President Al Gore have developed their own eco-theology. Critics claim that policies that reflect the environmental faith are a violation of separation of church and state. They warn of a state eco-religion, which will strip away freedoms and become despotic.

Private religious beliefs will affect individual policy makers. Furthermore, concern for the environment should compel the formation of policies to preserve nature for future generations. However, as journalist Robert Sirico states, the driving force for policy should not be "for the sake of an ethic that mistakenly places a higher value on material things than on people" (Sirico, 1994).

References

Barker, Rocky. "Chenoweth's Logic Aimed at Environment is Flawed," *Idaho Falls Post Register*, February 18, 1996, C-1.

Chase, Alston. "Environmentalism Has Not-So-Suddenly Become a Religion," *Denver Post*, January 28, 1996, E-5.

Epstein, Keith. "Preaching in the Park," *The Plain Dealer* (Cleveland, OH), April 9, 1995.

Ferguson, Andrew. "Gorby Talks Up a Brave New World," *Sunday Times*, October 22, 1995.

McKibben, Bill. *The End of Nature*. New York: Doubleday, 1989.

Nelson, Robert H. "Bruce Babbitt, Pipeline to the Almighty," *Weekly Standard*, Vol. 1, (1992): 17.

———. "Does 'Existence Value' Exist?" *The Independent Review*. Vol. 1, 4: 499-521.

Sirico, Robert A. "The Greening of American Faith," *National Review*, August 29, 1994, 42.

Stamer, Larry B. "Tom Hayden Finds Spiritual Roots for Green Message," *Los Angeles Times*, October 5, 1996.

Starr, Roger. "Against Environmentalism as a Religion," *Fortune*, April 23, 1979, 135.

St. Francis of Assisi, *Canticle of the Brother Sun*. Available On-line:http://www. stfrancis.com/prayers.html. March 19, 1997.

Sugg, Ike C. "Lords of the Flies," *The National Review*, May 5, 1997, 45.

Thomas, Cal. Syndicated Column. *St. Louis Post-Dispatch*, February 20, 1996.

Witham, Larry. "Nature Worship Strays from God, Some Worry," *Washington Times*, April 25, 1992, D-4.

Index

About the Authors

Jason Annan is a 1996 engineering graduate of Duke University. He received his M.S. degree in environmental science and engineering from Clemson University in 1998, and is currently employed as an engineering consultant in Charlotte, North Carolina.

Sean Blacklocke has worked in water pollution control at the S.C. Department of Health and Environmental Control and was employed by the S.C. Department of Natural Resources Marine Resources Institute and the National Marine Fisheries Service in Alaska. He earned his B.S. degree in marine biology from the College of Charleston in 1990 and his M.S. in environmental studies from the Medical University of South Carolina in 1996. Blacklocke is currently pursuing a Ph.D. in applied economics at Clemson University.

Angela Ives received her B.S. degree in economics from Clemson in 1998 and is currently pursuing a graduate degree in education at the University of Charleston in Charleston, South Carolina.

Brian Kropp is a Ph.D. candidate in public policy analysis at the University of North Carolina at Chapel Hill. Prior to attending UNC, Kropp worked for Resources for the Future as a research assistant. Kropp received his M.A.. degree in economics from Clemson University in 1995.

Mariela Mercedes Nino Restrepo was employed as an environmental engineer in Colombia prior to entering graduate studies at Clemson University. She received her M.S. degree in environmental engineering and science from Clemson in 1998 and is entering the graduate program in applied economics at Clemson University.

David W. Riggs received his B.S. degree in economics from the University of North Carolina–Wilmington and his Ph.D. in applied economics from Clemson University in 1994. He held a joint appointment at Texas A&M University as an economist for a state-level agency and was Senior Fellow for Economic and Environmental Studies at the Center of the American Experiment in Minneapolis, Minnesota. Riggs is now Director of Land and Natural Resources Policy at the Competitive Enterprise Institute in Washington.

Matt Ryan received his B.S. degree in management from Clemson University in 1997 and worked as a research assistant in the Center for Policy & Legal Studies. Ryan is now a market analyst for for Harrah's Entertainment, Inc. in Memphis, Tennessee.

Jeffrey C. Terry received his B.S. and M.S. degrees in applied economics from Clemson University. He has worked as an economist with the Chemical Manufacturers Association, as a member of the congressional relations staff for the Society of Plastics Institute, and is now Director of Environmental and Health Effects Activities for the Engine Manufacturers Association in Chicago.

Stacie Thomas is currently employed as an economist on the staff of Senator Phil Gramm on the Banking, Housing and Urban Affairs Committee. She received her M.A. degree in economics from Clemson University in 1999 and her undergraduate degree in Spanish and International Trade, also from Clemson, in 1996. She was an intern at the Competitive Enterprise Institute in 1997 and a fellow at the Political Economy Research Center in 1998.

Alec Watson graduated magna cum laude from Clemson University in 1998 with a B.S. degree in economics. While at Clemson, he earned departmental honors and was named both the outstanding junior and senior economics major in his class. He is currently a student at the University of North Carolina Law School.